CHARLES R. SWINDOLL

SWINDOLL'S
LIVING
INSIGHTS

NEW TESTAMENT COMMENTARY

MATTHEW 1-15

Tyndale House Publishers
Carol Stream, Illinois

Swindoll's Living Insights New Testament Commentary, Volume 1A

Visit Tyndale online at www.tyndale.com.

Insights on Matthew 1–15 copyright © 2020 by Charles R. Swindoll, Inc.

Cover photograph of sunrise copyright © KEEP_THE_MOMENT/Shutterstock. All rights reserved.

All images are the property of their respective copyright holders and all rights are reserved.

Maps copyright © 2019 by Tyndale House Publishers. All rights reserved.

Photograph of notebook copyright © jcsmilly/Shutterstock. All rights reserved.

Designed by Nicole Grimes

Published in association with Yates & Yates, LLP (www.yates2.com).

Library of Congress Cataloging-in-Publication Data
Names: Swindoll, Charles R., author.
Title: Insights on Matthew / Charles R. Swindoll.
Description: Carol Stream, Illinois : Tyndale House Publishers, Inc., 2020.
| Series: Swindoll's living insights New Testament commentary | Includes
bibliographical references. | Contents: Part 1: 1-15
Identifiers: LCCN 2019034800 (print) | LCCN 2019034801 (ebook) | ISBN
9781414393827 (vol. 1 ; hardcover) | ISBN 9781414393971 (kindle edition)
| ISBN 9781496410689 (epub) | ISBN 9781496410672 (epub)
Subjects: LCSH: Bible. Matthew—Commentaries.
Classification: LCC BS2575.53 .S95 2020 (print) | LCC BS2575.53 (ebook) |
DDC 226.2/077—dc23
LC record available at https://lccn.loc.gov/2019034800
LC ebook record available at https://lccn.loc.gov/2019034801

Printed in China

26   25   24   23   22   21   20
7   6   5   4   3   2   1

CONTENTS

AUTHOR'S PREFACE

For more than sixty years I have loved the Bible. It was that love for the Scriptures, mixed with a clear call into the gospel ministry during my tour of duty in the Marine Corps, that resulted in my going to Dallas Theological Seminary to prepare for a lifetime of ministry. During those four great years I had the privilege of studying under outstanding men of God, who also loved God's Word. They not only held the inerrant Word of God in high esteem, they taught it carefully, preached it passionately, and modeled it consistently. A week never passes without my giving thanks to God for the grand heritage that has been mine to claim! I am forever indebted to those fine theologians and mentors, who cultivated in me a strong commitment to the understanding, exposition, and application of God's truth.

For more than fifty years I have been engaged in doing just that—*and how I love it!* I confess without hesitation that I am addicted to the examination and the proclamation of the Scriptures. Because of this, books have played a major role in my life for as long as I have been in ministry—especially those volumes that explain the truths and enhance my understanding of what God has written. Through these many years I have collected a large personal library, which has proven invaluable as I have sought to remain a faithful student of the Bible. To the end of my days, my major goal in life is to communicate the Word with accuracy, insight, clarity, and practicality. Without informative and reliable books to turn to, I would have "run dry" decades ago.

Among my favorite and most well-worn volumes are those that have enabled me to get a better grasp of the biblical text. Like most expositors, I am forever searching for literary tools that I can use to hone my gifts and sharpen my skills. For me, that means finding resources that make the complicated simple and easy to understand, that offer insightful comments and word pictures that enable me to see the relevance of sacred truth in light of my twenty-first-century world, and that drive those truths home to my heart in ways I do not easily forget. When I come across such books, they wind up in my hands as I devour them and then place them in my library for further reference . . . and, believe me, I often return to them. What a relief it is to have these resources to turn to when I lack fresh insight, or when I need just the right story or illustration, or when I get stuck in the tangled text and cannot find my way out. For the serious expositor, a library is essential. As a mentor of mine once said, "Where else can you have ten thousand professors at your fingertips?"

In recent years I have discovered there are not nearly enough resources like those I just described. It was such a discovery that prompted me to consider becoming a part of the answer instead of lamenting the problem. But the solution would result in a huge undertaking. A writing project that covers all of the books and letters of the New Testament seemed overwhelming and intimidating. A rush of relief came when I realized that during the past fifty-plus years I've taught and preached through most of the New Testament. In my files were folders filled with notes from those messages that were just lying there, waiting to be brought out of hiding, given a fresh and relevant touch in light of today's needs, and applied to fit into the lives of men and women who long for a fresh word from the Lord. *That did it!* I began to work on plans to turn all of those notes into this commentary on the New Testament.

I must express my gratitude to Mike Svigel for his tireless and devoted efforts, serving as my hands-on, day-to-day editor. He has done superb work as we have walked our way through the verses and chapters of all twenty-seven New Testament books. It has been a pleasure to see how he has taken my original material and helped me shape it into a style that remains true to the text of the Scriptures, at the same time interestingly and creatively developed, and all the while allowing my voice to come through in a natural and easy-to-read manner.

I need to add sincere words of appreciation to the congregations I have served in various parts of these United States for more than five decades. It has been my good fortune to be the recipient of their love, support, encouragement, patience, and frequent words of affirmation as I have fulfilled my calling to stand and deliver God's message year after year. The sheep from all those flocks have endeared themselves to this shepherd in more ways than I can put into words . . . and none more than those I currently serve with delight at Stonebriar Community Church in Frisco, Texas.

Finally, I must thank my wife, Cynthia, for her understanding of my addiction to studying, to preaching, and to writing. Never has she discouraged me from staying at it. Never has she failed to urge me in the pursuit of doing my very best. On the contrary, her affectionate support personally, and her own commitment to excellence in leading Insight for Living for more than three and a half decades, have combined to keep me faithful to my calling "in season and out of season." Without her devotion to me and apart from our mutual partnership throughout our lifetime of ministry together, Swindoll's Living Insights would never have been undertaken.

I am grateful that it has now found its way into your hands and, ultimately, onto the shelves of your library. My continued hope and prayer is that you will find these volumes helpful in your own study and personal application of the Bible. May they help you come to realize, as I have over these many years, that God's Word is as timeless as it is true.

The grass withers, the flower fades,
But the word of our God stands forever. (Isa. 40:8, NASB)

Chuck Swindoll
Frisco, Texas

THE STRONG'S NUMBERING SYSTEM

Swindoll's Living Insights New Testament Commentary uses the Strong's word-study numbering system to give both newer and more advanced Bible students alike quicker, more convenient access to helpful original-language tools (e.g., concordances, lexicons, and theological dictionaries). The Strong's numbering system, made popular by the *Strong's Exhaustive Concordance of the Bible*, is used with the majority of biblical Greek and Hebrew reference works. Those who are unfamiliar with the ancient Hebrew, Aramaic, and Greek alphabets can quickly find information on a given word by looking up the appropriate index number. Advanced students will find the system helpful because it allows them to quickly find the lexical form of obscure conjugations and inflections.

When a Greek word is mentioned in the text, the Strong's number is included in square brackets after the Greek word. So in the example of the Greek word *agapē* [26], "love," the number is used with Greek tools keyed to the Strong's system.

On occasion, a Hebrew word is mentioned in the text. The Strong's Hebrew numbers are completely separate from the Greek numbers, so Hebrew numbers are prefixed with a letter "H." So, for example, the Hebrew word *kapporet* [H3727], "mercy seat," comes from *kopher* [H3722], "to ransom," "to secure favor through a gift."

INSIGHTS ON MATTHEW 1–15

Though God may not show up exactly the way
we're expecting or through the means we think
He should, God does show up. *Matthew's*
Gospel not only reveals that Jesus is the King,
Israel's long-awaited Messiah, but it also
reminds us that Jesus is our Immanuel—"God
with us"—now resurrected and ascended,
yet with us still, even to the end of the age.

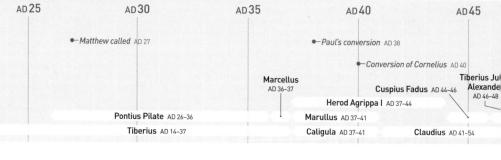

Matthew called AD 27

Paul's conversion AD 38

Conversion of Cornelius AD 40

Marcellus AD 36–37

Cuspius Fadus AD 44–46

Tiberius Ju Alexande AD 46–48

Herod Agrippa I AD 37–44

Pontius Pilate AD 26–36

Marullus AD 37–41

Tiberius AD 14–37

Caligula AD 37–41

Claudius AD 41–54

Map of Jesus' Life and Ministry. Matthew's story begins with the birth of Jesus in Bethlehem. It then traces Jesus' ministry throughout Galilee. After Jesus continued His ministry en route from Galilee to Judea, He was met with rejection in Jerusalem, ultimately resulting in His death.

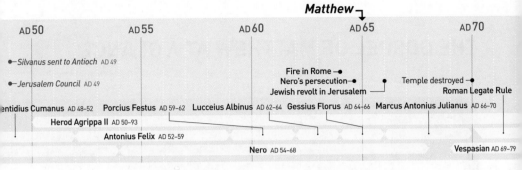

Matthew

AD 50   AD 55   AD 60   AD 65   AD 70

●—Silvanus sent to Antioch AD 49

●—Jerusalem Council AD 49

Fire in Rome —●
Nero's persecution—●
Jewish revolt in Jerusalem ——

Temple destroyed —●
Roman Legate Rule

ntidius Cumanus AD 48–52   Porcius Festus AD 59–62   Lucceius Albinus AD 62–64   Gessius Florus AD 64–66   Marcus Antonius Julianus AD 66–70

Herod Agrippa II AD 50–93

Antonius Felix AD 52–59

Nero AD 54–68   Vespasian AD 69–79

MATTHEW

INTRODUCTION

The backgrounds of the four Gospel writers present a fascinating study in contrasts. John Mark had likely been a teenage hanger-on accompanying the disciples. He may have been the young man who fled the scene of Jesus' arrest in an embarrassing fashion (Mark 14:51-52).[1] Then, after a shaky start in ministry with Paul and his own cousin, Barnabas (Acts 12:25–13:13; 15:36-41; see Col. 4:10), Mark went on to become a faithful assistant to the apostle Peter (1 Pet. 5:13), ultimately penning what was probably the earliest written Gospel, based on Peter's firsthand testimony.

Luke, on the other hand, was a physician (Col. 4:14). As a well-educated Gentile skilled in Greek, Luke applied his meticulous, critical mind to collecting, verifying, and arranging information so as to write a careful, orderly account of the life of Christ (Luke 1:1-4). Then he wrote a sequel recounting the earliest decades of the church, partly based on his own firsthand participation in ministry (Acts 1:1-2).

John, the "disciple whom Jesus loved" (John 20:2), started out as a young fisherman willing to cast off the entanglements of fishing nets and become a fisher of men (Matt. 4:18-22). By the time John penned his Gospel around AD 97, he not only likely had access to the other three Gospels but also had had a lifetime to reflect on the deep theological truths concerning who Jesus was and what that really meant.

This brings us to Matthew. Not a blue-collar fisherman like John. Not a sophisticated, white-collar physician like Luke. And not a young hanger-on like Mark. Matthew had been a tax collector.

A TAX COLLECTOR!

It's hard for us to picture what that meant to a first-century Jewish audience. Banish from your mind the image of a well-dressed IRS auditor just

THE GOSPEL OF MATTHEW AT A GLANCE

SECTION	ANNOUNCEMENT AND ARRIVAL OF THE KING	PROCLAMATION AND RECEPTION OF THE KING
PASSAGE	1:1–4:25	5:1–15:39
THEMES	Jesus' Credentials Birth Baptism Temptation	Jesus' Message Miracles Discourses Parables
KEY TERMS	Baptize Christ Proclaim	Righteousness Authority Blessed Parable

OPPOSITION AND REJECTION OF THE KING	PASSION AND TRIUMPH OF THE KING
16:1–25:46	26:1–28:20
Jesus' Suffering	Jesus' Victory
Opposition Rejection Second Coming	Passover and Arrest Suffering and Death Resurrection Ascension
Tribulation Woe Stumble	Hand Over Suffer

doing their job to keep taxpayers honest, or a matter-of-fact customs officer reviewing goods to make sure nobody exceeds duty-free limits. Matthew was not some hourly cashier collecting coins for local officials. The Greek term *telōnēs* [5057], translated "tax collector," is used quite negatively in the New Testament—often associated with such terms as "sinners" and "prostitutes."[2] Involved in the collection of money for an oppressive government, tax collectors were regarded as unpatriotic . . . and they were known to engage in extortion for personal gain.[3] If we picture a low-ranking mobster fleecing honest, hardworking citizens for a local cartel, we probably wouldn't be far from the truth. Michael Green notes that tax collectors, known in Latin as *publicani*, "were much hated as social pariahs, and the Jews classed them with murderers. They were not even tolerated in the synagogues."[4]

Who else but God would choose a hated, greedy tax collector not only to become one of Jesus' twelve disciples but also to pen what would become the first book of the New Testament canon? What a surprising example of the mercy and grace of God! When the presumably dishonest tax collector named Levi (Matthew) met the Lord Jesus and recognized Him as the long-awaited King of Israel, everything changed. His whole life would now be about proclaiming the Messiah to his fellow Jews—both through his living testimony and through his written words. I love what one man writes about Matthew: "When Jesus called Matthew, as he sat in the office where he collected the customs duty, Matthew rose up and followed him and left everything behind him except one thing—his pen."[5]

MATTHEW AMONG THE FOUR GOSPELS

God chose to reveal the life, works, teachings, death, and resurrection of Jesus Christ through four written accounts—those of Matthew, Mark, Luke, and John. Why four Gospels? Why not just one? Or seven? Because God has seen fit to reveal Himself in this way. His Spirit has told us the pivotal story of Jesus, the God-man, through the eyes of four unique writers with four distinct but complementary perspectives. The following chart summarizes these four Gospels, demonstrating the various contributions of their writers.

COMPARISON OF THE FOUR GOSPELS			
	MATTHEW	**MARK**	**LUKE**	**JOHN**
PORTRAIT OF JESUS	Promised King	Suffering Servant	Perfect Man	God the Son
ORIGINAL AUDIENCE	Jews	Romans	Greeks	The World
AUTHOR	Tax collector, one of the twelve disciples	Close associate of and assistant to the disciples	Gentile physician, early convert	Fisherman, one of the twelve disciples
THEME	The messianic King has come, fulfilling Old Testament promises.	The Son of God has come to seek, to serve, and to save.	The Son of Man has come to redeem all of humanity.	The eternal Son of God has become incarnate.
RESPONSE	Worship Him!	Follow Him!	Imitate Him!	Believe in Him!

Though all four Gospel accounts together harmoniously present the good news of the person and work of Jesus Christ in His first coming, Matthew, Mark, and Luke relate to each other in a unique way. These three are called "synoptic" Gospels, from a Greek term meaning "seeing together." In many places these first three Gospels can be read side by side, giving distinct but complementary accounts of events that, when "seen together," provide a fuller picture of what Jesus said and did. In contrast, the apostle John's account, written several decades after the synoptic Gospels were composed, covers elements from John's own eyewitness testimony that the preceding Gospels don't treat.

Though the synoptic Gospels present the life of Christ in similar ways, the Gospel according to Matthew stands out as the most Jewish. This is evident from the opening words of the narrative, in which Matthew traces the genealogy of Jesus in typically Jewish ways. This unique attribute of Matthew's account explains why we see so many references of Jewish significance throughout the book—references to the Law, to Jewish customs, to feasts, to Old Testament prophecies fulfilled by Jesus. Matthew contains a large number of direct quotations from, allusions to, and paraphrases of Old Testament passages—many more than Mark, Luke, or John. By some estimates, Matthew has over sixty-five references to the Old Testament, compared to about thirty

DID MATTHEW ORIGINALLY WRITE AN ARAMAIC GOSPEL?

According to Papias of Hierapolis, a second-century pastor who had been a disciple of the apostle John and knew many first-generation disciples of the original apostles, "Matthew wrote the oracles in the Hebrew language, and every one interpreted them as he was able."[6] This early second-century testimony is also confirmed later by Irenaeus of Lyons, a disciple of Polycarp of Smyrna, who himself had been a disciple of the apostle John. Irenaeus wrote, "Matthew also issued a written Gospel among the Hebrews in their own dialect."[7] Most early church fathers believed this early tradition that Matthew had originally written an account of the gospel in the language of the Jews—Aramaic—that was later translated into Greek.[8]

Many modern scholars doubt this early testimony, however. Many consider it more likely that Matthew wrote his Gospel based on the earlier and shorter Gospel of Mark, expanding the account in ways that would appeal more to a Jewish audience. To date, no Aramaic or Hebrew-language version of Matthew has been found, so even if such a text once existed, the Greek version of Matthew is the one the Holy Spirit has preserved as part of the New Testament canon.

each for Mark and Luke and as few as fifteen for John. Clearly, Matthew wanted to convince his Jewish readers that Jesus was their long-awaited Messiah, who did not come to abolish the Law or the Prophets but to fulfill them (5:17).

OVERVIEW OF MATTHEW'S GOSPEL

Matthew wrote his account of Jesus' birth, life, teachings, death, resurrection, and ascension to demonstrate to Jewish readers that Jesus is the King, Israel's long-awaited Messiah. The opening line of the book makes this clear: "The record of the genealogy of Jesus the Messiah, the son of David, the son of Abraham" (1:1). Every chapter contributes in some way to this overarching theme.

However, Matthew also delves deeper into a question that would have especially nagged his first-century Jewish readers who had already become convinced of the messiahship of Jesus: "If Jesus is our King, where is the promised kingdom?" Part of the plot of Matthew's Gospel is that Jesus did, in fact, offer the kingdom to Israel, but the offer was rejected by almost all Jewish political and religious leaders as well as a majority of the people (4:17; 16:13-28; 21:42-43). Matthew thus sets up the unexpected plot twist that Israel's rejection of Jesus would lead to the establishment of the church of baptized disciples from all nations (8:10-12; 28:19-20). Nonetheless, Christ's fulfillment of the original kingdom promises to Israel would still one day be fulfilled at His second coming (19:28; cf. 25:31).

Matthew develops his plot in two distinct parts: Chapters 1 through 15 address the *identity of the King*; chapters 16 through 28 address the *destiny and victory of the King.* The scope of the crowd also shifts between chapters 15 and 16 from Jesus teaching the vast multitudes to Jesus narrowing His focus to teach primarily the Twelve. In the first half of the Gospel, Jesus' popularity among the people increases; in the second half, the hostility against Jesus rises. Geographically, the first fifteen chapters emphasize Jesus' ministry in Galilee; the second half focuses on His ministry in Judea and especially Jerusalem.

The first half of Matthew's Gospel, which will be the subject of the present half volume, can be further divided into two parts.

Announcement and Arrival of the King (1:1–4:25). These opening chapters develop Jesus' credentials and qualifications as the long-awaited Messiah. His identity is demonstrated through His messianic genealogy (1:1-17), the fulfillment of Old Testament prophecies and types related to His birth and childhood (1:18–2:23), His baptismal consecration and commissioning (3:1-17), His victory over the devil's temptations (4:1-11), His calling of disciples (4:12-22), and the commencement of His public ministry (4:23-25).

Proclamation and Reception of the King (5:1–15:39). These eleven chapters recount Jesus' teaching, preaching, and miracles in inauguration and anticipation of His kingdom. This section includes the well-known "Sermon on the Mount" (5:1–7:29), accounts of various miracles (8:1–9:38), discourses on a number of practical, moral, and spiritual themes amid growing controversy (10:1–12:50), the exposition of the kingdom through parables (13:1-58), and additional miracles accompanied by greater resistance to Jesus' teachings (14:1–15:39).

The second half of the Gospel of Matthew, chapters 16 through 28, which chronicles the *Opposition and Rejection of the King* (16:1–25:46) as well as the *Passion and Triumph of the King* (26:1–28:20), will be discussed in the second half volume of this commentary. Suffice it to say that we have a lot of ground to cover in the first half of this Gospel before we examine the growing opposition to and rejection, crucifixion, and resurrection of Jesus in the second half.

What a profound and powerful message to kick off the opening pages of the New Testament! After four hundred years of prophetic silence during which God's people pored over the Old Testament writings for clues pointing to the coming Messiah, many may have wondered whether God had forgotten His promises and deserted them. Seeming silence from God can feel that way sometimes. However, John the Baptizer broke the silence with a call to repentance in preparation for the coming Messiah . . . and then Jesus Himself arrived with an offer of the kingdom, based on one condition—*faith*. Faith in a Messiah who met very few people's expectations. Faith in a kingdom that advanced through peace rather than war. Faith in a God who cared not only for His people, Israel, but for the whole world.

For anybody who feels like God forgets His people, Matthew speaks loudly in the silence. He will never forsake His people and never break His promises. Though God may not show up exactly the way we're expecting or through the means we think He should, *God does show up*. Matthew's Gospel not only reveals that Jesus is the King, Israel's long-awaited Messiah, but it also reminds us that Jesus is our Immanuel—"God with us"—now resurrected and ascended, yet with us still, even to the end of the age (see 28:20).

Get ready to meet your King!

ANNOUNCEMENT AND ARRIVAL OF THE KING (MATTHEW 1:1-4:25)

The four Gospels all begin differently. The Gospel according to Mark, probably the earliest written account, drops us right into the middle of the action, with John the Baptizer's proclamation of the coming of the kingdom, followed by the baptism of Jesus, His temptation, and the start of His preaching in Galilee (Mark 1:1-15). The careful, studious physician Luke opens with a kind of preface addressing a specific person, Theophilus, and setting forth in a formal fashion as assurance of the orderliness of the account. The account then begins by outlining the birth of John the Baptizer and relaying events from the birth and childhood of Jesus, providing historical details (Luke 1:1–2:52). Meanwhile, the Gospel of John starts with a soaring theological hymn about the eternal Word made flesh, exalting the God-man and the miracle of the Incarnation (John 1:1-18).

The Gospel of Matthew begins not with the immediate action of Mark, the historical context of Luke, or the glorious hymn of John, but with a genealogy tracing Jesus' legal ancestry back to the patriarch Abraham and through King David (Matt. 1:1-17). Prior to recounting the commencement of Jesus' public ministry, Matthew provides details spanning two chapters about Jesus' birth and childhood, much of which is not included in any other account—the angelic visitation to Joseph (1:18-25); the arrival of the magi, or "wise men," and their gifts of gold, frankincense, and myrrh (2:1-12); and the flight to Egypt and murder of the children of Bethlehem (2:13-23).

The purpose of these unique details is to point us to the announcement and arrival of the King (1:1–4:25). By the end of these opening chapters, no reader will be confused about who this Jesus of Nazareth really is. He's the King, Israel's long-awaited Messiah.

KEY TERMS IN MATTHEW 1:1–4:25

baptizō (βαπτίζω) [907] "to bathe," "to wash," "to immerse"

The English word *baptize* is not a translation so much as a transliteration of the Greek verb *baptizō*, which refers to the act of dipping something underwater for the purpose of washing it. In the ancient world, the act of immersion underwater was used by both Jewish and pagan religious groups for ritual cleansing—initiation into a sacred community, consecration for a particular vocation, or the symbolic washing away of sin or guilt in anticipation of worship. To be "baptized into" a community was to become identified with the collective group, to share the benefits of membership in it, and to help shoulder its responsibilities.

christos (χριστός) [5547] "messiah," "anointed one"

The Greek translation of the Hebrew Bible, the Septuagint, used *christos* to translate the Hebrew word *mashiach* [H4899] (from which we get the English word *messiah*), meaning "anointed one." In the Old Testament, an actual anointing ceremony with olive oil was used to consecrate prophets (1 Kgs. 19:16), priests (Exod. 28:41), and kings (1 Sam. 10:1). While Israel had many anointed prophets, priests, and kings throughout its history, these all came to be seen as anticipating the ultimate Prophet, Priest, and King—*the* Messiah, or "Christ."

kēryssō (κηρύσσω) [2784] "to preach," "to proclaim," "to announce"

In the first century, this verb generally referred to the making of official, public proclamations, as a herald might cry out an announcement from a king.[1] In the New Testament, it carries this sense, emphasizing the proclamation of God's kingdom with a call to repentance and faith (e.g., 3:1; 4:17). After Christ's death and resurrection, this proclamation of the good news would focus specifically on Christ as not only the King of the coming kingdom but also the Son of God who died and rose again (Acts 9:20; 28:30-31; 1 Cor. 1:22-24; 15:12).

The Genesis of Jesus
MATTHEW 1:1-17

NASB

¹The ᵃrecord of the genealogy of ᵇJesus ᶜthe Messiah, the son of David, the son of Abraham:

²Abraham ᵃwas the father of Isaac, ᵇIsaac the father of Jacob, and Jacob

NLT

¹This is a record of the ancestors of Jesus the Messiah, a descendant of David and of Abraham*:

² Abraham was the father of Isaac. Isaac was the father of Jacob.

the father of ᶜJudah and his brothers.
³Judah was the father of Perez and
Zerah by Tamar, Perez was the father
of Hezron, and Hezron the father of
ªRam. ⁴Ram was the father of Amminadab, Amminadab the father of
Nahshon, and Nahshon the father
of Salmon. ⁵Salmon was the father
of Boaz by Rahab, Boaz was the father of Obed by Ruth, and Obed the
father of Jesse. ⁶Jesse was the father
of David the king.

David was the father of Solomon
by ªBathsheba who had been the
wife of Uriah. ⁷Solomon was the father of Rehoboam, Rehoboam the
father of Abijah, and Abijah the father of ªAsa. ⁸Asa was the father of
Jehoshaphat, Jehoshaphat the father
of ªJoram, and Joram the father of Uzziah. ⁹Uzziah was the father of ªJo-
tham, Jotham the father of Ahaz, and
Ahaz the father of Hezekiah. ¹⁰Heze-
kiah was the father of Manasseh,
Manasseh the father of ªAmon, and
Amon the father of Josiah. ¹¹Josiah
became the father of ªJeconiah and
his brothers, at the time of the deportation to Babylon.

¹²After the deportation to Babylon: Jeconiah became the father of
ªShealtiel, and Shealtiel the father

Jacob was the father of Judah and
his brothers.
³ Judah was the father of Perez
and Zerah (whose mother was
Tamar).
Perez was the father of Hezron.
Hezron was the father of Ram.*
⁴ Ram was the father of
Amminadab.
Amminadab was the father of
Nahshon.
Nahshon was the father of
Salmon.
⁵ Salmon was the father of Boaz
(whose mother was Rahab).
Boaz was the father of Obed
(whose mother was Ruth).
Obed was the father of Jesse.
⁶ Jesse was the father of King
David.
David was the father of Solomon
(whose mother was Bathsheba,
the widow of Uriah).
⁷ Solomon was the father of
Rehoboam.
Rehoboam was the father of
Abijah.
Abijah was the father of Asa.*
⁸ Asa was the father of
Jehoshaphat.
Jehoshaphat was the father of
Jehoram.*
Jehoram was the father* of
Uzziah.
⁹ Uzziah was the father of Jotham.
Jotham was the father of Ahaz.
Ahaz was the father of Hezekiah.
¹⁰ Hezekiah was the father of
Manasseh.
Manasseh was the father of
Amon.*
Amon was the father of Josiah.
¹¹ Josiah was the father of
Jehoiachin* and his brothers
(born at the time of the exile
to Babylon).
¹² After the Babylonian exile:
Jehoiachin was the father of
Shealtiel.

NASB

of Zerubbabel. ¹³Zerubbabel was the father of ᵃAbihud, Abihud the father of Eliakim, and Eliakim the father of Azor. ¹⁴Azor was the father of Zadok, Zadok the father of Achim, and Achim the father of Eliud. ¹⁵Eliud was the father of Eleazar, Eleazar the father of Matthan, and Matthan the father of Jacob. ¹⁶Jacob was the father of Joseph the husband of Mary, by whom Jesus was born, who is called ᵃthe Messiah.

¹⁷So all the generations from Abraham to David are fourteen generations; from David to the deportation to Babylon, fourteen generations; and from the deportation to Babylon to ᵃthe Messiah, fourteen generations.

1:1 ᵃLit *book* ᵇHeb *Yeshua* (*Joshua*), meaning *The* LORD *saves* ᶜGr *Christos* (*Christ*), Gr for *Messiah*, which means *Anointed One* 1:2 ᵃLit *fathered*, and throughout the genealogy ᶜGr *Judas;* names of people in the Old Testament are given in their Old Testament form 1:3 ᵃGr *Aram* 1:6 ᵃLit *her of Uriah* 1:7 ᵃGr *Asaph* 1:8 ᵃAlso Gr for *Jehoram* in 2 King 8:16; cf 1 Chron 3:11 1:9 ᵃGr *Joatham* 1:10 ᵃGr *Amos* 1:11 ᵃ*Jehoiachin* in 2 Kin 24:15 1:12 ᵃGr *Salathiel* 1:13 ᵃGr *Abioud*, usually spelled *Abiud* 1:16 ᵃGr *Christos* (*Christ*) 1:17 ᵃGr *Christos* (*Christ*)

NLT

Shealtiel was the father of Zerubbabel.
¹³ Zerubbabel was the father of Abiud.
Abiud was the father of Eliakim.
Eliakim was the father of Azor.
¹⁴ Azor was the father of Zadok.
Zadok was the father of Akim.
Akim was the father of Eliud.
¹⁵ Eliud was the father of Eleazar.
Eleazar was the father of Matthan.
Matthan was the father of Jacob.
¹⁶ Jacob was the father of Joseph, the husband of Mary.
Mary gave birth to Jesus, who is called the Messiah.

¹⁷All those listed above include fourteen generations from Abraham to David, fourteen from David to the Babylonian exile, and fourteen from the Babylonian exile to the Messiah.

1:1 Greek *Jesus the Messiah, Son of David and son of Abraham.* 1:3 Greek *Aram,* a variant spelling of Ram; also in 1:4. See 1 Chr 2:9-10. 1:7 Greek *Asaph,* a variant spelling of Asa; also in 1:8. See 1 Chr 3:10. 1:8a Greek *Joram,* a variant spelling of Jehoram; also in 1:8b. See 1 Kgs 22:50 and note at 1 Chr 3:11. 1:8b Or *ancestor;* also in 1:11. 1:10 Greek *Amos,* a variant spelling of Amon; also in 1:10b. See 1 Chr 3:14. 1:11 Greek *Jeconiah,* a variant spelling of Jehoiachin; also in 1:12. See 2 Kgs 24:6 and note at 1 Chr 3:16.

Do you know the names of your great-grandparents? How about your great-great-grandparents? Chances are good that even the most avid genealogy enthusiasts among us couldn't trace their ancestries back more than a few generations before things get fuzzy. With countless hours of research using internet resources and a cotton swab in the cheek for a genetic test, you might be able to uncover your family history back another generation or two. But I'm not sure I know anybody who could draw a line back forty generations. In fact, I'm not sure anybody would want to!

Unless you're royalty.

The present royal family of England can trace their lineage back over thirty-five generations through numerous Georges, Edwards, Williams, Fredericks, Charleses (that's my favorite), Jameses, Henrys, Johns, and others. For royal families, genealogy is everything, because in monarchies, political power isn't conferred by vote or achieved by victory . . . it's inherited by birth.

So it is in the opening verses of the Gospel of Matthew. Remember, the overarching purpose in this account of the life of Christ is to demonstrate that Jesus is the King, Israel's long-awaited Messiah. It makes perfect sense, then, that Matthew would begin with documented proof that Jesus was not only the legal heir of the royal line of David but also the heir of the covenant blessing of Abraham.

Anyone who makes the decision to read through the New Testament in order for the first time immediately encounters a daunting challenge. Right out of the gate, the reader has to wade through a long list of names. To make matters worse, most of the names are unfamiliar, and some are even difficult to pronounce! The first reaction of someone who has no clue about the value and purpose of genealogies in Scripture is to think something like, *Why in the world does the very first book in the New Testament start like this?*

However, what appears to us to be of little interest and, frankly, rather boring information is, in fact, the most fundamental starting point for a Jewish reader. To a Jewish audience, if a man were to claim that he was the Messiah but didn't have the royal pedigree, it would all be over. One commentator writes it this way: "It is important not to think that this is a waste of time. For many cultures ancient and modern, and certainly in the Jewish world of Matthew's day, this genealogy was the equivalent of a roll of drums, a fanfare of trumpets, and a town crier calling for attention. Any first-century Jew would find this family tree both impressive and compelling."[2]

For these opening verses, put yourself in the place of a first-century Jewish skeptic—arms folded, eyes narrowed in suspicion, doubt written on your face. You want to see for yourself whether this Jesus of Nazareth is even worth considering as a candidate for the Messiah. You want to see documented proof.

— 1:1 —

The first verse of the Gospel of Matthew begins, literally, "The book of the genesis of Jesus the Messiah." To qualify as the long-awaited Messiah, or anointed king, a person would have to be an heir of the promise of Abraham and a legal descendant of King David. If Jesus of Nazareth had been from some other race of people—for instance, a Roman—or if He had been from a tribe and family different from the tribe of Judah and the family of David, He would have been automatically disqualified.

In Genesis 12:7, God said to Abram, "To your descendants [or *off-spring* or *seed*] I will give this land." Thus, none other than a descendant of Abraham could be the ultimate recipient of the kingdom of Israel. Then, centuries later, God made a covenant with David and swore, "Your house and your kingdom shall endure before Me forever; your throne shall be established forever" (2 Sam. 7:16). So only an heir from the house (family) of David would have the credentials to reign as the messianic King.

This is why Matthew begins his Gospel account with a straight-forward and simple—but vitally important—thesis for his Jewish readers: "This is a record of the ancestors of Jesus the Messiah, a descendant of David and of Abraham" (Matt. 1:1, NLT). The list of names that follows becomes Exhibit A—proof that Jesus really does have the pedigree to be the long-awaited Messiah.

Realizing the value of the genealogical record of Matthew, we can now look at the unique way he organized the information. He didn't just present a roll of names in chronological order like one might dig up in the basement of a public archives building. Rather, he divided the history from Abraham to Jesus into three clusters—from Abraham to David (1:2-6a), from David to the Babylonian captivity (1:6b-11), and from the Babylonian captivity to Jesus (1:12-16). Within each of these three groups, Matthew selected fourteen names, intentionally leaving some lesser-known individuals out of the record and unexpectedly including some specific women in the list.

It's clear that this genealogy isn't meant to present an exhaustive, precise, "just the facts" presentation of Jesus' lineage. While providing a summary of the ancestry of Jesus sufficient to satisfy those who would doubt His legal right to the Davidic throne, Matthew seems to have been even more interested in teaching his Jewish readers some things *about* Jesus—using a method of presenting material that would have particularly appealed to them as Jews.

Instead of examining every name in Matthew's genealogy, let's focus on some of the unique features of each cluster.

— 1:2-6a —

The first cluster of fourteen generations takes us from Abraham to David. This era, spanning roughly from 2000 BC to 1000 BC, included the patriarchs Abraham, Isaac, Jacob, and Judah, from whom the line of Israelite kings was to come (see Gen. 49:10). This period also spanned the time during the enslavement in Egypt, the Exodus under Moses, the giving of the covenant of the Law and the establishment of the tabernacle and sacrifices, and the conquest of the Promised Land.

But Matthew doesn't focus on these events. He doesn't even mention Moses or the Law. Nor does he simply transcribe from his sources a straight genealogy of father to son. Rather, he intentionally mentions that Judah fathered Perez and Zerah by Tamar (Matt. 1:3), that Salmon fathered Boaz by Rahab (1:5), that Boaz fathered Obed by Ruth (1:5), and—in the first entry of the second cluster of names—that David fathered Solomon by Bathsheba (1:6).

The four women Matthew mentions in Jesus' genealogy in 1:3-6 aren't just random wives thrown into the mix to prove that Matthew respected women. Matthew highlighted women who were probably all of Gentile—that is, non-Jewish—stock.[3] All of them entered the messianic lineage through less-than-ideal means. Tamar feigned being a prostitute to sleep with her father-in-law. Rahab was a prostitute prior to being incorporated into the community of Israel. Ruth came from Moab, a country often at odds with Israel. And Bathsheba became the wife of David only after David committed adultery with her and arranged for her husband to be killed. Think about it. Each of these women would have been viewed by pious Jewish readers as "tainted" or "stained" in some way. Why is this observation important? What was Matthew trying to demonstrate? One commentator puts it well: "The presence of these four persons in the lineage of the King emphasizes a genealogy of grace."[4] Because of their ignoble—rather than noble— pedigrees, none of the women fit comfortably in the family of the Messiah. But then again, none of us do either.

— 1:6b-11 —

The second cluster of fourteen generations selected by Matthew includes such major figures as Solomon, who built the temple in Jerusalem; Rehoboam, under whom the kingdom split between north (Israel) and south (Judah); Uzziah; and Hezekiah. In the first cluster (1:2-6a), Matthew added the names of four women who had been "grafted into" the family tree of Jesus despite their Gentile backgrounds. In this second set of fourteen, Matthew intentionally omitted the names of four men who appear in the more precise and detailed Old Testament genealogies— Kings Ahaziah, Joash, Amaziah, and Jehoiakim. Matthew's rationale for dropping these four names may have related either to their insignificance or to their infamous character.[5] In any case, a genealogy didn't need to include every single ancestor in order to demonstrate one's legal lineage; it was acceptable practice at this time for genealogies to skip generations.[6] It seems that the importance of maintaining the "fourteen generations" in each cluster prompted Matthew to make decisions regarding intentional omissions from the list.

In the first movement of Matthew's rhythmic symphony of generations (1:2-6a), we may get the impression that the long story beginning with Abraham built to a grand crescendo in the person of David. However, in the second movement, from David to the Babylonian captivity (1:6b-11), the rousing melody seems to have deteriorated into a cacophony of random clashes, out-of-tune instruments, and rogue band members either playing their own music or dropping out entirely. The history leading up to the exile in Babylon includes decline, degeneracy, apostasy, and idolatry, ultimately ending in defeat, destruction, and deportation.

But God had neither given up on His people nor broken His promises.

— 1:12-16 —

After things fall apart in the generations leading up to Israel's deportation to Babylon, the history of God's people declines into obscurity. We hardly know the people named in the third section of the genealogy. We can read about Zerubbabel, who took the lead in the return to Jerusalem to rebuild the temple (see Ezra 5:1-2; Neh. 12:1). But the rest are just names.

In picturing the four centuries of prophetic silence leading up to John the Baptizer's cries in the wilderness in the first century, we can imagine quiet, pious Jews living in the land of Israel, eagerly longing for their Messiah. As the royal line passed from generation to generation under the radar of successive oppressive nations—Babylon to Persia to Greece to Rome—the candle of messianic hope would continue to flicker until its enduring flame set the torch of the Messiah ablaze.

Matthew notes the final generation in a peculiar way that demonstrates Jesus' identity both as the legal heir of the royal line of David and as a child born of the Virgin Mary without having physically descended from Joseph. Literally, Matthew 1:16 says, "And Jacob brought forth Joseph, the husband of Mary, from whom was brought forth Jesus, who is called the Messiah." A few things are noteworthy about the way Matthew phrases this relationship. Previous entries in the genealogy connected names like Abraham and Isaac or Jesse and David with the Greek verb *gennaō* [1080] to indicate that the first person literally "brought forth" the second—that is, he became his ancestor. Even when women are named in the genealogy, it's clear that the man was considered the ancestral source through normal procreation—for example, "Boaz brought forth Obed by Ruth" (1:5, my translation). However, Matthew describes the origin of Jesus in a way that disconnects His physical generation from Joseph and instead links it to Mary. In 1:16, Matthew says that Joseph was the husband of Mary, from whom (Mary) Jesus was brought forth (still using the term *gennaō*). The tiny Greek phrase *ek hēs* [1537 + 3739], "from whom," uses the singular feminine relative pronoun, making Mary the sole source of Jesus' physical origin. However, Joseph is called Mary's *anēr* [435] ("husband"), making Jesus the legal (though not physical) son of Joseph . . . and thus the heir of the Davidic throne!

— 1:17 —

Matthew ends his stylized rendition of the Messiah's genealogy from Abraham with a summary statement noting that he intentionally limited each of the three movements to fourteen generations. In its most technical sense, the Greek term rendered "generation" (*genea* [1074]) can mean an actual physical descent from one person to another—the generation from a father to a son. However, it can also refer to "a period of time,"[7] just as we might say, "Back in my parents' generation, things were simpler." This appears to be the way Matthew is using the term in 1:17 when he says that fourteen generations passed from Abraham to David, from David to the deportation to Babylon, and from the deportation to Babylon to the Messiah. To arrive at the number fourteen for each era, Matthew appears to have counted David's pivotal reign itself as both the end of the first era and the beginning of the second.[8]

The division of these three clusters into fourteen "ages" or "eras" was entirely Matthew's doing. It isn't found in the Old Testament, nor do the genealogical lists immediately lend themselves to such a division. So why would Matthew go out of his way to present the legal ancestry of Jesus in three groups of fourteen? It has everything to do with Matthew's presentation of the genealogy in a style that would appeal to his original Jewish audience. Stan Toussaint explains one appealing possibility: "This was a common rabbinic device. Matthew may have derived the number fourteen from the Hebrew spelling of David's name. In the Hebrew language the letters of the alphabet have numerical value. . . . These three letters [making up David's name in Hebrew] have the numerical value of four, six, four, respectively, their total being fourteen."[9]

Hebrew "David"	ד ו ד
Transliteration	D V D
Numerical Value	4 + 6 + 4 = 14

What's the message behind Matthew's clever device? Jesus is the "second David"—the long-awaited Messiah who was to restore the power, glory, and kingdom promised to the first David.

In arranging his genealogy, Matthew wasn't merely presenting dry historical facts; he also embedded important theological truths using rhetorical devices that his fellow Jews would have caught. It's as if Matthew was hiding "Easter eggs" in his text for Jews to find . . . if they would only take the time to look carefully and think deeply. Throughout this book, we'll see that Matthew repeatedly invites his readers to go beyond the surface level of the narrative to think about who Jesus is by examining Old Testament patterns and prophecies and ultimately to see the truth that Jesus is the King, Israel's long-awaited Messiah.

THE THREE DRAMATIC MOVEMENTS OF MATTHEW'S GENEALOGY		
FIRST MOVEMENT	**SECOND MOVEMENT**	**THIRD MOVEMENT**
Crescendo	*Cacophony*	*Climax*
"From Abraham to David"	**"From David to the Deportation to Babylon"**	**"From the Deportation to Babylon to the Messiah"**
Abraham to Isaac	David to Solomon by Bathsheba	Jeconiah to Shealtiel
Isaac to Jacob	Solomon to Rehoboam	Shealtiel to Zerubbabel
Jacob to Judah and his brothers	Rehoboam to Abijah	Zerubbabel to Abihud
Judah to Perez and Zerah by Tamar	Abijah to Asa	Abihud to Eliakim
Perez to Hezron	Asa to Jehoshaphat	Eliakim to Azor
Hezron to Ram	Jehoshaphat to Joram	Azor to Zadok
Ram to Amminadab	Joram to Uzziah	Zadok to Achim

Amminadab to Nahshon	Uzziah to Jotham (skipping Ahaziah, Joash, and Amaziah)	Achim to Eliud
Nahshon to Salmon	Jotham to Ahaz	Eliud to Eleazar
Salmon to Boaz by Rahab	Ahaz to Hezekiah	Eleazar to Matthan
Boaz to Obed by Ruth	Hezekiah to Manasseh	Matthan to Jacob
Obed to Jesse	Manasseh to Amon	Jacob to Joseph
Jesse to David the king	Amon to Josiah	Joseph to Jesus the Messiah, born of Mary
David's reign as king	Josiah to Jeconiah and his brothers, at the time of the deportation to Babylon	

APPLICATION: MATTHEW 1:1-17

A Genealogy of Grace

At first glance, Matthew's genealogy looks like a boring list of barely pronounceable names—verses to be skipped in a daily reading schedule and definitely not a passage to preach from on a Sunday morning! However, on closer examination, we recognize an important practical truth woven into the fabric of this list of the Messiah's ancestors.

With the exception of Jesus Himself, every person in this list was a sinner—frail and foolish. Each one—from the very well known to the virtually unknown—had a life marred by sin and guilt. We can't name each one's sin. But we know of Abraham's deceptions. And Judah's conspiring with his brothers against Joseph. And Tamar's seduction. And Rahab's prostitution. And David's adultery. And Manasseh's wickedness. And the on-again, off-again, halfhearted faith and obedience of the line of Judah's kings.

So what does this list tell us? That God's grace excludes no one. If these men and women could be included in God's past story, sinners like you and me can be included in His present story. Humanly speaking, nobody deserved a place in Christ's legal and physical family line. Likewise, none of us deserves a branch in His spiritual family tree! Matthew's genealogy reminds us all of God's amazing grace.

Standing in Joseph's Sandals
MATTHEW 1:18-25

NASB

¹⁸Now the birth of Jesus ^aChrist was as follows: when His mother Mary had been ^bbetrothed to Joseph, before they came together she was found to be with child by the Holy Spirit. ¹⁹And Joseph her husband, being a righteous man and not wanting to disgrace her, planned ^ato send her away secretly. ²⁰But when he had considered this, behold, an angel of the Lord appeared to him in a dream, saying, "Joseph, son of David, do not be afraid to take Mary as your wife; for ^athe Child who has been ^bconceived in her is of the Holy Spirit. ²¹She will bear a Son; and you shall call His name Jesus, for ^aHe will save His people from their sins." ²²Now all this ^atook place to fulfill what was spoken by the Lord through the prophet: ²³"BEHOLD, THE VIRGIN SHALL BE WITH CHILD AND SHALL BEAR A SON, AND THEY SHALL CALL HIS NAME ^aIMMANUEL," which translated means, "GOD WITH US." ²⁴And Joseph ^aawoke from his sleep and did as the angel of the Lord commanded him, and took *Mary* as his wife, ^{25a}but kept her a virgin until she gave birth to a Son; and he called His name Jesus.

1:18 ^aI.e. The Messiah ^bThe first stage of marriage in Jewish culture, usually lasting for a year before the wedding night, more legal than an engagement   1:19 ^aOr *to divorce her*   1:20 ^aLit *that which*   ^bLit *begotten*   1:21 ^aLit *He Himself*   1:22 ^aLit *has happened*   1:23 ^aOr *Emmanuel*   1:24 ^aLit *got up*   1:25 ^aLit *and was not knowing her*

NLT

¹⁸This is how Jesus the Messiah was born. His mother, Mary, was engaged to be married to Joseph. But before the marriage took place, while she was still a virgin, she became pregnant through the power of the Holy Spirit. ¹⁹Joseph, to whom she was engaged, was a righteous man and did not want to disgrace her publicly, so he decided to break the engagement* quietly.

²⁰As he considered this, an angel of the Lord appeared to him in a dream. "Joseph, son of David," the angel said, "do not be afraid to take Mary as your wife. For the child within her was conceived by the Holy Spirit. ²¹And she will have a son, and you are to name him Jesus,* for he will save his people from their sins."

²²All of this occurred to fulfill the Lord's message through his prophet:

²³ "Look! The virgin will conceive a child!
She will give birth to a son,
and they will call him
Immanuel,*
which means 'God is with us.'"

²⁴When Joseph woke up, he did as the angel of the Lord commanded and took Mary as his wife. ²⁵But he did not have sexual relations with her until her son was born. And Joseph named him Jesus.

1:19 Greek *to divorce her.*   1:21 *Jesus* means "The LORD saves."   1:23 Isa 7:14; 8:8, 10 (Greek version).

The Bible records several conceptions and births that we could describe as amazing, unexpected, or even miraculous. The long-drawn-out promise of Abraham's "seed" was finally fulfilled when Isaac was born to a ninety-year-old mother, Sarah (Gen. 21:2). The wife of Elkanah, Hannah, previously unable to have children, was finally blessed with a child who became the great prophet Samuel (1 Sam. 1:19-20). And Elizabeth, the wife of the priest Zacharias, gave birth to John the Baptizer at a very old age (Luke 1:36).

However, none of these stories can compare to the birth of Jesus from the womb of the Virgin Mary. At Christmastime every year, people around the world rehearse that well-known yet always amazing story of the Savior's birth. Though we're acquainted with virtually all the details, we can often overlook one very important person in the story—the man named Joseph, "the husband of Mary" (Matt. 1:16). Mary had been visited by an angel who informed her of the miraculous conception (see Luke 1:26-38), but Joseph was unprepared for the hard-to-believe news of Mary's pregnancy.

All Joseph knew was that the baby was not his, biologically speaking. He hadn't touched Mary intimately. This could only mean that somebody else had. That was the only logical, natural explanation, *unless* . . . unless something supernatural had happened. (But Joseph assumed those things only happened in the Bible—what we call the Old Testament.)

Put yourself in Joseph's sandals. Which would be easier to believe: the natural or the supernatural?

— 1:18-19 —

Matthew makes a sharp transition from the genealogy of Jesus in 1:1-17 with the phrase "Now the birth of Jesus Christ was as follows" (1:18). This line reaches back to 1:16, where Joseph was described as "the husband of Mary, by whom Jesus was born." By the time Matthew wrote his Gospel in the AD 60s, the doctrine of the virgin conception of Jesus had been firmly established in Christian churches. It was part of the earliest creeds and baptismal confessions. At the same time, however, whispered rumors conceived in unbelief and birthed in slander began to circulate regarding Jesus' conception through either sexual immorality or assault.[10] Matthew includes a true and detailed account of the miraculous conception of Jesus to lay to rest such malicious gossip.

In his account of the birth of Jesus, Matthew places us squarely within the point of view of Joseph. Remember, Joseph was the one who stood in the line of succession for the Davidic kingship according to the genealogy, so Jews would have been particularly interested in the story of Jesus' birth from Joseph's perspective. But as we, the readers, are placed in Joseph's sandals, we immediately sense the uncomfortable situation: Sometime during the approximately one-year period of betrothal between Joseph and Mary, "she was found to be with child" (1:18). Matthew clarifies for the reader that this unexpected pregnancy was "by the Holy Spirit," but the account makes it clear that Joseph didn't know this.

At this point—that is, after the initial betrothal arrangement—the events recorded in Luke 1:26-56 had already occurred. The angel Gabriel had announced to Mary, "You will conceive in your womb and bear a son, and you shall name Him Jesus. . . . The Holy Spirit will come upon you, and the power of the Most High will overshadow you; and for that reason the holy Child shall be called the Son of God" (Luke 1:31, 35). After this, Mary traveled from Nazareth to visit her relative Elizabeth—the mother of John the Baptizer—in Judea, and stayed with her for three months, until around the time that Elizabeth gave birth to John. It was probably during this absence that Joseph wrestled with how to handle the potentially scandalous situation of his pregnant fiancée.

I have a feeling Mary had told Joseph about her visitation by the angel Gabriel, as recorded in Luke. That would explain why Matthew's Gospel mentions that "she was found to be with child by the Holy Spirit" (Matt. 1:18). But, of course, such an explanation for her pregnancy would have seemed to Joseph far-fetched to say the least!

The alternatives, though heartbreaking and humiliating, would have clearly been more reasonable. Mary had either been unfaithful or had been violated. If the latter, why wouldn't she just tell Joseph the truth, name her assailant, and appeal to Deuteronomy 22:25-27? The Law provided legal protection to women who had been taken advantage of in circumstances where no one could step in. However, if she had willingly engaged in sexual immorality, what kind of woman would add to the sin of adultery the blasphemous claim that her child of fornication was actually the Son of God?

None of this seemed to add up. Joseph had likely known Mary and her family for years, and he would have known that neither immorality nor deception was part of her character. Perhaps she had gone mad!

You can imagine the agony Joseph was going through.

From Joseph's perspective, he had three options in dealing with this dilemma. First, he could accept her as a scandalous liar and marry her anyway. But to do so would be to overlook offenses that God condemns. Second, Joseph could publicly condemn Mary as an adulteress, and she would be stoned to death under the Law (see Deut. 22:23-24). Or third, Joseph could divorce Mary privately and quietly, finding a way to deflect attention from the embarrassing situation. Perhaps Joseph

BETROTHAL IN THE FIRST CENTURY

MATTHEW 1:18

Though we may be aware of arranged marriages in some traditional cultures, especially in the East, most of us in the Western world are much more familiar with the practice of engagement—a man and woman meet, date, get serious, and then announce that they have chosen to be married. They set a date, make plans, and have a wedding. This whole process can generally last anywhere from a few months to several years. And depending on the couple's religious and moral convictions, they may live together or apart during that time; in today's world of loosened moral standards and on-and-off commitments, living together doesn't necessarily equate to being married, nor does being engaged necessarily mean there will ever be a wedding.

Regardless, our modern, Western approach to courtship and marriage would have seemed bizarre to the first-century Jewish way of thinking. Rather than undergoing a process in which a period of dating was followed by engagement and then a wedding, men and women in the first century approached marriage via the concept of betrothal. The Jewish marriage process can be divided into three stages.[11] First, a man and woman were matched together, usually by their fathers. The couple and their families then took time to become acquainted and approve the match, after which they entered a formal contractual agreement that included some kind of dowry or exchange of property passed from the woman's family to the man's family. Once the contract was signed and sealed, the man and woman entered the second stage: betrothal. Betrothal essentially amounted to a waiting period, somewhat similar to what we might call engagement, but with the important distinction that a contract had already been signed, making betrothal final in a sense similar to what we think of as marriage itself.

When the waiting period had elapsed and the groom's new living quarters had been prepared to receive the bride, the third stage transpired: the wedding ceremony. This included a public presentation of the bride and groom before family and friends, the sealing of their union, and a celebration with a grand feast.[12]

The severing of an arrangement of betrothal would have been a big deal in Jewish culture—essentially a breach of contract!

thought her extended stay with her relative Elizabeth in Judea would be a perfect opportunity to "send her away secretly" (Matt. 1:19). He could just send word that Mary should stay in Judea and not return to Nazareth. Perhaps Joseph could move out of town himself and relocate to his family's ancestral land in Bethlehem. Before long, nobody would remember that he had been betrothed to Mary. Or by the time they realized she had given birth out of wedlock, nobody would care . . . maybe.

But even this strategy to maintain his own righteousness and save her from public disgrace had its risks. Was it a realistic possibility that the truth wouldn't surface in a small town like Nazareth?

— 1:20-21 —

Joseph certainly faced a troubling dilemma. We shouldn't skate quickly over the surface of the opening words of 1:20, which state, literally, "While thinking on these things . . ." The Greek word used here for "thinking" (*enthymeomai* [1760]) means "to process information by thinking about it carefully."[13] We might say that Joseph "ruminated on" or "pondered" his decision. It kept him up at night and distracted him during the day. Even after he planned to divorce Mary discreetly, something didn't sit well with his decision. He *knew* her. This was *Mary*! She wouldn't do something like this . . . and then make up a story about an angel! But how else could he explain what was happening? *And why was this happening to him?*

Besides the irreconcilable facts bouncing around in his head, Joseph had to deal with the agonizing emotions churning in his stomach. He loved Mary, and he was brokenhearted thinking about the prospect of her unfaithfulness. Or he was devastated by her madness, if he thought she had lost her mind. But he also loved the Lord and couldn't just sweep the facts under the rug like wood shavings from his workshop! Trying to handle these vivid emotions probably drove Joseph to exhaustion.

And on one occasion of his falling asleep, it happened.

An angel of the Lord appeared to Joseph in a dream. What Joseph couldn't figure out through ponderous calculations and careful strategizing, God cleared up through a messenger from heaven. The word from the Lord was simple and direct. It settled the spinning of Joseph's mind and calmed the pounding of his heart: "Do not be afraid to take Mary as your wife"—that addressed his emotions; "for the Child who has been conceived in her is of the Holy Spirit"—that answered his questions (1:20). Then Joseph was presented with what was, in embryonic form, the gospel of salvation: "She will bear a Son; and you shall call His name Jesus, for He will save His people from their sins" (1:21). Joseph's response of immediate obedience (1:24) demonstrates not only that he believed the angel's message but also that he faced his fears and acted on his faith in the striking message about the child.

— 1:22-23 —

At this point in the dramatic narrative, Matthew pushes the pause button and makes an editorial comment for the benefit of his intended

Jewish audience—especially those who would be likely to roll their eyes and say, "Gimme a break! Conceived by the Holy Spirit? Born of a virgin? Who's ever heard of such a thing?" Matthew knew his skeptical audience well. To preempt their objections, he asserted that the virgin conception of the Messiah was, in fact, in keeping with a prophecy in the Old Testament book of Isaiah.

When it comes to Old Testament texts related to the Messiah, some passages might be what we would call *direct and clear* prophecies. In this category, the single, direct referent of the prophecy is the future Messiah. This would include passages like Isaiah 9:6-7, in which the child to be born who would reign on the throne of David is none other than Jesus, and Isaiah 52:13–53:12, which refers to a suffering, dying, and rising righteous Servant, a prophecy clearly fulfilled in the death and resurrection of Jesus.

Other Old Testament passages could be called *direct but veiled* prophecies, in which the referent is the Messiah, but the original audience may not have seen this clearly without the help of additional revelation. The reference to the seed of the woman in Genesis 3:15 falls into this category, as does the reference to the seed ("descendants") in Genesis 12:7, which Paul tells us is a veiled but direct reference to Jesus (Gal. 3:16).

Another category of messianic Old Testament passages may be called *indirect and veiled* prophecies. This would include types in the Old Testament that find their parallels in Christ, such as the Passover lamb, the sacrificial system, and certain figures (like Moses and David) who prefigure the Messiah either by comparison or contrast. Additionally, it may include prophecies that had a near or partial fulfillment at the time of the original prophecy but that also point forward to a greater fulfillment in the future at the coming of the Messiah.

Matthew's reference to Isaiah 7:14 and its application to Jesus' virgin conception falls most comfortably in the third category.[14] To grasp how Matthew understood this passage, we need to explore its significance to the original audience in the days of King Ahaz of Judah. At that time, Ahaz feared that his kingdom—and indeed, the entire line of David—would be terminated by an alliance of his enemies, the northern kingdom of Israel and its neighbor Syria (Isa. 7:1-9). To strengthen Ahaz's confidence, God offered that the king ask for a sign, which he refused to do. In response, God provided His own sign of His enduring faithfulness against the threat. He told Ahaz that a woman who was a virgin at the time would conceive and bring forth a child who would be called "Immanuel," meaning "God is with us" (Isa. 7:14). Before that child grew to be old enough to know right from wrong, the enemies threatening the line of David would have been defeated (Isa. 7:15-25).

After announcing this sign of the near destruction of Judah's enemies, Isaiah alludes to its fulfillment: "So I approached the prophetess, and she conceived and gave birth to a son. Then the LORD said to me, 'Name him Maher-shalal-hash-baz; for before the boy knows how to cry out "My father" or "My mother," the wealth of Damascus and the spoil of Samaria will be carried away before the king of Assyria'" (Isa. 8:3-4). This child, born to Isaiah and his wife, is also addressed in Isaiah 8:8 as "Immanuel," a sign that reminded God's people of His presence and protection against any enemies who would try to destroy the line of David. Finally, in Isaiah 8:10, the prophet taunts Judah's enemies by saying, "Devise a plan, but it will be thwarted; state a proposal, but it will not stand, for God is with us."

So, after the sign is announced in Isaiah 7 ("a virgin will be with child and bear a son"), the sign arrives in Isaiah 8: The maiden gives birth to "Immanuel," and the enemies of Israel are thwarted before he reaches adulthood. However, Isaiah also further develops the crucial themes of the birth of a child, "God with us," and the preservation of the Davidic throne. In the very next chapter, Isaiah incorporates these themes in a message that would find its ultimate fulfillment in the future Messiah:

> For a child will be born to us, a son will be given to us;
> And the government will rest on His shoulders;
> And His name will be called Wonderful Counselor,
>   Mighty God,
> Eternal Father, Prince of Peace.
> There will be no end to the increase of His government or
>   of peace,
> On the throne of David and over his kingdom,
> To establish it and to uphold it with justice and
>   righteousness
> From then on and forevermore.
> The zeal of the LORD of hosts will accomplish this.
>   (Isa. 9:6-7)

Stan Toussaint sums up the way in which Matthew, under the inspiration of the Spirit, understands the double fulfillment of Isaiah's "Virgin Birth" prophecy. He writes,

The virgin of Isaiah 7:14 was first then a virgin of Isaiah's time who would marry, conceive, and bear a child. . . . When the predicted events came to pass in a few years the sign was proven true. However, the ultimate fulfillment of the Immanuel prophecy is seen in the Messiah. In other words, the Isaiah 7:14 prophecy has a double fulfillment—a near and a far accomplishment of the prediction with the ultimate being the final fulfillment in the care of the virgin Mary and the virgin birth of Jesus Christ.[15]

In the original (near) fulfillment of the prophecy in Isaiah's day, the woman gave birth to the son by natural means (Isa. 8:3-4); the son was then symbolically called "Immanuel" to remind the people that God was with them (Isa. 8:8, 10). However, when Matthew read Isaiah 7 and 8 through the messianic lens of Isaiah 9 by the illumination of the Spirit, he understood that in the ultimate (far) fulfillment, Isaiah 7:14 points to a *literal* birth from a virgin—Mary—and refers to the *literal* "God with us"—the incarnation of God the Son, Jesus Christ, the God-man.

Matthew's original Jewish readers would have understood this kind of explanation of Old Testament prophecy, and it would have resonated with them. They would have been able to readily grasp the near/far implications of the prophecy of Isaiah 7 as they were unfolded in Isaiah 8 (near) and Isaiah 9 (far). And they would have expected an intensification of its fulfillment in its application to the Messiah. Throughout the rest of Matthew's Gospel, we'll see similarly profound insights into the ways Jesus fulfilled Old Testament prophecies—both directly and indirectly, both clearly and veiled.

Fulfillment of Isaiah 7:14

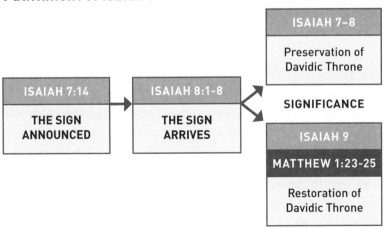

— 1:24-25 —

When Joseph awoke from his life-changing encounter with an angel, he knew exactly what he had to do. His mind was made up, his fear checked, his will submitted to God's. However, this didn't make the days and years ahead of him easier. We can be sure that some of the more observant neighbors and relatives would have "done the math" related to the marriage of Mary and Joseph and the birth of Jesus. Whispered rumors would have spread either about Mary's premarital infidelity or about Joseph's inability to keep himself pure prior to the consummation of their wedding. In fact, Matthew goes out of his way to mention that Joseph didn't have sexual relations with Mary as her husband "until she gave birth" (1:25). So honorable and righteous was Joseph that he kept Mary sexually pure through the birth of the Messiah.

Joseph not only behaved as Mary's faithful protector, but he presumably also took on the role of her advocate. He adjusted his life in a totally new direction once he realized what God was doing in their lives and what part he was meant to play. Together Mary and Joseph would likely bear the brunt of whispered rumors, backbiting gossip, and ugly condemnation—from friends, family, and especially enemies. But Joseph knew the truth, and he made a tough, life-altering decision based on that truth. Being a righteous man, he did what was right, regardless of the personal cost.

APPLICATION: MATTHEW 1:18-25

Doing What's Right, Regardless

As a descendant of David, Joseph's veins flowed with royal blood; but he showed his true nobility not in the purity of his pedigree but in the rightness of his actions. He believed and acted on what he had heard from the angel, taking Mary as his wife and resolving to serve as her advocate through the weeks, months, and years ahead of potential ridicule by those who didn't have the privilege of a heavenly revelation.

In light of Joseph's courageous actions, I'd like us to consider three questions to help us identify with him—to put ourselves in his sandals, as it were. Think through each of these questions carefully, not hastily, in relation to your own decision making. Then get off the fence of indecision and determine to do what's right, not just what's comfortable.

First, *are you being forced to make a tough, life-altering decision? One that calls for sacrifice in order to obey the Lord?* I know that some of you reading this find yourselves facing unbelievably difficult decisions that can literally change your life. They may call for great sacrifice. My counsel to you is this: When it's a matter of obeying God, *do it!* You can count the costs and seek godly counsel, but once you've determined what it is God wants you to do, follow the model of Joseph: Do the hard thing. I've learned in my years in ministry that the right thing is rarely the easy thing. As I look back over my life, some of the best decisions I ever made were also some of the hardest decisions I ever made. You may be facing one of those kinds of decisions. (I'm deliberately leaving the circumstances vague so that this principle can be applied in whatever life-altering situation you may be experiencing.) Don't be afraid.

Second, *are you now experiencing the brunt of others' criticism and judgmental attitudes because of a decision to do what is right?* You may have made a tough decision and are now living in the backwash of others' tongue wagging and headshaking. Perhaps you've chosen an unpopular path, like giving up a promising, lucrative career to pursue what many think is a fool's quest. Maybe you've stayed faithful to your spouse when you could have bolted. Maybe you've admitted your inability to break free from an addiction and have taken courageous steps toward recovery . . . and your old "friends" don't like it. Whatever it is, my counsel to you is to *keep at it!* You've done what's right. Yes, there will probably be those who won't let you off the hook or commend you for doing what is hard. But stay with it. Don't run from it. Keep at it.

Third, *are you aware of someone who needs an advocate to help support them through a difficult time?* Maybe your prodigal child is suffering through an excruciating experience. Maybe your spouse needs you at their side to walk through a trial. Maybe the leaders of your church need a few more allies and encouragers. My advice to you is to *go there!* It's not easy. It requires sacrifice and discomfort, and their problems will certainly become yours. Perhaps their enemies will begin to attack you. But being an advocate is the right thing to do. Go there.

Wise Men and Wicked Men
MATTHEW 2:1-12

NASB

¹Now after Jesus was born in Bethlehem of Judea in the days of Herod the king, ªmagi from the east arrived in Jerusalem, saying, ²"Where is He who has been born King of the Jews? For we saw His star in the east and have come to worship Him." ³When Herod the king heard *this,* he was troubled, and all Jerusalem with him. ⁴Gathering together all the chief priests and scribes of the people, he inquired of them where the ªMessiah was to be born. ⁵They said to him, "In Bethlehem of Judea; for this is what has been written ªby the prophet:

⁶ 'AND YOU, BETHLEHEM, LAND OF
     JUDAH,
ARE BY NO MEANS LEAST AMONG
     THE LEADERS OF JUDAH;
FOR OUT OF YOU SHALL COME
     FORTH A RULER
WHO WILL SHEPHERD MY PEOPLE
     ISRAEL.'"

⁷Then Herod secretly called the magi and determined from them ªthe exact time the star appeared. ⁸And he sent them to Bethlehem and said, "Go and search carefully for the Child; and when you have found *Him,* report to me, so that I too may come and worship Him." ⁹After hearing the king, they went their way; and the star, which they had seen in the east, went on before them until it came and stood over *the place* where the Child was. ¹⁰When they saw the star, they rejoiced exceedingly with great joy. ¹¹After coming into the house they saw the Child with Mary His mother; and they ªfell to the ground and worshiped Him. Then, opening their treasures, they presented to Him gifts of gold, frankincense, and myrrh. ¹²And having

NLT

¹Jesus was born in Bethlehem in Judea, during the reign of King Herod. About that time some wise men* from eastern lands arrived in Jerusalem, asking, ²"Where is the newborn king of the Jews? We saw his star as it rose,* and we have come to worship him."

³King Herod was deeply disturbed when he heard this, as was everyone in Jerusalem. ⁴He called a meeting of the leading priests and teachers of religious law and asked, "Where is the Messiah supposed to be born?"

⁵"In Bethlehem in Judea," they said, "for this is what the prophet wrote:

⁶ 'And you, O Bethlehem in the
     land of Judah,
are not least among the ruling
     cities* of Judah,
for a ruler will come from you
who will be the shepherd for
     my people Israel.'*"

⁷Then Herod called for a private meeting with the wise men, and he learned from them the time when the star first appeared. ⁸Then he told them, "Go to Bethlehem and search carefully for the child. And when you find him, come back and tell me so that I can go and worship him, too!" ⁹After this interview the wise men went their way. And the star they had seen in the east guided them to Bethlehem. It went ahead of them and stopped over the place where the child was. ¹⁰When they saw the star, they were filled with joy! ¹¹They entered the house and saw the child with his mother, Mary, and they bowed down and worshiped him. Then they opened their treasure chests and gave him gifts of gold, frankincense, and myrrh.

¹²When it was time to leave, they

NLT

been warned *by God* in a dream not to return to Herod, the magi left for their own country by another way.

2:1 ªA caste of wise men specializing in astronomy, astrology, and natural science 2:4 ªGr *Christos (Christ)* 2:5 ªOr *through* 2:7 ªLit *the time of the appearing star* 2:11 ªLit *prostrated;* i.e. face down in a prone position to indicate worship

returned to their own country by another route, for God had warned them in a dream not to return to Herod.

2:1 Or *royal astrologers;* Greek reads *magi;* also in 2:7, 16. 2:2 Or *star in the east.* 2:6a Greek *the rulers.* 2:6b Mic 5:2; 2 Sam 5:2.

I'm convinced that most people—including many Bible-believing Christians—get many of their "facts" about the birth of Jesus not from the Bible itself but from cheap Christmas cards, cute Christmas pageants, traditional Christmas carols, and sentimental Nativity sets. Typical Nativity sets—from expensive olive wood to cheap plastic—have certain elements in common. In the center of donkeys, sheep, and other barnyard animals, Mary and Joseph dote over a newborn babe in a wooden manger. Behind them, a few shepherds lean on their staffs in wonder. Angels are posted on top of the thatched roof or are dangling on a string. And, of course, three wise men dressed in opulent robes and crowns kneel before baby Jesus, offering Him priceless gifts.

We also know those wise men were three kings from the Orient . . . just like the song says. They rode three camels by night . . . like all those greeting cards depict. When they arrived at the well-constructed stable, the wise men got a glimpse of the baby's divine halo glowing from the manger. I saw that in a painting. Oh, and their names were Balthasar, Melchior, and Gaspar, from Arabia, Persia, and India, respectively. We get that from church tradition. And, as the story goes, their bones are interred in Cologne, Germany. (Don't ask me why.)

Or so we're led to believe.

However, when we read Matthew's inspired biblical account (2:1-12), we realize that none of these things are actually taught in Scripture. In fact, these details distract us from the real point of the account of the magi from the east. The truth of the matter is far more insightful and relevant than the layers of legend that have almost smothered the high drama of the narrative of the wise men.

— 2:1-3—

If we stick with what the Bible clearly reveals, we'll need to make some significant adjustments to our Nativity sets. We won't have to change the location—Bethlehem of Judea (2:1). And we won't have to change the date—the time of Herod the Great, who reigned as king from 37 BC until his death in 4 BC. (Yes, as odd as it may sound, Jesus was born several years BC—*before Christ*. Most date His birth around 6 BC, about two years before the end of Herod's reign.)

But this is where familiar facts begin to give way to countless legends. Though we've been programmed to believe that "three kings of Orient" came, bearing the three gifts, the Bible makes no such statement. Rather, Matthew doesn't tell us how many men came from the east. He refers to them in the plural, which means there had to have been at least two. But there could have been four or five—or more—traveling together. This certainly isn't a detail to lose any sleep over. But if you accidentally drop one of the three wise-men figurines from your Nativity set and it shatters, you don't have to rush to the store to replace it.

More significant is the fact that Matthew never identifies the visitors from the east as kings. This idea is pure speculation and doesn't actually stand up to historical reasoning. Think about it. What three eastern realms in the first century BC would so easily do without their monarchs while they took a journey to Jerusalem? And if actual kings from Armenia, Parthia, Arabia, Scythia, or even India traveled to Judea, they would have been accompanied by such a horde of guards, servants, officials, and other attendants that it would have looked like an invading army making its way to the Promised Land!

The travelers from the east are identified not as kings, but as "magi." The Greek word *magos* [3097] refers to a "wise man and priest, who was expert in astrology, interpretation of dreams and various other occult arts."[16] But we would be wrong to identify the magi as magicians or sorcerers. Rather, we should probably think of them as philosopher-sages or astrologers who engaged in the interpretation of dreams, sought signs in the heavens, and practiced other such forms of primitive science mixed with folklore.[17] It is possible that they had also become familiar with Old Testament messianic prophecies through exposure to Jewish Scriptures like the books of Isaiah and Daniel, which would have been known among Jewish communities spread through Arabia, Persia, and Babylon (see the eastern regions represented in Acts 2:9-11).[18]

These stargazers weren't kings, but they likely belonged to the upper echelons of society, perhaps serving in a royal court. How else could they have afforded such a long journey and brought such expensive gifts? And if they were well-to-do, they would also have been accompanied by at least a modest entourage that would have made their sudden arrival in Judea noticeable.

HEROD THE GREAT

MATTHEW 2:1

Herod the Great ruled Judea at the time of Jesus' birth, but he had no legitimate right to the title "King of the Jews." Far from having a place in the bloodline of the Davidic dynasty, Herod's ancestors were Idumean converts to Judaism. His father, Antipater, was a wealthy and politically connected Idumean who had been appointed by Rome to a high position in Judea.[19] The Idumeans were descendants of Esau, who had forfeited his birthright to his brother, Jacob, also called "Israel" (Gen. 25:33-34; 32:28). Thus, ironically, in becoming "King of the Jews," Herod seemed to reverse the ancient fortunes of Jacob and Esau, giving the natural firstborn the upper hand. Political support from Rome and a strategic marriage to a Jewish royal gave Herod the crown around 40 BC, and he kept it through bloody intrigue for more than thirty years.[20]

So desperate was Herod to maintain his questionable hold on the title "King of the Jews" that he was known to execute even his own family members. Herod's ruthless madness was legendary. A fifth-century historian, Macrobius, wrote, "When [Caesar Augustus] heard that Herod king of the Jews had ordered boys in Syria under the age of two years to be put to death and that the king's son was among those killed, he said, 'I'd rather be Herod's pig than Herod's son!'"[21]

Archaeologists' reconstruction of **Herod's tomb** at the Herodium near Bethlehem

Beyond the infamy of his brutality, Herod was well known as a builder. His magnificent building projects impressed the masses in his day, and clear remnants of many of those structures are still visible in Israel today. Among these is the retaining wall of the great temple mount in Jerusalem, upon which Herod completely reconstructed and beautified the temple and its surrounding structures. He also constructed fortresses like the Antonia in Jerusalem, Masada near the Dead Sea, and the Herodium near Bethlehem.[22] Despite these valiant attempts to wow the masses and woo their favor, the carnage and mayhem Herod inflicted upon the people of Judea would give him the reputation of one of the most brutal kings in their history.

When they appeared in Jerusalem, the magi immediately got down to business. They were probably expecting to find a young toddler recently added to the royal family—"Where is He who has been born King of the Jews?" (Matt. 2:2). In their inquiry, they revealed that they had been guided all the way from the east by a heavenly light that they identified as "His star," and they were eager to "worship Him." Understandably, King Herod was "troubled" when he heard such things (2:3). In the mind of Herod the Great, only one person in Judea was "King of the Jews" and worthy of worship—*Herod the Great!* And, as Matthew makes clear, when Herod wasn't happy, nobody was happy.

— 2:4-8 —

Herod's reaction to the arrival of the magi looks like frantic damage control. He called together his own cadre of wise men—"chief priests and scribes (2:4)—to give him a crash course akin to Messianic Prophecy 101. He started with the most basic question: Where was the Messiah to be born? On the surface, Herod's actions could be interpreted as sincere, as if he were simply trying to provide an answer to the magi's question or discover the truth of the matter himself. In reality, however, Herod only wanted to preempt any potential threat to his own power, even if this meant killing small children.

One commentator characterizes Herod as "incredibly jealous, suspicious, and afraid for his position and power. Fearing his potential threat, he had the high priest Aristobulus, who was his wife Mariamne's brother, drowned. . . . He then had Mariamne herself killed, and then her mother and two of his own sons. Five days before his death . . . he had a third son executed."[23] Clearly, Herod wasn't trying to locate the Messiah's birthplace so he could throw a baby shower for the King. He was out for blood!

The priests and scribes obliged King Herod and pointed to Micah 5:2, which gave a clear prophecy in which God said that from the seemingly insignificant town of Bethlehem in Judea, "One will go forth for Me to be ruler in Israel." Interestingly, besides presenting King Herod with a somewhat loose paraphrase of the passage from Micah that seemed to simplify the wording for the king, they also left off an important line from the original text that would have exalted the coming Messiah to the position of deity. The messianic prophecy of Micah 5:2 concludes, "His goings forth are from long ago, from the days of eternity."

Having learned the *place* of the Messiah's birth, Herod next wanted to narrow in on the *time*. In a secret meeting, he interviewed the magi themselves, who naively informed King Herod of the moment when the miraculous star announcing the Messiah's birth first appeared in the sky (Matt. 2:7). With knowledge of both the place and the time, Herod sent the well-meaning wise men on a fact-finding mission in service of his wickedness: Find the child and report back. Hiding his true, malevolent intentions, King Herod feigned piety: "Go and search carefully for the Child . . . so that I too may come and worship Him" (2:8).

— 2:9-12 —

The magi wouldn't need to spend any effort searching for Jesus. The miraculous guiding light in the form of a roaming star immediately "went on before them" until it hovered over the exact location of Jesus' home (2:9-10). By this time, Jesus would have been a little over a year old—no longer a swaddled baby lying in a manger. Herod deduced that the child would have been under the age of two "according to the time which he had determined from the magi" (2:16). By this time, then, Mary, Joseph, and Jesus would have settled in a more permanent home in Bethlehem, possibly a home belonging to relatives—descendants of the line of David. After all, Bethlehem had been the family's ancient hometown.

I'm sure Joseph and Mary would not have expected the knock on the door and the visitors they received that day—wealthy foreigners decked out in opulent clothing, not only bringing greetings and gifts but also doing something even more surprising: "They fell to the ground and worshiped Him" (2:11)! The term translated "worshiped" is *proskyneō* [4352], which refers to an act with much greater significance than merely showing honor or respect to a human ruler. One lexicon notes that "Persians did this in the presence of their deified king," and "by this act [the object of worship is] to be recognized as belonging to a superhuman realm."[24]

With their worship, the magi brought offerings not only fit for a king but also appropriate for the worship of God. Gold would have been a standard treasure offered to a king as a tribute or a sign of honor. It was, at the time, regarded as the most precious metal. But beyond gold, they gave Him the eastern spices of frankincense and myrrh. John Peter Lange offers a description of these spices: *"Frankincense, a resin of bitter taste, but fragrant odor, was used chiefly in sacrifices and in the services of the temple. . . . Myrrh, an aromatic of a similar kind . . . was employed for fumigation and for improving the taste of wine, but especially as an ingredient of a very precious ointment."*[25] Many commentators have suggested that the frankincense pointed to Christ's deity or to His function as priest and that the myrrh—associated with burial (John 19:38-42)—served as a foreshadowing of Christ's suffering and death (see Mark 15:23).

Sputnikcccp/English language Wikipedia

Gold, frankincense, and myrrh, the gifts brought to Jesus by the magi

The response of the wise men from the east stands in stark contrast to the reaction of the wicked king in Jerusalem. Herod sought to kill the child; the magi sought to worship Him.

By the time the magi were ready to leave Bethlehem, the Lord warned them in a dream of the true intentions of Herod the Great. So instead of returning to Jerusalem and reporting to the king, the magi slipped off unnoticed and returned to their own country.

APPLICATION: MATTHEW 2:1-12

Responding to the Messiah

Over and over we've been led to believe that three kings visited baby Jesus in the manger. After looking at a few short verses from Matthew's Gospel, we can lay that fairy tale to rest. In fact, only two kings appear in these twelve verses—one a wicked wannabe who had zero legitimate claim to the throne, Herod the Great; the other the true Messiah, the Son of David and Son of God, Jesus. The monstrous Herod manipulated, lied, and schemed to "search and destroy" any threat to his power (2:13). Yet the real center of attention in this passage—whether indifference, hostility, or worship—was the young Messiah. Let's briefly consider each of the responses to Jesus in this passage. I think we'll find that they're similar to the responses people have to Jesus today.

First, we find *indifference*. When Herod called together the high priests and scribes, those religious teachers and Bible scholars knew without hesitation the facts surrounding the coming of the Messiah. They could have won first place in a Bible trivia contest. Perhaps they patted themselves on the back for being able to answer the king's scriptural question with such ease. But assuming they found out the reason why Herod was asking, these religious leaders didn't seem interested in checking it out for themselves. They had the book knowledge, but they had no passion. The truth of Scripture hadn't moved from their heads to their hearts, and it had certainly not made it to their hands and feet.

Second, we find *hostility*. Herod, though veiling his true motives in false piety and curiosity, sought to destroy the child before He became a threat to his rule. People today similarly find the claims of Christ's lordship threatening. Nobody's threatened by a tiny baby in a manger or a moral teacher or a Cynic sage or a religious philosopher. Such descriptions refer to a mere man who can be either respected or ignored. But the God-man, the King with authority over heaven and earth who deserves full obedience and submission? Unbelievers who have everything to lose in the realm of personal power will fight such a Messiah with venom and vehemence. Just like Herod the Great.

Finally, we find *worship*. Wise women and men today have chosen to follow the guiding light of the Spirit of God and fall down to worship and adore Jesus Christ as God and King. Like the magi of old, they acknowledge Him as worthy of worship, honor, trust, obedience, and total allegiance. And they won't betray their true King for short-term gains found in the favor of a temporal king.

Each of us today must choose how we'll respond to the Messiah—like the wise or the wicked?

Destination-Driven Dreams
MATTHEW 2:13-23

NASB

13 Now when they had gone, behold, an angel of the Lord appeared to Joseph in a dream and said, "Get up!

NLT

13 After the wise men were gone, an angel of the Lord appeared to Joseph in a dream. "Get up! Flee to Egypt

NASB

Take the Child and His mother and flee to Egypt, and remain there until I tell you; for Herod is going to search for the Child to destroy Him."

¹⁴So ᵃJoseph got up and took the Child and His mother while it was still night, and left for Egypt. ¹⁵He ᵃremained there until the death of Herod. *This was* to fulfill what had been spoken by the Lord through the prophet: "OUT OF EGYPT I CALLED MY SON."

¹⁶Then when Herod saw that he had been tricked by the magi, he became very enraged, and sent and slew all the male children who were in Bethlehem and all its vicinity, from two years old and under, according to the time which he had determined from the magi. ¹⁷Then what had been spoken through Jeremiah the prophet was fulfilled:

¹⁸ "A VOICE WAS HEARD IN RAMAH,
WEEPING AND GREAT MOURNING,
RACHEL WEEPING FOR HER
    CHILDREN;
AND SHE REFUSED TO BE
    COMFORTED,
BECAUSE THEY WERE NO MORE."

¹⁹But when Herod died, behold, an angel of the Lord appeared in a dream to Joseph in Egypt, and said, ²⁰"Get up, take the Child and His mother, and go into the land of Israel; for those who sought the Child's life are dead." ²¹So ᵃJoseph got up, took the Child and His mother, and came into the land of Israel. ²²But when he heard that Archelaus was reigning over Judea in place of his father Herod, he was afraid to go there. Then after being warned *by God* in a dream, he left for the regions of Galilee, ²³and came and lived in a city called Nazareth. *This was* to fulfill what was spoken through the prophets: "He shall be called a Nazarene."

2:14 ᵃLit *he*   2:15 ᵃLit *was*   2:21 ᵃLit *he*

NLT

with the child and his mother," the angel said. "Stay there until I tell you to return, because Herod is going to search for the child to kill him."

¹⁴That night Joseph left for Egypt with the child and Mary, his mother, ¹⁵and they stayed there until Herod's death. This fulfilled what the Lord had spoken through the prophet: "I called my Son out of Egypt."*

¹⁶Herod was furious when he realized that the wise men had outwitted him. He sent soldiers to kill all the boys in and around Bethlehem who were two years old and under, based on the wise men's report of the star's first appearance. ¹⁷Herod's brutal action fulfilled what God had spoken through the prophet Jeremiah:

¹⁸ "A cry was heard in Ramah—
    weeping and great mourning.
Rachel weeps for her children,
    refusing to be comforted,
    for they are dead."*

¹⁹When Herod died, an angel of the Lord appeared in a dream to Joseph in Egypt. ²⁰"Get up!" the angel said. "Take the child and his mother back to the land of Israel, because those who were trying to kill the child are dead."

²¹So Joseph got up and returned to the land of Israel with Jesus and his mother. ²²But when he learned that the new ruler of Judea was Herod's son Archelaus, he was afraid to go there. Then, after being warned in a dream, he left for the region of Galilee. ²³So the family went and lived in a town called Nazareth. This fulfilled what the prophets had said: "He will be called a Nazarene."

2:15 Hos 11:1.   2:18 Jer 31:15.

When people try to discern the Lord's leading, they often do strange things. I read about a man in Washington, DC, who was seeking the Lord's will for his life. His car stalled in front of the Philippine embassy, and he took that as a sure sign that God was calling him to be a missionary to the Philippines.

A woman, not sure she should take a trip to Israel, read a brochure one evening before going to bed. She noticed that the flight from New York to Tel Aviv would be on a 747. She folded up the brochure and prayed, *Lord, make it clear whether I should do this or not.* The next morning, she woke up and her digital clock read "7:47." She took that to mean she should go to Israel on that airplane.

I could tell about a dozen more stories like this—all of them true, but many hard to believe. It's amazing how many Christians believe God leads through means that are superstitious or are borderline occult practices. God doesn't lead His children through stars in the night or cloud formations passing in the sky during the day. Nor does He reveal His will through horoscopes, the zodiac, or random verses found by plopping open a Bible and pointing with a finger.

Dawson Trotman, founder of The Navigators, used to say, "The Lord gave you a lot of leading when He gave you a brain." God didn't give us brains so we could switch them off when we have to make decisions. We don't kick our reason into neutral in order to seek His will. God leads through clear thinking based on the information and resources He gives us on our journey.

However, when we turn the pages of our Bibles to Matthew 2:13-23, we encounter a time when God led His people in some clear, direct, and astonishing means. We read of dreams, voices, and angels—supernatural experiences that communicated God's specific will loud and clear. Before God inspired all sixty-six books of the Bible and sent His Spirit at Pentecost to indwell believers (Acts 2), He often revealed His will in unique, supernatural ways. One of those ways—dreams—we see over and over again in connection with the birth and early life of the Messiah.

Though we don't expect God to use dreams and visions as a normal way of revealing Himself to us, we can learn a lot from the way Joseph and Mary responded to God's clear revelation of His will. Hopefully, our own responses to the revealed will of God will be as immediate and complete as theirs.

— 2:13-15 —

This next scene in Matthew's account of the dramatic events surrounding Jesus' birth occurred immediately after the magi departed secretly to their country in response to a warning from God in a dream (2:12). And that wasn't the first time in Matthew's Gospel that the Lord revealed His specific will through a dream. Remember? Joseph had already received in a dream a revelation about Mary's miraculous conception (1:19-21). Three more times God would use this same means to guide the steps of Joseph and his family (2:13, 19, 22).

The Lord was clearly orchestrating events during these crucial years of the Messiah's childhood, guiding Joseph and Mary in the protection of their young child. What I find particularly interesting is the timing and order of events. The Greek text of 2:13 indicates a very close connection between the departure of the magi and the appearance of the angel. In fact, we might render the text, "Upon the departure of the wise men, an angel of the Lord appeared." Picture it. Joseph and Mary had just packed away the expensive gifts from the magi and had turned in to sleep when an angel prompted Joseph to wake up, flee to Egypt with his family, and stay there until the coast was clear from Herod's madness.

The prospect of suddenly fleeing to Egypt in the middle of the night would have been utterly daunting to a young family with limited means . . . had the magi not just loaded the family down with gold, frankincense, and myrrh! As the adage goes, "Where the Lord guides, He provides!" So, gathering their limited belongings and packing the treasures securely, Joseph obeyed the angel's instruction instantly. Matthew indicates in 2:14 that they left "while it was still night." Joseph didn't call a family meeting to weigh the angel's words, didn't begin a week of planning and packing, and didn't go ahead to find suitable lodging in Egypt for his family. He fled immediately because the angel had warned him that Herod would soon be searching for the child to destroy Him (2:13). Because of the dangerous prospect of a pursuit, Joseph and his family no doubt left Bethlehem in a manner similar to the magi—quietly and secretly, without a word to anyone. They left without a trace.

The treasure provided by the magi probably enabled the family to remain in Egypt until the dust settled back home after the death of Herod, perhaps two or three years later. We know nothing of their stay in Egypt, not even the city where they dwelled, though many believe it was the large city of Alexandria. The specific place isn't important. What's important is that Joseph had probably never been to Egypt before and was thus stepping into a whole host of unknowns, trusting God to continue to guide and provide while he simply obeyed.

Matthew concludes this brief scene of the flight to Egypt by drawing

Five Principles for Discerning God's Leading

MATTHEW 2:13

Throughout my life, I've had seasons in which numerous decisions and opportunities have driven me to seek the will of God. Never has the Lord sent an angel or spoken to me in a dream or guided me with a star, as He did in the second chapter of Matthew. However, I have learned a handful of principles for discerning God's will through both my study of Scripture and my reflection on how God has led me—and others—through the years.

First, God leads those who have chosen to follow Him. You need to be a Christian if you hope to be led by God. Romans 8:14 says, "For all who are being led by the Spirit of God, these are sons of God." Christians enjoy a personal relationship with Christ through the indwelling Spirit. One of the great benefits believers have that non-Christians don't is the privilege of being led by the Spirit.

Second, God leads through His written Word. Careful, intelligent, and diligent study of the Bible helps us to learn God's mind on moral and practical matters, informs a Christian view of the world, and imparts wisdom and virtue in keeping with the heart of God. Psalm 119:105 says, "Your word is a lamp to my feet and a light to my path." The Bible may not directly address your specific question, like "Should I accept this job offer or that job offer?" But as God's values and priorities become yours through careful meditation on His Word, you will be able to more critically think through the values and priorities involved in even seemingly neutral decisions like these.

Third, God leads through the inner promptings of the Holy Spirit. I don't mean tingling, butterflies, or warm sensations. I mean something inexpressible and, yes, even mysterious. The Spirit of God truly—not metaphorically—lives in us. He will work to convict you when you're doing wrong and give you a sense of confidence and

(continued on next page)

relief when you do what's right. He'll illuminate the truth of Scripture and open your eyes to see things you didn't see before. When you pray for wisdom and insight, He'll give it (Jas. 1:5). In, with, and through the inspired Word of God, the Spirit works in, with, and through you as you genuinely and humbly seek Him.

Fourth, God leads through the counsel of wise, qualified, mature, trustworthy Christians who love and care for you (see Prov. 11:14). All these adjectives are important. Don't ask just anybody you know to share their perspective and insight; seek those who exhibit Christlike character, have years of experience walking with God, know you intimately, and have your best interests in mind. You want counselors who are objective, who have no personal or vested interest in the outcome of your decision, and who will ask hard questions and not let you get away with weak answers.

Fifth, God leads by replacing restlessness and fear with confidence and calmness. He gives us inner peace. Colossians 3:15 says, "Let the peace of Christ rule in your hearts." Of course, the feeling of peace over a decision can't be separated from the other four principles. I've met people in total rebellion against God's clearly revealed will in Scripture who claimed to have had peace over their sinful decisions. But if your process for discerning God's will renders several equally good and viable alternatives, there's nothing wrong with humbly taking steps toward the one that brings peace and relieves restlessness.

a fascinating parallel between the sojourn of Jesus in Egypt and the sojourn of the nation of Israel prior to the Exodus. In 2:15, Matthew quotes Hosea 11:1, which in its original context did not refer to the incarnate Son of God as a direct prophecy, nor to a family leaving Egypt after hiding from a wicked king. Rather, it referred to the nation of Israel, figuratively and corporately called God's "son" because the nation had been adopted as His special people, watched over in their bondage in Egypt, and called out of Egypt during the Exodus. Hosea 11:1 says, "When Israel was a youth I loved him, and out of Egypt I called My son." The passage goes on to describe both the apostasy of Israel in going after idols and sacrificing to foreign gods and the chastisement that fell upon them as a result (Hos. 11:2-11). The figure of speech in Hosea 11:1 is clearly a personification. It also involves a concept called *corporate solidarity*, in which the many are represented by the one (here, the nation is represented by the expression "My son").

In what way, then, does Jesus' flight to and return from Egypt fulfill this passage?

In a creative way, Matthew is communicating that the Messiah is the true Israel in the grandest sense—the epitome, or climax, of everything Israel was supposed to have been. In this connection, Jesus is the fulfillment of the figurative "son." While Israel may have been an adopted son of God, their continual disobedience caused them to fall under discipline, including exile from the land. The literal Son, Jesus, represents the nation in a spiritual way, undoing their disobedience through His own obedience. By citing Hosea 11:1, Matthew is drawing from the Exodus motif as well as pointing out the sharp contrast between the "son" of the Old Testament and the Son of the New.

— 2:16-18 —

It didn't take long for Herod, the paranoid megalomaniac, to realize he'd been "tricked by the magi" (2:16). In response, he sent soldiers to slaughter all the boys under two years old in Bethlehem and the surrounding region. He hoped he would thereby destroy the child the magi had hailed as "King of the Jews" (2:2). Little did he know, of course, that Joseph, Mary, and Jesus had already fled, perhaps only a matter of hours earlier.

As heinous as it seems to us today, Herod's rage against the innocent children of Bethlehem would have probably drawn shrugs from many of those who knew Herod. Such brutality was business as usual for that monster. Michael Green notes that Herod "slaughtered the last remnants of the Hasmonean dynasty of Jewish high-priestly kings who had ruled before him. He executed more than half the Sanhedrin. He killed 300 court officers out of hand. He executed his own Hasmonean wife, Mariamne, her mother Alexandra, and his sons Aristobulus, Alexander and Antipater. Finally, as he lay dying, he arranged for all the notable men of Jerusalem to be assembled in the hippodrome and killed as soon as his own death was announced."[26]

Though the death of the innocents—perhaps as many as two or three dozen—wasn't enough to get a single secular historian to use their ink on it, the Holy Spirit moved Matthew to tap into the pain and anguish of those parents who lost those who were their pride and joy at the hands of a madman. Quoting Jeremiah 31:15, Matthew illustrates the kind of weeping and mourning that was heard and felt in Bethlehem by comparing it to the lamenting of mothers in Ramah who had lost their children when they were dragged into exile (Matt. 2:18).

This is the third instance of Matthew's use of the "fulfillment" formula for an Old Testament passage that was being completed in some sense by a New Testament event. Among the similarities between the two passages is the weeping and mourning that took place during both tragedies because of the loss of children. Among the differences is the fact that the locations of the events were not the same. Ramah, mentioned in the Jeremiah passage, is nowhere near Bethlehem. In addition, in the Old Testament situation, a figurative "Rachel" wept for her children; in the New Testament, many mothers mourned for theirs. In the New Testament account, the cause of mourning was the death of sons; in the Old Testament story, it was the children lost to the Exile.

But if we try to envision how a first-century Jewish reader would have read Matthew, we are invited to deeper reflection on the two events placed side by side in 2:18. In the original context of Jeremiah 31:15, God was comforting His people with words of promise: regathering, rebuilding, returning of the remnant, and rejoicing (Jer. 31:1-12). God would one day "turn their mourning into joy" (Jer. 31:13), and His people would be satisfied with His goodness (Jer. 31:14). The Lord God contrasted this coming joy with the previous state of despair by declaring the words that Matthew would one day quote, which begin, "A voice is heard in Ramah" (Jer. 31:15). Immediately after this verse come the words "'Restrain your voice from weeping and your eyes from tears; for your work will be rewarded,' declares the LORD, 'and they will return from the land of the enemy. There is hope for your future,' declares the LORD, 'and your children will return to their own territory'"

(Jer. 31:16-17). God then elaborated on this promise (Jer. 31:18-25) and followed it with the promise of the new covenant, which, as we know from the New Testament, is fulfilled in a direct way through Christ (Jer. 31:27-34; see Matt. 26:26-28). It is with an understanding of this broad, messianic, new-covenant context that Matthew cites this passage.

EXCURSUS: THE MEANING OF "FULFILL" IN MATTHEW

MATTHEW 2:15, 17, 23

In Matthew, the word *plēroō* [4137] and its prefixed form, *anaplēroō* [378]—both translated "to fulfill"—are used eleven times with various forms of a fulfillment formula: "[This event] fulfills what was written [in that Old Testament Scripture]."[27] One standard Greek lexicon gives six nuances for *plēroō*: (1) to make full; (2) to complete a period of time; (3) to finish something already begun; (4) to fulfill a prophecy, obligation, promise, law, or request; (5) to complete or bring to an end; and (6) to have the number completed.[28] The general meaning of the term, then, is to fill up what is lacking.

Matthew himself understood the flexibility of the word *plēroō*. He uses it in 3:15, where Jesus submits to John's baptism because it was necessary to "fulfill all righteousness." The "thing lacking" was Jesus' baptism. In 5:17, Jesus declares that He came not to abolish the Law but to "fulfill" it, meaning that He came to meet the requirements of the commands. The "thing lacking" was the obedient response to the commands of the Law. A very interesting use of the word emerges in 23:32, where Jesus says that the Israelites would "fill up" the measure of their fathers' wickedness; that is, they attained to the same degree of evil as their ancestors. The "thing lacking" was more wickedness! Matthew evidently understood the primary meaning and the various nuances of the term.

In light of the various ways *plēroō* can be used, what does Matthew mean when he says an event or circumstance in the life of Christ "fulfilled" an Old Testament Scripture? In a broad sense, the "thing that is lacking" in the Old Testament text that is "fulfilled" by the New Testament event is first and foremost *a more complete revelation in Jesus Christ*. A type of Christ may lack its antitype in the life of Christ; an illustration may lack its referent; a prophecy may lack its accomplishment; a promise may lack its fulfillment; a series of events may lack its ultimate climax. The New Testament authors saw in the person and work of Jesus Christ the ultimate revelation of God (see, e.g., Luke 24:27; John 5:39; Heb. 1:1-2). In other words, the body of revelation contained in the Old Testament Scriptures was lacking the further revelation that comes through Christ, similar to the way a question may have an incomplete answer.

This kind of notion of the Old Testament—through its use of pattern, type, illustration, or anticipation—being "fulfilled" in the New Testament would have been familiar to Matthew's Jewish readers. This approach invites readers to mull over passages of Scripture, thinking more carefully about what Matthew is doing in each individual "fulfillment" passage.

Certainly, Matthew wasn't suggesting that Jeremiah 31:15 was a clear and direct prophecy about male children dying in Bethlehem. Rather, Matthew uses this parallel as a springboard into the broad picture of comfort, redemption, and future joy under the new covenant. The type in history was fulfilled by the messianic antitype. Matthew's Jewish readers would have understood and appreciated his use of literary and theological parallels that point to deeper truths.

— 2:19-23 —

Just as God brought the nation of Israel out of Egypt, He also called His Son, Jesus, out of Egypt at the right time. In another dream, an angel informed Joseph that Herod had died and told him to return with Mary and Jesus to the land of Israel (2:19-20). Instantly Joseph obeyed (2:21). It seems that at first Joseph hoped to return to the house he had left in Bethlehem of Judea. However, as he neared, he caught wind of the new ruler in Jerusalem—the son of Herod named Archelaus. F. F. Bruce notes, "Archelaus had all his father's defects of character with but little of his administrative and diplomatic ability."[29] No wonder Joseph "was afraid to go there" (2:22).

Yet Joseph had learned not to question God's clear leading. He headed for the hills of Judea, confident that God would protect him and his family as He always had. But then the Lord stepped in again through another dream and steered Joseph in a different direction—toward Galilee, to a small village called Nazareth (2:22-23). This was the city where Mary and Joseph had originally lived before traveling to Bethlehem during her pregnancy (Luke 1:26-27; 2:4). At that time, the region of Galilee was being governed by another of Herod's sons, Antipas, who was "the ablest of Herod's sons," able to maintain relative peace and order in his territories for over forty years.[30]

Matthew concludes this section on the divinely directed journeys of Joseph, Mary, and Jesus with one last parallel drawn between the Old Testament Scriptures and circumstances in the life of Christ. Matthew says that Jesus spent most of His childhood years as a resident of Nazareth in fulfillment of prophecy—"He shall be called a Nazarene" (Matt. 2:23).

On the surface, this appears problematic because there is no verse in the Old Testament that contains this prophecy. However, we should note that Matthew doesn't cite any particular prophet, or even *one* prophet. Rather, he says that this description of the Messiah as a "Nazarene" was spoken through the *prophets*—plural. The prophets spoke many things

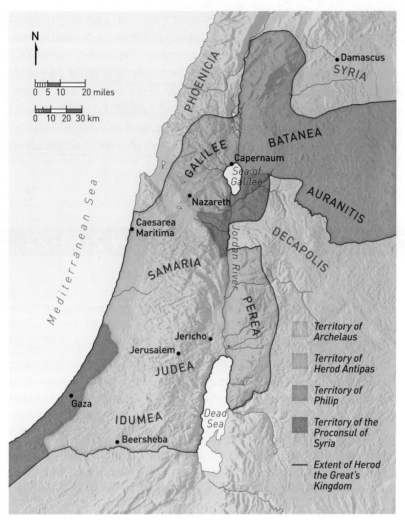

The regions ruled by Herod the Great were divided between his sons when he died in 4 BC.

that aren't recorded in the Old Testament, so it's possible that this was one of those things. However, some commentators suggest that perhaps Matthew was pointing out the fact that the Old Testament indicated the Messiah would come from humble, despised origins—a perfect description of somebody from Nazareth. For example, R. T. France suggests that "Matthew saw in the obscurity of Nazareth the fulfilment of Old Testament indications of a humble and rejected Messiah," such as Psalm 22; Isaiah 53; and Zechariah 11:4-14.[31]

Throughout this series of upheavals in the early life of Jesus, we clearly see the providential and protective hand of God, who provided for the family of the Messiah in amazing ways. God gave supernatural guidance just when it was needed most. But more importantly, Matthew repeatedly points out how the seemingly disjointed, reactionary movements of Joseph and his family were anything but a desperate attempt by God to stay just one step ahead of the forces of evil. Rather, Matthew shows how events in the life of Christ fulfilled Old Testament types, parallels, and prophecies beautifully.

From Bethlehem to Egypt to Nazareth, Joseph heard God's leading, trusted His guidance, and obeyed His word.

APPLICATION: MATTHEW 2:13-23

Three Disciplines of the Will of God

We've tracked the journeys of Joseph, Mary, and Jesus over many miles and through various situations. We've seen God lead them out of danger, into unexpected places, and to new places called "home." The landscapes changed, the cultures changed . . . even the languages changed. And, no doubt, each move taught them a new lesson on what it means to trust and obey God. As I look at how and why the Lord led this little family as He did, I am reminded of three specific disciplines of the Christian life that relate to following God's will.

First, *we need the discipline of trusting.* Remember, Joseph was given clear instructions to get up and go (2:13). Joseph had no clue how close he was to danger at the time. Had he lingered or delayed or weighed alternatives, he would have put his family in harm's way. Sometimes, God's clear will comes suddenly and requires an immediate response. That response is to trust Him enough to obey Him right away and completely. We trust that God knows best, that His timing is right, and that maybe later we'll be able to know *why* He chose a particular path for us.

Second, *we need the discipline of waiting.* The Lord told Joseph to pull up stakes in Egypt probably right about the time he and the family had been getting used to the strange environment (2:19-20). Then they found out that a king had taken over in Judea who was about as monstrous as Herod the Great! God's will can be surprising and confusing. It no doubt seemed to Joseph that this time God was leading his family straight *into* harm's way. Yet it was clearly God's will that Joseph face that danger without knowing exactly how God would deal with it.

Joseph learned how to wait on the Lord to intervene in the midst of his confusion. Joseph's job was simply to do the will of God, letting Him work out the details in His own time.

Third, *we need the discipline of humility.* Remember, when God led this little family back to the Promised Land, it wasn't to the City of David, Bethlehem—little more than a stone's throw from Jerusalem. Instead, God sent them to Nazareth, an obscure, little-known village in Galilee, more than 60 miles away from Jerusalem. Occasionally, God's will requires us to accept obscurity, insignificance, and the mundane while He is working on us—possibly over the course of many years—to prepare us for the next step in the journey He has for us.

Trusting, waiting, and humility—the journeys of Joseph, Mary, and Jesus give us a glimpse of these qualities, which are needed to trust and obey God when we have discerned His will.

Strange Preacher, Strong Proclamation
MATTHEW 3:1-17

NASB

¹Now in those days John the Baptist ªcame, ᵇpreaching in the wilderness of Judea, saying, ²"Repent, for the kingdom of heaven ªis at hand." ³For this is the one referred to ªby Isaiah the prophet when he said,

"THE VOICE OF ONE ᵇCRYING IN
THE WILDERNESS,
'MAKE READY THE WAY OF THE
LORD,
MAKE HIS PATHS STRAIGHT!'"

⁴Now John himself had ªa garment of camel's hair and a leather belt around his waist; and his food was locusts and wild honey. ⁵Then Jerusalem was going out to him, and all Judea and all the district around the Jordan; ⁶and they were being baptized by him in the Jordan River, as they confessed their sins.

⁷But when he saw many of the

NLT

¹In those days John the Baptist came to the Judean wilderness and began preaching. His message was, ²"Repent of your sins and turn to God, for the Kingdom of Heaven is near.*"
³The prophet Isaiah was speaking about John when he said,

"He is a voice shouting in the
wilderness,
'Prepare the way for the LORD's
coming!
Clear the road for him!'"*

⁴John's clothes were woven from coarse camel hair, and he wore a leather belt around his waist. For food he ate locusts and wild honey. ⁵People from Jerusalem and from all of Judea and all over the Jordan Valley went out to see and hear John. ⁶And when they confessed their sins, he baptized them in the Jordan River.

⁷But when he saw many Pharisees

NASB

Pharisees and Sadducees coming for baptism, he said to them, "You brood of vipers, who warned you to flee from the wrath to come? ⁸Therefore bear fruit in keeping with repentance; ⁹and do not suppose that you can say to yourselves, 'We have Abraham for our father'; for I say to you that from these stones God is able to raise up children to Abraham. ¹⁰The axe is already laid at the root of the trees; therefore every tree that does not bear good fruit is cut down and thrown into the fire.

¹¹"As for me, I baptize you ªwith water for repentance, but He who is coming after me is mightier than I, and I am not fit to remove His sandals; He will baptize you ªwith the Holy Spirit and fire. ¹²His winnowing fork is in His hand, and He will thoroughly clear His threshing floor; and He will gather His wheat into the barn, but He will burn up the chaff with unquenchable fire."

¹³Then Jesus arrived from Galilee at the Jordan *coming* to John, to be baptized by him. ¹⁴But John tried to prevent Him, saying, "I have need to be baptized by You, and do You come to me?" ¹⁵But Jesus answering said to him, "Permit *it* at this time; for in this way it is fitting for us to fulfill all righteousness." Then he permitted Him. ¹⁶After being baptized, Jesus came up immediately from the water; and behold, the heavens were opened, and ªhe saw the Spirit of God descending as a dove *and* ᵇlighting on Him, ¹⁷and behold, a voice out of the heavens said, "This is ªMy beloved Son, in whom I am well-pleased."

3:1 ªOr *arrived*, or *appeared* ᵇOr *proclaiming as a herald* 3:2 ªLit *has come near* 3:3 ªOr *through* ᵇOr *shouting* 3:4 ªLit *his garment* 3:11 ªThe Gr here can be translated *in, with* or *by* 3:16 ªOr *He* ᵇLit *coming upon Him* 3:17 ªOr *My Son, the Beloved*

NLT

and Sadducees coming to watch him baptize,* he denounced them. "You brood of snakes!" he exclaimed. "Who warned you to flee the coming wrath? ⁸Prove by the way you live that you have repented of your sins and turned to God. ⁹Don't just say to each other, 'We're safe, for we are descendants of Abraham.' That means nothing, for I tell you, God can create children of Abraham from these very stones. ¹⁰Even now the ax of God's judgment is poised, ready to sever the roots of the trees. Yes, every tree that does not produce good fruit will be chopped down and thrown into the fire.

¹¹"I baptize with* water those who repent of their sins and turn to God. But someone is coming soon who is greater than I am—so much greater that I'm not worthy even to be his slave and carry his sandals. He will baptize you with the Holy Spirit and with fire.* ¹²He is ready to separate the chaff from the wheat with his winnowing fork. Then he will clean up the threshing area, gathering the wheat into his barn but burning the chaff with never-ending fire."

¹³Then Jesus went from Galilee to the Jordan River to be baptized by John. ¹⁴But John tried to talk him out of it. "I am the one who needs to be baptized by you," he said, "so why are you coming to me?"

¹⁵But Jesus said, "It should be done, for we must carry out all that God requires.*" So John agreed to baptize him.

¹⁶After his baptism, as Jesus came up out of the water, the heavens were opened* and he saw the Spirit of God descending like a dove and settling on him. ¹⁷And a voice from heaven said, "This is my dearly loved Son, who brings me great joy."

3:2 Or *has come*, or *is coming soon.* 3:3 Isa 40:3 (Greek version). 3:7 Or *coming to be baptized.* 3:11a Or *in.* 3:11b Or *in the Holy Spirit and in fire.* 3:15 Or *for we must fulfill all righteousness.* 3:16 Some manuscripts read *opened to him.*

Through the years, there have been some unusual preachers who have delivered powerful messages. Consider some who lived in biblical days. Noah built a giant boat while proclaiming a message of coming judgment for well over a century. His hearers were disinterested, to say the least. In fact, every intention of the thoughts of their hearts was "only evil continually" (Gen. 6:5). I'm sure from the vantage point of those wicked unbelievers Noah's preaching seemed strange . . . until the flood came.

Moses didn't get started in his ministry as a prophet until he was eighty years old. Then he made up for lost time over the next forty years. He challenged the power of the false gods of the Egyptians, freed the Hebrews from bondage to the pharaoh, and stunned the nations with powerful signs. Yet most of the time he delivered his messages through his brother, Aaron, rather than directly to the people (see Exod. 4:28-30).

Elijah came out of nowhere, but he became one of the most admired prophets in Israel's history, largely on account of his boldness. Yet he retreated in a weak moment and even asked God to kill him when Jezebel threatened to have him assassinated (1 Kgs. 19:1-4). Even the most powerful preachers can find themselves in the pit of despair!

In the Old Testament, God seemed to delight in using imperfect, weak, unlikely, and, yes, even strange people to deliver strong proclamations. Nothing had changed at the close of the Old Testament era and the dawn of the New Testament. The last great old-covenant preacher of repentance—John the Baptizer—certainly fit the bill of a strange preacher with a strong proclamation.

— 3:1-4 —

With John the Baptizer, it was "what you see is what you get." He was raw, authentic, real. He didn't spiff himself up, put on a flowing white robe, and craft scripted sermons to be sensitive to the seekers. He didn't avoid words like *sin*, *repent*, or even *judgment* and *fire*! He didn't care what people thought of him, what he wore, or what he ate (3:4). And he certainly didn't adjust his message to accommodate influential or wealthy members of his audience. He had one mission—to preach the message God gave him to preach.

What was that message? Matthew summarizes it: "Repent, for the kingdom of heaven is at hand" (3:2). The word translated "repent" is the Greek term *metanoeō* [3340], which means to "change one's mind," resulting in a change of allegiances, lifestyle, or trajectory.[32] It doesn't mean "change your ways." True repentance doesn't start with external actions or mere behavior modifications. We've all seen outwardly compliant children do what's right while harboring rebellion in their hearts. The kind of repentance John preached was a change of mind that was followed by a change of lifestyle.

The urgency for John's call to repentance was the imminent coming of the kingdom of heaven. John's original Jewish audience—as well as Matthew's Jewish readers—would most likely have understood the coming kingdom of God as the messianic kingdom described in such passages as Daniel 2:44: "The God of heaven will set up a kingdom which will never be destroyed, and that kingdom will not be left for another people; it will crush and put an end to all these kingdoms, but it will itself endure forever." Daniel's dramatic vision itself hearkens back to other messianic prophecies, such as Isaiah 9:7: "There will be no end to the increase of His government or of peace, on the throne of David and over his kingdom, to establish it and to uphold it with justice and righteousness from then on and forevermore. The zeal of the LORD of hosts will accomplish this."

So, the "kingdom of heaven," Matthew's expression for the "kingdom of God" (see Mark 1:15), is the long-anticipated kingdom that would come with the arrival of the Messiah. With the kingdom would come righteousness, peace, justice, deliverance, and blessing for God's people. The coming of the kingdom would also bring judgment and wrath upon unbelievers, the wicked, and those who rejected God and His Messiah. This is why repentance was necessary. "John's message . . . was that a change of mind and heart (*metanoeite,* 'repent') was necessary before they could qualify for the kingdom. They did not realize how far they had drifted from God's Law and the requirements laid down by the prophets (e.g., Mal. 3:7-12)."[33]

Matthew doesn't give us any background regarding John's origins. The Gospel of Luke, however, tells us that John was the son of a priest, Zacharias, whose wife was a relative of Mary, the mother of Jesus (Luke 1:5-25, 39-45, 57-80). It's quite likely that John and Jesus knew of each other during their childhood years—though probably not well. In any case, Matthew doesn't focus on John's family and background. Instead, he introduces John via his preaching ministry, which anticipated the coming of the Messiah. Matthew presents John's message as a fulfillment of Isaiah 40:3, in which a voice cries out, "Clear the way for the LORD in the wilderness; make smooth in the desert a highway for our God." From Matthew's perspective, if John's preaching was to prepare the way for the Messiah, Jesus, and if that ministry fulfilled Isaiah's reference to a voice preparing the way for the Lord God, then in some way the coming of Jesus was the coming of God Himself! R. T. France notes, "It is one of several places in Matthew (and throughout the New Testament) where Old Testament passages about the coming of God are seen as fulfilled in Jesus."[34]

— 3:5-12 —

How did the Jews respond to John's preaching of repentance and the coming kingdom? Matthew tells us that word of this strange preacher and his strong proclamation had reached Jerusalem, Judea, and all around the Jordan River. People from all walks of life wanted to see and hear for themselves what this famed prophet had to say. And in response, they were being baptized in the Jordan "as they confessed their sins" (3:6).

This act of being immersed in water had particular significance for first-century Jews. Against the backdrop of Old Testament purification rites (e.g., Exod. 29:4; 2 Kgs. 5:14), Judaism had likely incorporated a single act of ceremonial cleansing as part of the initiation process for a Gentile converting to Judaism. After passing an examination, the males were circumcised, and all converts were immersed in water. Baptism became a symbol of a once-for-all cleansing from sin, undertaken before entering the Jewish covenant community. To be "baptized into" Judaism was to become a "son of the covenant" along with natural-born Jews.[35]

When John the Baptizer took up the rite of immersion, he "infused into the ritual act of initiation and purification an ethical quality that baptism had not had before. His was a moral community of penitent souls seeking personal righteousness, and he associated with the act of baptism the imperative necessity for a thorough change in the condition of the soul."[36] Or, as one commentator states, "Baptism for John was a symbol of repentance, a symbol of cleansing from sin and turning away from the old life to a new life."[37] So, like proselyte baptism, John's baptism was an outward symbol of inward devotion to God, submission to His will, and identity with the true people of God. And it was more than just a mark of repentance from sin; it was also a consecration to a life of loving service to God and to holiness. Take note, however, that the audience of John's address was not morally and spiritually "filthy" Gentiles, but Jews! He was saying, in effect, "Because of your sin, you are outside of Abraham's covenant with God—*unclean!* You must repent like a Gentile and come to God as if for the first time."

THE PHARISEES AND SADDUCEES

MATTHEW 3:7

A. T. Robertson has noted, "One cannot properly understand the theological atmosphere of Palestine at this time without an adequate knowledge of both Pharisees and Sadducees."[38] In the same way that twenty-first-century Christianity has its conservative and progressive wings, first-century Judaism had its right-wing (Pharisee) and left-wing (Sadducee) branches. The Pharisees were more traditional and orthodox in their doctrine and practice. They were the much larger party, having the respect and favor of the general population, who mostly saw eye to eye with them on theological matters. The Sadducees, on the other hand, tended to be much more secular in their doctrine, yet they generally had control of the priesthood and worked in close association with the prevailing political powers.

Most likely, the term "Pharisee" means "separated one."[39] Many historians trace this strict branch of Judaism back to the remnant of orthodox, observant Jews who lived during the Babylonian exile, represented by figures like Daniel and his three friends (see Dan. 1:8–20). While in exile, these Jews had to preserve their culture, religion, language, and identity by separating themselves from the world and maintaining strict attention to detailed traditions.[40] However, after several centuries, the methods used to preserve purity in faith and practice had turned into a legalistic, judgmental, and hypocritical approach to religion. This group also came to believe that the traditional teachings and practices that were developed in the course of their study of the Law were as authoritative as the Law of Moses itself, leading many to argue that this "oral law" had actually been passed down to the rabbis from Moses through oral tradition.[41]

The Sadducees, meanwhile, were on a different end of the theological spectrum. They accepted no oral teaching or tradition beyond what could be found in the five books of Moses (the Pentateuch). In this way, they represent a kind of early form of biblical criticism that found a "canon within the canon" and tried to reform Judaism based on this rationalistic approach. Furthermore, while the Pharisees believed in the sovereignty of God and in predestination regarding many matters, the Sadducees rejected the notion of predestination altogether in favor of a strong view of human free will.[42] The Sadducees also denied the reality of angels, spirits, and life after death, emphasizing instead the blessings received in *this* life for faithfulness to the covenant—especially with regard to the sacrificial system. They resembled in some ways the progressive deists of the eighteenth century—skeptical to the core of anything supernatural or fatalistic.[43]

Not all reacted to John's call to repentance and baptism with broken hearts and humble spirits. When some Pharisees and Sadducees came to be baptized, John saw through their hypocrisy. Calling them a "brood of vipers," he castigated them for claiming to have repented but failing to actually live in keeping with that claim (Matt. 3:7-8). He pointed out the pride they had in their privileged status as children of Abraham, urging that judgment and wrath would come upon any—even outwardly pious Jews—who failed to respond in true repentance (3:9-10).

John's preaching was saturated with language and images of coming judgment. He warned listeners to "flee from the wrath to come" (3:7). He threatened the unrepentant children of Abraham, indicating that they were in danger of being cut down like trees and "thrown into the fire" (3:10). And he pointed forward to the coming Messiah, who would baptize "with the Holy Spirit and fire" (3:11). In all likelihood, this imagery of fire is related to the coming judgment, as seen in Malachi 3:1-3:

> "Behold, I am going to send My messenger, and he will clear the way before Me. And the Lord, whom you seek, will suddenly come to His temple; and the messenger of the covenant, in whom you delight, behold, He is coming," says the LORD of hosts.
>
> "But who can endure the day of His coming? And who can stand when He appears? For He is like a refiner's fire and like fullers' soap.
>
> He will sit as a smelter and purifier of silver, and He will purify the sons of Levi and refine them like gold and silver, so that they may present to the LORD offerings in righteousness."

By the power of the Holy Spirit, the coming Messiah would use refining fire to test and separate the righteous from the wicked. Fire not only purifies precious metals like gold and silver, but it also burns up the dross—the impurities that don't belong. It's no wonder the Gospel of Mark points to this very passage in Malachi with reference to John the Baptizer's ministry of preparation for the Messiah (Mark 1:2).[44] John was that messenger sent to clear the way before the Lord.

John preached that when the Messiah comes as Judge, He will sort out the saved righteous and the unsaved wicked like a winnower on a threshing floor (Matt. 3:12). This image refers to workers during the grain harvest who would use a tool called a winnowing fork—like a rake or pitchfork—to separate grain kernels from their husks. Workers would toss the grain stalks into the air, and the heavy seeds would fall to the ground while the chaff would blow away in the wind.

Winnowing to separate grain from chaff

— 3:13-17 —

It's hard for me to imagine what John the Baptizer felt when, at the climax of his preaching ministry, he looked up and saw the Savior—Jesus Himself—standing in line to be baptized (3:13). Jesus had come down from Nazareth in Galilee, walked through the Jordan Valley in Judea, and stood in line for His turn in the water. Those of us who have read the Gospels, seen movies that include this story, or heard sermons on the baptism of Jesus in the Jordan have probably lost the sense of wonder in this moment. But John? *He couldn't believe his eyes.*

Remember, John had been preaching that with the coming of the Messiah, the kingdom of heaven was coming. Judgment was near. John's baptism of water was only a sign of repentance to prepare the way of the long-expected One, who would arrive with refining fire to separate the wicked and the righteous. John didn't seem to have room in his end-times expectations for a Messiah standing in line for baptism!

John's actions and words reveal his confusion and embarrassment. Why would the Judge and King, the Son of God and Son of David, whose sandals John was not even worthy to remove (3:11), permit Himself to be immersed by John in an act that represented consecration for repentant sinners? Matthew says that John "tried to prevent Him" (3:14). I'm not sure if John held out his hand as Jesus stepped into the water or backed away to communicate that he would have no part of this. His words reveal the humble posture he took: "I have need to be baptized by You, and do You come to me?" In other words, even as the greatest of the prophets, John the Baptizer needed the baptism of the Holy Spirit that only the Messiah could impart. And as the great God-man, Jesus had no need to participate in a baptism of repentance!

At this point, Jesus opened His mouth and uttered His first words recorded in the Gospel of Matthew: "Permit it at this time; for in this way it is fitting for us to fulfill all righteousness" (3:15). By submitting to baptism like everyone else, the Son of God from heaven was fully identifying Himself with humanity. By describing His actions as fulfilling "all righteousness," Jesus was adding even greater significance to the rite of baptism. Jesus' submission to John's baptism also communicated His approval of the rite and its adoption by His own disciples, who would continue to carry on the practice with those who responded to Jesus' teaching (John 4:1-3).

Furthermore, Jesus presented Himself for baptism in order to give the symbol an even deeper theological meaning: With that simple ceremony of cleansing and consecrating, heaven itself revealed the work of the triune God—the Father, the Son, and the Holy Spirit. As soon as Jesus came up from the water after baptism, heaven opened and the Spirit of God descended upon Him as a dove would light upon a branch (Matt. 3:16). At the same time, a voice spoke from heaven, saying, "This is My beloved Son, in whom I am well-pleased" (3:17). These two verses and their parallels (Mark 1:10-11; Luke 3:22) feature all three persons of the Trinity at Jesus' baptism. God the Father spoke from heaven; God the Holy Spirit descended like a dove; and God the Son received the approval of the Father and the sign of the Holy Spirit.

Matthew doesn't develop the doctrine of the Trinity in this passage. Rather, he gives us a glimpse of the three persons—Father, Son, and Holy Spirit—in association with the practice of baptism. The doctrine of the Trinity would be more fully explored, explained, and explicated as believers reflected on God's revelation of Himself in Scripture. The biblical "data" for this doctrine includes eight straightforward statements:[45]

- There is one God. (Deut. 6:4)
- The Father is God. (John 6:27)
- The Son is God. (John 1:1)
- The Spirit is God. (Acts 5:3-4)
- The Son is not the Father. (John 20:17)
- The Son is not the Spirit. (John 14:16)
- The Spirit is not the Father. (John 14:26)
- There is one God, not three. (1 Cor. 8:6)

The baptism of Jesus, with the accompanying phenomena of the Father's voice from heaven and the Spirit's descent, clearly indicates the distinction between the three divine persons. They work together in the plan of salvation but are not three different names for the same person. The three-in-one relationship of Father, Son, and Spirit may be difficult to comprehend with our finite minds, but we believe it by faith in the revelation of God's Word. B. B. Warfield masterfully summarized the awesome mystery of the Trinity this way, and the brevity of his statement makes it worth memorizing: "There is one only and true God, but in the unity of the Godhead there are three coeternal and coequal Persons, the same in substance but distinct in subsistence."[46]

APPLICATION: MATTHEW 3:1-17
Responding to the Strong Proclamation

The hoped-for response to the preaching of John the Baptizer was straightforward: *Repent!* That is, *Change your mind about your relationship with God!* To those who were just going through the motions, depending on their Jewish religious heritage to save them, this meant coming to a *true* personal conviction of sin, trusting in God's mercy, and living with a deeper, higher standard of righteousness. To those who had strayed from their covenant faithfulness, it meant turning to God in faith and obedience, letting go of their lifestyles of sin and instead serving Him with attentiveness to His kingdom priorities. For Jesus, who had neither harbored unbelief and rebellion nor had any stain of original or personal sin, baptism was a sign—a representation of His full consecration to the service of God and an association with the Father and Holy Spirit.

Each of us reading this today needs to likewise respond to the proclamation. We may have a deeper understanding of the significance of baptism today, but the basic message is still the same. It's an invitation to life with God, to an intimate association with Him and with His community of saints—that is, the "set-apart ones."

So, which group do you find yourself in today?

Are you like the Pharisees and Sadducees, carrying on a religious tradition inherited from your parents or grandparents but never experiencing an authentic, personal relationship with God through Jesus

Christ by the power of the Spirit? Do you do religious activities, say religious things, and go to religious places but lack the relationship that makes all these things worthwhile? God is calling you to a change of heart, to a genuine relationship with Christ. All you need to do is admit to Him the shallowness and emptiness of your religion and ask Him for a real relationship.

Or are you like the wayward, wandering Jews who had departed from the faith, needing to cleanse themselves from unbelief and wickedness? You can do that today! God doesn't need you to wash yourself clean from every sin committed and every blasphemous word spoken before entering a permanent relationship with Him. He'll forgive you, cleanse you by the blood of Christ, and seal you with His Spirit. His calling to a life of faith—and a life of righteousness consistent with that faith—will be accompanied by the inner working of the Spirit, which will equip you for this new life.

Or, finally, are you a believer who has experienced God's free grace and forgiveness but need to make up your mind to follow Him where He leads? Jesus stepped into the water as the carpenter's son from Nazareth and stepped out of the water ready to begin His mission with the commendation of the Father and the power of the Spirit. Do you need to change direction in your own life? Do you need to answer His call to service in the church, on the mission field, in your family, or in your work—with a personal decision of consecration and commitment to serve Him alone?

Whatever your personal situation, step forward now. Respond to the strong proclamation of the gospel.

Acing the Devil's Tests
MATTHEW 4:1-11

NASB

[1] Then Jesus was led up by the Spirit into the wilderness to be tempted by the devil. [2] And after He had fasted forty days and forty nights, He [a]then became hungry. [3] And the tempter came and said to Him, "If You are the Son of God, command that these stones become bread."

NLT

[1] Then Jesus was led by the Spirit into the wilderness to be tempted there by the devil. [2] For forty days and forty nights he fasted and became very hungry.

[3] During that time the devil* came and said to him, "If you are the Son of God, tell these stones to become loaves of bread."

NASB

⁴But He answered and said, "It is written, 'MAN SHALL NOT LIVE ON BREAD ALONE, BUT ON EVERY WORD THAT PROCEEDS OUT OF THE MOUTH OF GOD.'"

⁵Then the devil took Him into the holy city and had Him stand on the pinnacle of the temple, ⁶and said to Him, "If You are the Son of God, throw Yourself down; for it is written,

'HE WILL COMMAND HIS ANGELS
    CONCERNING YOU';
and
'ON *their* HANDS THEY WILL BEAR
    YOU UP,
SO THAT YOU WILL NOT STRIKE
    YOUR FOOT AGAINST A
    STONE.'"

⁷Jesus said to him, "ᵃOn the other hand, it is written, 'YOU SHALL NOT PUT THE LORD YOUR GOD TO THE TEST.'"

⁸Again, the devil took Him to a very high mountain and showed Him all the kingdoms of the world and their glory; ⁹and he said to Him, "All these things I will give You, if You fall down and ᵃworship me." ¹⁰Then Jesus said to him, "Go, Satan! For it is written, 'YOU SHALL WORSHIP THE LORD YOUR GOD, AND ᵃSERVE HIM ONLY.'" ¹¹Then the devil left Him; and behold, angels came and *began* to minister to Him.

4:2 ᵃLit *later became;* or *afterward became*
4:7 ᵃLit *Again* 4:9 ᵃLit *prostrate Yourself*
4:10 ᵃOr *fulfill religious duty to Him*

NLT

⁴But Jesus told him, "No! The Scriptures say,

'People do not live by bread
    alone,
but by every word that comes
    from the mouth of God.'*"

⁵Then the devil took him to the holy city, Jerusalem, to the highest point of the Temple, ⁶and said, "If you are the Son of God, jump off! For the Scriptures say,

'He will order his angels to
    protect you.
And they will hold you up with
    their hands
so you won't even hurt your
    foot on a stone.'*"

⁷Jesus responded, "The Scriptures also say, 'You must not test the LORD your God.'*"

⁸Next the devil took him to the peak of a very high mountain and showed him all the kingdoms of the world and their glory. ⁹"I will give it all to you," he said, "if you will kneel down and worship me."

¹⁰"Get out of here, Satan," Jesus told him. "For the Scriptures say,

'You must worship the LORD your
    God
and serve only him.'*"

¹¹Then the devil went away, and angels came and took care of Jesus.

4:3 Greek *the tempter.* 4:4 Deut 8:3. 4:6 Ps 91:11-12. 4:7 Deut 6:16. 4:10 Deut 6:13.

Jesus' identity as the Messiah was confirmed at His baptism. It must have been an emotional high mark in His life—especially when He heard those loud, affirming words from the Father in heaven: "This is My beloved Son, in whom I am well-pleased" (3:17). But as we'll see in a moment, another eavesdropper on the ministry of John the Baptizer heard the astonishing proclamation that Jesus of Nazareth was the Son of God . . . and he wanted to put that theology to the test!

Immediately on the heels of that magnificent moment, Jesus found

Himself alone in the wilderness. The Gospel of Mark has the briefest account of this episode: "Immediately the Spirit impelled Him to go out into the wilderness. And He was in the wilderness forty days being tempted by Satan; and He was with the wild beasts, and the angels were ministering to Him" (Mark 1:12-13). Mark gives no details of the kinds of temptations Jesus endured in the wilderness, but both Matthew and Luke fill in the gaps with some eye-opening descriptions.

During this time, Jesus fasted for forty days and, naturally, became extremely hungry. While He was in that vulnerable setting, alone and physically drained, the archenemy of God's people—Satan himself—arrived on the scene with sinister plans to lay three strong temptations before the Son of God. Using his supernaturally subtle and persuasive skills, the devil's plan was to take Jesus out before His ministry even got off the ground.

Think about what hung in the balance. Were Christ to yield to the temptations, not only would He disqualify Himself from being the perfect, innocent sacrifice for the sins of the world, but He would also allow the devil to declare himself victor, thereby claiming once and for all total dominion over humanity and the world. However, by withstanding the tests, Jesus would retain His rightful position as the victorious Ruler of all creation . . . and also leave us an example to follow when we, too, are tempted.

— 4:1-2 —

Tests of our faith and obedience are part of growing in the Christian life. Hebrews 11:17 says, "By faith Abraham, when he was tested, offered up Isaac." We know what Abraham didn't—that God had always intended to provide a substitute for Isaac. But God tested Abraham to demonstrate that His servant would obey even when he didn't understand. James 1:2-3 says, "Consider it all joy, my brethren, when you encounter various trials, knowing that the testing of your faith produces endurance." The trials God allows in our lives are not for our ruin, but for our benefit.

When God brings tests to strengthen our faith and obedience, we can be sure we're in the hands of a loving Father. The tests are specially crafted for us alone, uniquely prepared to build us up, not to tear us down. In every test, God's desire is the same: He wants us to pass. He never gives a test He secretly hopes we'll fail, and the tests are never designed to utterly defeat or destroy us. Never. God also equips us to pass the tests. But even when we fail, He picks us up, brushes us off, and through the failure strengthens us. Being a God of grace, He always has our best interests in mind.

Not so with the devil. The devil also throws tests our way, along with trials and temptations. His tests are always designed to lead us into failure, to weaken our faith, to bring about disobedience, and to fill us with despair. His great hope is to see us yield to his temptations over and over again. And if we resist his temptations and pass a test, we can be sure that he's ready to throw another one our way whenever he gets the opportunity. Satan hates us, and he never has our best interests in mind.

Against this backdrop, Jesus was led by the Spirit of God directly "into the wilderness to be tempted by the devil" (Matt. 4:1). Practically speaking, Jesus was all alone in a desolate place. The Judean wilderness is barren beyond belief. Cold at night, hot in the morning. Hardly anything to eat or drink. In this bleak place devoid of people and occupied by wild animals, Jesus fasted for forty days and nights (4:2). In this place, even if Jesus' fast included eating very small amounts, He would have had access only to a meager offering of edible plants and the small amount of water that might rarely drop from the sky.

By the end of this period, He would have been extremely hungry—to the point of starvation.

In many cases, this kind of silence, solitude, and disciplining of one's body can lead to deep experiences with God. When Christians

Barry Beitzel

The Judean Wilderness

fast, they typically focus on prayer and meditation. Yet fasting can eventually debilitate the body, weaken the mind, and undermine the will. This is likely the state Jesus was in when Satan came calling. It wasn't until *after* the forty days of fasting and the onset of extreme hunger that the devil appeared on the scene.

Though wicked to the core, the devil's no dummy. He knows that the best chance he has at successfully hooking victims with temptation and dragging them into sin is when they are weakened in mind, emotion, and will. When Satan catches us alone in a weakened state, he can more easily get us to justify our evil desires. And he can craft his temptations in such a way that the path toward destruction appears like the road to glory. His temptations can seem not only reasonable but even downright good and right.

— 4:3-4 —

Matthew reports three temptations by Satan aimed at Jesus, as well as Jesus' responses. Each temptation was progressively aimed at Jesus from a different angle, trying to find a weakness in His spiritual armor. The first temptation related to Christ's physical needs as a man. Satan tried to get Jesus to distrust the Father's providential care. Notice that Satan presented Jesus with a challenge to His identity: "If You are the Son of God . . ." (4:3). Where did the devil get the idea that Jesus might be "the Son of God"? Just forty-one days earlier at Jesus' baptism by John in the Jordan, a voice had announced, "This is My beloved Son, in whom I am well-pleased" (3:17). This makes me wonder whether Satan spent day after day hanging out with the crowds of Jews coming to John to be baptized, waiting for this anticipated Messiah to show up. I wonder if Satan heard the proclamation from heaven and thought he'd put this so-called "Son of God" to the test.

The nature of the temptation tells us that the devil thought the potential powers of the Son of God would be remarkable. No matter how famished I've gotten in my life, I've never been tempted to turn rocks into bread. But the devil knew that if Jesus was really the Son of God, as the voice from heaven stated, then such a feat would clearly be within His power. Besides this, wouldn't God the Father approve of such a miraculous display of power, considering that Jesus was famished? The temptation *seems* to have Jesus' best interests in mind: "If You are the Son of God, command that these stones become bread" (4:3). But Satan's subtle suggestion was designed to make the Son doubt the Father's love for Him and concern for His physical welfare. Didn't the

Son have every right to use His divine power and authority to meet the basic needs of His life?

Jesus responded immediately by quoting a Scripture passage from Deuteronomy: "He humbled you [Israel] and let you be hungry, and fed you with manna which you did not know, nor did your fathers know, that He might make you understand that man does not live by bread alone, but man lives by everything that proceeds out of the mouth of the LORD" (Deut. 8:3; cf. Matt. 4:4). As the perfect, sinless Redeemer of Israel, Jesus would succeed where the nation of Israel had failed in the wilderness. He would not forsake His dependence upon God for His very existence. Instead, He knew God would provide for Him in His timing.

Having passed the first temptation, Jesus faced two more.

— 4:5-7 —

The second temptation put the Father's love and power to the test. Here Satan used a completely different strategy. This time it wasn't about satisfying Jesus' physical needs; instead, it was about attracting a crowd, instantly promoting His fame, and gaining the attention and adoration He rightly deserved as the Son of God. For this temptation, Satan took Jesus into the city of Jerusalem, where He mingled anonymously among the crowds of worshipers at the temple. Satan then had Jesus make His

During the time of Jesus, the southwestern corner of the temple overlooked busy thoroughfares below.

way to the "pinnacle" of the temple (4:5), probably the southwest corner of the towering retaining wall that supported the massive temple mount complex. This ledge overlooked the busiest roads and entrances up to the temple on both its southern and western sides.

From there, Satan urged Jesus, "If You are the Son of God, throw Yourself down" (4:6). If Jesus really was the Messiah, surely God would protect Him from harm in front of the observing crowds below. To bolster his temptation, Satan even quoted Scripture, just as Jesus had done to resist the first temptation. Satan quoted the first of two lines in Psalm 91:11 ("For He will give His angels charge concerning you") and then Psalm 91:12 ("They will bear you up in their hands, that you do not strike your foot against a stone"). The devil conveniently left out an important part in the middle: "to guard you in all your ways." The text thus indicates that the promise of protection was related to

EXCURSUS: COULD JESUS HAVE SINNED?

MATTHEW 4:1-11

The episode of Jesus' temptation by Satan in Matthew 4 leads to a hypothetical question often used by seminary professors who are trying to get their students to think through their doctrinal convictions: "Could Jesus have sinned in the wilderness?" The two responses are often posed this way: "Yes, Jesus could have sinned, being fully human—the temptation wouldn't have been real if He was guaranteed victory." Or, "No, Jesus couldn't have sinned, being fully divine—it is impossible for God to sin."

The answer to this question reveals everything about the soundness of one's Christology—that is, the doctrine concerning Christ. The Bible teaches that Jesus is not just a man but is also God the Son. On the other hand, He is not just God but is also fully human. He is the God-man, fully God and fully human in one person (John 1:1, 14; Phil. 2:5-11). The Christian church has therefore definitively taught that Jesus has "two undiminished natures—human and divine—in one person, and that the unity of the two natures is 'without confusion, without change, without division, without separation.'"[47]

So the question as to whether Jesus could have sinned is solved by an understanding of the nature of His incarnation as the God-man. Because Jesus was fully human, He could be tempted by Satan and feel the full force of this temptation. However, because Jesus was simultaneously fully God, He could not sin but would be victorious over the temptation. This doesn't make the temptation less real. A person can pummel a 12-inch-thick steel wall with a sledgehammer over and over again with every ounce of might he or she has, but the nature of the steel wall is such that it will not succumb to the pounding. In the same way, Satan unleashed a genuine attack on the God-man, but His nature is such that He was able to be tempted but unable to sin.

accidents that would occur in the course of a person's normal comings and goings—not to intentional, attention-grabbing stunts that put oneself in danger.

If Jesus had done this, it would have been quite the spectacle . . . but completely contrary to God's plan and outside Scripture's intended promise of protection. It would have put God Himself to the test. So Jesus again responded to Satan with the Word of God: "On the other hand, it is written, 'You shall not put the Lord your God to the test'" (Matt. 4:7, quoting Deut. 6:16). This quote comes from Moses' farewell address to the nation of Israel, warning them against their habit of trying the patience and providential care of the Lord God. I wonder, though, whether Jesus' words might have been a sort of double entendre. Perhaps Jesus quoted Deuteronomy 6:16 as a sharp rebuke to Satan himself, indicating that, in tempting Jesus, the devil was putting the Lord God to the test!

— 4:8-11 —

In his third temptation, the devil attempted to coax Jesus into worshiping him for a magnificent but short-term gain. Really, it was just a shortcut to what would one day be the Messiah's anyway: a glorious position over the kingdoms of the world. At this point, Satan was no longer interested in being subtle or tactful or masking his true intentions: "Fall down and worship me!" In return for doing so, the devil offered Him "all the kingdoms of the world and their glory" (4:8-9).

Now, on the one hand, Satan was offering something he had no power to give. We know that God alone is sovereign over all nations and that no king or kingdom can reign apart from His will (Ps. 103:19; Dan. 2:37). Furthermore, God Himself will one day set up a kingdom of His own under the Messiah to replace the wicked kingdoms of the world (Dan. 2:44). On the other hand, until the coming of the Messiah's kingdom, the kingdoms of this world will be under the sway of the evil one (1 Jn. 5:19). The implication is that the kingdoms that Satan offered to Jesus were the corrupt, impure, and rebellious worldly empires of the present age—and Jesus could have these kingdoms without having to endure the suffering and death predicted of the Messiah in Isaiah 53!

But Jesus is no fool. With His fast and sharp response to the devil's "best offer yet," Jesus made it clear to Satan just who it was he was dealing with. Jesus was no mortal pushover. He wasn't a fallen, depraved man who would sell his soul if the price was right. He wasn't an angelic being like one of the heavenly host that had followed the devil in his fall. And He wasn't the kind of "son of the gods" we find in Greek and Roman mythologies that can be manipulated, deceived, or lured into wickedness. No, Jesus is the God-man, fully human and fully divine—able to be tempted because of His humanity, but always empowered to conquer temptation because of His divinity.

Jesus commanded, "Go, Satan!" (Matt. 4:10). Just as He had done in response to the previous temptations, Jesus paraphrased another Scripture, this time from Deuteronomy 6:13, which says, "You shall fear only the LORD your God; and you shall worship Him and swear by His name." Matthew notes that in response to Jesus' third appeal to the truth of Scripture, "the devil left Him" (Matt. 4:11). What else could he do? The God-man passed the tests, demonstrating not only His true identity as the Messiah but also His power as God in the flesh.

After Satan departed, God provided Jesus with blessed relief in His weakness. Matthew simply says, "Angels came and began to minister to Him" (4:11). We aren't told what form this ministry took, but we can imagine they brought Him food and drink, strengthening Him in body, soul, and spirit. In passing these tests, Jesus didn't *become* worthy of the task set before Him but *proved* that He was worthy as the Messiah— the God-man who was qualified to be the Savior of the world.

APPLICATION: MATTHEW 4:1-11

When the Devil Leads into Temptation . . .

When we ponder Satan's strategies and goals in leading us into temptations that test our faith and obedience, we need to keep some important principles in mind: something about Satan, something about Scripture, something about the Savior, and something about sin. These reminders and warnings aren't complicated. They're simple enough to memorize; in fact, I'd suggest that you do.

First, *regarding Satan, remember that he's a defeated enemy—so don't fear and don't be intimidated in the face of his temptations.* Scripture says, "Greater is He who is in you than he who is in the world" (1 Jn. 4:4). Christ has defeated Satan, and the Spirit who dwells within you is God Almighty—not some equal-but-opposite force wrestling with Satan in a conflict that could go either way. Satan's doom is sure. Every move on the chessboard of history puts Satan closer to the lake of fire prepared for him and his demons (Matt. 25:41; Rev. 20:10). As a disciple of Jesus Christ, you're on the winning side—not by your own strength or power, but by His Spirit. You can have the victory because Satan is a defeated enemy.

Second, *regarding Scripture, remember that it's alive and powerful—so don't hesitate to stand on it.* Hebrews 4:12 says, "The word of God is living and active and sharper than any two-edged sword." You can rely on it. Read it. Study it. Memorize it. Use it in times of trial and temptation. Post it on the wall beside your desk. Tape it to your mirror to see as you face the morning. Keep it in front of you throughout the day. Now, don't do this in a superstitious way, treating Scripture like a good-luck charm that will ward off wicked spirits just by its physical presence. Rather, let the Word of God enter your mind and heart throughout the day so you can be reminded of its unfailing truth and power. When temptation comes, wield Scripture.

Third, *regarding the Savior, remember that He's our Shield and Sustainer—so don't lean on your own strength.* Psalm 18:2 says, "The LORD is my rock and my fortress and my deliverer, my God, my rock, in whom I take refuge; my shield and the horn of my salvation, my stronghold." Don't forget that Jesus isn't just some great guy who happened to pass the test and prove that it can be done. He's the God-man, who passed the test by His divine power, who passed on our behalf, and who offers us the same divine power so that we can share His victory! Just as He shared in our infirmities, we can share in His victory. In the midst of our temptations, He will liberate us over and over. Just call on Him to see you through by His grace, mercy, and power. He'll never leave you in the lurch. He is your Shield and Sustainer.

Fourth, *regarding sin, remember that you don't have to yield to temptation—so resist its call.* Scripture says, "Submit therefore to God. Resist the devil and he will flee from you" (Jas. 4:7). You have a choice to submit to God—to step aside and let Him fight the spiritual battle against temptation and sin. Call on His name, quote His powerful Word, and claim His victory. Unfortunately, as fallen, frail humans, we so often forget to do this. Instead of resisting, we partake. And then we find ourselves taking steps deeper and deeper into sin and temptation. When this happens, remember that you have a way out through forgiveness and cleansing: "If we confess our sins, He is faithful and righteous to forgive us our sins and to cleanse us from all unrighteousness" (1 Jn. 1:9). You can be picked up, cleaned up, and built up to continue the lifelong battle against sin, knowing that, ultimately, the hope of heaven and the release from bondage will bring victory!

Where and How It All Began
MATTHEW 4:12-25

NASB

¹²Now when Jesus heard that John had been taken into custody, He withdrew into Galilee; ¹³and leaving Nazareth, He came and settled in Capernaum, which is by the sea, in the region of Zebulun and Naphtali. ¹⁴*This was* to fulfill what was spoken through Isaiah the prophet:

¹⁵ "THE LAND OF ZEBULUN AND THE LAND OF NAPHTALI,
ᵃBY THE WAY OF THE SEA, BEYOND THE JORDAN, GALILEE OF THE ᵇGENTILES—
¹⁶ "THE PEOPLE WHO WERE SITTING IN DARKNESS SAW A GREAT LIGHT,
AND THOSE WHO WERE SITTING IN THE LAND AND SHADOW OF DEATH,
UPON THEM A LIGHT DAWNED."

¹⁷From that time Jesus began to ᵃpreach and say, "Repent, for the kingdom of heaven is at hand."

¹⁸Now as Jesus was walking by the Sea of Galilee, He saw two brothers, Simon who was called Peter, and Andrew his brother, casting a net into the sea; for they were fishermen. ¹⁹And He said to them, "ᵃFollow Me, and I will make you fishers of men." ²⁰Immediately they left their nets and followed Him. ²¹Going on from there He saw two other brothers, ᵃJames the *son* of Zebedee, and ᵇJohn his brother, in the boat with Zebedee their father, mending their nets; and He called them. ²²Immediately they left the boat and their father, and followed Him.

²³Jesus was going throughout all Galilee, teaching in their synagogues and proclaiming the ᵃgospel of the kingdom, and healing every kind of disease and every kind of sickness among the people.

NLT

¹²When Jesus heard that John had been arrested, he left Judea and returned to Galilee. ¹³He went first to Nazareth, then left there and moved to Capernaum, beside the Sea of Galilee, in the region of Zebulun and Naphtali. ¹⁴This fulfilled what God said through the prophet Isaiah:

¹⁵ "In the land of Zebulun and of Naphtali,
beside the sea, beyond the Jordan River,
in Galilee where so many Gentiles live,
¹⁶ the people who sat in darkness have seen a great light.
And for those who lived in the land where death casts its shadow,
a light has shined."*

¹⁷From then on Jesus began to preach, "Repent of your sins and turn to God, for the Kingdom of Heaven is near.*"

¹⁸One day as Jesus was walking along the shore of the Sea of Galilee, he saw two brothers—Simon, also called Peter, and Andrew—throwing a net into the water, for they fished for a living. ¹⁹Jesus called out to them, "Come, follow me, and I will show you how to fish for people!" ²⁰And they left their nets at once and followed him.

²¹A little farther up the shore he saw two other brothers, James and John, sitting in a boat with their father, Zebedee, repairing their nets. And he called them to come, too. ²²They immediately followed him, leaving the boat and their father behind.

²³Jesus traveled throughout the region of Galilee, teaching in the synagogues and announcing the Good News about the Kingdom. And he healed every kind of disease and

NASB

24The news about Him spread throughout all Syria; and they brought to Him all who were ill, those suffering with various diseases and pains, demoniacs, ªepileptics, paralytics; and He healed them. 25Large crowds followed Him from Galilee and *the* Decapolis and Jerusalem and Judea and *from* beyond the Jordan.

4:15 ªOr *Toward the sea* ᵇLit *nations,* usually non-Jewish 4:17 ªOr *proclaim* 4:19 ªLit *Come here after Me* 4:21 ªOr *Jacob;* James is the Eng form of Jacob ᵇGr *Joannes,* Heb *Johanan* 4:23 ªOr *good news* 4:24 ªLit *moonstruck*

NLT

illness. 24News about him spread as far as Syria, and people soon began bringing to him all who were sick. And whatever their sickness or disease, or if they were demon possessed or epileptic or paralyzed—he healed them all. 25Large crowds followed him wherever he went—people from Galilee, the Ten Towns,* Jerusalem, from all over Judea, and from east of the Jordan River.

4:15-16 Isa 9:1-2 (Greek version). 4:17 Or *has come,* or *is coming soon.* 4:25 Greek *Decapolis.*

Many things about Jesus' first thirty years on earth remain subject to mere speculation. We just don't know what His home life was like. We have virtually no details about His relationship with His mother, Mary, or with Joseph. We don't know how Mary and Joseph managed to rear all their other children alongside an older brother who never disobeyed. How did Jesus interact with other children in Nazareth? Or with adults? How did He know when to leave His home in Nazareth and start His ministry? Did He ever sit down with His mother and siblings to explain what was about to happen?

Those three decades of Jesus' growth into mature manhood are shrouded in obscurity. But we *do* know where He went when God gave the green light to launch His ministry. As soon as Jesus submitted to baptism in the Jordan and aced the devil's tests in the wilderness, He traveled from one area, town, or city to another, making His message known. Without exception, He attracted large crowds through His astonishing words and actions. Many believed in Him and His message; others were hangers-on or lookie-loos—eager to linger among the throngs but unwilling to fully commit.

From among those who heard His message, Jesus singled out a handful to become part of a small group with whom He would spend a great deal of personal time. That calling would require commitment and personal sacrifice. This select group would need to leave their occupations and receive training to carry out the ministry Jesus had for them as disciples. Jesus called them to something deeper than being simply hearers, believers, or followers. He called them to be full-on disciples with a single passion—serving their Savior.

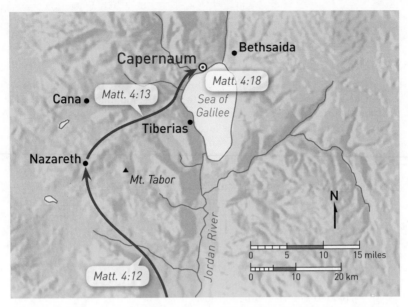

After departing the Jordan River Valley in the vicinity of Jericho, Jesus returned briefly to Nazareth, then ministered around the Sea of Galilee, establishing His base in the city of Capernaum. He would call His first disciples along the seacoast.

— 4:12-17 —

Shortly after Jesus' forty days of fasting and His temptation in the wilderness, He emerged from the Judean desert and returned to the location of John the Baptizer's ministry, somewhere near the Jordan River in the vicinity of Jericho. The events of this period are passed over between Matthew 4:11 and 4:12, but they are recorded in some detail in John 1:19–4:3. During that space of time—about a year—John the Baptizer continued to point people to Jesus as "the Lamb of God who takes away the sin of the world" (John 1:29), also stating, "He must increase, but I must decrease" (John 3:30).

The Gospel of Luke informs us that John the Baptizer's preaching got him into trouble with Herod Antipas, the ruler of Galilee: "When Herod the tetrarch was reprimanded by [John] because of Herodias, his brother's wife, and because of all the wicked things which Herod had done, Herod also added this to them all: he locked John up in prison" (Luke 3:19-20). Though Herod Antipas had wed a Nabataean princess, to whom he was married for two decades, he fell in love with Herodias, his niece and sister-in-law, the daughter of one half-brother and wife of another half-brother (her uncle)! When his Nabataean wife returned home to her father in dismay, Antipas took advantage of her absence and brought Herodias into his home to live with him as his wife.[48] This

CAPERNAUM

MATTHEW 4:13

When Jesus wanted to launch His public ministry, He moved from the out-of-the-way village of Nazareth to the bustling lakeshore town of Capernaum. The city was a center of commerce with a busy fishing industry and a trade center for local agriculture. It was located on an international trade route that ran all the way from Egypt in the south through Syria and on to Mesopotamia in the north.[49]

This town was no small fishing and farming village. It housed the residence of a high government official, a tax office, and even a large synagogue, the foundation of which is still present today.[50] When Jesus made Capernaum His base of ministry, it was a practical and strategic move. From here, Jesus

- called Peter, Andrew, James, and John;
- called Matthew, the tax collector;
- taught in the synagogue;
- healed Peter's mother-in-law;
- healed a centurion's servant;
- healed a paralytic who was lowered through the roof;
- raised Jairus's daughter from the dead;
- healed a woman who had experienced twelve years of bleeding; and
- healed two blind men and a mute demoniac.

Barry Beitzel

These ruins of a fourth-century synagogue in Capernaum rest on the foundation of the black-basalt synagogue in which Jesus taught in the first century.

Though Jesus did numerous miracles in Capernaum that clearly tes-
tified to His power and Godhead, He condemned the city along with
others in the region for rejecting His call to repentance (11:23). The
effects of that condemnation can be seen in the fact that Capernaum
has stood in ruins for a millennium and a half. Today, the once bustling
town, and center of Jesus' Galilean ministry, is simply an impressive
archaeological site—the destination of tourists who want to catch a
glimpse of the lingering footprint of that once impressive city.

blatant infidelity and immorality led John to speak out against Herod;
in turn, he had John arrested (Matt. 4:12).

Upon John's arrest, Jesus moved the center of His ministry to Capernaum. Though Jesus had already been active in Galilee, the Jordan Valley, and even Jerusalem up to this time (see John 1–4), Matthew informs
us that the arrest of John the Baptizer marked what may be regarded
as the official launching of His public ministry. He settled in the large,
bustling town of Capernaum on the north shore of the Sea of Galilee,
which was a fulfillment of Isaiah 9:1-2 (Matt. 4:14-16). That prophecy
foresaw a time when a great light would shine in the darkness of "Galilee of the Gentiles." This light would be none other than Jesus—the
"Wonderful Counselor, Mighty God, Eternal Father, Prince of Peace"
who was destined to reign "on the throne of David" (Isa. 9:6-7).

At this point, Jesus picked up the message that had been John the
Baptizer's mainstay and made it His own: "Repent, for the kingdom of
heaven is at hand" (Matt. 4:17). (See commentary on 3:2.) Those who
heard Jesus' preaching had never heard anything like it in their lives.
They had sat through many monotonous lectures by the elders in the
synagogues, who tended to pit opinions against opinions and interpretations against interpretations as the men discussed, debated, and dia-
logued with each other over what this Scripture meant or what that rabbi
said. But when Jesus stepped into the synagogue and opened His mouth,
His word came with power. He preached "as one having authority, and
not as their scribes" (7:29). This difference between the authoritative,
powerful preaching of Jesus and the speculative, tedious discussions of
the elders reminds me of the wise words of one pastor: "Preaching is the
proclamation of certainties, not the suggestion of possibilities."[51]

— 4:18-22 —

In the midst of Jesus' itinerant preaching about the coming kingdom
of God and the call to repentance, He walked the rocky, breezy shore

of the Sea of Galilee to officially call a handful of permanent companions. He first found two brothers, Simon (Peter) and Andrew, casting their nets into the lake (4:18). Now, we sometimes get the impression from reading just the account of Matthew or Mark that Jesus stepped into those fishermen's lives as a total stranger, mesmerized them with His magnetic personality, and called them away from their livelihood, with the result that they miraculously followed this strange, itinerant prophet.

In actuality, this scene isn't the first time these men encountered Jesus. Sometime earlier, before John the Baptizer had been imprisoned, Andrew, and probably John, had been following the locust-eating prophet from the Jordan Valley (John 1:35-40). When the Baptizer pointed Jesus out as "the Lamb of God" (John 1:36), they shadowed the mysterious figure to His abode (John 1:39). Afterward Andrew introduced Jesus to his brother Simon as "the Messiah," and at this point, Jesus gave Simon the nickname Peter (John 1:41-42). The next day, Philip and Nathanael both joined John, Andrew, and Peter, accompanying Jesus to Galilee.

Around this time, Jesus and some of His followers also attended a wedding in Cana, just a short distance from Nazareth. There Jesus turned water into wine, "and His disciples believed in Him" (John 2:11). From there, Jesus traveled to Capernaum with His disciples (John 2:12) and later spent some time in Jerusalem (John 2:13–3:21). Jesus and a handful of disciples even began baptizing in Judea while John the Baptizer was still preaching and baptizing (John 3:22-36), eventually withdrawing again to Galilee so as not to draw too much attention from the Pharisees in the region (John 4:1-3).

Then John the Baptizer was arrested, marking a clear, clean break between John's ministry of preparation and Jesus' own full-time, open, public proclamation. It was in this context, then, that Jesus found four of His erstwhile followers and presented them with a new commission. Though they had been following Jesus for some months prior to this event, the fact that they were hard at work fishing in the Sea of Galilee that day indicates that they had not seen their following of Jesus as a full-time, permanent calling. Jesus' words changed that for good: "Follow Me, and I will make you fishers of men" (Matt. 4:19).

Perhaps anticipating this very day when the Messiah would call them to service, Andrew and Peter literally dropped what they were doing and followed Jesus—without discussion, without debate, without hesitation (4:20). A little farther down the shoreline, the three men

My Calling

MATTHEW 4:18-22

When I read about the calling of Andrew, Peter, James, and John, I can't help but remember my own calling into full-time ministry. I was in the Marine Corps, 8,000 miles from home and family. Thanks to the ministry of a man named Bob Newkirk, with The Navigators, I got some of my first real tastes of Christian ministry serving under his mentorship.

I remember Bob putting me on the back of a flatbed truck so I could lead songs while he preached the gospel. The next time we had a meeting, he had me do the preaching while he led the singing. Looking back, I have to admit the preaching was better the first time. Bob was a better preacher by far. But he was a teacher and mentor, and he knew the kinds of experiences that were needed to teach me what I needed to learn. I remember thinking after those meetings were over, I would love to do this. I told Bob my desire, and he said, "Chuck, you may be called to preach."

Nonetheless, I initially resisted the idea of a call to full-time ministry. An occasional, short-term stint? Certainly. But committing my life to preaching? Chuck, who do you think you are? But over time, the Holy Spirit worked on me through experiences and encouragement from others—and by His inner guidance and conviction. Eventually, I knew God was calling me to preach.

I remember writing to Cynthia back home something like this: "You're not going to believe this, but when I get out of the Marine Corps, I want to find a way to get to Dallas Seminary to get the training I need to be a preacher." To my surprise, she never once said, "No way!" or "What's the salary?" or "Are there benefits?" or "Where are we going to go?" or "What's the retirement plan like?'" Not once. Instead, she said, "Let's do it!"

So, when I was discharged from the Marines, we packed up what we had, took the seventy-five dollars in our bank account, and moved

(continued on next page)

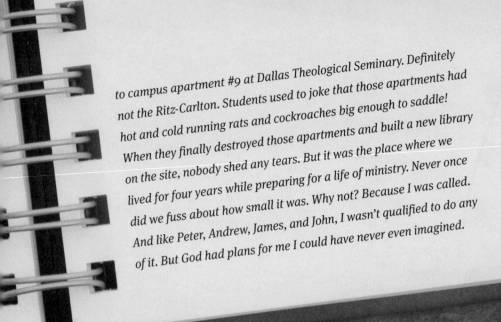

to campus apartment #9 at Dallas Theological Seminary. Definitely not the Ritz-Carlton. Students used to joke that those apartments had hot and cold running rats and cockroaches big enough to saddle! When they finally destroyed those apartments and built a new library on the site, nobody shed any tears. But it was the place where we lived for four years while preparing for a life of ministry. Never once did we fuss about how small it was. Why not? Because I was called. And like Peter, Andrew, James, and John, I wasn't qualified to do any of it. But God had plans for me I could have never even imagined.

found James and John along with their father, Zebedee, and the hired hands. Matthew mentions that they were "in the boat . . . mending their nets" (4:21). Normally, after a day of casting nets, fishermen would pull in their boats, wash and hang their nets out to dry, and mend them while on shore (see Luke 5:2). The fact that these men were mending nets *while still in the boat* may suggest that they had been catching so many fish that the nets had torn. As such, they may have been quickly mending the nets while in the boat in order to cast them out again as soon as they could. If this is the case, we could say that business was booming!

Yet, in the middle of frantically repairing the nets, James and John immediately "left the boat and their father, and followed Him" (Matt. 4:22). We shouldn't characterize James and John as lousy sons who abandoned their father when he needed them most. Nor should we picture Zebedee sitting alone in that boat with a torn fishing net in his hands while his zealous sons chased after a roving rabbi. The Gospel of Mark clarifies that Zebedee was "in the boat with the hired servants" (Mark 1:20).

The sons of Zebedee may not have left their father in the lurch, but they did leave a presumably lucrative family business, from which they were no doubt receiving a handsome share of the profits. Jesus offered no salary, no benefits, no pension plan. Following a thirty-something rabbi who had never been to the equivalent of rabbinical college certainly wasn't a résumé builder. Those four men—Andrew, Peter, James, and John—weren't hired as ministry interns; they were called into a life of service to Christ. And they responded instantly.

— 4:23-25 —

Matthew 4:23 serves as a summary statement that gives a broad preview of Jesus' ministry. Throughout the four Gospels, we see specific examples of each of these three dimensions of Jesus' public ministry: teaching, preaching, and healing. He *taught* in the synagogues, and He *proclaimed* the gospel. Note that Matthew distinguishes teaching and preaching. *Teaching* primarily conveys information, addressing the hearers' minds. It offers facts, insights, and truth from God's Word. *Preaching*, or *proclaiming*, takes the truth of God's Word and addresses the will, calling for a decision, a response. Jesus did both.

Since the practices of teaching and preaching were able to convey Jesus' central message, why did He engage in healing sickness and disease? First, the miracles Jesus did proved that He had divine authority in His teaching and preaching. People couldn't reject His message without rejecting God Himself. Second, the miracles demonstrated that God is compassionate; He cares about not only spiritual needs but also physical needs. Third, the miracles verified that Jesus was the prophesied Messiah, whose mission included the ushering in of a kingdom in which sickness, disease, suffering, and death would be vanquished. Finally, His miracles proved that the offer of the kingdom to Israel was legitimate—the One who had authority over sickness, disease, and demonic forces could be taken seriously when He offered the kingdom of God to those who repented and accepted Him as Messiah.

As a result of Christ's ministry of teaching, preaching, and healing, huge crowds came to see Him from throughout Syria, Galilee, the Decapolis,

While Jesus' ministry was based in Galilee, His fame spread throughout the surrounding areas.

79

Jerusalem, Judea, and the region east of the Jordan (4:24-25). No doubt many were enthralled by His teaching and convicted by His preaching. Numerous men and women who suffered from physical ailments and spiritual oppression experienced life-changing deliverance that resulted in lifelong discipleship. But I'm sure the crowds also included plenty of uncommitted and purely curious people—impressed but not convinced.

How things had changed, though, since Jesus stepped out of the waters of the Jordan after His baptism by John! From anonymity to fame . . . from obscurity to popularity . . . from citizen of small-town Nazareth to regional celebrity! By the time we get to the end of Matthew 4, there's no question that Christ's ministry has been launched and things will never be the same for Him—or for the world.

APPLICATION: MATTHEW 4:12-25

Answering His Call

Jesus' call to follow Him as a disciple isn't something that occurred only during those opening weeks of His public ministry. Jesus still calls people today to believe in Him and follow Him. Some are called to serve more deeply in their local congregations. Others are called to full-time ministry beyond the walls of their churches.

Everyone reading this is called to be a disciple. The first step in answering the call is to trust in Christ and Christ alone as your Savior. Salvation comes by grace alone through faith alone in the person and work of Christ alone. Without answering that first call to salvation, the deeper call to self-sacrificial service for Christ won't make any sense.

Beyond the call to salvation, the call to discipleship involves surrendering to Christ's will for your life, willingly following Him wherever He leads you. Sometimes this involves simply stepping into the opportunities before you—stepping out of the lingering crowd, moving from spectator to team member, from audience to participant. Sometimes it may even involve "dropping your nets" and making a complete break from your former life and livelihood.

I know a man who left a very successful engineering position and, to the surprise of many around him, went into full-time ministry. When he did so, his salary dropped to one-fourth of what it had been. But when you're called, the money doesn't matter. God provides. When you answer His call, it makes no difference what people think or say. All that matters is that you're faithful in the role God asks you to play in the proclamation of the gospel.

When God calls us, we can't say, "I'm untrained" or "I already have a job" or "I have a family." So did most of those original disciples. When God calls, we need to answer. He'll provide for our families. He'll see to it that we get the experience and training necessary to do what He has called us to. And He'll give us the grace we need to carry out His work.

PROCLAMATION AND RECEPTION OF THE KING (MATTHEW 5:1–15:39)

In many ways, the first four chapters of Matthew can be regarded as prologue, preamble, and preparation for the rest of the book. But this doesn't mean that they aren't important. They established the vital foundation of Jesus' genealogy, demonstrating that He has the proper messianic qualifications (1:1-17). They also laid the groundwork for proving that Jesus fulfilled the hopes, anticipations, and yearnings of the Old Testament Scriptures through His birth and childhood (1:18– 2:23). And these chapters concluded with His consecration to ministry (3:1-17), His testing for ministry (4:1-11), and His public launch into ministry (4:12-25).

Upon this strong foundation, Matthew continues to build his case that Jesus is the King, Israel's long-awaited Messiah. In this second major section, which I've titled *Proclamation and Reception of the King* (5:1–15:39), we will follow Jesus as He teaches, preaches, and performs miracles—all of which invites His hearers to place their faith in Him as their Lord. We'll hear Jesus' famous Sermon on the Mount (5:1–7:29), calling His followers to a depth of righteousness unheard of in other religions. We will witness astonishing miracles the likes of which nobody had ever seen (8:1–9:38). We'll be captivated by teaching on theological and practical truths by "one having authority" (10:1–12:50; see 7:29). As controversy and opposition grow, we will see Jesus maintain His single focus—to teach and preach concerning the kingdom of God, confirming His teaching with miraculous signs (13:1–15:39).

Along with growing numbers of disciples, the Lord Jesus will gain a growing number of detractors. As He preaches, they seethe. As He heals, they scheme. And as He publicly demonstrates His messiahship, they'll privately plot His demise. These enemies of the gospel will mostly be operating in the shadows. Meanwhile, in the light of day, we'll see men, women, and children flocking to the Savior, joyously receiving Him as their King, Israel's long-awaited Messiah.

KEY TERMS IN MATTHEW 5:1–15:39

dikaiosynē (δικαιοσύνη) [1343] "righteousness," "justice," "fairness"

The term *dikaiosynē* has numerous nuances in the New Testament. At its root is the sense of "uprightness" or "rectitude." In Matthew, the term "righteousness" is used to emphasize the visible manifestation of a right disposition or moral uprightness reflected in one's attitudes and actions (5:6, 10; 6:1). Throughout this Gospel, the superficial and humanly impossible righteousness of the Pharisees is contrasted with God's righteousness (6:33), for which we are to "hunger and thirst" (5:6). The apostle Paul uses the term in a more legal sense: a right standing before God as a result of a declaration of righteousness (Rom. 1:17; 3:22; see also Rom. 5:1-21). Such righteousness "comes from God on the basis of faith" (Phil. 3:8-11).

exousia (ἐξουσία) [1849] "authority," "dominion," "jurisdiction," "control"

Those who heard Jesus' teaching marveled that He taught "as one having authority [*exousia*], and not as their scribes" (7:29). One who has *exousia* has unrestricted ability to act based on their own discretion. This authority almost always implies power to enforce one's will, a power either delegated by a higher-ranking authority or possessed in one's own right. In Matthew's Gospel, the question "Who has authority?" is paramount, as Jesus challenges the existing religious and political authorities and asserts—by word and deed—that He has authority over all realms of life (see 9:6), an authority that He can also delegate to others (10:1).

makarios (μακάριος) [3107] "blessed," "happy," "privileged"

The very first word in the Greek translation of the book of Psalms is *makarios*: "Blessed [*makarios*] is the man that walketh not in the counsel of the ungodly" (Ps. 1:1, KJV). The theme of blessing is carried on throughout the collection of songs, with the term appearing twenty-five times in the Psalms. It expresses the positive benefits of a life of faithfulness. The Greek term originally conveyed "the happy estate of the gods above earthly sufferings and labors. Later it came to mean any positive condition a person experienced."[1] From the Latin word *beatus*, a translation of *makarios*, we get the term "Beatitudes," used to describe the repeated use of the adjective in Jesus' Sermon on the Mount (Matt. 5:1-12). Here the term describes transcendent happiness, the kind that neither depends upon earthly fortunes nor falters before temporal hardships. A "blessed" person possesses what we would call true joy.

parabolē (παραβολή) [3850] "parable," "figure," "illustrative comparison"

The word *parabolē* has the basic sense of "setting alongside," with the idea that two concepts, stories, or ideas are placed beside each other to

83

draw out comparisons.² In teaching, parables most often use everyday images and scenarios familiar to listeners and are intended to illustrate big-picture spiritual or moral truths. As such, any incidental details are intended to make the story vivid, not to communicate detailed, hidden truths. Jesus used parables both to reveal truth to His followers and to conceal it from those who are spiritually blind (13:10-17).

Ingredients for Lasting and Contagious Joy
MATTHEW 5:1-16

NASB

¹When Jesus saw the crowds, He went up on the ᵃmountain; and after He sat down, His disciples came to Him. ²He opened His mouth and *began* to teach them, saying,

³"ᵃBlessed are the ᵇpoor in spirit, for theirs is the kingdom of heaven.

⁴"Blessed are those who mourn, for they shall be comforted.

⁵"Blessed are the ᵃgentle, for they shall inherit the earth.

⁶"Blessed are those who hunger and thirst for righteousness, for they shall be satisfied.

⁷"Blessed are the merciful, for they shall receive mercy.

⁸"Blessed are the pure in heart, for they shall see God.

⁹"Blessed are the peacemakers, for they shall be called sons of God.

¹⁰"Blessed are those who have been persecuted for the sake of righteousness, for theirs is the kingdom of heaven.

NLT

¹One day as he saw the crowds gathering, Jesus went up on the mountainside and sat down. His disciples gathered around him, ²and he began to teach them.

³ "God blesses those who are poor and realize their need for him,*
for the Kingdom of Heaven is theirs.

⁴ God blesses those who mourn,
for they will be comforted.

⁵ God blesses those who are humble,
for they will inherit the whole earth.

⁶ God blesses those who hunger and thirst for justice,*
for they will be satisfied.

⁷ God blesses those who are merciful,
for they will be shown mercy.

⁸ God blesses those whose hearts are pure,
for they will see God.

⁹ God blesses those who work for peace,
for they will be called the children of God.

¹⁰ God blesses those who are persecuted for doing right,
for the Kingdom of Heaven is theirs.

11 "Blessed are you when *people* insult you and persecute you, and falsely say all kinds of evil against you because of Me. 12Rejoice and be glad, for your reward in heaven is great; for in the same way they persecuted the prophets who were before you.

13 "You are the salt of the earth; but if the salt has become tasteless, how aᶜan it be made salty *again?* It is no longer good for anything, except to be thrown out and trampled under foot by men.

14 "You are the light of the world. A city set on a ahill cannot be hidden; 15nor does *anyone* light a lamp and put it under a abasket, but on the lampstand, and it gives light to all who are in the house. 16Let your light shine before men in such a way that they may see your good works, and glorify your Father who is in heaven.

5:1 aOr *hill*   5:3 aI.e. fortunate or prosperous, and so through v 11   bI.e. those who are not spiritually arrogant   5:5 aOr *humble, meek*   5:13 aLit *will*   5:14 aOr *mountain*   5:15 aOr *peck-measure*

11 "God blesses you when people mock you and persecute you and lie about you and say all sorts of evil things against you because you are my followers. 12Be happy about it! Be very glad! For a great reward awaits you in heaven. And remember, the ancient prophets were persecuted in the same way.

13 "You are the salt of the earth. But what good is salt if it has lost its flavor? Can you make it salty again? It will be thrown out and trampled underfoot as worthless.

14 "You are the light of the world—like a city on a hilltop that cannot be hidden. 15No one lights a lamp and then puts it under a basket. Instead, a lamp is placed on a stand, where it gives light to everyone in the house. 16In the same way, let your good deeds shine out for all to see, so that everyone will praise your heavenly Father.

5:3 Greek *poor in spirit.*   5:6 Or *for righteousness.*

Of the millions of sermons that have been preached through the centuries, none is more famous, more convicting, or more enduring than the one Jesus delivered shortly after beginning His ministry. We know it as the Sermon on the Mount. Though Jesus preached this sermon in the first half of the first century AD, it remains timeless, relevant, and practical even in the twenty-first century.

Through these words, Jesus—with penetrating insight—exposed the brittle veneer of all self-righteousness prevalent in His day . . . and in ours. He explained the essence of true righteousness, which leads to a deep-seated joy. Weaving threads from the Old Testament throughout this garment of truth, the heir of the throne of David set forth principles that must never be ignored by subjects of His kingdom. Yet how few truly embrace Jesus' words!

We may observe and outline these words, analyze and interpret them, admire and quote them, even frame them and build churches to commemorate them! But we rarely apply them with earnestness and obey them with seriousness. Because of that, we miss the point entirely.

Jesus preached this sermon to bring about permanent life change, and His concern was (and still is) that we live in stark contrast to the world's system. He desires that His followers be Christlike to the core—a divine minority who live differently from the rest of the world.

Perhaps the best-known part of this message as recorded in Matthew 5 through 7 is the set of opening lines, known as the Beatitudes (5:1-12).

— 5:1-2 —

Jesus' miracles had drawn crowds from all over the regions of Galilee, Syria, the Decapolis, Jerusalem, Judea, and even beyond the Jordan (4:23-25). A group this large would have had not only diverse backgrounds and beliefs but also different life experiences, different struggles, and different levels of commitment to spiritual things. In addition to regional differences, Jesus' audience contained people old and young, male and female, well-off and poor, religious and rebellious. With such a diverse group of people, what would Jesus preach? What lessons could He possibly teach that would minister to all of them together and each of them individually? *The fundamentals of life.* These essential principles would transcend language, culture, gender, age, and class.

Matthew tells us that with such a large crowd following Him, Jesus led them up a mountain. The Greek word for this (*oros* [3735]) could also be translated "hill," so this may not have entailed a sizable climb. The purpose was to give Jesus an elevated place from which to preach so the hundreds—maybe even thousands—of listeners would be better able to hear. If you were to travel to Israel today, you'd likely visit the traditional location referred to as the Mount of Beatitudes on the north shore of the Sea of Galilee, not too far from Capernaum. You'd feel the cool breeze coming off the lake, smell the flowers in bloom, and ponder what it may have been like that day when Jesus took a seat on the edge of that ridge and faced the gathered crowds. The mount and corresponding slope formed a natural theater to carry Christ's voice to the ears and hearts of His listeners.

The "disciples" (5:1) who had come to Him to hear the message included many more than just Jesus' inner circle of Peter, James, John, Andrew, and select others. This is evidenced at the end of the sermon, where Matthew reports, "When Jesus had finished these words, the crowds were amazed at His teaching" (7:28).

The content of the first part of His teaching has traditionally been called the Beatitudes, which derives from the Latin word *beatus,*

Fallaner/Wikimedia

The traditional location for the Sermon on the Mount provides plenty of room for thousands of people to hear a message preached from the ridge.

meaning "blessed." The Greek word usually translated "blessed"—*makarios* [3107]—doesn't have a precise English equivalent and has thus been rendered by numerous roughly synonymous words: "fortunate," "contented," "blissful," "privileged," "peaceful," "serene," "joyful," "happy," and "blessed." We might define it as "an inward contentment or abiding joy unaffected by outer circumstances." The Beatitudes are pronouncements, not possibilities. They are statements of celebration, like the worshipful psalms or parts of the Wisdom Literature, not commands, like the Law of Moses dictated from Mount Sinai.

Yet, as one commentator notes, "The Beatitudes, far from being passive or mild, are a gauntlet flung down before the world's accepted standards."[3] The ethical underpinnings of the Beatitudes are essentially those of the future kingdom of Christ—but lived out in the present interim of the church by His people. When we live out the values and virtues of the coming kingdom prior to Christ's return, the world will be stunned by the contrast and will be insatiably curious. It will blow their minds! As Christians engage in kingdom living in a depraved world, Christ's character will be revealed through believing sinners transformed by the Holy Spirit.

Let's briefly walk through each of the eight beatitudes (5:3-12) and see how they apply to us today. Once we've done this we can then note the effect this Christlike, kingdom living will have on the world around us when we embrace it (5:13-16).

— 5:3-12 —

Blessed are the poor in spirit, for theirs is the kingdom of heaven (Matt. 5:3). The first beatitude refers not to the financially poor, but to "the poor in spirit"—those who realize their own utter helplessness and absence of spiritual merit. The only response to such realization is total dependence on the Lord God for spiritual riches. Pride, arrogance, and haughtiness are banished in the life of true happiness, contentment, and joy. This is the attitude expressed in the great hymn of Augustus Toplady, "Rock of Ages":

> Nothing in my hand I bring,
> Simply to the cross I cling;
> Naked, come to Thee for dress;
> Helpless, look to Thee for grace;
> Foul, I to the fountain fly;
> Wash me, Savior, or I die.[4]

By giving up the foolish agenda of building our *own* kingdoms of dirt here on earth, we truly participate in Christ's kingdom agenda. We serve under His sovereign rule, allowing Him to direct our steps while He gets the glory He deserves.

Blessed are those who mourn, for they shall be comforted (Matt. 5:4). The Greek word for "mourn" is *pentheō* [3996]. It refers to a passionate lament or the anguish felt because of some sorrowful event, condition, or circumstance, such as death (see Mark 16:10).[5] Believers in a right relationship with God will mourn over the wrongs of our world and be grieved over the destructiveness of sin (see Rom. 7:24). This doesn't mean that God calls us to permanent depression or to hum a constant dirge. As Ecclesiastes wisely affirms, "There is an appointed time for everything. . . . A time to weep and a time to laugh; a time to mourn and a time to dance" (Eccl. 3:1, 4). What Jesus is saying is that when we mourn for the woes and wrongs of this world, we can take comfort in the here and now that one day the wrongs will be righted, death will be dealt a death blow itself, and God will wipe away every tear from our eyes (Rev. 21:4).

Blessed are the gentle, for they shall inherit the earth (Matt. 5:5). The world has some less-than-flattering descriptions for the gentle or meek person: wimp, doormat, milquetoast, spineless, weak, yellow, pushover. But the biblical term used here, *praus* [4239], means "not being overly impressed by a sense of one's self-importance, *gentle, humble, considerate.*"[6] The word is used in the Greek version of the Old Testament to describe Moses (Num. 12:3)—hardly somebody we would picture in a constant state of kowtowing to those around him. Meekness doesn't mean weakness, but strength under control. Those who keep their anger in check, who don't flaunt their power or constantly claim their rights, who put others' interests before their own—these are the kind who will "inherit the earth" (Matt. 5:5). In the future, they will be fellow heirs with Christ, ruling with Him in the kingdom (Rom. 8:16-17; 2 Tim. 2:12). But even in the present, God may place them in positions of influence, knowing they can be trusted to handle authority with integrity and humility.

Blessed are those who hunger and thirst for righteousness, for they shall be satisfied (Matt. 5:6). True disciples of Christ have an insatiable appetite for spiritual truth and a life of holiness. The "righteousness" here is both positional—having a right relationship with God by grace through faith—and practical—living out that right relationship in our just acts of love toward God and others. Jesus is referring to a passionate desire to know and walk intimately with the Lord. When we have this desire, we can't get enough of His Word, devouring it, digesting it, and putting it into practice. We can't drink deeply enough from the fount of truth, letting it flow into us, through us, and out of us as we refresh the lives of others. Such a desire for righteousness has its own reward, the fruit of righteousness being a clean conscience, a deeper love for God and others, and a life free from fear, regret, and shame.

Blessed are the merciful, for they shall receive mercy (Matt. 5:7). The "merciful" are those whose hearts are moved for those in need, having a desire to step in and assist in relieving their pain. This kind of mercy goes beyond merely feeling sorry for people or having pity or sympathy. It may start with such emotions, but it doesn't end there. The merciful person empathizes with those who suffer and then actually *does something* to help. James 2:15-16 says, "If a brother or sister is without clothing and in need of daily food, and one of you says to them, 'Go in peace, be warmed and be filled,' and yet you do not give them what is necessary for their body, what use is that?" Similarly, 1 John 3:17 admonishes, "Whoever has the world's goods, and sees his brother in need and closes his heart against him, how does the love of God abide in him?" The effects of a lifestyle of mercy are both future (heavenly) and present (earthly). In light of the fact that God has had mercy on us and will, in the future, show us mercy through Christ (Jude 1:21), we are called to show mercy to others; and when we engage in acts of mercy, others will show mercy toward us.

Blessed are the pure in heart, for they shall see God (Matt. 5:8). Being "pure in heart" probably refers to having a clean conscience or a sincere mind (see 2 Tim. 2:22; Titus 1:15; Heb. 10:22). Such people are honest, trustworthy, faithful, and loyal. Lying and deceit are far from them. They don't have to keep track of little white lies in order to avoid being found out as fibbers, and they maintain integrity of actions even when nobody is looking. The pure in heart will see God. Again, like the other beatitudes, this is true with respect to both the future and the present. True purity of heart, which is available only through the salvation that comes through Christ, guarantees us a place in heaven before the awesome presence of God. But the pure in heart will also witness God at work in the here and now, feeling His presence even amid present trials and temptations.

Blessed are the peacemakers, for they shall be called sons of God (Matt. 5:9). Those who make peace relieve tensions and don't feed fuel to fires of controversy. A peacemaker seeks resolutions to arguments and debates. A peacemaker works hard to keep offenses from festering into fractured relationships. A peacemaker's words generate light but not heat. Proverbs 15:1 says, "A gentle answer turns away wrath, but a harsh word stirs up anger." It is important to note, however, that being a peacemaker does not amount to being a passive person who lies down like a doormat and lets people walk all over them. The kind of peacemaking referred to here is *active*, not *passive*. Peacemakers are engaged in a ministry of reconciliation and restoration, entering troubled waters to help bring calm. In this way, they model in this life the ministry of Jesus, the Son of God, who came preaching peace and reconciliation to those willing to hear.

Blessed are those who have been persecuted for the sake of righteousness, for theirs is the kingdom of heaven. Blessed are you when people insult you and persecute you, and falsely say all kinds of evil against you because of Me. Rejoice and be glad, for your reward in heaven is great; for in the same way they persecuted the prophets who were before you (Matt. 5:10-12). Some commentators see the statements of 5:10-11 as the eighth and ninth beatitudes, but I understand 5:11-12 as expanding on the beatitude of 5:10 regarding persecution. These statements provide a surprising conclusion to the previous seven beatitudes, and the association between persecution and joy seems counterintuitive. This is why in this case Jesus expends a few words of explanation beyond the pithy principle.

In 5:10 Jesus refers to those who are persecuted and harassed for living lives in keeping with God's ethical standards and for promoting these moral truths in their teaching and preaching. Though the kingdoms of the world grow weary of righteousness and seek to have it labeled as narrow, outdated, bigoted, and even hateful, Christ assures us that the kingdom of heaven belongs to the righteous. That is, God is on *their* side, even when the world isn't.

Then, in 5:11-12, Jesus focuses on the persecution that occurs against believers simply because they are Christians. People with different religious beliefs can sometimes be hostile to Christianity. This was the case in the first century, and it remains the case today. People may insult, slander, and persecute Christians not for any wrong they have done but simply because they are Christians. In some parts of the world today, we hear of official, government-sponsored persecution of Christians—especially those who outwardly proclaim the gospel of Christ. Add to this the unofficial social and religious persecution that occurs in many non-Christian and post-Christian cultures, and the situation seems overwhelming.

However, Jesus encourages those who are enduring such persecutions to "rejoice and be glad" (5:12). Why? Because historically, the persecuted belong to a noble group—the prophets of old were themselves persecuted by the wicked. And ultimately, a great heavenly reward awaits those who endure persecution in this life.

— 5:13-16 —

When disciples of Jesus Christ live out the surprising, countercultural principles of the Beatitudes, people in the world will take note. The poor in spirit will demonstrate to others the need for the grace that only Christ can offer. Those who are comforted by the Spirit in their mourning will grab the attention of those who mourn without hope (see 1 Thes. 4:13). Because of their acts of mercy toward those in need, the merciful will draw people to themselves and point people to the God of mercy. Peacemakers will be sought out by those who are weary of being embroiled in constant conflict. And in numerous other ways, Christians engaged in kingdom living as described in the Beatitudes will influence others' opinions, prompt their decisions, and encourage their actions in a positive direction. This kind of influence occurs without coercion, force, or command. It happens by example. The influence we can have doesn't come by being just like the world around us, but by being different from the world around us.

In Matthew 5:13-16, Jesus uses two metaphors to describe how Christians function in the world when they live out the principles of the Beatitudes. These metaphors are salt (5:13) and light (5:14-16). Why these particular metaphors? First, Jesus uses the metaphor of salt because its properties and usefulness provide an excellent analogy. Salt adds flavor to food, and it also serves as a preservative, keeping meat from spoiling. Furthermore, when people consume salt, it makes them thirsty. Finally, salt can serve as a kind of detergent, making things clean. I think all these ideas lie behind Christ's description of kingdom-living believers as "salt of the earth" (5:13). If we allow ourselves to be watered-down, tasteless, bland, just-like-the-world-around-us Christians, we will lose our testimony and thus our ability to add meaning to people's lives. We will become ineffective in slowing down moral decline in families and communities, in creating a thirst for spiritual things, and in operating as a cleansing agent for those seeking to start new lives in Christ.

Second, Jesus uses the metaphor of light because the world is filled with darkness. Immorality, unbelief, corruption, violence, pain, and death engulf us. When believers exhibit kingdom living like that described in the Beatitudes, their light dispels darkness. They're like the light of a city set on a hill—people from miles around who dwell in deep darkness will have a beacon of hope toward which to move (5:14). When the light of the Christian life does what it's supposed to do, it can't be hidden or extinguished; instead, it stands tall, shines clearly, and is shared with others (5:15).

Jesus ends the analogies with an admonition: "Let your light shine" (5:16). When we let our lives reflect the glory of God and His coming kingdom, more people in the darkness around us will see our good works and glorify God the Father—perhaps by even converting and committing their own lives to Christ. They'll observe how we react to pressure and trials and will want that same kind of fortitude. They'll see how we treat others with love, dignity, and respect and will want to have the power to do the same. They'll see mercy and peacemaking exemplified in our lives and will find themselves drawn to the Prince of Peace, who can show mercy to even the most hardened hearts.

APPLICATION: MATTHEW 5:1-16

Being the Beatitudes

We don't want to be those whose salt has lost its saltiness—and with it the ability to positively influence those around us for the kingdom of God. And we don't want to dim our lights or snuff out our witness by hiding our kingdom living so the world can't see it. Rather, we want to shake the salt and shine the light, avoiding extremes of over-salting with "holier than thou" attitudes or over-shining in ways that blind people and turn them away from the truth rather than invite them to the warm glow of the gospel.

But how can we make the Beatitudes part of our everyday lives? How could we, as sinners saved by grace, ever live up to the high calling described in these eight challenging statements? Let me give two suggestions for how we can "be" the Beatitudes.

First, *apply one beatitude each day.* Just take small steps, tiny bites. Don't try to juggle all the beatitudes in the air at once. Meditate on one each day. On Monday, focus on what it means to be "poor in spirit"—having total dependence on God. On Tuesday, work through mourning for your sinful condition, and regard with thankfulness Christ's forgiveness. On Wednesday, think about how you can maintain gentleness in all your interactions. Do this each day of the week, constantly running through the eight beatitudes day after day for at least a month. By the end of the month, see how it affects your daily walk with Christ and your witness to others; then commit to continuing.

Second, *pay closer attention to the contrast between the world's system and Christ's teaching.* Put up your radar of discernment when you watch TV, browse the internet and social media, or look at the news. Listen for the opposites of the Beatitudes that so pervasively fill this world. Imagine what it would be like if everybody lived their lives in ways completely opposed to the Beatitudes. Then decide, each day, which kind of world you want to live in: the kind of world that anticipates the coming kingdom, in which people live as salt and light in keeping with that kingdom's ideals, or the kind of world where life is bland and decaying fast, with people heading into the darkness of twilight and having no light on the horizon?

You can make a difference. Don't neglect any chance to do it.

Real Righteousness
MATTHEW 5:17-48

NASB

17 "Do not think that I came to abolish the Law or the Prophets; I did not come to abolish but to fulfill. 18 For truly I say to you, until heaven and earth pass away, not ªthe smallest letter or stroke shall pass from the Law until all is accomplished. 19 Whoever then annuls one of the least of these commandments, and teaches ªothers *to do* the same, shall be called least in the kingdom of heaven; but whoever ᵇkeeps and teaches *them,* he shall be called great in the kingdom of heaven.

20 "For I say to you that unless your righteousness surpasses *that* of the scribes and Pharisees, you will not enter the kingdom of heaven.

21 "You have heard that ªthe ancients were told, 'YOU SHALL NOT COMMIT MURDER' and 'Whoever commits murder shall be ᵇliable to the court.' 22 But I say to you that everyone who is angry with his brother shall be ªguilty before the court; and whoever says to his brother, 'ᵇYou good-for-nothing,' shall be ªguilty before ᶜthe supreme court; and whoever says, 'You fool,' shall be ªguilty *enough to go* into the ᵈfiery hell. 23 Therefore if you are presenting your ªoffering at the altar, and there remember that your brother has something against you, 24 leave your ªoffering there before the altar and go; first be reconciled to your brother, and then come and present your ªoffering. 25 Make friends quickly with your opponent at law while you are with him on the way, so that your opponent may not hand you over to the judge, and the judge to the officer, and you be thrown into prison. 26 Truly I say to

NLT

17 "Don't misunderstand why I have come. I did not come to abolish the law of Moses or the writings of the prophets. No, I came to accomplish their purpose. 18 I tell you the truth, until heaven and earth disappear, not even the smallest detail of God's law will disappear until its purpose is achieved. 19 So if you ignore the least commandment and teach others to do the same, you will be called the least in the Kingdom of Heaven. But anyone who obeys God's laws and teaches them will be called great in the Kingdom of Heaven.

20 "But I warn you—unless your righteousness is better than the righteousness of the teachers of religious law and the Pharisees, you will never enter the Kingdom of Heaven!

21 "You have heard that our ancestors were told, 'You must not murder. If you commit murder, you are subject to judgment.'* 22 But I say, if you are even angry with someone,* you are subject to judgment! If you call someone an idiot,* you are in danger of being brought before the court. And if you curse someone,* you are in danger of the fires of hell.*

23 "So if you are presenting a sacrifice* at the altar in the Temple and you suddenly remember that someone has something against you, 24 leave your sacrifice there at the altar. Go and be reconciled to that person. Then come and offer your sacrifice to God.

25 "When you are on the way to court with your adversary, settle your differences quickly. Otherwise, your accuser may hand you over to the judge, who will hand you over to an officer, and you will be thrown into prison. 26 And if that happens,

you, you will not come out of there until you have paid up the last ᵃcent. ²⁷"You have heard that it was said, 'YOU SHALL NOT COMMIT ADULTERY'; ²⁸but I say to you that everyone who looks at a woman with lust for her has already committed adultery with her in his heart. ²⁹If your right eye makes you ᵃstumble, tear it out and throw it from you; for it is better for you ᵇto lose one of the parts of your body, ᶜthan for your whole body to be thrown into ᵈhell. ³⁰If your right hand makes you ᵃstumble, cut it off and throw it from you; for it is better for you ᵇto lose one of the parts of your body, ᶜthan for your whole body to go into ᵈhell.

³¹"It was said, 'WHOEVER SENDS HIS WIFE AWAY, LET HIM GIVE HER A CERTIFICATE OF DIVORCE'; ³²but I say to you that everyone who ᵃdivorces his wife, except for *the* reason of unchastity, makes her commit adultery; and whoever marries a ᵇdivorced woman commits adultery.

³³"Again, you have heard that ᵃthe ancients were told, 'ᵇYOU SHALL NOT ᶜMAKE FALSE VOWS, BUT SHALL FULFILL YOUR ᵈVOWS TO THE LORD.' ³⁴But I say to you, make no oath at all, either by heaven, for it is the throne of God, ³⁵or by the earth, for it is the footstool of His feet, or ᵃby Jerusalem, for it is THE CITY OF THE GREAT KING. ³⁶Nor shall you make an oath by your head, for you cannot make one hair white or black. ³⁷But let your statement be, 'Yes, yes' *or* 'No, no'; anything beyond these is ᵃof evil.

³⁸"You have heard that it was said, 'AN EYE FOR AN EYE, AND A TOOTH FOR A TOOTH.' ³⁹But I say to you, do not resist an evil person; but whoever slaps you on your right cheek, turn the other to him also. ⁴⁰If anyone wants to sue you and take your

you surely won't be free again until you have paid the last penny.*

²⁷"You have heard the commandment that says, 'You must not commit adultery.'* ²⁸But I say, anyone who even looks at a woman with lust has already committed adultery with her in his heart. ²⁹So if your eye—even your good eye*—causes you to lust, gouge it out and throw it away. It is better for you to lose one part of your body than for your whole body to be thrown into hell. ³⁰And if your hand—even your stronger hand*—causes you to sin, cut it off and throw it away. It is better for you to lose one part of your body than for your whole body to be thrown into hell.

³¹"You have heard the law that says, 'A man can divorce his wife by merely giving her a written notice of divorce.'* ³²But I say that a man who divorces his wife, unless she has been unfaithful, causes her to commit adultery. And anyone who marries a divorced woman also commits adultery.

³³"You have also heard that our ancestors were told, 'You must not break your vows; you must carry out the vows you make to the LORD.'* ³⁴But I say, do not make any vows! Do not say, 'By heaven!' because heaven is God's throne. ³⁵And do not say, 'By the earth!' because the earth is his footstool. And do not say, 'By Jerusalem!' for Jerusalem is the city of the great King. ³⁶Do not even say, 'By my head!' for you can't turn one hair white or black. ³⁷Just say a simple, 'Yes, I will,' or 'No, I won't.' Anything beyond this is from the evil one.

³⁸"You have heard the law that says the punishment must match the injury: 'An eye for an eye, and a tooth for a tooth.'* ³⁹But I say, do not resist an evil person! If someone slaps you on the right cheek, offer the other cheek also. ⁴⁰If you are sued in court

NASB

ashirt, let him have your bcoat also. 41Whoever aforces you to go one mile, go with him two. 42Give to him who asks of you, and do not turn away from him who wants to borrow from you.

43 "You have heard that it was said, 'YOU SHALL LOVE YOUR NEIGHBOR and hate your enemy.' 44But I say to you, love your enemies and pray for those who persecute you, 45so that you may abe sons of your Father who is in heaven; for He causes His sun to rise on *the* evil and *the* good, and sends rain on *the* righteous and *the* unrighteous. 46For if you love those who love you, what reward do you have? Do not even the tax collectors do the same? 47If you greet only your brothers, what more are you doing *than others?* Do not even the Gentiles do the same? 48Therefore ayou are to be perfect, as your heavenly Father is perfect.

5:18 aLit one iota (Heb yodh) or one projection of a letter (serif)   5:19 aGr anthropoi   bLit does   5:21 aLit it was said to the ancients   bOr guilty before   5:22 aOr liable to   bOr empty-head; Gr Raka (Raca) fr Aram reqa   cLit the Sanhedrin   dLit Gehenna of fire   5:23 aOr gift   5:24 aOr gift   5:26 aLit quadrans (equaling two mites); i.e. 1/64 of a daily wage   5:29 aI.e. sin   bLit that one... be lost   cLit not your whole body   dGr Gehenna   5:30 aI.e. sin   bLit that one...be lost   cLit not your whole body   dGr Gehenna   5:32 aOr sends away   bOr sent away   5:33 aLit it was said to the ancients   byou and your are singular here   cOr break your vows   dLit oaths   5:35 aOr toward   5:37 aOr from the evil one   5:40 aLit tunic; i.e. a garment worn next to the body   bLit cloak; i.e. an outer garment   5:41 aLit will force   5:45 aOr show yourselves to be   5:48 aLit you shall be

NLT

and your shirt is taken from you, give your coat, too. 41If a soldier demands that you carry his gear for a mile,* carry it two miles. 42Give to those who ask, and don't turn away from those who want to borrow.

43 "You have heard the law that says, 'Love your neighbor'* and hate your enemy. 44But I say, love your enemies!* Pray for those who persecute you! 45In that way, you will be acting as true children of your Father in heaven. For he gives his sunlight to both the evil and the good, and he sends rain on the just and the unjust alike. 46If you love only those who love you, what reward is there for that? Even corrupt tax collectors do that much. 47If you are kind only to your friends,* how are you different from anyone else? Even pagans do that. 48But you are to be perfect, even as your Father in heaven is perfect.

5:21 Exod 20:13; Deut 5:17.   5:22a Some manuscripts add without cause.   5:22b Greek uses an Aramaic term of contempt: If you say to your brother, 'Raca.'   5:22c Greek if you say, 'You fool.'   5:22d Greek Gehenna; also in 5:29, 30.   5:23 Greek gift; also in 5:24.   5:26 Greek the last kodrantes [i.e., quadrans].   5:27 Exod 20:14; Deut 5:18.   5:29 Greek your right eye.   5:30 Greek your right hand.   5:31 Deut 24:1.   5:33 Num 30:2.   5:38 Greek the law that says: 'An eye for an eye and a tooth for a tooth.' Exod 21:24; Lev 24:20; Deut 19:21.   5:41 Greek milion [4,854 feet or 1,478 meters].   5:43 Lev 19:18.   5:44 Some manuscripts add Bless those who curse you. Do good to those who hate you. Compare Luke 6:27-28.   5:47 Greek your brothers.

Nobody spoke more clearly than Jesus. Without any attempt at parading His wisdom or flaunting His role, He moved quietly into the ranks of humanity and confidently explained truth like none other before or since. What courage that took in a religious culture that touted human traditions as the truth of God!

For many long years, faulty information had been taught by the religious aristocracy. With unquestioned authority, these religious leaders twisted the meaning of Holy Scripture, offered interpretations that were simply wrong, and demanded applications that were frankly impossible. Not content to let God's Word speak for itself, they added to the commandments of God and required that everyone obey their additions without hesitation. When Jesus sat down and delivered His illustrious Sermon on the Mount, jaws must have dropped as His audience heard an entirely different interpretation, delivered in an entirely different mode of communication.

With boldness and clarity, He explained crucial truths in such a way that anyone could grasp the meaning. His teachings were both insightful and convicting. They stood in sharp contrast to the traditional religious instructions the people had been taught throughout their lives. And just as these truths were impactful among Jesus' original audience, they have immense bearing for us today.

— 5:17-20 —

In the first century, those who read, interpreted, and applied the Word of God in the synagogues were the scribes and Pharisees—leaders of the religious elite. The Jewish people were reared in synagogues, participated in temple worship, and learned the Old Testament Law from teachers and scholars steeped in traditional religion. The role of the average, everyday layperson was simply to believe and obey what the official teachers taught. They had no opportunity or authority to question, doubt, or challenge their views.

But when Jesus arrived on the scene, He began to set the record straight. He didn't come to throw out the Law and the Prophets themselves! After all, the Old Testament Scriptures were the very Word of God in written form—inspired and inerrant, true in everything they affirmed. The problem wasn't with the Law and the Prophets but with the faulty interpretation and application of them.

The critics felt threatened by the bold, authoritative teaching of Jesus. Their own high position in society was under attack, so of course they looked at Him with contempt. Jesus' interpretation of the Bible differed from theirs, and because they assumed their reading was right, they pitted Jesus' words *against* the Bible and tried to accuse Him of unfaithfulness to Scripture. They wanted to brand Him as a heretic!

Jesus made it clear that He didn't come to "abolish the Law or the Prophets" (5:17). In fact, in case anybody might think He was soft on Holy Scripture, He affirmed that not even the "smallest letter or stroke" of the Law would pass away (5:18). The terms used in 5:18 highlight the precision and perfection of the inspired Word. Literally, it says, "not one iota or one horn." The *iota* (ι) was the smallest Greek vowel, sometimes even located beneath another letter. The "horn" probably referred to a tiny mark like a hook or tail that distinguished one letter from another, as in the case of the Hebrew letters *yod* (י) and *waw* (ו), or *daleth* (ד) and *resh* (ר).[7] Furthermore, using a play on words, Jesus warned that any teacher who annuls even one of the "least" of the commandments will be "least" in the kingdom of God. On the contrary, "whoever keeps and teaches" the commandments will be "great" (5:19). Clearly, nobody could accuse Jesus of having a low regard for the inspiration, inerrancy, and accuracy of Scripture!

So, rather than setting aside, rejecting, or replacing the Word of God, Jesus had come to "fulfill" and to "accomplish" it (5:17-18). Jesus Himself would fulfill God's Word doctrinally, ethically, prophetically, and personally. He would live its laws and interpret its words as God originally intended. He would fulfill its prophecies and promises as predicted.

As the long-expected King of Israel, Jesus was, by definition, the *greatest* in the kingdom of God. Therefore, He would keep and teach the commandments in purity and perfection. However, He would *not* live up to the man-made rules of the Pharisees or cater to the false interpretations of the scribes. His righteousness would be authentic, not like the fake, outward righteousness of the scribes and Pharisees of His day. What's the difference? John Stott puts it this way: "Christian righteousness is greater than pharisaic righteousness because it is deeper, being a righteousness of the heart. . . . Pharisees were content with an external and formal obedience, a rigid conformity to the letter of the law. . . . The righteousness which is pleasing to him is an inward righteousness of mind and motive."[8]

For the remainder of chapter 5, Matthew recounts six examples of the "deeper righteousness" Jesus expects from those who truly know the Lord, who love and obey Him with true hearts. These examples reflect topics that often sparked controversial discussion in Jesus' day:

- murder (5:21-26)
- adultery (5:27-30)
- divorce (5:31-32)
- oaths (5:33-37)
- retaliation (5:38-42)
- love (5:43-48)

For each of these six topics, Jesus used a repeated pattern: "You have heard" (the teaching from rabbis with which His listeners were familiar)

. . . "but I say to you" (the correct interpretation or application of the biblical truth). With this rhythmic rhetorical device, Jesus struck at the very center of the man-made veneer of the religious authorities of His day. At the same time, He shifted the emphasis from merely external, observable conformity to internal transformation.

— 5:21-26—

Murder. The outward act is straightforward—unjustly taking the life of another. This act is condemned in one of the Ten Commandments (Exod. 20:13), which Jesus quotes in Matthew 5:21, adding an allusion to the justice demanded by the courts that were established in Israel for "righteous judgment" (Deut. 16:18). Chances are good that not a single soul among Jesus' listeners had ever been brought before the village courts to stand trial for murder. So they were probably feeling pretty good about themselves.

But right at this point the Messiah caught them off guard with His "but I say to you" statement (Matt. 5:22). He moved from the outward act that none of them had committed to the inner attitude that went deeper—to the actual *cause* of the chain reaction of attitudes, thoughts, emotions, and actions that leads people to commit murder. Ever been angry with your brother? You may be innocent before the city magistrate, but you are guilty before God's court. Ever call your brother useless or a fool? You're guilty before God's bench of perfect justice and are liable to eternal fire! You've murdered that person in your heart or slain that person with your tongue. Though no physical wounds are visible, the words themselves leave a mark on the mind and emotions.

In contrast to seething anger and poisonous words that damage relationships and can even lead to rancor, violence, and ultimately murder, Jesus offers an antidote: *reconciliation.* When we find ourselves engaged in worship of the Lord, we should take that opportunity to reflect on the relationships we have with others. And if we recognize that we're harboring bitter feelings toward another person or that we've had a falling out or dispute with someone, we are to seek reconciliation immediately (5:23-24).

By now Jesus' hearers were probably a bit uncomfortable. Who hasn't had some rocky relationships with their physical or spiritual brothers or sisters? Nonetheless, what Jesus said made sense. I'm sure within a few minutes, He had hundreds of nodding heads from people pondering how they would make amends with their closest companions. But then Jesus took the admonition one level deeper—from reconciliation with a brother to reconciliation with an opponent! This time, the context of the illustration is not that of making one's way to worship but rather of making one's way to court to settle a debt or lawsuit (5:25). Jesus urged His listeners to maintain an attitude of reconciliation even in legal disputes. They should be peacemakers, eager to settle. The truth is, a court's decision doesn't always go your way—you could end up losing the suit, and then your harboring of bitterness and demands for vengeance will end with you losing everything (5:26)!

Here Jesus applies the principles of the Beatitudes—particularly the ones involving mercy and peacemaking—to very concrete situations. The basic truth of Jesus' deep message that murder includes the harboring of hatred and the seeking of vengeance is straightforward: We can't be right with God unless we're right with others; or, to reverse the phrasing, our relationships with others have an impact on our relationship with God.

— 5:27-30 —

Adultery. Again Jesus tossed out to His hearers one of the great "Thou shalt nots" (see 5:27). Like many raised in Christian homes today, the Jews in the first century had heard over and over again, "You shall not commit adultery" (Exod. 20:14). While committing adultery is more common than committing murder, it is still one of those big infractions that many readers of Matthew 5 believe they can scratch off their lists of sins . . . until Jesus' "but I say to you" (5:28). In His deep reading of the command, Jesus said that to look with lust at someone who is not your spouse is tantamount to committing adultery in your heart. To underscore the seriousness with which we should take this, Jesus employed a figure of speech called *hyperbole*—obviously exaggerated language intended to make an emotional impact on an audience and to drive a principle deep into their hearts and minds. Jesus said to tear out your eye if you can't control its lustful gazing or to cut off your hand if you can't keep it to yourself. Being thus maimed in this life is better than being dragged into condemnation in the next (5:29-30).

Let me make a few clarifying statements regarding Jesus' teaching here. First, He didn't give the slightest hint that the natural sexual relations within marriage between a man and woman are anything but God-given and fitting. Jesus was talking not about sexual relations between a husband and wife but about unlawful intimacy between two people who are not married.

Second, His teaching has to do with all forms of sexual immorality, not just the one specific example He used to illustrate the deeper principle. Yes, He referred to a man looking in lust at a woman, but He could have used a different example of lust.

Third, Jesus wasn't advocating literal self-mutilation as a solution for sexual lust. However, the hyperbolic figure of speech does point to a severe, uncompromising moral self-control and self-denial. Lust enters through the eyes and sends a message to the mind, where the imagination takes over. So we shouldn't look at things we know are treacherous, like pornographic images, and we shouldn't stare at people as if they are merely objects of physical attraction. We should, to interpret Jesus' figure of speech, be "blind" to them! Likewise, through the act of touching, lust is stimulated. If your hands go where they shouldn't, then you have ignited your imagination and poured gasoline on the fire. Keep your hands to yourself!

> **BIBLICAL PASSAGES ON MARRIAGE, DIVORCE, AND REMARRIAGE**
>
> Genesis 2:18-25
> Deuteronomy 24:1-4
> Malachi 2:13-16
> Matthew 5:27-32
> Matthew 19:3-12
> 1 Corinthians 7:1-16
> Ephesians 5:22-33
> 1 Peter 3:1-7

— 5:31-32 —

Divorce. Probably no two verses in Matthew 5 have been more debated, commented on, interpreted, reinterpreted, pored over, wept over, and argued about than the brief statement on divorce in 5:31-32. Deuteronomy 24:1-4 includes the proper principles and procedures for handling a divorce when a husband finds some "indecency" in his wife (Deut. 24:1). But the views regarding what the Law meant by "indecency" diverged in two opposite directions in Jesus' day. A conservative school of thought, following the rabbi Shammai, restricted this language to include only sexual immorality proven by witnesses. However, the more liberal school of the rabbi Hillel understood "indecency" to include anything that displeased a husband, including burning dinner.[9] The first-century Jewish historian Josephus summed up this common liberal view of his day: "He that desires to be divorced from his wife for any cause whatsoever (and many such causes happen among men), let him in writing give assurance that he will never use her as his wife any more."[10]

Jesus quite clearly steered far from this liberal, permissive, and unjust application of divorce. Those who divorce "except for the reason of unchastity"—sexual unfaithfulness—would be unlawfully divorcing and therefore be guilty of adultery if they were to marry another. Jesus was a firm believer in marital fidelity and was opposed to a flippant, casual approach to divorce, which God hates (Mal. 2:16). However, though divorce was never commanded (God always prefers reconciliation), it was a divine concession in the Law, allowable under certain circumstances. In this passage, Jesus didn't get into all the various scenarios and exceptions. (We will address this topic much more directly and deeply in our discussion of Matthew 19:1-12.)[11]

— 5:33-37 —

Oaths. If the rabbis in Jesus' day were lax and liberal on divorce, imagine how permissive they were when it came to taking vows to seal the earnestness of their words. An oath was a promise, pure and simple. But it wasn't just a "See you at the market in a little while" kind of promise. It was specific, intentional, clear, and solemn: "I promise I will be at the market at the sixth hour to deliver the three sheep you purchased." Jesus stressed the importance of keeping our vows. He first paraphrased Leviticus 19:12, then stripped the first-century practice of oath taking of its elaborate forms.

Apparently, people had become untrustworthy in their promises and nonchalant about actually following through on commitments. To get others to take their promises seriously, people had to swear by heaven, by the earth, by Jerusalem, or by their own lives, in an almost superstitious sort of way (see Matt. 5:34-36). But even in this swearing, there was a catch—none of them actually used the name of God. As such, some were interpreting these oaths as allowing for a bit of flexibility. If a man broke a vow sworn "by Jerusalem," only Jerusalem would be offended, but not God. Stan Toussaint puts it well: "The Jewish concept of taking oaths was based on a false interpretation of Leviticus 19:12, 'You shall not swear falsely by My name.' They thought that any oath, therefore, which did not include the name of God was not binding. Sometimes these oaths even came to be used as a means of deceit."[12]

Jesus' answer to this culture of subtlety and deception was simple: "Let your statement be, 'Yes, yes' or 'No, no'; anything beyond these is of evil" (Matt. 5:37). Just a single word will do. When we agree to pay a debt, we shouldn't need to sign thirty pages of contracts; we should just pay it. When we vow to be faithful to a husband or wife, our simple "I do" should serve as a permanent seal of our fidelity. If we say we'll meet somebody at five o'clock, we should follow through on our commitment unless uncontrollable circumstances prevent it. An elaborate "oath" isn't needed to buttress the word of a believer who values truth and commitment. Just tell the truth and keep your promises!

— 5:38-42 —

Retaliation. All of Jesus' hearers knew the Old Testament law of retribution:

If a man takes the life of any human being, he shall surely be put to death. The one who takes the life of an animal shall make it good, life for life. If a man injures his neighbor, just as he has done, so it shall be done to him: fracture for fracture, eye for eye, tooth for tooth; just as he has injured a man, so it shall be inflicted on him. Thus the one who kills an animal shall make it good, but the one who kills a man shall be put to death. (Lev. 24:17-21)

The wheels of justice turned on the principle of payback. However, God gave these guidelines to govern civil and criminal justice. They prevented judges and courts from exacting excessive punishments on people. They also served as a deterrent to criminal acts because people could be sure that, in such a system of justice, what they did to others would come back upon them in equal measure.

This law of retribution was not intended to govern personal, every-day relationships between family members, friends, and neighbors. Yet many were applying this principle in a tit-for-tat, this-for-that style of vigilante "justice." Such an interpretation left no room for grace and mercy, forgiveness and forbearance. Jesus knew human nature. He knew that if all individuals felt it was their legal obligation to retaliate against every little wrong, it would lead to an escalation of aggression and a breakdown of society.

So Jesus urged His listeners to respond to personal offenses with grace and mercy. When an evil person insults you, take the insult. If they take their aggression one step further and slap you on the cheek, refuse to retaliate (Matt. 5:39). If somebody tries to unjustly take from you or force you to do something, voluntarily give up your right to personal dignity and respect, and cooperate (5:40-42). Jesus knew that such alarming and unexpected responses to wicked behavior often disarm and disorient people and lead not to an escalation of wickedness and violence but to repentance and reconciliation.

However, Jesus' statements must be understood in their overall context. Nowhere in Scripture are we instructed to be submissive victims to physical, verbal, or sexual abuse, rape, terrorism, murder, or other threats of true harm. It's noble to bite your tongue when some guy insults you in the checkout lane, or to refuse to lean on the horn when an aggressive driver cuts you off in traffic, or to take a step back when an upset mother slaps you for scolding her out-of-control child. But it's deplorable to sit back passively as a bully injures a defenseless victim, or to refuse to defend your children if a kidnapper tries to drag them off, or to raise the flag of surrender if an army of terrorists rolls across your nation's border. John Stott puts Jesus' words into perspective: "Christ's illustrations are not to be taken as the charter for any unscrupulous tyrant, ruffian, beggar or thug. His purpose was to forbid revenge, not to encourage injustice, dishonesty or vice. . . . True love, caring for both the individual and society, takes action to deter evil and to promote good."[13]

— 5:43-48 —

Love. Jesus sums up this portion of His message with the principle of loving your enemies. What Jesus' audience heard while growing up in the synagogue was "Love your neighbor and hate your enemy" (5:43). The command to love is from Leviticus 19:18, but the command to hate is found nowhere in Scripture. Human reason tainted by depravity made the logical leap that if you were to love your neighbor, there must be non-neighborly people—namely, your enemies—who must be hated. But Jesus' response toppled such human reasoning: Love your enemies and pray for your persecutors (Matt. 5:44). The word for "love" used here is *agapaō* [25], the verb form of *agapē* [26]— not an emotional, endearing kind of love, but a one-way, no-strings-attached kind of love that flows from grace and mercy. Nobody really deserves *agapē* love; but by the power of God and by following the example of Christ, we can show this kind of love even to outsiders and adversaries.

Jesus' original audience would have understood this to refer particularly to the Romans, who were their pagan oppressors. Notice that Jesus didn't say that His followers should love the way their enemies live, love their beliefs, love the way they treat them, or love their plans and motives. They are to love them by praying for them (5:44), by showing them the same general grace and mercy as God does (5:45), and by greeting them cordially and kindly (5:47).

To love only members of one's own family or tribe is natural—any wicked unbeliever does that (5:46-47). Jesus called His audience to a greater love, a love that was *supernatural*. Such a love requires a work of the Spirit in our hearts to transcend our normal human tendency to love only our own. Because of the transcendent nature of this *agapē*, Jesus said that those who love in such a way are like children of their heavenly Father (5:45) and are to be, in fact, "perfect," as He is (5:48). This doesn't refer to sinless perfection. One commentator explains the real significance of the word translated "perfect" this way: "The Greek word is *teleios*, a word which carries the meaning of culmination, of maturity, of achievement in function. . . . It is an active word, and, in context, means that our love must be all-inclusive as God's is all-inclusive."[14]

APPLICATION: MATTHEW 5:17-48

Just Be Perfect, That's All!

Jesus' summary statement in Matthew 5:48 would have sounded as shocking to His original hearers as it does to today's readers: "Therefore you are to be perfect, as your heavenly Father is perfect." If you're like me, that kind of jolts you out of your spiritual slumber, doesn't it? Doing your best, trying hard, taking baby steps—we can relate to that. But "be perfect"? Just like God the Father? Is that all?

The term *teleios* [5046], translated here as "perfect," doesn't mean being godlike. It means living up to our created purpose. A man who has reached full-grown stature is *teleios*, no longer a little boy. A student who now grasps mature knowledge of a subject is *teleios*, unlike a kindergartner. The related noun, *telos* [5056], refers to the end, aim, goal, or purpose for which something is created. You and I are *teleios* when we fulfill the purpose for which we were created—bearing the image of God and reflecting His love, justice, grace, and mercy in the world. Jesus' statement doesn't mean that we are to be as perfect as our heavenly Father but that we are to be perfect, complete, and mature in our actions in accordance with our purpose as humans—just as the Father is perfect, complete, and mature in His actions in accordance with His divine nature.

So, what are the typical human responses to Jesus' desire that we be "perfect"? I can think of three.

An immature response is "This is easy!" If Jesus said we should live out the Sermon on the Mount in this life, it must mean that anybody can do it. He wouldn't tell us to do something that's impossible, would He? To respond in this overly optimistic way is to forget our own depravity, weakness, and sinfulness. The standard of righteousness Jesus set isn't adjusted for our fallen condition. God's standard of right living, even in a fallen world, isn't on a sliding scale . . . He doesn't grade on a curve. Those who think the principles of the Sermon on the Mount are easy and that we should be able to achieve sinless perfection in this life are going to have to redefine *sin* like the Pharisees did, or they'll be constantly depressed and disappointed.

A second response might go something like this: "This is extremely difficult, so I'll need to work really hard at it, to give it my all. After all, practice makes perfect." This approach also sees the principles of the Sermon on the Mount as achievable, but only through great self-discipline and constant effort; by incremental steps, we can get more and more holy, closer and closer to God's standard, and therefore merit commendation and reward. In this response, the emphasis is still on *our own efforts*. Like the Pharisees of old, we strive to be perfect in our own strength.

A third, proper response, is "This is impossible." Yes, the depth of sincerity, love, righteousness, discernment, and holiness Jesus has in mind in the Sermon on the Mount is impossible . . . in our own strength. But the great truth is that when we become Christians, we're not left to ourselves. Now we have the Holy Spirit living within us, who works in us both to help us to desire and to carry out a level of righteousness impossible to an unbeliever (Phil. 2:12-13). The Lord Jesus releases His power through you, enabling you to love rather than hate, to keep your promises, to maintain your fidelity, to restrain your desire for revenge, to surrender your rights for the sake of reconciliation, and to wisely discern when it's proper to take a stand against wickedness or let things slide for a greater outcome. We can do none of these things on our own. But we don't have to! The author of Hebrews sums up this truth perfectly: "Now the God of peace, who brought up from the dead the great Shepherd of the sheep through the blood of the eternal covenant, even Jesus our Lord, *equip you in every good thing to do His will, working in us that which is pleasing in His sight,* through Jesus Christ, to whom be the glory forever and ever. Amen" (Heb. 13:20-21, emphasis mine).

Piety and Prayer minus the Pizzazz
MATTHEW 6:1-18

NASB

1 "Beware of practicing your righteousness before men to be noticed by them; otherwise you have no reward with your Father who is in heaven.

2 "So when you ªgive to the poor, do not sound a trumpet before you, as the hypocrites do in the synagogues and in the streets, so that they may be honored by men. Truly I say to you, they have their reward in full. 3 But when you ªgive to the poor, do not let your left hand know what your right hand is doing, 4 so that your ªgiving will be in secret; and your Father who sees *what is done* in secret will reward you.

5 "When you pray, you are not to be like the hypocrites; for they love to stand and pray in the synagogues and on the street corners ªso that they may be seen by men. Truly I say to you, they have their reward in full. 6 But you, when you pray, go into your inner room, close your door and pray to your Father who is in secret, and your Father who sees *what is done* in secret will reward you.

7 "And when you are praying, do not use meaningless repetition as the Gentiles do, for they suppose that they will be heard for their many words. 8 So do not be like them; for your Father knows what you need before you ask Him.

9 "Pray, then, in this way:
'Our Father who is in heaven,
Hallowed be Your name.
10 'Your kingdom come.
Your will be done,
On earth as it is in heaven.
11 'Give us this day ªour daily bread.
12 'And forgive us our debts, as
we also have forgiven our
debtors.

NLT

1 "Watch out! Don't do your good deeds publicly, to be admired by others, for you will lose the reward from your Father in heaven. 2 When you give to someone in need, don't do as the hypocrites do—blowing trumpets in the synagogues and streets to call attention to their acts of charity! I tell you the truth, they have received all the reward they will ever get. 3 But when you give to someone in need, don't let your left hand know what your right hand is doing. 4 Give your gifts in private, and your Father, who sees everything, will reward you.

5 "When you pray, don't be like the hypocrites who love to pray publicly on street corners and in the synagogues where everyone can see them. I tell you the truth, that is all the reward they will ever get. 6 But when you pray, go away by yourself, shut the door behind you, and pray to your Father in private. Then your Father, who sees everything, will reward you.

7 "When you pray, don't babble on and on as the Gentiles do. They think their prayers are answered merely by repeating their words again and again. 8 Don't be like them, for your Father knows exactly what you need even before you ask him! 9 Pray like this:

Our Father in heaven,
may your name be kept holy.
10 May your Kingdom come soon.
May your will be done on earth,
as it is in heaven.
11 Give us today the food we need,*
12 and forgive us our sins,
as we have forgiven those who
sin against us.

NASB

¹³ 'And do not lead us into temptation, but deliver us from ªevil. ᵇ[For Yours is the kingdom and the power and the glory forever. Amen.']

¹⁴For if you forgive ªothers for their transgressions, your heavenly Father will also forgive you. ¹⁵But if you do not forgive ªothers, then your Father will not forgive your transgressions.

¹⁶"Whenever you fast, do not put on a gloomy face as the hypocrites do, for they ªneglect their appearance so that they will be noticed by men when they are fasting. Truly I say to you, they have their reward in full. ¹⁷But you, when you fast, anoint your head and wash your face ¹⁸so that your fasting will not be noticed by men, but by your Father who is in secret; and your Father who sees *what is done* in secret will reward you.

6:2 ªOr *give alms*   6:3 ªOr *give alms*   6:4 ªOr *alms*   6:5 ªLit *to be apparent to men*   6:11 ªOr *our bread for tomorrow*   6:13 ªOr *the evil one*   ᵇThis clause not found in early mss   6:14 ªGr *anthropoi*   6:15 ªGr *anthropoi*   6:16 ªLit *distort their faces,* i.e. discolor their faces with makeup

NLT

¹³ And don't let us yield to temptation,* but rescue us from the evil one.*

¹⁴"If you forgive those who sin against you, your heavenly Father will forgive you. ¹⁵But if you refuse to forgive others, your Father will not forgive your sins.

¹⁶"And when you fast, don't make it obvious, as the hypocrites do, for they try to look miserable and disheveled so people will admire them for their fasting. I tell you the truth, that is the only reward they will ever get. ¹⁷But when you fast, comb your hair* and wash your face. ¹⁸Then no one will notice that you are fasting, except your Father, who knows what you do in private. And your Father, who sees everything, will reward you.

6:11 Or *Give us today our food for the day;* or *Give us today our food for tomorrow.*   6:13a Or *And keep us from being tested.*   6:13b Or *from evil.* Some manuscripts add *For yours is the kingdom and the power and the glory forever. Amen.*   6:17 Greek *anoint your head.*

Few things were more of a turnoff to Jesus than religion on parade. He reserved His severest criticism for religious hypocrites who liked to be seen showing off their piety in order to impress others. Jesus was a master at exposing what lay beneath the veneer of all that nonsense. And frequently He urged His followers to practice total honesty, authenticity, and simplicity.

Dropping in again on His Sermon on the Mount, we find Jesus addressing three of the disciplines that His followers would later practice regularly: giving (6:2-4), praying (6:5-15), and fasting (6:16-18). In the treatment of each, Jesus functioned more as a prophet than as a priest or teacher. Teachers relay information; Jesus called for transformation. Priests comfort the afflicted; Jesus afflicted the comfortable. Prophets not only told the truth, but they also boldly confronted error. As a prophet, Jesus' preaching naturally provoked the pseudoreligious elites of His day with a meddlesome message of true faith, sincere love, and a life of righteousness that flew in the face of the pious performers' pizzazz. His timeless words continue to address today's hypocrisy and religiosity as powerfully as they did in the first century.

— 6:1 —

In classic prophetic style, Jesus began with a strong word of warning: "Beware!" You can imagine any complacent listeners suddenly snapping to attention. *Take heed! Watch out! Warning!* Jesus was about to discuss an aspect of life in which it is easy for well-meaning folks to veer off into danger: practicing righteousness for the purpose of being noticed (6:1). When we do this, Jesus said, we already have our reward in the esteem and applause of others. But our heavenly Father? Not impressed.

In what areas are we tempted to show off? They're essentially the same now as they were then: when we give (6:2), when we pray (6:5), and when we fast (6:16). In these outward activities, which can be easily flaunted, exaggerated, and even faked, God sees through to the heart. Hebrews 4:13 reminds us, "There is no creature hidden from His sight, but all things are open and laid bare to the eyes of Him with whom we have to do." Therefore, we are to "walk humbly" with our God (Mic. 6:8). And while we are to be "salt" and "light" (Matt. 5:13-14), we shouldn't parade our piety noisily. Note that salt and light both reflect quiet manifestations of righteousness. When we carry out these practices rightly, people will notice and glorify God. But when we do these things in order to be noticed by other people, we rob God of His glory.

— 6:2-4 —

The first area where we may be tempted to parade our piety is giving. Jesus contrasted a wrong approach to giving (6:2) with the proper approach (6:3-4). He begins with how *not* to give. The Pharisees would give their alms in such a way that it was noticeable. They might as well have been sounding trumpets to draw attention to themselves. This kind of attention drawing isn't limited to the first century. As a kid, I saw people thump the bottom of the offering plate to ensure that others knew they had put something in. I've seen people wave large bills high enough for others to see before dropping them in the offering plate. Such people "love the approval of men rather than the approval of God" (see John 12:43).

Ideally, our giving is not only to be joyful and generous, but it's also to be done with a right motive and attitude. The result will be giving in secret—not in ways that draw attention to ourselves, but in ways that keep our own attention on God. This is the direction Jesus moved when He described how we're to give. When you give to those in need, you should not let your left hand know what your right hand is doing (Matt. 6:3). This idiom probably refers to a kind of "sleight of hand" move, similar to what a magician might do to make a coin or handkerchief disappear. Metaphorically, it means simply to give in secret, without drawing attention to yourself in any way. In fact, go out of your way to avoid attention.

This approach to giving results in a personal, private moment of giving as an act of worship that finds pleasure with God, who knows what you're doing and will reward you for your generosity (6:4). How are we rewarded? For one thing, the gracious, sincere giver is rewarded by the knowledge that a need has been met—the naked clothed, the sick healed, the weak encouraged, the building finished, the lost saved, the forgotten found, the wayward restored. Such acts of generous love in action bring with them their own private, spiritual rewards. Only the generous soul who gives as an act of worship can enjoy this satisfaction and receive this kind of reward.

— 6:5-15 —

The second area where people tend to parade their piety is prayer. The structure of this warning is similar to the one on giving, but here Jesus goes into greater depth and detail. In the first century, the prayers of the Pharisees had become formalized, repetitive, regulated, localized, long, overdone, and on display. Jesus countered this with a few statements for His listeners concerning how *not* to pray.

First, they are not to pray "like the hypocrites" (6:5), who loved to perform their prayers in public places where they couldn't be missed. They wanted more than to be observed; they wanted to be applauded. And they didn't want simply to inform onlookers; they wanted to impress them. Hypocrites don't love God or love to pray; they love to be seen. In getting what they're seeking—public approval—they get their reward. Today, we see people praying in the end zone after scoring a touchdown, on a busy street corner for pedestrians to see, or loudly at a restaurant so all the "heathen" customers around them can see that they're religious. Our prayers should not be on display.

Second, they are not to pray with constant repetition, gibberish, mumblings, and mutterings (6:7). I can't help but think of those who pray repetitiously through a prayer book or liturgy without thinking

Caught in the Act

MATTHEW 6:6

One night, long ago, I caught my mentor, Bob Newkirk, in the act. He never knew it, and I never told him. But that moment, I accidentally witnessed him doing something that has had a profound impact on me for the rest of my life.

I was in the Marines, stationed on the island of Okinawa, at a pretty low point emotionally and spiritually. On a rainy night, I went to see Bob, the Navigator representative on the island. When I knocked on the door to his home, his wife, Norma, answered.

"Is Bob here?" I said.

"No, I'm sorry you missed him. I think he might be at his office, but—"

"Well, I don't . . . I don't want to bother him," I said. (His office was a bus ride away.)

"You know, he said he had a lot of things on his mind and needed to be down there for a while, so . . ."

I said goodbye and thought about it for a bit. I decided I really needed to see Bob, even if only for a few minutes. So I picked up the local jitney bus and took a ride over to his part of town. I splashed through a few mud puddles and came to his little office. It was made of bamboo, with tiny spaces between the stalks. As I approached, I saw candlelight seeping through the cracks and heard Bob singing inside:

> Come, Thou Fount of every blessing,
> Tune my heart to sing Thy grace;
> Streams of mercy, never ceasing,
> Call for songs of loudest praise.[15]

The rain was dripping off my nose and dropping in pools around me, but still I heard him:

(continued on next page)

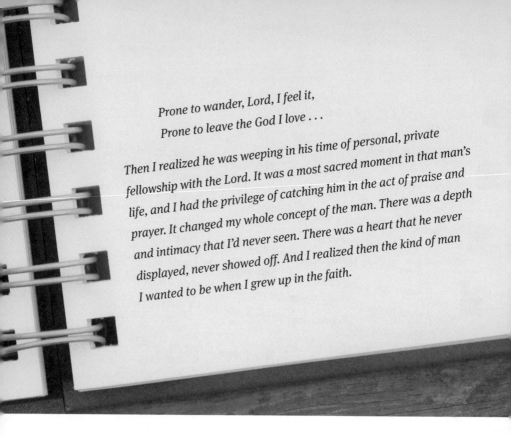

Prone to wander, Lord, I feel it,
Prone to leave the God I love . . .

Then I realized he was weeping in his time of personal, private fellowship with the Lord. It was a most sacred moment in that man's life, and I had the privilege of catching him in the act of praise and prayer. It changed my whole concept of the man. There was a depth and intimacy that I'd never seen. There was a heart that he never displayed, never showed off. And I realized then the kind of man I wanted to be when I grew up in the faith.

about what the prayers actually say, or the use of some form of ecstatic speech in which neither the speaker nor those around them know what's being said, or even some repetitive choruses in churches that have congregations singing the same lines over and over and over. God isn't impressed by many words. In fact, He already knows what we need before we ask (6:8). I'd say it's a good rule of thumb to keep our prayers simple, original, brief, and sincere.

Having stated how we *shouldn't* pray, Jesus also prescribed how we *ought* to pray. First, we should pray privately, in an "inner room," behind closed doors (6:6). This contrasts with the behavior of those who loudly, publicly prayed in the streets and synagogues in order to be seen. Jesus wasn't forbidding corporate prayer in churches, but He was pointing out that those who love to parade their prayers in public likely never pray at home, where only God can see. That is, they have a feigned, false piety, not a personal, intimate relationship with God. And just as God honors those who give in secret (6:4), so also will He reward with rich fellowship those who pray in secret (6:6).

Second, in contrast to the verbose, rambling, and meaningless prayers of the hypocrites, Jesus instructed His disciples on how to pray by giving a model prayer to follow (6:9-13). We know it as "the Lord's

Prayer," which indicates that it comes from the Lord Himself. Perhaps more accurately, we could call it "the Disciples' Prayer," since Jesus used it to instruct His audience on how to pray in a way that was appropriate. There's nothing wrong with memorizing this prayer. After all, this is Holy Scripture, the inspired, inerrant Word of God. However, as a model prayer, it wasn't Jesus' intention for His followers to simply repeat the words verbatim, in a way that was thoughtless. To do that would be to miss the point Jesus was making. Rather, this is an *exemplary* prayer—an outline or general model to follow as we learn to pray to our heavenly Father in our own words.

Notice some important things about this prayer. First, it focuses on the Lord. It's *His* name, *His* kingdom, *His* will. If our prayers focus only on ourselves, our problems, our needs, our desires, and our hopes and dreams, something's wrong. Our prayers should center on God the Father and His character, kingdom, and purposes.

Following this pattern, we address our prayers to God the Father (6:9). There's nothing doctrinally wrong with singing praises to Jesus or the Holy Spirit, but the normal practice of prayer in the New Testament is to address the Father, in the name of the Son, by the power of the Holy Spirit. We talk to Him as our heavenly Father, who hears our prayers as a dad listens to the words of his child. In our relationship with the heavenly Father, there's freedom, openness, love, acceptance, compassion, and understanding. However, we also acknowledge Him as holy, or "hallowed." In our prayers, we should never forget that God is almighty and doesn't cease to be holy when He stoops down to hear our heartfelt prayers.

Notice also that we pray for God's kingdom to come, not our own kingdom (6:10). We want His plan and purpose, not our own agendas and priorities, to be achieved in heaven and on earth. In fact, in prayer we should seek to conform our wills to His will, not His will to ours. By doing so, we implicitly confess His power, His wisdom, and His goodness. His will and kingdom purposes are always superior to our own foolish notions of what's good for us. In the original context of the prayer, this desire for the kingdom of God to come probably would have been understood as including an appeal for the Messiah to subdue His enemies and usher in His kingdom. And we still yearn for this. Yet at the same time we can live out kingdom principles and priorities even today, as we invite Christ to reign in our hearts and lives, such that our own families and churches become models of God's kingdom rule.

From talking about adoration and humility, Jesus transitioned to the topic of petitioning for everyday needs: physical, spiritual, and social. We can ask the Father to provide for our daily food (6:11)—not for a daily feast, but for basic needs. We can also ask God to provide for our deep spiritual needs, like forgiveness (6:12). We'd know nothing of inner cleansing if it were not for our Father, who gives us freedom from guilt as a free gift of grace. When we experience this kind of forgiveness in our vertical relationship with God, it has a healing power in our horizontal relationships with others.

We can also pray that God will provide us with the ability to escape the temptations we face (6:13), delivering us from the evil one, Satan. We know that apart from God's grace and mercy, we will always be victim to the wiles of the devil, never able to subdue our sinful nature. But by the power of His Holy Spirit, we can experience victory and growth in holiness.

Before moving on from an example of genuine prayer to the issue of fasting, Jesus briefly added a parenthetical statement regarding the forgiveness mentioned in 6:12 ("And forgive us our debts, as we also have forgiven our debtors"). He emphasized the importance of an attitude of forgiveness toward others, which is necessary for enjoying an unhindered personal intimacy with the almighty God in prayer (6:14-15). If we withhold forgiveness, grace, and mercy from people in our horizontal relationships, God will withhold the same in our vertical relationship with Him. This isn't about our eternal salvation and right standing with God before the court of heaven. It refers to our day-to-day fellowship and communion with God. Stan Toussaint puts it well: "Judicial forgiveness is not in view (Acts 10:43) but fellowship (1 John 1:5-9). It is impossible for one to be in fellowship with God as long as he harbors ill will in his heart."[16]

— 6:16-18 —

A final area where we may be tempted to parade our piety is fasting. Jesus said, "whenever you fast" (6:16), thus assuming that this practice would be a normal part of one's spiritual life. And it should be! I know that fasting feels like a thing of the past—or like a rigid ritual of "high church" denominations prescribed for certain holidays. But the kind of legalistic fasting Jesus condemned here does not take away from the value of proper fasting.

Those who fast should do so without drawing attention to themselves. The hypocrites who liked to make a show of things would exaggerate their weakness and gloominess, neglect to tidy up, and put on a super-pious glower to show how committed they were. If getting attention was their goal, they got their reward in full.

But Jesus said there's nothing spiritual about walking around looking like an unmade bed! To fast properly, you should take care of yourself and maintain good hygiene (6:17). If you normally shave, shave. If you normally put on makeup, do so. In other words, make sure you don't do anything with your appearance that would draw attention to yourself. Remember, you're fasting and praying not for the sake of those around you but for your heavenly Father, who rewards discreet, sincere spiritual disciplines (6:18). A good test of our motives is to fast and say nothing to anyone about it. Such a personal spiritual discipline is between you and the Lord.

SEVEN BENEFITS OF FASTING

- Fasting helps us concentrate attention on issues that require prayer.
- Fasting enables us to rearrange our priorities in order to focus on things that really matter.
- Fasting encourages us to examine our lives and inspect our motives.
- Fasting assists us when we're seeking the Lord's will.
- Fasting strengthens our self-control and discipline.
- Fasting brings us back to basics and simplifies our lives.
- Fasting equips us to recover from grief and endure sorrow.

APPLICATION: MATTHEW 6:1-18
Beware of Religious Performances

Whether we're giving, praying, or fasting, it's easy to slip into "performance mode." We forget that our heavenly Father is to be our main focus, not the people around us. And we forget that our secret place—not some public space—is our primary platform. Very quickly our motives can become driven by the horizontal plane—what people around us think of our piety—rather than by our desire to have fellowship with God and please Him alone. I have three final warnings regarding the temptation toward religious performance that will help us apply the principles of Matthew 6:1-18.

First, *when our devotion becomes a performance, we lapse into hypocrisy.* This can happen to any of us, especially those in ministry or leadership. We can lose our awe for God. And with such casual familiarity comes contempt. Instead of nurturing a deep, personal intimacy with the Almighty, we fall into going through the motions. Our audience becomes the people around us; our motive becomes making them think we're more holy and spiritual than we really are.

Second, *when our giving lacks anonymity, we miss the reward of satisfaction.* We don't give to our churches, to ministries, or to individuals in need because of some material blessing or a heavenly gem in a golden crown. God may bless us financially so we can bless others, and there are rewards in heaven, but proper, private giving that pleases God also has its own reward—the peace and joy that comes from knowing we're investing in eternal things rather than temporal things. The kind of spiritual contentment that comes through such anonymous, quiet giving is inexpressible.

Third, *when our praying and fasting is done to impress others, we fail to do what is pleasing to God.* He knows our hearts. He's fully aware of our true motives. We can't deceive Him. In fact, when we put on a show with our long monologues in prayer or our long faces in fasting, we grieve the Spirit, who wants simplicity and sincerity. Remember, the Father is looking for those who will worship Him in spirit and truth (John 4:23).

The Troubling Temptations of the World's Wares
MATTHEW 6:19-34

NASB

19 "Do not store up for yourselves treasures on earth, where moth and rust destroy, and where thieves break in and steal. 20 But store up for yourselves treasures in heaven, where neither moth nor rust destroys, and where thieves do not break in or steal; 21 for where your treasure is, there your heart will be also.

22 "The eye is the lamp of the body; so then if your eye is ªclear, your whole body will be full of light. 23 But if your eye is ªbad, your whole body

NLT

19 "Don't store up treasures here on earth, where moths eat them and rust destroys them, and where thieves break in and steal. 20 Store your treasures in heaven, where moths and rust cannot destroy, and thieves do not break in and steal. 21 Wherever your treasure is, there the desires of your heart will also be.

22 "Your eye is like a lamp that provides light for your body. When your eye is healthy, your whole body is filled with light. 23 But when your eye is unhealthy, your whole body is

will be full of darkness. If then the light that is in you is darkness, how great is the darkness!

24"No one can serve two masters; for either he will hate the one and love the other, or he will be devoted to one and despise the other. You cannot serve God and ªwealth.

25"For this reason I say to you, ªdo not be worried about your ᵇlife, *as to* what you will eat or what you will drink; nor for your body, *as to* what you will put on. Is not life more than food, and the body more than clothing? 26Look at the birds of the ªair, that they do not sow, nor reap nor gather into barns, and *yet* your heavenly Father feeds them. Are you not worth much more than they? 27And who of you by being worried can add a *single* ªhour to his ᵇlife? 28And why are you worried about clothing? Observe how the lilies of the field grow; they do not toil nor do they spin, 29yet I say to you that not even Solomon in all his glory clothed himself like one of these. 30But if God so clothes the grass of the field, which is *alive* today and tomorrow is thrown into the furnace, *will He* not much more *clothe* you? You of little faith! 31Do not worry then, saying, 'What will we eat?' or 'What will we drink?' or 'What will we wear for clothing?' 32For the Gentiles eagerly seek all these things; for your heavenly Father knows that you need all these things. 33But ªseek first ᵇHis kingdom and His righteousness, and all these things will be ᶜadded to you.

34"So do not worry about tomorrow; for tomorrow will ªcare for itself. ᵇEach day has enough trouble of its own.

filled with darkness. And if the light you think you have is actually darkness, how deep that darkness is!

24"No one can serve two masters. For you will hate one and love the other; you will be devoted to one and despise the other. You cannot serve God and be enslaved to money.

25"That is why I tell you not to worry about everyday life—whether you have enough food and drink, or enough clothes to wear. Isn't life more than food, and your body more than clothing? 26Look at the birds. They don't plant or harvest or store food in barns, for your heavenly Father feeds them. And aren't you far more valuable to him than they are? 27Can all your worries add a single moment to your life?

28"And why worry about your clothing? Look at the lilies of the field and how they grow. They don't work or make their clothing, 29yet Solomon in all his glory was not dressed as beautifully as they are. 30And if God cares so wonderfully for wildflowers that are here today and thrown into the fire tomorrow, he will certainly care for you. Why do you have so little faith?

31"So don't worry about these things, saying, 'What will we eat? What will we drink? What will we wear?' 32These things dominate the thoughts of unbelievers, but your heavenly Father already knows all your needs. 33Seek the Kingdom of God* above all else, and live righteously, and he will give you everything you need.

34"So don't worry about tomorrow, for tomorrow will bring its own worries. Today's trouble is enough for today.

6:22 ªOr *healthy;* or *sincere* 6:23 ªOr *evil*
6:24 ªGr *mamonas,* for Aram *mamon* (mammon);
i.e. wealth, etc., personified as an object of
worship 6:25 ªOr *stop being worried* ᵇLit *soul*
6:26 ªLit *heaven* 6:27 ªLit *cubit* (approx 18 in.)
ᵇOr *height* 6:33 ªOr *continually seek* ᵇOr *the
kingdom* ᶜOr *provided* 6:34 ªLit *worry about itself*
ᵇLit *Sufficient for the day is its evils*

6:33 Some manuscripts do not include *of God.*

The path of Christianity is strewn with the litter of straying saints. Those men and women lured by a lesser loyalty surprise us—perhaps even shock us. More often than not, we don't see it coming. The passionate pursuit of worldly wares leads to a slow and steady erosion of the passionate pursuit of Christ.

The roots of this kind of erosion go deep into the soil of humanity. No one is immune—neither the young, nor the middle aged, nor even those who have walked with the Lord for decades. Someone who was once a model of spiritual zeal and strong faith can be lured away from a close relationship with Christ and become tainted and tortured within by greed for money and lust for more. How quickly we can come to live a bold-faced lie while appearing genuinely holy!

And ironically, with the accumulation of possessions like money, property, treasures, and toys, we almost always sink deeper and deeper into worry. Those who have more tend to worry more.

Jesus addresses these very real problems in His Sermon on the Mount as He singles out the corrupting effects of wealth, warning us of the subtle yet powerful tentacles of greed and the futility of worry.

— 6:19-21 —

Jesus began this section with a contrast related to possessions—"Do not store up for yourselves treasures on earth. . . . But store up for yourselves treasures in heaven" (6:19-20). He explained the contrast by spelling out the folly of choosing to invest time, energy, and resources in earthly, material excesses and by pointing to the wisdom of investing in eternal things.

An important point needs to be made here: Jesus wasn't prohibiting possessions per se. Nowhere does the Bible forbid ownership of property or having possessions. Riches and honor come from God, who ought to be thanked for material blessings when He graciously gives them (1 Chr. 29:12-13). Nor was Jesus warning against planning for the future. Those who would use this passage to teach that buying insurance or investing for retirement constitutes a lack of faith are reading this in a way the Lord didn't intend. Scripture exhorts us to plan wisely and especially to provide for our families (1 Tim. 5:8; Jas. 4:13-15). The Lord also was not dissuading us from enjoying the gifts He gives us (see 1 Tim. 6:17).

Rather, Jesus was denouncing a life focused on the accumulation of more and more, warning against selfishness and an extravagant lifestyle. He used the term translated "treasures" purposefully. The Greek term *thēsauros* [2344] is used to refer to the gold, frankincense, and myrrh given to Jesus by the magi (Matt. 2:11) and to "the treasures of Egypt" that Moses forsook (Heb. 11:26). What is being condemned is a this-worldly hoarding of wealth and riches, setting one's heart and mind on these things. The Bible is clear that "those who trust in their wealth and boast in the abundance of their riches" are wicked (Ps. 49:5-6).

Why is it so foolish to focus on acquiring material wealth on earth rather than investing in spiritual reward in heaven? Because the things of this world are subject to corruption, deterioration, and tragic loss, while every deposit in the heavenly storehouse is eternally protected (Matt. 6:19-20). Why would anybody but a fool place all their faith, hope, and love in something as unreliable and ultimately disappointing as material possessions?

Jesus summed up the message in 6:21: "Where your treasure is, there your heart will be also." Those words should prompt us to do some soul-searching. Ask yourself some questions: *Am I living unselfishly? Do I demonstrate generosity and care for others? Or am I tightfisted and reluctant to help those in need? Do I know when I have acquired enough? Or am I stuck in an endless race grasping for more and more? Do I allow things to lure me into a materialistic lifestyle? Am I just plain greedy? Or am I content with what God has given me and satisfied with His provision for my simple needs?*

When we make wealth our master, we'll be lured deeper and deeper into blind loyalty to it. It'll change us. We'll become greedy, competitive, and envious. But if we swear allegiance to the King and let His eternal kingdom priorities guide us, our earthly possessions will be conscripted into *His* service.

— 6:22-24 —

In the second part of His teaching on this topic, Jesus addressed our focus. Admittedly, taken out of context, this saying of Jesus is difficult to understand. However, we need to remember that Jesus hadn't changed topics. He was still talking about the deceptive allure of riches. This is evidenced by the very clear statement of 6:24: "No one can serve two masters. . . . You cannot serve God and wealth." The theme hadn't changed. When Jesus spoke of the eye as "the lamp of the body" (6:22), He was still talking about how we deal with riches in this world and where our hearts and priorities lie.

In this section, Jesus was essentially talking about the need for a singularity of mind-set. We know how sight works—light reflected from objects enters our eyes and the images then enter our minds. The goal of the righteous is that the light that enters their eyes is "clear." The word translated "clear" is *haplous* [573], which means "motivated by singleness of purpose so as to be open and aboveboard, *single, without guile, sincere, straightforward.*"[17]

In other words, we need to have clarity of focus, not double-sightedness or double-mindedness. One commentator puts it well: "Jesus, using this language metaphorically, affirms that if a man's spiritual sense is healthy and his affections directed towards heavenly treasure, his whole personality will be without blemish; but if that spiritual sense is diseased by a false sense of values, or by covetousness, or by a grudging ungenerous spirit, he will rapidly become disingenuous."[18]

Seen in this light, the need for a single-minded focus on the things of heaven instead of a blurred double vision held captive by the things of earth leads directly to Jesus' clear conclusion in 6:24: "You cannot serve God and wealth." Many Christians believe they can balance the passionate pursuit of Christ with the passionate pursuit of riches, or give equal time to both of these. But in the Christian life that has enthroned Jesus alone as Lord, there is no room for competing loyalties. Our possessions and pursuits must be submitted to Christ's plans and priorities, not the other way around.

— 6:25-34 —

Jesus began His famous discussion of anxiety with the words "For this reason . . ." That is, in light of what He had been teaching concerning the folly of storing up treasures on earth (6:19-21) and the warnings about trying to split our loyalty between God and riches (6:22-24), the Lord unpacked some very practical principles concerning earthly possessions and the worry that goes along with them.

Worry. It's one of our favorite pet sins. Anxiety, worry, fretting—these vices have been domesticated by modern Christians. We've adopted them into the family, so to speak. Rarely do we hear of anybody rebuking or correcting a brother or sister in Christ over excessive worry—probably because most of us are guilty of it, too, at some level. Yet Christ is clear in Matthew 6:25-34 that worrying can be extremely detrimental to our lives. That's because at the heart of worry is a distrust of God's promises and providence.

The command of Christ is straightforward: "Do not be worried about your life" (6:25). This isn't a suggestion. Not one bit of take-it-or-leave-it advice that you might want to apply if you feel so inclined. It's an imperative. Stop the self-tormenting anxiety that corrodes your inner peace; stop being obsessed with fear!

Jesus then specified areas of life that cause particular anxiety: our daily provisions of food and drink and our need for clothing (6:25, 31). Here Jesus employed a typical Jewish way of arguing from the lesser to the greater. First, He urged His anxious audience to consider the fact that God provides for the birds of the air everything they need to survive and thrive, even though they engage in no great labor of sowing, reaping, and hoarding of possessions. The point is this: If God takes care of the birds, how much more will He take care of His children, who are fashioned in His image (6:26)?

He then turned the people's attention to the temporary wildflowers growing in the fields, which spring up gloriously and then pass off the scene. God adorns them with beauty that would rival royalty even though they do nothing but fall under His providential care (6:28-30). Certainly, if God can clothe the plants of the field with such splendor and beauty, He'll eagerly provide for those He loves.

Beyond this, Jesus noted that nothing can be accomplished by such worry. Not a single hour can be added to our lives (6:27). In fact, we know that stress and anxiety can lead to all sorts of mental, emotional, and physical ailments that actually shorten our lives . . . or at least make the few days we have on this earth more miserable! Worrying is not only a waste of energy, a drain on our contentment, and a damper on our gratitude, but it also signifies a lack of faith in God's character as our Provider. This is why Jesus rebuked worriers with the stinging exclamation "You of little faith!" (6:30). This kind of fretting was typical of Gentiles, whose fickle and flaky gods couldn't be trusted. By contrast, our heavenly Father knows what we need even before we ask (6:8, 32).

Of course, our whole first-world culture is fueled by anxiety over food and clothing and by the discontent that comes from worrying about tomorrow (6:34). Marketers try to convince us that the things we *don't* have are the things we really need . . . and that the things we *do* have aren't really that good. Open any magazine or sit through a string of commercials while watching a show, and you'll see a parade of ads for food, drink, and clothing. Media outlets often boost their ratings by scaring us into believing the world is spinning out of control. And many politicians manipulate our fears to get us to thoughtlessly buy into their half-baked agendas.

Scripture, however, gives us an alternative: "Be anxious for nothing, but in everything by prayer and supplication with thanksgiving let your requests be made known to God. And the peace of God, which surpasses all comprehension, will guard your hearts and your minds in Christ Jesus" (Phil. 4:6-7). When we pray, we can have a real contentment that comes from trusting in God's provision in every circumstance. Paul learned this: "Not that I speak from want, for I have learned to be content in whatever circumstances I am. I know how to get along with humble means, and I also know how to live in prosperity; in any and every circumstance I have learned the secret of being filled and going hungry, both of having abundance and suffering need. I can do all things through Him who strengthens me" (Phil. 4:11-13).

Christ Himself provided the inoculation for the disease of worry in Matthew 6:33. We would all do well to memorize this verse and remind ourselves of it whenever we begin to worry over whether God will provide for our needs: "Seek first His kingdom and His righteousness, and all these things will be added to you." What is the righteousness we're to pursue as the focus of our lives? The kingdom living described already in the Sermon on the Mount (5:1–6:24). And what are the things that God will provide for those who seek His kingdom priorities? *Everything we need*—which includes food, drink, and clothing. A promise made to the Philippians still stands for all those engaged in the work of building up the church: "God will supply all your needs according to His riches in glory in Christ Jesus" (Phil. 4:19).

APPLICATION: MATTHEW 6:19-34

First Things First

Our world is filled with worry. Think about the things that keep people up at night, the themes trending on social media, and the stories trumpeted on news outlets. If it's not the threat of an economic recession, it's the fear of global terrorism. If we aren't anxious about going to war with the latest totalitarian regime, we're fretting over reports of climate change and hurricanes. We worry about our children, our spouses, our churches, our friends, our health, our investments, our job security . . . *it's always something!*

How can we possibly break free from this cycle of worry? Jesus made it clear in the climax of His sustained treatment of keeping our focus on the things of heaven rather than the things of this world. We can summarize His cure for worry in two words: *priorities* and *simplicity*.

First, *we need to start putting first things first* (6:33). This relates to setting the right priorities. We put Christ's kingdom first, trusting Him because He is the sovereign King and living righteous lives because He is the worthy Lord. Worry is incompatible with putting the things of the kingdom and eternity first. What does this prioritization look like in practical terms? It means spending time in God's Word, reading it, understanding it, and applying it. It also means making prayer a priority, bringing your concerns, worries, and needs to God rather than fretting about them alone or complaining about them to others (Phil. 4:6-7). Put first things first.

Second, *we need to stop living more than one day at a time* (Matt. 6:34). Each day has sufficient struggles, Jesus says. We have responsibilities and obligations to take care of, and if we don't address those sufficiently, guess what? They roll over into the next day and we'll just increase our stress. Jesus' words here shouldn't be taken as a warning against wise planning for the future. In fact, just the opposite. If we have a big project due in a few weeks, we should plan to do a little at a time each day—and stay faithful to those daily goals. What a relief it is when we nibble away bit by bit at each day's bite-sized concerns rather than obsess over the looming problems that may or may not be on the horizon. When you neglect the day-to-day activities and instead fret about the future, you become paralyzed by fear, and procrastination kicks in.

These may seem like small things—putting first things first and living one day at a time. But the Lord promises to honor that lifestyle of proper priorities and simplicity. The benefits may not make the headlines, but you'll reap what you sow—confidence in God's providence and provision as well as contentment and peace that surpass all understanding.

Powerful Principles
of the Golden Rule
MATTHEW 7:1-12

NASB

1 "Do not judge so that you will not be judged. 2 For in the way you judge, you will be judged; and ᵃby your standard of measure, it will be measured to you. 3 Why do you look at the speck that is in your brother's eye, but do not notice the log that is

NLT

1 "Do not judge others, and you will not be judged. 2 For you will be treated as you treat others.* The standard you use in judging is the standard by which you will be judged.*

3 "And why worry about a speck in your friend's eye* when you have a

NASB

in your own eye? [4]Or how [a]can you say to your brother, 'Let me take the speck out of your eye,' and behold, the log is in your own eye? [5]You hypocrite, first take the log out of your own eye, and then you will see clearly to take the speck out of your brother's eye.

[6]"Do not give what is holy to dogs, and do not throw your pearls before swine, or they will trample them under their feet, and turn and tear you to pieces.

[7]"[a]Ask, and it will be given to you; [b]seek, and you will find; [c]knock, and it will be opened to you. [8]For everyone who asks receives, and he who seeks finds, and to him who knocks it will be opened. [9]Or what man is there among you [a]who, when his son asks for a loaf, [b]will give him a stone? [10]Or [a]if he asks for a fish, he will not give him a snake, will he? [11]If you then, being evil, know how to give good gifts to your children, how much more will your Father who is in heaven give what is good to those who ask Him!

[12]"In everything, therefore, [a]treat people the same way you want [b]them to treat you, for this is the Law and the Prophets.

7:2 [a]Lit *by what measure you measure*   7:4 [a]Lit *will*   7:7 [a]Or *Keep asking* [b]Or *keep seeking* [c]Or *keep knocking*   7:9 [a]Lit *whom his son will ask* [b]Lit *he will not give him a stone, will he?*   7:10 [a]Lit *also will ask*   7:12 [a]Lit *you, too, do so for them* [b]Lit *people*; Gr *anthropoi*

NLT

log in your own? [4]How can you think of saying to your friend,* 'Let me help you get rid of that speck in your eye,' when you can't see past the log in your own eye? [5]Hypocrite! First get rid of the log in your own eye; then you will see well enough to deal with the speck in your friend's eye.

[6]"Don't waste what is holy on people who are unholy.* Don't throw your pearls to pigs! They will trample the pearls, then turn and attack you.

[7]"Keep on asking, and you will receive what you ask for. Keep on seeking, and you will find. Keep on knocking, and the door will be opened to you. [8]For everyone who asks, receives. Everyone who seeks, finds. And to everyone who knocks, the door will be opened.

[9]"You parents—if your children ask for a loaf of bread, do you give them a stone instead? [10]Or if they ask for a fish, do you give them a snake? Of course not! [11]So if you sinful people know how to give good gifts to your children, how much more will your heavenly Father give good gifts to those who ask him.

[12]"Do to others whatever you would like them to do to you. This is the essence of all that is taught in the law and the prophets.

7:2a Or *For God will judge you as you judge others.* 7:2b Or *The measure you give will be the measure you get back.*   7:3 Greek *your brother's eye*; also in 7:5.   7:4 Greek *your brother.*   7:6 Greek *Don't give the sacred to dogs.*

Without realizing it, we frequently quote from the Sermon on the Mount. Many of the statements in it punctuate our speech and are familiar to all of us—so familiar, in fact, that they stand as mottoes in our minds. Most are better known than Benjamin Franklin's wit and wisdom, Mark Twain's clever aphorisms, or Shakespeare's most memorable lines. And certainly, Jesus' words are far more personal and penetrating:

- "Let your light shine."
- "Every jot and tittle."

- "Turn the other cheek."
- "Where your treasure is, there your heart will be also."
- "You cannot serve both God and mammon."
- "Oh, ye of little faith!"
- "Judge not, lest ye be judged."
- "Don't cast your pearls before swine."
- "Seek, and you will find."

Even unbelievers who have never cracked open a Bible are familiar with many of these sayings. Without doubt, Jesus was the greatest of all wordsmiths. His choice of words, placement of emphasis, and memorable metaphors can't be matched.

Jesus' rapid-fire delivery of powerful principles in Matthew 7:1-12 builds up to a profound climax in what we know today as the Golden Rule—"Treat people the same way you want them to treat you" (7:12). These unforgettable and convicting words have the same impact on our lives as they did on the lives of the original audience on the mountain by the Sea of Galilee nearly two thousand years ago. And they come to us with the same authority of the same King.

— 7:1-5 —

The first principle Jesus expounded relates to judging others: *Exhortation must come from a position of love and humility rather than hypocritical pride.* Far too many Christians, however, like to play a game I'll call "Let's Label," also known as "The Judging Game." The gameplay is pretty simple: Someone finds something they don't like or agree with about a person, usually by quickly and superficially surveying the person's external qualities. Then they jump to negative, critical opinions about that person. These self-proclaimed judges never take the time to dig deeply, get the facts straight, and draw fair conclusions about a person. Instead, they slap the person with a label and then interpret all that person's words and actions through that grid. Finally—and this is key—they share their inaccurate observations and conclusions openly and freely with others.

In the Christian life, if worry is our favorite pet sin, then judging is our favorite pastime. Worry represents a lack of faith and trust in God; judging flows from a lack of love and acceptance of others. Even though Jesus spoke firmly against judging others, we go right on playing this wicked, destructive game. How much clearer could Jesus have been than "Do not judge" (7:1)?

Why is it wrong to judge others? First, we can never know all the facts about a person or see into their hearts to know their motives. Only God can do that. First Samuel 16:7 says, "God sees not as man sees, for man looks at the outward appearance, but the LORD looks at the heart." Second, in our fallen, frail, and finite condition, we are necessarily prejudiced people, which means we're never able to be completely objective. We prejudge based on our limited perspective and little information. Third, when we judge others, we place ourselves in a position we're not qualified to fill. God is the all-knowing, just Judge; we're in no position to play God.

With this background, we need to clear up what Jesus did *not* mean when He said "Do not judge" in Matthew 7:1. He didn't mean for us to be naïve and lack discernment. In fact, the Lord would soon warn His listeners to "beware of the false prophets" (7:15), which requires discernment. Likewise, 1 John 4:1 says believers are to "test the spirits to see whether they are from God." This requires observation, weighing facts, and drawing conclusions. Jesus' warning in the Sermon on the Mount against hypocritically judging others doesn't mean we're to support false teachers blindly or neglect our responsibility to call out genuine deception or wickedness when we see it. In fact, local churches have a responsibility to "judge" a so-called brother or sister who claims the name of Christ but is clearly engaged in unrepentant and ongoing sin (1 Cor. 5:11-13). But the calm, careful, corporate discipline of a local church is very different from the labeling and judging that occurs between individuals who are fueled by hypocritical pride.

What Jesus *is* condemning in the Sermon on the Mount is a judgmental, negative, haughty attitude that assesses others with a suspicious spirit. People who have such an attitude are always on the hunt for faults, mistakes, or imperfections in others. And they find them! There are always petty flaws and failures to be exposed. They do this out of an attitude of superiority, presumption, prejudice, and pride. The result is a destructive, condemning attitude and a blindness to one's own faults. This is the glaring hypocrisy that Jesus emphasizes here.

Judging others is not only destructive for the person who is unjustly and prematurely labeled and condemned. Jesus made it clear that playing the role of judge also has harmful effects on the person doing the judging! First, the attitude we demonstrate will result in the same attitude from others toward us (Matt. 7:1-2). We'll get back what we dish out. You've probably heard the saying "What goes around comes around." Jesus affirmed the basic proverbial truth of this, but not in a karmic sense. The reality is that if we exhibit a hypocritical, judgmental spirit, it will come back to bite us. When we fail to show grace to others, it will be more difficult for others to show grace to us when we need it. When we point our fingers at others, we'll draw the attention of those with critical attitudes. When we apply unjust standards to others, we shouldn't be surprised when others apply unjust standards to us.

Second, a hypocritical, judgmental attitude can result in our own condemnation before God. By acting like we're qualified to pass quick, merciless judgment, we're placing ourselves in a position of moral superiority. The apostle Paul says, "Therefore you have no excuse, everyone of you who passes judgment, for in that which you judge another, you condemn yourself; for you who judge practice the same things" (Rom. 2:1). Those who play "Let's Label" are equally as guilty before God as those with whom they find fault, because "all have sinned and fall short of the glory of God" (Rom. 3:23).

To illustrate the folly of this kind of mean-spirited, myopic, and self-destructive judgment, Jesus used a brilliant—and funny—illustration (Matt. 7:3-5). Jesus wanted His listeners to picture one man informing another that he has a tiny particle in his eye. The word translated "speck" refers to a tiny piece of dried wood, like a splinter, that causes irritation.[19] But while the man is pointing out his brother's fault, he doesn't notice the "log" in his own eye. Jesus used intentional, unrealistic exaggeration here so we would catch the ridiculousness of the "helpful" brother pointing out the tiny source of the speck bearer's blind spot. The word translated "log" refers to the rafters or joists that hold up the walls and roof of a building![20]

How can somebody with a support beam the size of a pillar in their eye see clearly enough to help somebody else remove their own source of irritation and blindness? It can't be done! The solution is to take care of our own character issues and faults that blind us (the "logs" in our eyes) so we can see more objectively and clearly to help others work through their issues (the "specks" in their eyes). To do anything less is to be hypocritical, which won't actually help anybody.

Notice that Jesus didn't tell us we should just mind our own business when we see the blind spot in somebody else's life. He didn't say, "Live and let live" or "Who am I to judge?" Rather, He acknowledged the rightness of wanting to help a brother or sister overcome a struggle. This kind of mutual love and accountability is what we're called to as Christians. However, Jesus wants us to be better equipped to lovingly, carefully, and unhypocritically help others.

— 7:6 —

The second powerful principle in 7:1-12 has to do with speaking and restraining: *Discernment must temper our declaration.* The judgmental type in 7:1-5 errs on the side of giving harsh, unjust condemnation where it isn't deserved. Such people speak too quickly when they should be more patient. They pick and poke too harshly when they should show more grace. In 7:6, however, Jesus considers those who swing to the opposite extreme: wastefully lavishing precious and priceless things upon those who aren't ready, willing, or wanting them. Here Jesus cautioned believers against sharing holy things with others indiscriminately.

To make His point, Jesus used the illustrations of a person giving a "holy" thing—probably consecrated food—to dogs and of casting precious "pearls" before pigs. In the same way that we wouldn't bless these wild and unclean animals with holy food or adorn them in fine pearls, we should be wise and prudent about the people we bless with spiritual things. R. T. France expresses the thought thus: "Holy and valuable things (the reference is primarily to teaching, probably) must be given only to those who are able to appreciate them. . . . God's gifts are not to be laid open to abuse, or his truth to mockery. There is a right discrimination which is different from the censorious judging of vv. 1–2."[21]

— 7:7-11 —

The third principle of Matthew 7:1-12 relates to praying and receiving: *Persistence must characterize our prayers.* Here Jesus begins with three commands (7:7). Each of these is conveyed in Greek by a present-tense imperative verb, which can be construed as a command of continual activity: Keep on asking . . . keep on seeking . . . keep on knocking.[22] In this context, Jesus was talking about being consistent and persistent in prayer. If we genuinely seek the Lord's will and earnestly pursue His intervention on our behalf, we will receive what we ask for, find what we're looking for, and gain access to the places we want to go. But we must stay at it, keep it up, and press on. If the situation worsens, we need to intensify our prayers. If our need persists, we need to return to our knees and petition God all the more.

Does this mean that God will give us anything we ask for, that we'll find whatever we're seeking, and that He'll open any doors we want? Not quite. The apostle John wrote, "This is the confidence which we have before Him, that, if we ask anything *according to His will*, He hears us" (1 Jn. 5:14, emphasis mine). Jesus' encouragement to be fervent in

DOGS AND PIGS

MATTHEW 7:6

Today in the West, dogs are pampered pets, and pork is "the other white meat." But in the Old and New Testament periods, Jews generally considered both dogs and pigs unclean and deplorable.

In the first century, as in many third-world countries today, dogs ran wild, usually in packs, and they were often vicious and dangerous.[23] They were known as scavengers that roamed the streets. They were certainly unclean. The term "dog" was sometimes used as a metaphor for wicked people (Isa. 56:10-11)—those outside the community of faith (Rev. 22:15).

Swine were also considered unclean and were often intrusive; they damaged property, and many were aggressive and dangerous. With regard to first-century swine, we should picture the wild boar, not the modern domestic pig. Jews so abhorred the pig that many would not even say the name of the animal, referring to it simply as "the abomination."[24]

prayer shouldn't be taken to mean that God is our heavenly vending machine, dispensing the things we want just because we want them. Rather, Christ emphasized that the relationship we have with the perfect heavenly Father through prayer is a privilege (Matt. 7:9-11). Jesus used the common Jewish practice of arguing from the lesser to the greater to demonstrate His point. Though our earthly fathers are fallen and depraved, they still love us enough to give us bread or fish when we ask; they don't give us harmful things instead, like stones or snakes.

Notice that Jesus referred to requests for reasonable daily sustenance, things we *need* to live, which are clearly part of God's will for us. As we ask for these things "according to His will" (1 Jn. 5:14), He will hear us. And because He loves us infinitely better than our earthly fathers are able to, God will "give what is good to those who ask Him" (Matt. 7:11). This is vitally important. God, who is good and does only good, will never withhold from us that which we truly need . . . and He certainly won't maliciously afflict us with what will be harmful. Everything He does for us in response to our prayers is for our good (see Rom. 8:28).

— 7:12 —

The fourth and final principle of Matthew 7:1-12 sums up everything that has come before: *Modeling must accompany our message.* Here Jesus introduced His hearers to what has become known as the

Golden Rule. William Barclay says concerning Matthew 7:12, "This is probably the most universally famous thing that Jesus ever said. With this commandment, the Sermon on the Mount reaches its summit. ... It is the topmost peak of social ethics, and the Everest of all ethical teaching."[25] This ethical principle wasn't new with Jesus. Something similar had been taught by Confucius, Greek philosophers, and Jewish rabbis.[26] It also appears in a negative form in the apocryphal book Tobit: "Don't do to others what you would hate to have them do to you" (Tobit 4:15).[27] Yet Jesus turned this principle around and expressed it in the positive, saying, in essence, "What you love, do for others." At the heart of this lofty ethic, then, is a spirit of other-centered, unconditional love.

This capstone serves as a fitting summation of the previous three principles. Treating people the way we want to be treated would mean not judging others unjustly—because to the degree we judge others, we ourselves will be judged (Matt. 7:1-5). Treating people the way we want to be treated would also mean not dumping our declaration of the message on those whom God has not prepared; to do so could sour them to the truth and cause them to treat the things of God with hardened contempt (7:6). Further, treating others the way we want to be treated would mean modeling for others the rich, loving benevolence God the Father has poured out on us (7:7-11). In other words, because of the inexpressible, unconditional grace God bestows upon us, we ought to show the same kind of unconditional grace toward others.

To live in this selfless, other-centered way is to fulfill "the Law and the Prophets" (7:12)—that is, the whole heart and soul of the Old Testament. When we live like this, we're broadcasting Christlikeness, modeling our message of grace for the world to see.

APPLICATION: MATTHEW 7:1-12

Doing for Others

From Jesus' teachings in Matthew 7:1-12, we gain four life-changing principles to help us on our journey of discipleship in service of the King. Let's return to each of these and consider how we can integrate them into our lives.

First, *exhortation must come from a position of love and humility rather than hypocritical pride* (7:1-5). Whenever we're on the verge of speaking about another's behavior, we need to examine ourselves first. Then we can acknowledge our own faults, weaknesses, and failures to make sure we are in a spiritual and moral position to understand a person's struggles and to be humble and gentle rather than harsh and hurried. And we must always remember that the goal in correction is restoration and recovery, not probation and condemnation.

Second, *discernment must temper our declaration* (7:6). The application of Jesus' second principle in this passage is to be alert, sensitive, and discerning as we share the gospel with others. If there's no interest—or you detect hostility or scorn—back off. This principle also applies to sharing material blessings with others. It may seem that the best thing we can do to help somebody with a financial need is to give them money. That may be true, but it isn't self-evident. Sometimes giving money to a fool or a wicked person or an addict will harm the person, not help them. In sharing our lives, our resources, our time, and our message, we need to be wise and prudent.

Third, *persistence must characterize our prayers* (7:7-11). We are to be tireless in our prayers, offering up our genuine needs before the Lord and trusting in His wisdom, goodness, and power to give us what we pray for. But we should also seek the things that *He* wants for us, humbly surrendering our own wills to His. As we pray fervently for something over a period of days, weeks, months, or even years—a prodigal child, a chronic illness, a hard-hearted family member, or a dying church—sometimes God will use the passage of time and the earnestness of our prayers to change *us*. We may find our own hearts moving, our wills bending, and our whole lives conforming to His will. In the process, we learn how good and wise and powerful God is.

Fourth, *modeling must accompany our message* (7:12). We apply the principle of the Golden Rule when we get into the habit of constantly evaluating our actions toward others with a few important questions. First, *what action would reflect the kind of grace, mercy, and love shown to me by my loving heavenly Father—doing for others what God has done for me?* Second, *what action would best represent Christ's own gracious work in the world—doing for others what Christ wants to do through me?* And third, *what actions would I like to have shown toward me if I were in the same situation—doing for others what I would want others to do for me?* Think about how your personal life, your family life, your community and church life, and even the world could be transformed if more people interacted with each other according to this ethic! But without a genuine experience of the love of Christ and the power of the Holy Spirit, such a revolutionary ethic is impossible. Thankfully, what is impossible with people is possible with God (Luke 18:27).

Secrets of an Unshakable Life
MATTHEW 7:13-29

NASB

13 "Enter through the narrow gate; for the gate is wide and the way is broad that leads to destruction, and there are many who enter through it. 14For the gate is small and the way is narrow that leads to life, and there are few who find it.

15 "Beware of the false prophets, who come to you in sheep's clothing, but inwardly are ravenous wolves. 16You will ªknow them by their fruits. ᵇGrapes are not gathered from thorn *bushes* nor figs from thistles, are they? 17So every good tree bears good fruit, but the bad tree bears bad fruit. 18A good tree cannot produce bad fruit, nor can a bad tree produce good fruit. 19Every tree that does not bear good fruit is cut down and thrown into the fire. 20So then, you will ªknow them by their fruits.

21 "Not everyone who says to Me, 'Lord, Lord,' will enter the kingdom of heaven, but he who does the will of My Father who is in heaven *will enter.* 22Many will say to Me on that day, 'Lord, Lord, did we not prophesy in Your name, and in Your name cast out demons, and in Your name perform many ªmiracles?' 23And then I will declare to them, 'I never knew you; DEPART FROM ME, YOU WHO PRACTICE LAWLESSNESS.'

24 "Therefore everyone who hears these words of Mine and ªacts on them, ᵇmay be compared to a wise man who built his house on the

NLT

13 "You can enter God's Kingdom only through the narrow gate. The highway to hell* is broad, and its gate is wide for the many who choose that way. 14But the gateway to life is very narrow and the road is difficult, and only a few ever find it.

15 "Beware of false prophets who come disguised as harmless sheep but are really vicious wolves. 16You can identify them by their fruit, that is, by the way they act. Can you pick grapes from thornbushes, or figs from thistles? 17A good tree produces good fruit, and a bad tree produces bad fruit. 18A good tree can't produce bad fruit, and a bad tree can't produce good fruit. 19So every tree that does not produce good fruit is chopped down and thrown into the fire. 20Yes, just as you can identify a tree by its fruit, so you can identify people by their actions.

21 "Not everyone who calls out to me, 'Lord! Lord!' will enter the Kingdom of Heaven. Only those who actually do the will of my Father in heaven will enter. 22On judgment day many will say to me, 'Lord! Lord! We prophesied in your name and cast out demons in your name and performed many miracles in your name.' 23But I will reply, 'I never knew you. Get away from me, you who break God's laws.'

24 "Anyone who listens to my teaching and follows it is wise, like a person who builds a house on solid

rock. ²⁵And the rain fell, and the ᵃfloods came, and the winds blew and slammed against that house; and *yet* it did not fall, for it had been founded on the rock. ²⁶Everyone who hears these words of Mine and does not ᵃact on them, will be like a foolish man who built his house on the sand. ²⁷The rain fell, and the ᵃfloods came, and the winds blew and slammed against that house; and it fell—and great was its fall."

²⁸ᵃWhen Jesus had finished these words, the crowds were amazed at His teaching; ²⁹for He was teaching them as *one* having authority, and not as their scribes.

7:16 ᵃOr *recognize* ᵇLit *They do not gather*
7:20 ᵃOr *recognize* 7:22 ᵃOr *works of power*
7:24 ᵃLit *does* ᵇLit *will* 7:25 ᵃLit *rivers* 7:26 ᵃLit *do* 7:27 ᵃLit *rivers* 7:28 ᵃLit *And it happened when*

rock. ²⁵Though the rain comes in torrents and the floodwaters rise and the winds beat against that house, it won't collapse because it is built on bedrock. ²⁶But anyone who hears my teaching and doesn't obey it is foolish, like a person who builds a house on sand. ²⁷When the rains and floods come and the winds beat against that house, it will collapse with a mighty crash."

²⁸When Jesus had finished saying these things, the crowds were amazed at his teaching, ²⁹for he taught with real authority—quite unlike their teachers of religious law.

7:13 Greek *The road that leads to destruction.*

I can't imagine Jesus licking His finger, raising it to the wind, and molding His message around whichever way the breeze of popular opinion seemed to be blowing. He didn't simply listen to the Pharisees and read the commentaries by the scribes so He could align His teachings squarely with those of the respected rabbis of the day. Nor did He ask for government approval or seek congregational affirmation. Rather, He spoke the truth—plainly, clearly, and directly. His messages were insightful and captivating, timeless and timely, convicting, courageous, and compelling—"Out with hypocrisy!" (5:1-48) . . . "Down with performance!" (6:1-34) . . . "In with acceptance!" (7:1-5) . . . "On with commitment!" (7:6-12).

As we conclude our exploration of the Sermon on the Mount, we realize that Jesus saved His most passionate words for the finale. Matthew 7:13-27 expresses the Lord's most intense feelings of the sermon. We could call this part the application section of His sermon. In light of everything He preached leading up to this point, Jesus says, essentially, "Now that you've heard all this, what are you going to do about it?" As He drove His audience to application, Jesus presented His listeners with four paired alternatives:

- *two gates*—the narrow one leading to life or the wide one leading to destruction (7:13-14)

- *two trees*—the good one bearing good fruit or the bad one bearing bad fruit (7:15-20)
- *two responses*—the genuine disciple who does the will of God or the hypocritical hearer who only gives lip service (7:21-23)
- *two foundations*—the one built on rock or the one built on sand (7:24-27)

Jesus' call to a decision in response to His message is really a call to faith for unbelievers and a call to discipleship for believers. It's a call to repentance, to trust in and obey the King, the long-awaited Messiah and only rightful Lord.

— 7:13-14 —

Two gates. In the first set of paired alternatives, Jesus ruled out the view—popular today—called pluralism. Pluralism can be defined as "the view that all religions include some truth and that there are many paths to God. Christians are saved through following the Christian path, Buddhists through following the Buddhist way, Muslims through faithfulness to Islam, etc."[28] In opposition to this viewpoint, Jesus noted that the popular gate through which many enter is a wide and broad way that "leads to destruction" (7:13).

The great twentieth-century Christian thinker and author C. S. Lewis describes his walk along the wide, broad path in his youth: "I was soon (in the famous words) 'altering "I believe" to "one does feel."' And oh, the relief of it! . . . From the tyrannous noon of revelation I passed into the cool evening twilight of Higher Thought, where there was nothing to be obeyed, and nothing to be believed except what was either comforting or exciting."[29] Think about it. When someone has a "broad mind" and runs with sophists equally as "bright," they will only be impressed with opinions of the learned, scholarly achievements, academic credentials, deep thoughts, and nuanced articulations. To that person, any talk of a small gate leading to a narrow way that only a few will find sounds absolutely ridiculous and naïve.

But Jesus' teaching concerning the narrowness of the way that leads to life (7:14) is in perfect harmony with the rest of God's revelation. Proverbs 14:12 says, "There is a way which seems right to a man, but its end is the way of death." The *only* right way God has provided for people to be saved and enter eternal life with Him is through the Son, as Jesus Himself said: "I am the way, and the truth, and the life; no one comes to the Father but through Me" (John 14:6). Likewise, years later, Paul would remind his understudy Timothy that "there is one

God, and one mediator also between God and men, the man Christ Jesus" (1 Tim. 2:5).

— 7:15-20 —

Two trees. With the second set of paired alternatives, Jesus addressed the problem of false teachers. Because most who follow the broad path through the wide gate have been drawn away from the true path by some teacher, author, preacher, or leader spouting deceptive lies, false teaching is the subject of a contrast designed to help hearers discern the differences among those they listen to.

EXCURSUS: THE "TWO WAYS"

MATTHEW 7:13-14

When Jesus taught about the two gates leading to two different "ways," or "paths," He was drawing on a very well-known pattern of teaching in the first century referred to as the "Two Ways." This pattern of teaching contrasted the way of life, light, truth, wisdom, and righteousness with the way of death, darkness, falsehood, folly, and wickedness. In various early Jewish and Christian texts that discussed the Two Ways, the "way of life" section explained the virtuous lifestyle expected of a man or woman of God. In contrast, the "way of death" section explained the sinful and destructive lifestyles of unbelievers. The first-century writing called *The Didache*, which may be the oldest Christian writing outside the inspired New Testament, begins this way: "There are two paths: the path of life and the path of death, and there is a vast difference between these two paths" (*Didache* 1.1).

While the Two Ways teaching pattern was used by the early church, it has roots in biblical and rabbinical teaching before the birth of Christianity. The Two Ways pattern can be seen in the Hebrew Scriptures (see Deut. 30:15; Pss. 1:6; 139:24; Prov. 2:8-22; Jer. 21:8), in the Dead Sea Scrolls literature,[30] and in other early Jewish literature.

Jesus described Himself as "the way" (John 14:6), indicating that all life, light, truth, wisdom, and righteousness is ultimately found in a relationship with Him. For the believer, the journey on the way of life begins with faith in Christ and continues until we reach our final, glorious destination: heaven. As John Bunyan portrays so vividly in his cherished work *The Pilgrim's Progress*, this path is laden with hardship, struggle, and suffering; but it is also traveled with a company of joyous, confident, and victorious saints. The path swarms with persecutors, tempters, and discouragers; but its travelers are accompanied by the Lord Jesus Christ, who bears our burdens and provides His Holy Spirit to reinvigorate our weak steps. In Jewish-Christian thought, the path of life, though narrow and difficult, leads to a destination that will make any road hazards, pitfalls, or setbacks along the journey well worth it.

Jesus began with a startling warning: "Beware of the false prophets" (7:15). Though they look like soft, gentle sheep on the outside, their true nature is that of ravenous wolves. They appear with soothing smiles, sweet words, and caring attitudes. They're approachable, thoughtful, interesting, charming, suave, and clever. Charismatic, attractive, and toting an impressive résumé of education and experience, these "sheep" have qualities that are merely fleece-deep! Peel back the fake veneer and you'll find a vicious monster that wants to gobble you up! The apostle Paul similarly develops this theme in 2 Corinthians 11:13-15, where he writes, "For such men are false apostles, deceitful workers, disguising themselves as apostles of Christ. No wonder, for even Satan disguises himself as an angel of light. Therefore it is not surprising if his servants also disguise themselves as servants of righteousness, whose end will be according to their deeds."

When it comes to false teachers, we can't immediately detect their true nature. However, by closely observing their "fruits," we can see through the disguise: "You will know them by their fruits" (Matt. 7:16, 20). Thorn bushes don't bring forth grapes, and thistles don't produce figs. Jesus appealed to the self-evident fact of nature that plants produce fruit "after their kind" (Gen. 1:12). We know that good fruit will only come from good trees and that bad trees will produce bad fruit—useless and only to be discarded and destroyed (Matt. 7:17-19).

— 7:21-23 —

Two responses. In the third set of paired alternatives, Jesus described two different responses to His teaching. He thus moved from unsound teachers (7:15-20) to unsound hearers (7:21-23). These verses can easily be misunderstood unless we read them very closely and consider them very carefully. Here we see the danger of a merely verbal profession of faith that lacks substance in reality. Some people may say things believers say and do things believers do—but it can all be fake.

Such people may be able to recite creeds and pray prayers that call Jesus "Lord, Lord" (7:21), but just because they claim the name of the King doesn't mean they're members of the kingdom. Now, we must never forget that we're saved by grace alone through faith alone. But the faith that saves doesn't remain alone. By that same grace that saves us, God produces in us fruit of the new birth. Not only do we genuinely know the Lord as an intimate friend, but we also practice righteousness rather than lawlessness (Jas. 2:14-26).

But here's where we need to be careful. False prophets and

professors of fake faith can stage a convincing performance. They say the right things and may even perform jaw-dropping feats. They can recite orthodox doctrines, exhibit passion and fervency in their deeds, and claim spectacular experiences that clearly seem to be supernatural, such as prophesying, casting out demons, and performing many miracles (Matt. 7:22). Notice that Jesus never says they were actually able to do these things in an authentic way. The false followers only *claim* to have done these things. However, all these things can be faked; they can also be claimed falsely. In my many years of ministry, I've seen both fraudulent and exaggerated claims of supernatural works done by deluded preachers.

Jesus can see through this façade. He will respond to the fakes with the chilling words "I never knew you; depart from Me, you who practice lawlessness" (7:23). These fakes stand in contrast to the genuine followers of Jesus, who *do* know Him truly and who do the will of the Father (7:21). Though false believers can fool people—including those in the church—God is never fooled.

— 7:24-29 —

Two foundations. In the fourth set of paired alternatives, Jesus described two very different foundations upon which people build their lives. He began this last segment of the Sermon on the Mount with the word "therefore" (7:24), signaling that everything He had been teaching the crowd up to this point had been leading to this final statement. And He left them with a dramatic image to drive home His point.

Jesus constructed side by side in the minds of His hearers two different homes. The first home Jesus described was built on solid, immovable bedrock (7:24). Against this house an inevitable storm unleashed its fury with rain, floods, and winds, "yet it did not fall, for it had been founded on the rock" (7:25). In contrast, the second home was built on shifting sand (7:26). When the same storm struck that home, "great was its fall" (7:27). The image is simple enough; the contrast vivid. Yet Jesus isn't primarily interested in construction techniques. He's interested in the quality of our lives.

The house built on a rock is a metaphor for, in Jesus' words, "everyone who hears these words of Mine and acts on them" (7:24). Which words? The words He had been teaching them throughout the Sermon on the Mount. In contrast, the house built foolishly on sand represents "everyone who hears these words of Mine and does not act on them" (7:26). When the unavoidable troubles of life come, those who

137

have lived lives in keeping with Christ's teaching will be able to sustain the bombardment. Those who have failed to follow His principles and example will suffer a great fall.

Storms and life go together. There's no place on earth where we can be completely free from trauma, tension, or trouble. What Job said was spot-on: "Man, who is born of woman, is short-lived and full of turmoil" (Job 14:1). Steering clear of all turmoil is only a fantasy. Our need, therefore, is to learn the secret of enduring without sinking, standing strong without collapsing. As Jesus drew His powerful and practical Sermon on the Mount to a close, He used this vivid picture of the two houses and two foundations to urge His listeners to action.

Jesus' words made quite an impact on the crowd. In fact, the people were left speechless. They were "amazed at His teaching" (Matt. 7:28). And rightly so! These weren't the words of some scribe struggling to grasp the nuances of a grammatical construction or the speculations of some Pharisee laboring to convince his fellow scholars that his opinion of this or that law was correct. No, Jesus taught the truth as the One who *is* Truth incarnate. He taught the Law as the One who originally delivered it at Sinai. That is, He taught from His divine authority, not like the scribes (7:29).

APPLICATION: MATTHEW 7:13-29

Getting off the Fence

The conclusion of Jesus' Sermon on the Mount was intended to motivate His listeners to get off the fence. The message is the same for us. And it's just as urgent today as it was in the first century. Only you can determine where you stand on the issues.

Between two gates. Each person stands before two gates and two paths. One gate is small, leading to a path that's narrow and found by few, but this gate leads to life. The other gate is wide, leading to a path that's broad and followed by many, but it leads to destruction. Have you chosen which gate to enter and which path to follow? Remember, Jesus is the Way, the Truth, and the Life; no one goes to the Father except through Him (John 14:6).

Between two trees. Jesus' teaching concerning the two trees underscores the fact that we must take care whose teaching we follow. What kind of fruit should we be looking for to help us spot the bad trees? We should pay attention to how teachers and leaders handle God's Word. Do they stand under it in a posture of total belief and obedience? Or do they stand over it and judge it, correct it, or neglect it? Do they have a high view of the person of Christ as the God-man? A devotion to His finished work on the cross as the substitute for sinners? An unswerving commitment to the miraculous bodily resurrection of Jesus from the dead? Do they embrace the doctrine of the Trinity—one God in three persons (Father, Son, and Holy Spirit)? Do they stand firmly on the foundational doctrines of the Christian faith?

Besides these doctrinal matters, look at their lifestyles. Do these teachers exalt Christ or themselves? Do they encourage followers to give their devotion to Jesus or to them? Do they promote a godly life-style, along with unity, grace, and mercy among their followers? Does their teaching lead to wickedness, schisms, legalism, or hurt?

Finally, ask some personal questions: *Is my walk with Christ getting deeper as a result of a particular teacher's influence? Am I enjoying closer harmony with others in the family of God? Am I growing in faith, love, and hope, and in the grace and knowledge of the Lord?* These things need to be considered whenever you do a careful fruit inspection of preachers and teachers who might seem to be a little "off."

Between two responses. Anybody can call Jesus "Lord, Lord" (see Matt. 7:21). Anybody can mouth the words of a "sinner's prayer" or recite the words of a creed. But a genuine relationship with God is more than a formula. Those who know the Lord and who are known by Him will demonstrate it by doing His will and rejecting a lifestyle of lawlessness. Ask yourself these questions: *Am I just going through the motions? Do I simply mimic the right words and play copycat with my actions? Or do I do the Lord's will—in and out of the spotlight?*

Between two foundations. Every day of our lives, we're building our house. As we trust Christ and obey His words in the Sermon on the Mount, we will have the spiritual resources necessary to withstand the storms of life that will come. These storms are inevitable and inescapable. Many times, they are severe. But if you've built your house on Christ and have striven to follow His teaching, you have nothing to fear. Here are a few more questions to ask yourself: *Do I act on what Jesus commands? Or do I walk away from His Word none the wiser? Do I face the trials and tribulations of life with confidence or with fear? Am I continuing, day after day, to build my life on the foundation of Christ and His Word? Or am I depending on other things, like the wisdom of the world, the advice of foolish teachers, or my own shaky emotions?*

We have choices to make every day. Christ is calling us off the fence and into the freedom we have in a life of faith and obedience.

Snapshots of Power Near and Far
MATTHEW 8:1-17

NASB

[1] When [a]Jesus came down from the mountain, [b]large crowds followed Him. [2] And a leper came to Him and [a]bowed down before Him, and said, "Lord, if You are willing, You can make me clean." [3] Jesus stretched out His hand and touched him, saying, "I am willing; be cleansed." And immediately his leprosy was cleansed. [4] And Jesus said to him, "See that you tell no one; but go, show yourself to the priest and present the [a]offering that Moses commanded, as a testimony to them."

[5] And when [a]Jesus entered Capernaum, a centurion came to Him, imploring Him, [6] and saying, "[a]Lord, my [b]servant is [c]lying paralyzed at home, fearfully tormented." [7] Jesus said to him, "I will come and heal him." [8] But the centurion said, "[a]Lord, I am not worthy for You to come under my roof, but just [b]say the word, and my [c]servant will be healed. [9] For I also am a man under authority, with soldiers under me; and I say to this one, 'Go!' and he goes, and to another, 'Come!' and he comes, and to my slave, 'Do this!' and he does *it.*" [10] Now when Jesus heard *this,*

NLT

[1] Large crowds followed Jesus as he came down the mountainside. [2] Suddenly, a man with leprosy approached him and knelt before him. "Lord," the man said, "if you are willing, you can heal me and make me clean."

[3] Jesus reached out and touched him. "I am willing," he said. "Be healed!" And instantly the leprosy disappeared. [4] Then Jesus said to him, "Don't tell anyone about this. Instead, go to the priest and let him examine you. Take along the offering required in the law of Moses for those who have been healed of leprosy.* This will be a public testimony that you have been cleansed."

[5] When Jesus returned to Capernaum, a Roman officer* came and pleaded with him, [6] "Lord, my young servant* lies in bed, paralyzed and in terrible pain."

[7] Jesus said, "I will come and heal him."

[8] But the officer said, "Lord, I am not worthy to have you come into my home. Just say the word from where you are, and my servant will be healed. [9] I know this because I am under the authority of my superior officers, and I have authority over my soldiers. I only need to say, 'Go,' and they go, or 'Come,' and they come. And if I say to my slaves, 'Do this,' they do it."

[10] When Jesus heard this, he was

He marveled and said to those who were following, "Truly I say to you, I have not found such great faith ªwith anyone in Israel. ¹¹I say to you that many will come from east and west, and ªrecline *at the table* with Abraham, Isaac and Jacob in the kingdom of heaven; ¹²but the sons of the kingdom will be cast out into the outer darkness; in that place there will be weeping and gnashing of teeth." ¹³And Jesus said to the centurion, "Go; ªit shall be done for you as you have believed." And the ᵇservant was healed that *very* ᶜmoment.

¹⁴When Jesus came into Peter's ªhome, He saw his mother-in-law lying sick in bed with a fever. ¹⁵He touched her hand, and the fever left her; and she got up and ªwaited on Him. ¹⁶When evening came, they brought to Him many who were demon-possessed; and He cast out the spirits with a word, and healed all who were ill. ¹⁷*This was* to fulfill what was spoken through Isaiah the prophet: "HE HIMSELF TOOK OUR INFIRMITIES AND ªCARRIED AWAY OUR DISEASES."

8:1 ªLit *He* ᵇLit *many*   8:2 ªOr *worshiped*   8:4 ªLit *gift*   8:5 ªLit *He*   8:6 ªOr *Sir* ᵇLit *boy* ᶜLit *thrown down*   8:8 ªOr *Sir* ᵇLit *say with a word* ᶜLit *boy*   8:10 ªOne early ms reads *not even in Israel*   8:11 ªOr *dine*   8:13 ªOr *let it be done;* i.e. a command ᵇLit *boy* ᶜLit *hour*   8:14 ªOr *house*   8:15 ªOr *served*   8:17 ªOr *removed*

amazed. Turning to those who were following him, he said, "I tell you the truth, I haven't seen faith like this in all Israel! ¹¹And I tell you this, that many Gentiles will come from all over the world—from east and west—and sit down with Abraham, Isaac, and Jacob at the feast in the Kingdom of Heaven. ¹²But many Israelites—those for whom the Kingdom was prepared—will be thrown into outer darkness, where there will be weeping and gnashing of teeth." ¹³Then Jesus said to the Roman officer, "Go back home. Because you believed, it has happened." And the young servant was healed that same hour.

¹⁴When Jesus arrived at Peter's house, Peter's mother-in-law was sick in bed with a high fever. ¹⁵But when Jesus touched her hand, the fever left her. Then she got up and prepared a meal for him.

¹⁶That evening many demon-possessed people were brought to Jesus. He cast out the evil spirits with a simple command, and he healed all the sick. ¹⁷This fulfilled the word of the Lord through the prophet Isaiah, who said,

"He took our sicknesses
and removed our diseases."*

8:4 See Lev 14:2-32.   8:5 Greek *a centurion;* similarly in 8:8, 13.   8:6 Or *child;* also in 8:13. 8:17 Isa 53:4.

The Gospel accounts of the life and ministry of Jesus are not a continuous story, like many feature films. Rather, they're periodic episodes put into writing, like short, two- or three-minute videos captured by people standing near the Savior. In different ways, from different angles, and for different reasons, these snapshots together tell the story of who Jesus is and what He did.

As Jesus wrapped up the message of His Sermon on the Mount (Matt. 5:1–7:29), He already had the rapt attention of the crowds because of the words He had spoken. They "were amazed at His teaching" because it had bold authority, not like the hesitant, hem-and-haw rambling of the so-called experts of the Law (7:28-29). So we shouldn't be surprised that those large crowds followed Jesus down the hill to hear more (8:1). However, what they got was not another sermon, but remarkable demonstrations of divine power: the cleansing of a leper by touch (8:2-4), the restoring of a paralyzed man from a distance (8:5-13), the healing of Peter's mother-in-law (8:14-15), and the providing of relief for many who were demon-possessed, ill, or suffering from other infirmities—all in fulfillment of the Old Testament expectations of the coming Messiah (8:16-17).

That day, not only did the crowds hear the preaching of the word of God, but they also experienced the power of the Word made flesh—God the Son come to earth as the long-awaited Messiah, the King of Israel.

— 8:1-4 —

Immediately prior to delivering the Sermon on the Mount (5:1–7:29), Jesus had been traveling throughout Galilee teaching, preaching, and "healing every kind of disease and every kind of sickness among the people" (4:23). Word of His amazing authority to relieve human suffering had spread throughout Galilee and the surrounding regions, drawing large crowds, no doubt including many who would make up the great number of those listening to the Sermon (4:24-25). On the heels of that message, just as in the period immediately before it, Jesus had no break, no nap, no time to slip away into a calm setting beside a quiet stream to get a little rest.

As soon as Jesus closed His compelling sermon and came down the hillside, the crowds closed in once again. As they pushed in toward Him, with their desperate pleas for healing, one man stood out among them—an outcast leper.

I can imagine the crowd parting like the Red Sea as the scarred, deformed leper made his way toward its center, potentially exposing everyone around him to infection, and certainly exposing them to ceremonial uncleanness. But that poor, humiliated, depressed, and desperate leper rightly believed that Jesus was his only hope. On reaching the man from Nazareth, the unnamed leper threw himself on the ground and worshiped Jesus. His words spoken from the ground said it all: "Lord, if You are willing, You can make me clean" (8:2).

What a gracious, humble request, full of faith and hope, respect and honor. The leper's act of total self-effacement revealed no hint of demanding—just confident expectation. He believed Jesus had the

God Alone Is Awesome

MATTHEW 8:2-3

Years ago, I made a commitment to use the word "awesome" exclusively for the triune God—the Father, Son, and Holy Spirit. Cars aren't awesome. Movies aren't awesome. Sports stars aren't awesome. Hamburgers aren't awesome. Fireworks aren't awesome. And preachers aren't awesome. All these things may be powerful, entertaining, impressive, delicious, exciting, or inspiring . . . but awesome is what we see when we read of the creation of heaven and earth in Genesis or the splitting of the Red Sea in Exodus or the miraculous works of Jesus in the Gospel of Matthew. Yes, God is awesome.

When we consider the power of Jesus, we're talking about awesome, divine power. He possesses all the attributes that are true of God the Father and God the Holy Spirit. As fully divine, Jesus is omnipotent—a word meaning "all-powerful." His divine power comprises the ability to do anything that is consistent with His character and according to His will. That's awesome!

This awesome power has given me immeasurable comfort over the years. No obstacle is insurmountable, no circumstance is impossible, no situation is unapproachable, no person is unchangeable, and no problem is unsolvable. Should it be His will, God is able to heal any sickness or disease, stop any addiction, and relieve any physical, mental, or emotional affliction. When He doesn't do so, it isn't because He lacks power, but because it isn't His will, which points to the fact that He is also all-knowing, all-wise, and all-good—not ignorant, foolish, or capricious. No force can resist what He wants to accomplish whenever He wants to accomplish it. No enemy is a threat, and no being, human or demonic, can withstand His sovereign control or alter His will. That's awesome!

The power of Jesus is unlimited, independent, absolute, and authoritative. Though it's often invisible, it's always invincible. Sometimes He exercises His sovereign will through His imperceptible

(continued on next page)

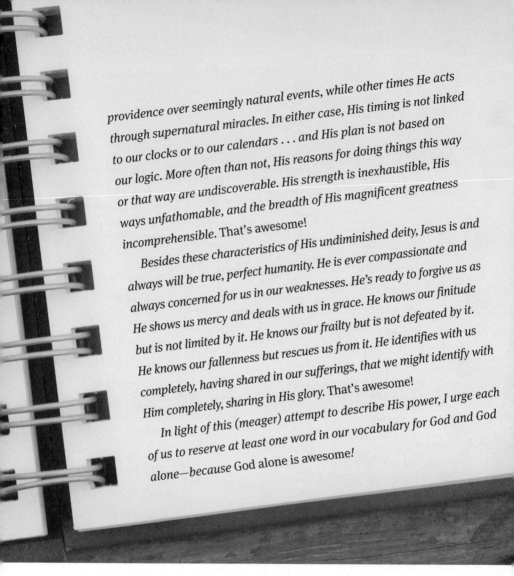

providence over seemingly natural events, while other times He acts through supernatural miracles. In either case, His timing is not linked to our clocks or to our calendars . . . and His plan is not based on our logic. More often than not, His reasons for doing things this way or that way are undiscoverable. His strength is inexhaustible, His ways unfathomable, and the breadth of His magnificent greatness incomprehensible. That's awesome!

Besides these characteristics of His undiminished deity, Jesus is and always will be true, perfect humanity. He is ever compassionate and always concerned for us in our weaknesses. He's ready to forgive us as He shows us mercy and deals with us in grace. He knows our finitude but is not limited by it. He knows our frailty but is not defeated by it. He knows our fallenness but rescues us from it. He identifies with us completely, having shared in our sufferings, that we might identify with Him completely, sharing in His glory. That's awesome!

In light of this (meager) attempt to describe His power, I urge each of us to reserve at least one word in our vocabulary for God and God alone—because God alone is awesome!

power to cleanse him, but he wasn't sure of His willingness to do so. No doubt this leper felt like the most unwanted and undeserving person in the crowd. He claimed no rights, had no hint of presumption, and understood that he was entirely at the mercy of Jesus. A. B. Bruce provides a great caption to this snapshot: "Men more easily believe in miraculous power than in miraculous love."[31]

Jesus' response to the man's plea for cleansing teaches something vital about His character. In this snapshot, we witness not only a confirmation of Jesus' divine power and authority but also a clear example of His compassion, grace, mercy, and love. Unlike a normal person who feared the hideous disease of leprosy, Jesus didn't take a step back to avoid accidental contact. Instead, He condescended to the man's

LEPROSY

MATTHEW 8:2-4

The word translated "leprosy" in the Old Testament is *tsaraath* [H6883]. This term describes a range of chronic or malignant skin infections (see Lev. 13–14). Both the Greek translation of the Hebrew Bible and the New Testament use the term *lepros* [3015], which means "scaly" or "scabby."[32] Like *tsaraath*, the word *lepros* is employed to describe various skin infections. One of these diseases is likely what we today call Hansen's disease, which manifests in discolored spots, skin ulcers, and the eventual loss of tissue and deformity.[33]

Because many (though not all) of the skin diseases labeled "leprosy" were debilitating and contagious, lepers were considered a health hazard and were isolated from the general population unless they were healed of their particular form of skin disease. Some forms were incurable and only led to worsening conditions, including blindness, paralysis, deafness, bleeding, and other obvious ailments.[34] Lepers were considered ceremonially unclean and, for all practical purposes, incurable (see 2 Kgs. 5:7).[35] Because of the insidious nature of the disease, those who were believed to have been cleansed of the condition had to receive official verification from the priests before being allowed to return to the general population (Lev. 14).

deplorable condition, reached out His hand, and touched him. Jesus touched him! I can imagine the gasps from the crowd. Maybe at that moment the Lord even lost a few disgusted hangers-on who couldn't follow somebody who would sink so low.

With His merciful action came words of divine power: "I am willing; be cleansed" (8:3). Just as light came into existence in obedience to the word of God (Gen. 1:3), the man's leprosy obeyed Jesus' word and left him instantly.

Among the inevitable oohs and aahs of the crowd, Jesus leaned in and instructed the former leper to follow the required protocols of the Law regarding leprosy described in Leviticus 14. Instead of telling everyone about the miracle, the cleansed leper was to fulfill the requirements before the priest and make the required offering (Matt. 8:4). Though Matthew doesn't recount what happened to the former leper, we can imagine the astonishment of the priest who examined him and heard that Jesus had healed the man instantly, demonstrating not only His divine power but also His divine goodness. This man of Nazareth was surely the long-awaited Messiah, the King of Israel . . . but also so much more!

— 8:5-13 —

With the next shift in the story, we also have a change of scenery. Jesus and His disciples—as well as the crowds of followers—made their way to the town of Capernaum. The walk would have taken less than an hour—it was just down the hill toward the lake. As Jesus entered the village, probably nearing the synagogue, a Roman centurion approached. If the leper in the hills was a crowd splitter, the Roman commander was a crowd stopper. With the way he was decked out in all the glories of soldiery, his approach would have drawn stares. William Barclay succinctly explains the function of first-century centurions:

> The centurions were the backbone of the Roman army. In a Roman legion there were 6,000 men; the legion was divided into 60 centuries, each containing 100 men, and in command of each century there was a centurion. These centurions were the long-service, regular soldiers of the Roman army. They were responsible for the discipline of the regiment, and they were the cement which held the army together. . . . The centurions were the finest men in the Roman army.[36]

No doubt word of Jesus' miraculous works and astonishing power had made its way through the ranks—all the way to the ears of Gentiles, and all the way up to the officers of the Roman army. Concerned for the life of his paralyzed, suffering servant, the centurion informed Jesus of the servant's condition (8:5-6). Interestingly, Matthew's account doesn't record the centurion actually asking or demanding that Jesus do anything. He simply shared the bad news of the servant's condition. This reflects an attitude of deference and respect. For a man used to giving orders, the subdued, indirect plea for mercy is astonishing. Here's a man of character who knew his place in the presence of the Lord.

Though Jesus offered to come to the centurion's home to heal the servant (8:7), the Roman soldier humbly demurred, expressing his unworthiness to have Jesus enter his home. In an amazing confession of faith in the power of Jesus, the centurion said, "Just say the word, and my servant will be healed" (8:8). Then, using his own position of authority as an illustration, the centurion expressed absolute confidence that Jesus had complete authority to do as He pleased (8:9).

No wonder the Lord commended the centurion for his deep faith: "Truly I say to you, I have not found such great faith with anyone in Israel" (8:10). The centurion didn't doubt in the least that Jesus could heal with just a word, from a distance, with no hocus-pocus, no incantations, and no application of herbs, balms, or antidotes, like those used by many of the wonder-workers or physicians of the day. In essence, the centurion was implicitly acknowledging that Jesus had divine power over the created realm itself.

Jesus then used this remarkable faith—from a *Gentile*, no less—as evidence that God's plan of redemption would ultimately include believers not only from Israel but also "from east and west"—that is, from among the Gentiles. They would find a place at the table with Abraham, Isaac, and Jacob in the kingdom of heaven, while the natural "sons of the kingdom"—Jews—would be cast far away if they remained in their unbelief (8:11-12).

The centurion's great faith foreshadowed the saving faith that would be found among the nations when the gospel of salvation would go forth from Jerusalem to Judea and Samaria and on to the ends of the earth (Acts 1:8). In response to the man's faith, Jesus simply affirmed, "Go; it shall be done for you as you have believed" (Matt. 8:13). That very moment, the servant was healed completely.

— 8:14-17 —

In the next snapshot of Jesus' power, we move from a display of His divine authority among the religiously remote and physically distant to a close, personal act of healing—a member of Peter's own family in Peter's own home. As soon as Jesus entered Peter's house, He saw Peter's

Ruins of a Byzantine church built over the likely location of Peter's house in Capernaum

mother-in-law lying in bed with a fever (8:14). Without hesitation and without being asked, Jesus touched the woman's hand. Immediately the fever left her, and she recovered instantly (8:15). In fact, she suddenly had enough energy to begin waiting on her weary guests!

Matthew's account implies that Jesus and His disciples actually had a chance to eat dinner. However, if any of them had been looking forward to a relaxing evening of rest over a quiet meal, this wasn't the time. When word got around that Jesus was staying at Peter's home in Capernaum, the crowds began flowing in. Many with spiritual and physical afflictions were delivered. If they were possessed by demons, Jesus cast out the demons with a word. If they were sick, He healed them instantly (8:16). The fact that Jesus could command demonic powers and get instant obedience demonstrated something about His awesome, divine power. Had Jesus been a mere, mortal human—or even a being at the level of an angel—He would not have had such authority over the spirits of wickedness that had been oppressing the people. Only the awesome God had that kind of authority.

Matthew ends this series of snapshots of power near and far by pointing to a prophecy in Isaiah 53:4: "This was to fulfill what was spoken through Isaiah the prophet: 'He Himself took our infirmities and carried away our diseases'" (Matt. 8:17). The quote not only identifies Jesus' person and work with the Suffering Servant of Isaiah 53, but it also reveals His character as the all-powerful, all-loving, all-merciful Savior. He is not only *able* to meet our spiritual and physical needs, but He is also *willing* to do so.

APPLICATION: MATTHEW 8:1-17

Whatever Your Need, Jesus Is Able

We've all faced desperate situations we lack the ability to change. You know the feeling—making the change you want is humanly impossible. You would if you could, but you have no supernatural power. Maybe you've tried everything to help yourself or to help somebody you love deeply. You've cared, reached out, and expended a lot of effort, but some situations simply defy human intervention. There are no steps toward a solution. You can't unravel it. It's too complicated.

You may see yourself in one of the snapshots of desperate need recorded in Matthew 8:1-17. A physician may have told you it's terminal. Remember, the power of Jesus is limitless. It may be a day-in, day-out struggle with deep emotional scars. Remember, the authority of Jesus is unfathomable. It may be an issue that surfaces in moments of shame when you reflect on the past and realize you can't change it. Remember, the mercy of Jesus is immeasurable.

The three snapshots of desperate need in this passage can help you turn to the Lord Jesus and cling to Him, whether He chooses to deliver you instantly here on earth or ultimately in heaven, and whether He does so through a gentle touch or a distant word. Perhaps you're like the leper (8:1-4) or those afflicted with deep spiritual oppression or physical torment (8:16). You've got it bad, and it feels like there's no way out, no hope. Remember, Jesus' power is awesome. Don't think your need is too extreme for Him—"He Himself took our infirmities and carried away our diseases" (8:17). Whether He chooses to deliver you from your affliction sooner or later, in this life or in the glorious, miraculous resurrection, His will is ultimately to deliver you. Turn to Him.

Or perhaps you're like the centurion. You're doing okay, but you're caring for somebody who's at the brink. You're worn out. You're desperate. You can't stop thinking about them and praying for them, hoping for a solution, a recovery, an answer. Maybe it's a relationship that's broken, and you just can't rebuild the bridge. Maybe there's spiritual distance; a friend or family member needs the Lord or has wandered from the right path, and you can't seem to say or do anything to bring them around. Take these needs to the Lord too. Commit that person or that situation—whatever the distance—to Him. Leave it with Him, like the centurion did. Know that the Lord can say a word and bring a change. Let it be. Leave it with Him.

Finally, perhaps you're like Peter's mother-in-law. Who knows how long she was on that bed with a high fever? Maybe you, too, are simmering in agony, wasting away in the dark—spiritually, emotionally, or physically. Lonely, depressed, silent, cut off from the world, and shut in, you need the Lord's touch, and it hasn't come. Don't be afraid to ask the Lord to reach out through the body of Christ on earth—through His people commissioned to be His arms and legs, to extend comfort, love, and kindness toward their brothers and sisters. And count on Him to take care of you, in His way, at His time, as He pleases. Don't be afraid to ask.

We need to live our lives in light of this promise: The Lord is for us, not against us. He is full of compassion and understanding. He's not some distant deity simply frowning and judging us. The Lord is intimately interested in the details of our lives—disfigured lepers, anonymous servants of pagans, family members of believers, and all those who are spiritually and physically afflicted. He cares for them; He cares for you, too. The Lord is capable of handling whatever we're struggling with. The love and power of Jesus is like nothing you've ever heard of or seen before. It's inexhaustible. And He's ready to hear us when we call. Rather than living your life behind the shades of depression, discouragement, doubt, and denial, open the blinds. Focus on the power of Jesus Christ, and let that power give you the strength to get up each morning and take on the day, whatever it may involve.

How Not to Follow Jesus
MATTHEW 8:18-27

NASB

18 Now when Jesus saw a crowd around Him, He gave orders to depart to the other side *of the sea.* 19 Then a scribe came and said to Him, "Teacher, I will follow You wherever You go." 20 Jesus said to him, "The foxes have holes and the birds of the ªair *have* ᵇnests, but the Son of Man has nowhere to lay His head." 21 Another of the disciples said to Him, "Lord, permit me first to go and bury my father." 22 But Jesus said to him, "Follow Me, and allow the dead to bury their own dead."

23 When He got into the boat, His disciples followed Him. 24 And behold, there arose ªa great storm on the sea, so that the boat was being covered with the waves; but Jesus Himself was asleep. 25 And they came to *Him* and woke Him, saying, "Save *us,* Lord; we are perishing!" 26 He said to them, "Why are you ªafraid, you men of little faith?" Then He got up

NLT

18 When Jesus saw the crowd around him, he instructed his disciples to cross to the other side of the lake. 19 Then one of the teachers of religious law said to him, "Teacher, I will follow you wherever you go."

20 But Jesus replied, "Foxes have dens to live in, and birds have nests, but the Son of Man* has no place even to lay his head."

21 Another of his disciples said, "Lord, first let me return home and bury my father."

22 But Jesus told him, "Follow me now. Let the spiritually dead bury their own dead.*"

23 Then Jesus got into the boat and started across the lake with his disciples. 24 Suddenly, a fierce storm struck the lake, with waves breaking into the boat. But Jesus was sleeping. 25 The disciples went and woke him up, shouting, "Lord, save us! We're going to drown!"

26 Jesus responded, "Why are you afraid? You have so little faith!" Then he got up and rebuked the wind and

and rebuked the winds and the sea, and ᵇit became perfectly calm. ²⁷The men were amazed, and said, "What kind of a man is this, that even the winds and the sea obey Him?"

waves, and suddenly there was a great calm. ²⁷The disciples were amazed. "Who is this man?" they asked. "Even the winds and waves obey him!"

8:20 ªOr *sky* ᵇOr *roosting places* 8:24 ªLit *a shaking* 8:26 ªOr *cowardly* ᵇLit *a great calm occurred*

8:20 "Son of Man" is a title Jesus used for himself.
8:22 Greek *Let the dead bury their own dead.*

Talk is cheap. Many people have the ability to use a lot of verbiage but say nothing of substance. They may utter a lot of words, but they either don't mean what they say or don't admit what they're hiding. The slang expression we have for this is "running off at the mouth." A superabundance of words can be a cover-up to hide a truth that's too painful to confess or to leave an impression that's too admirable to be real.

Words that sound right don't necessarily represent honest feelings that come from the heart. Cutting to the core of what's being said—or *not* being said—takes a great deal of insight and discernment. We refer to this as "seeing through" people or "seeing past" their words. Jesus was great at doing this. While He heard the same words others heard, He had the divine ability to hear what wasn't obvious to others. Being able to read between the lines, He could not only spot a phony in an instant but also detect the motives hidden behind someone's words.

Because of His supernatural discernment, Jesus often responded to people in ways that seem strange to us at first glance. As we journey with Jesus through this section of Matthew's account of His earthly ministry, we'll be able to see how He responded to people in four separate settings. If we pay close attention along the way, we'll learn how *not* to follow Jesus.

— 8:18 —

First, let's consider the crowd gathered around Jesus. We saw in Matthew 4:23 that the crowds were gathering around Jesus because of His reputation as a miracle worker. They were also in awe of His new, unique, and surprising teaching (7:28-29). It was more out of curiosity than out of conviction that the crowds followed Jesus to see what He might do or say next. This crowd apparently lingered throughout the evening, into the morning, and perhaps for several days.

In my experience, crowds are sort of self-perpetuating. When they get large enough and reach a critical mass, they develop their own gravitational pull. People first gather around some person or event, but then others gather simply because people are gathered. Sometimes people just want to be part of the action and experience the excitement; they aren't necessarily convinced of the cause.

Jesus was never interested in drawing a large crowd or being a celebrity. The fact that He told the cleansed leper, "See that you tell no one" (8:4) suggests that He wasn't primarily trying to build a public platform. He wasn't interested in followers for followers' sake, but in *making disciples for the kingdom of God.* Jesus discerned the mentality of the crowd. He knew most of them were not committed, dedicated followers, but riled-up fans with a shallow emotionalism. Instead of finding another high place from which to preach to the crowd or a way of organizing them to grow even more, Jesus did what seems unthinkable in our modern, Western mind-set: "He gave orders to depart to the other side of the sea" (8:18). He left them!

This move was ingenious. The act of leaving the crowds gathered around Him and heading across the Sea of Galilee with His handpicked disciples would sift out those who were unwilling to go out of their way to follow Him. Now, to see Him and hear Him, they would have to actually *do* something.

The principle here is simple: Don't follow Jesus because of the size of the crowd. Guard against becoming a "groupie" of a church, a ministry, or a celebrity preacher or teacher. Steer clear of becoming a "fan."

— 8:19-20 —

Second, let's look at the scribe who sounded spiritual. In that day, a scribe was essentially a Bible scholar and teacher. We might call him a "man of letters." F. F. Bruce notes, "The 'scribes' . . . were the accepted teachers and interpreters of the Torah, from the time of Ezra onwards."[37] It took intellect and skill—and probably a robust library and quiet place to study—to fulfill this work. For a scribe, following a rabbi meant placing himself under the master's tutelage, sitting at the feet of the esteemed teacher, and therefore partaking in his fame. As a rabbi's reputation advanced, so did the careers of his students. So when a scribe came to Jesus and said, "Teacher, I will follow You wherever You go" (8:19), the student's idea of discipleship wasn't what Jesus had in mind.

We have two firsts in this passage. It's the first time somebody of such a high social rank and influence—in this case, a scribe—indicated the desire to follow Jesus full-time. It's also the first time in the Gospel of Matthew that Jesus refers to Himself as "the Son of Man" (8:20).

Picture the scene. A highly respected, religiously orthodox, professional scholar was willing to enroll as a student in the School of Jesus.
Compared to Jesus' ragtag band of scruffy-looking fishermen, the addition of a real scholar and thinker could give Jesus the credibility He
"needed" in the eyes of the Jewish leaders.

Yet Jesus discerned what was going on and replied with a painful
jab at the man's limited willingness to follow. By identifying Himself as
the Son of Man, Jesus may have been making a lightly veiled reference
to the exalted messianic figure of Daniel 7:13-14—a reference that the
learned scribe no doubt would have caught:

> And behold, with the clouds of heaven
> One like a Son of Man was coming,
> And He came up to the Ancient of Days
> And was presented before Him.
> And to Him was given dominion,
> Glory and a kingdom,
> That all the peoples, nations and men of every language
> Might serve Him.
> His dominion is an everlasting dominion
> Which will not pass away;
> And His kingdom is one
> Which will not be destroyed.

But in the same breath that He claimed ultimate heavenly glory and
power, Jesus pointed out His earthly poverty and actual homelessness!
He noted that even foxes and birds had places to rest, while He Himself
had "nowhere to lay His head" (Matt. 8:20). Certainly, from the perspective of the scribe, that kind of wandering, rootless lifestyle wasn't con-
ducive to deep scholarly study of Scripture. For the kind of discipleship
Jesus had in mind, the mentality of the rugged fishermen was the way
to go. One author describes the encounter this way: "To a fisherman,
working all night in an open boat, homelessness was partly tolerable;
but to a scribe, accustomed to his scrolls and his home, homelessness
was a stern demand. Jesus doubtless had in mind a deeper homelessness: the scribe was 'safe' in his traditions."[38]

Jesus called the scribe's bluff. He was all talk but no follow-through.
The principle here is again simple: Don't follow Jesus full of yourself.
Don't be a person with lots of words but who's short on humility. There's
a saying among the seasoned ranchers in West Texas when they meet
up with a kid with a big mouth and a lot of ambition but no scars or

experience—"The kid's all hat and no horse." That was the scribe. He was all books, but no wisdom; all knowledge, but no courage.

— 8:21-22 —

Third, let's ponder the follower who had an excuse. This individual is referred to as "another of the disciples"—that is, a follower of Jesus. The Greek term rendered "disciple," *mathētēs* [3101], doesn't always refer to one of the twelve disciples or even necessarily to true, committed disciples. The term in its general sense simply means "one who engages in learning through instruction from another."[39] Its usage here implies that the man mentioned in 8:21-22 had been following Jesus for some time and had seen and heard a lot of astonishing things. He wanted "in"—but only on his own terms.

The man had a situation at home regarding his aging father. Evidently, he was the eldest son of his family, and thus responsible for his father's eventual burial. Contrary to what many readers assume, the father was not dead yet. If the man's father had already died and was awaiting burial, it's highly doubtful the son would have been out among the crowd of Jesus' followers, especially since burial generally took place the same day a death occurred. The expression "bury my father" (8:21) thus likely referred to staying at home for the remainder of his parent's life so he could settle the family estate. The man hoped that he could indefinitely defer enlistment among the ranks of Jesus' close disciples until his father died and he received his inheritance. Perhaps then, being fully funded from his family estate, he would be able to provide for himself and serve Jesus in style.

Taking care of one's family was a noble cause, to be sure. But Jesus saw past the smokescreen to the real issue: the man's need for comfort and security. Jesus' response was classic: "Follow Me, and allow the dead to bury their own dead" (8:22). I take "the dead" to be a reference to the spiritually dead, probably meaning any family members at home who had no desire to believe in and follow Jesus. One of these "dead" could do the job of burial. The only reason the man wanted a rain check from discipleship was because he wanted a piece of the pie back home!

Jesus' words were straightforward. There's no time to wait months or years to follow Him. If you want in, you need to be all in *now*. The principle is clear: Don't follow Jesus with reservations or with a hidden agenda. If there's reluctance because you have higher priorities of creaturely comforts and financial security, you're missing the point of discipleship. A call to follow Jesus is a call to urgency.

— 8:23-27 —

Finally, let's reflect on the disciples who thought they would die. Here we're talking about those disciples who were closest to Jesus. We don't know what happened to most of the crowd (8:18) or to the scribe (8:19-20) or to the man who wanted to go home to daddy (8:21-22). Maybe they counted the cost and turned away, or maybe they cleared their double-mindedness and became permanent, full-time disciples, possibly among the seventy (Luke 10:1) or the five hundred (1 Cor. 15:6). We just don't know. But we do know that the disciples who got into the boat with Jesus (Matt. 8:23) were the real thing. They were keepers.

This scene is fairly familiar to those of us who have known the Lord for some time. Jesus and His inner circle—Peter, James, John, Andrew, and the rest—were able to step into a boat and sail away from the crowd. They set sail across the Sea of Galilee, heading in a southeasterly direction toward the "country of the Gadarenes" on the other side of the lake (8:28). The journey from Capernaum was about 10 miles by boat, and the lake could potentially be crossed within a couple of hours. During this time, Jesus took the opportunity to get some much-needed rest (8:24). Understandably, He was exhausted from the overwhelming pace of the last few days.

Suddenly, though, a massive storm blew in. This is pretty typical, even today. What appears to be a clear, sunny, calm day on the lake can very quickly turn into a dark, stormy upheaval with high-velocity winds and crashing waves. I've personally been at the Sea of Galilee when these storms have come seemingly out of nowhere. The surrounding hills create a sort of gigantic funnel, generating potentially catastrophic winds that could easily topple a midsize fishing boat like the one carrying Jesus and the disciples across the lake.

In a sheer panic—understandable from a purely human point of view—the disciples woke Jesus up from His sleep. What surprises me the most about this event is not that the storm sprang up so suddenly and so violently that the boat was filling with water, but that Jesus was sound asleep through all of it! This reveals two things: First, Jesus, fully human, was so physically exhausted that He could apparently sleep through anything. Second, Jesus, fully divine, was utterly unworried about the violent storm. As long as the God-man was on board, nothing catastrophic would happen to that vessel.

Nevertheless, all of the disciples were at the peak of panic. They shouted, "Save us, Lord; we are perishing!" (8:25). The first line was a confession of great faith—they actually believed that Jesus could save them because He is Lord even of this storm. But the second line reveals their fear and doubt—"We'll never make it! We're going to drown!" In the midst of the panic, they awaken Jesus. And what does the Lord of glory do? Does He instantly jump to His feet and rebuke the storm? No. He shakes His finger at the disciples and scolds them for their "little faith" (8:26), manifested in their palpable fear. Only then does He take care of their problem with a word: "He got up and rebuked the winds and the sea, and it became perfectly calm."

In the Greek text, there's a great contrast between the conditions of the storm and what immediately followed Jesus' rebuke. In 8:24, Matthew describes the storm as a "mega shock" (*seismos megas* [4578 + 3173]); in 8:26, he describes the calm as a "mega sheen" (*galēnē megalē* [1055 + 3173]). No wonder the dripping wet disciples stood in astonishment, their fear finally focused on the right thing—the awesome, divine power of the God-man. They uttered, "What kind of a man is this, that even the winds and the sea obey Him?" (8:27). Finally, they were starting to get it.

The principle here is convicting: Don't follow Jesus if you fear the storms of life more than you fear the Lord of life. If rough-and-tumble circumstances cause us to buckle and crumble instead of drive us to call on the Lord, we need to get our theology straight. He alone is the divine Son of Man who has sovereign power over all things that could do us in. If the winds and sea obey Him, there's no situation—natural or supernatural—that He can't handle.

APPLICATION: MATTHEW 8:18-27

Finding Yourself among the Followers

In this section, we observed four different responses to following Jesus. First, we watched from a distance as Jesus saw a crowd gathered around Him (8:18). He discerned that most of them were just curious, not dedicated followers. Second, we listened to the scribe who spoke spiritual-sounding words but lacked true humility (8:19-20). Jesus discerned that this man was "all hat and no horse." Third, we observed the man who came reluctantly, unable to prioritize the kingdom of God over his duties at home (8:21-22). Jesus discerned that the man needed comfort and security before he could fully commit. Finally, we were in a boat as a storm turned a calm sea into a dangerous situation (8:23-27). Jesus discerned His disciples' panic, which was leading to unbelief and doubt.

Where are you among Jesus' followers? You—and you alone—are the one who can answer this. Be honest with yourself. Are you just a "fan"? One of the crowd? Do you just go through the motions, doing what the crowd does and saying what the crowd says, while Jesus is really at a distance? The screws are tightening on Christians in our increasingly secular world that is antagonistic to Christian beliefs and values. Only those who are true followers rather than groupies will stand.

Or are you like the scribe, who's long on verbiage but short on conviction? Are you full of yourself—your accomplishments, your Bible trivia, your memorized verses, the books you've read, the conferences you've attended, the degrees you've obtained? You're invited to love Jesus and follow Him *as He is*, not as you wish He would be. The real Jesus will surprise you. He may even disappoint you when your expectations are unrealistic. He will ask you to go where you don't want to go and do what you don't want to do. But following Him in humility and sincerity will be worth it.

Or are you like the man who had to bury his dead—that is, who had to settle his household affairs, including his inheritance? Are you following with reservations? Do you need to make sure you're well taken care of before committing to a life of discipleship and service? Do you have a lack of urgency? Are you holding out for a posh, comfortable, and low-risk calling, or are you willing to do whatever, whenever, wherever?

Or, finally, are you like the disciples in the boat, willing to stick close to Jesus in fair weather but crumbling into a panic when the storms blow in? Do dangerous situations cause you to doubt His sovereignty? Do catastrophes lead you to challenge His goodness and wisdom? Does your worry about the future consume you? Or do you place everything in His all-powerful, all-good, all-loving hands?

Jesus wants genuine, committed, bold disciples to carry on the work left for us in this world. Are you one?

Dealing with Demons
MATTHEW 8:28-34

NASB

28 When He came to the other side into the country of the Gadarenes, two men who were demon-possessed

NLT

28 When Jesus arrived on the other side of the lake, in the region of the Gadarenes,* two men who were possessed by demons met him. They

met Him as they were coming out of the tombs. *They were* so extremely violent that no one could pass by that way. ²⁹And they cried out, saying, "ᵃWhat business do we have with each other, Son of God? Have You come here to torment us before ᵇthe time?" ³⁰Now there was a herd of many swine feeding at a distance from them. ³¹The demons *began* to entreat Him, saying, "If You *are going to* cast us out, send us into the herd of swine." ³²And He said to them, "Go!" And they came out and went into the swine, and the whole herd rushed down the steep bank into the sea and perished in the waters. ³³The herdsmen ran away, and went to the city and reported everything, ᵃincluding what had happened to the demoniacs. ³⁴And behold, the whole city came out to meet Jesus; and when they saw Him, they implored Him to leave their region.

8:29 ᵃLit *What is to us and to you* (a Heb idiom) ᵇI.e. the appointed time of judgment **8:33** ᵃLit *and the things of*

came out of the tombs and were so violent that no one could go through that area. ²⁹They began screaming at him, "Why are you interfering with us, Son of God? Have you come here to torture us before God's appointed time?" ³⁰There happened to be a large herd of pigs feeding in the distance. ³¹So the demons begged, "If you cast us out, send us into that herd of pigs." ³²"All right, go!" Jesus commanded them. So the demons came out of the men and entered the pigs, and the whole herd plunged down the steep hillside into the lake and drowned in the water. ³³The herdsmen fled to the nearby town, telling everyone what happened to the demon-possessed men. ³⁴Then the entire town came out to meet Jesus, but they begged him to go away and leave them alone.

8:28 Other manuscripts read *Gerasenes;* still others read *Gergesenes.* Compare Mark 5:1; Luke 8:26.

The Bible is filled with amazing scenes and stories that almost take our breath away. When we picture ourselves being there, seeing through our own eyes the incredible events as they take place and wondering how everything will turn out, we're held in the grip of our imagination. The disciples of Jesus occupied front-row seats throughout His earthly ministry. How often they must have stared in amazement at what they saw and heard—mouths wide open, shocked beyond words!

This is where they were at the end of the previous story, having seen Jesus stop the waves, quiet the violent winds, and still the storm with just a word. Surrounded by eerie silence, a glistening sheen spread across the surface of the deep, they wondered aloud, "What kind of a man is this?" (8:27). Slowly but surely, step by step, episode by episode, the true identity of this man-like-no-other was beginning to be revealed to them.

Yet another shock awaited them as their boat slipped quietly across the surface of the still sea. It happened as soon as their boat pushed ashore. They had no idea that they would encounter raw evil in the flesh—an evil force that knew the answer to their question all too well.

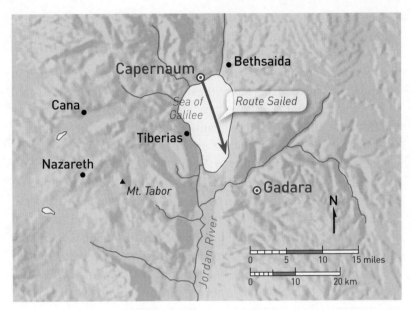

After departing from Capernaum, Jesus and the disciples sailed across the lake— encountering a fierce storm along the way—and landed on the southeastern coast. The town of Gadara was approximately 6 miles inland.

— 8:28 —

As the disciples landed their boat on the side of the Sea of Galilee opposite Capernaum (8:28), they arrived at the edge of the region of the Gadarenes, elsewhere called the Gerasenes (Mark 5:1; Luke 8:26). This region, associated with Gadara, a city of the Decapolis ("Ten Cities"), covered an area southeast of the Sea of Galilee. We can't be sure exactly where the disciples landed the boat, but a couple of places with steep shorelines on the southeast edge of the lake match the description of the event in Matthew 8:32.[40]

As soon as Jesus and the disciples climbed out of their boat, two demon-possessed men confronted them. The Greek term for their condition is *daimonizomai* [1139], literally translated "demonized." The word describes those who are so thoroughly under the control of demons that they can't control themselves. They engage in self-destructive behavior and exhibit supernatural strength and abilities. Robert Lightner offers this definition: "One is demon-possessed when a demon (or demons) takes up residence in that person's body, resulting in degrees of derangement and the inability of the possessed to free himself or herself from demonic control. . . . Possession occurs when the demons go beyond exerting influence and actually indwell their victims."[41]

The parallel accounts in Mark and Luke add a few more details. All three accounts point out that the demon-possessed men had been living in the tombs. Mark and Luke focus on just one of the demoniacs, who was probably the more prominent of the two mentioned in Matthew. He had amazing strength, such that those who tried to bind him in chains couldn't subdue him (Mark 5:3-4). Mark also mentions that the demoniac shrieked in anguish day and night and cut himself with sharp stones (Mark 5:5). Luke provides the detail that he had been naked for a long time, dwelling in the tombs like a savage animal (Luke 8:27). So violent were this demon-possessed man and his companion that they prevented people from passing that way toward the city (Matt. 8:28). People avoided them like they avoided stray, ravenous dogs.

What a sad, terrifying sight! Clearly the demons that possessed the man and his companion were attempting to destroy their basic humanity. Through the years, the men had reflected the image of God less and less, to the utter delight of the wicked spirits whose goal is to rob men and women of their dignity as God's image bearers.

But now they had come face-to-face with the One whose mission it is to lift the fallen children of Adam to their rightful place of glory as those created in God's image.

— 8:29-32 —

Though Matthew indicates that two demoniacs met Jesus and the disciples on the lakeshore, Mark and Luke suggest that one of them—likely the bigger and stronger of the two—confronted Jesus. Matthew records what was said: "What business do we have with each other, Son of God? Have You come here to torment us before the time?" (8:29). Mark and Luke add another detail regarding the conversation. At one point, Jesus asked, "What is your name?" The demoniac responded, "My name is Legion; for we are many" (Mark 5:9).

We can observe a few important points from this brief but dramatic encounter between Jesus and the demons. First, the demons were fully aware of Jesus' identity and His power. There was no doubt about it. Standing before them was "Jesus, Son of the Most High God," the One with complete authority over them (Mark 5:7; Luke 8:28). While the self-righteous religious leaders would doubt Jesus' messianic status, the spirits of wickedness knew whom they were dealing with: the God-man.

Second, the demons knew their ultimate destiny. They wondered whether Jesus was going to torment them "before the time" (Matt 8:29). Later, Jesus would teach His disciples that an "eternal fire . . . has been

EXCURSUS: DEMONOLOGY 101

MATTHEW 8:28

Popular portrayals of Satan and demons range from the cute and comical to the ghastly and horrifying. You can buy little red demons as stuffed plush toys or pay homage to them in heathen religions. You can reject their existence or run in fear of their influence. But mark my words: Demons are neither funny nor phony. They are real, and understanding just what they are and what they aren't—and what they can and can't do—is important for dealing with demons in a way that is biblical.

When it comes to demons, people often go to extremes. Some totally deny their existence. Even those who believe in a personal God and angelic beings will often reject other dimensions of the supernatural world—especially Satan and demons. Others treat the demonic in a lighthearted way, making jokes about spirits of wickedness or playing games with the occult, magic, or sorcery as if they were harmless hobbies. Still others nurture an inordinate preoccupation with the subject of demons, seeing Satan and his minions behind every mishap, every temptation, and every sin or sickness. Each of these distorted perspectives can be damaging to Christian living. Denial leads to lack of preparation for demonic attacks. Lack of seriousness leads to careless flirtation with things of spiritual wickedness. And obsession leads to blaming demons even for our own weaknesses and sins.

The Bible presents a clear picture of demons and what they can and can't do.

Demons are invisible, angelic beings in the service of Satan (Matt. 25:41; Rev. 12:9), and they are actively engaged in evil objectives through relentless deception (Matt. 4:1-11; 1 Cor. 10:20; 2 Cor. 11:13-15; 2 Thes. 2:8-10; Rev. 16:13-14). Demons clearly have supernatural powers, but as finite, created beings, they are not all-powerful, all-knowing, or omnipresent. They are limited by the sovereign power of God and are subject to His plan and purpose (Job 1:12; Dan. 10:12-13; Rev. 12:7-9). Because they crave worship and adoration, they inhabit temples and associate with idols; involvement with such pagan worship can result in communion with demonic forces (1 Cor. 10:14, 19-21). We also know that demons can sometimes inhabit living beings, both animals and humans, taking control of their victims' bodies and wreaking great havoc on their physical, mental, emotional, and especially spiritual well-being (Gen. 3:1; Matt. 8:16, 28).

A short summary of Demonology 101 will help put things in perspective: "While God's good angelic beings are spirits ministering on behalf of His people (Heb. 1:14), the wicked spirits attempt to undermine God's kingdom and the salvation of His people. And although, for His own purposes and according to His own plan, God allows evil spirits to continue to operate in this world, one day He will vanquish them forever, and never again will they inflict evil on His creation (Rev. 20:10)."[42]

prepared for the devil and his angels" (25:41). The demons knew that at some point their ability to roam the earth and tempt, afflict, oppress, and possess people would come to an end. Judgment was coming, and Jesus would be the Judge. Was it already beginning for them?

Third, the number of demons possessing the men was great. The man speaking claimed to have a "legion" of demons. The term "legion" referred to a Roman military unit consisting of approximately six thousand soldiers.[43] The demons may have been exaggerating their number, of course, but the point is clear: These men were not only indwelled by demons—they were infested with them! So many were there that they requested to be cast into a nearby herd of about two thousand swine (8:30-31; see Mark 5:13).

Fourth, Jesus transferred the demons from the demoniacs with a single word: "He said to them, 'Go!' And they came out and went into the swine" (Matt. 8:32). There was no fight, no argument, no sprinkling with holy water, no magic, no reading from a rite of exorcism. Jesus' authority was absolute. Had Jesus simply been a created, angelic being dwelling in a human body, as some false teachers would later believe, He would have been no match against thousands of wicked spirits of equal spiritual strength. But the Son of the Most High is no creature. He has divine power and authority over all created things—animate and inanimate—because He is the divine Creator Himself.

This episode reminds me of the words of the great Reformation hymn "A Mighty Fortress Is Our God," by Martin Luther:

> And tho this world, with devils filled,
> Should threaten to undo us,
> We will not fear, for God hath willed
> His truth to triumph thru us.
> The Prince of darkness grim,
> We tremble not for him—
> His rage we can endure,
> For lo, his doom is sure:
> One little word shall fell him.[44]

With one little word, Jesus felled the thousands of demons, casting them into the pigs. It seems that demons prefer inhabiting other living things on earth to remaining disembodied in the invisible spirit realm. However, their enjoyment of the new bodies was short-lived. The unclean animals roaming the area scrounging for food were instantly driven mad by the invasion of demons. They rushed headlong down a steep bank into the Sea of Galilee and drowned. In the end, not only were the demons vanquished, but a couple thousand nonkosher animals forbidden by the Mosaic Law to be eaten were also lost in the process!

— 8:33-34 —

The swineherds nearby were clearly not happy with their loss. Instead of marveling at the authority of Jesus and the restoration of the demon-possessed men, the people of the nearby village begged Jesus to leave the region (8:33-34). Rather than rejoicing over the relief and recovery of the victims of the demons, the townspeople drove Jesus out of town! What He had done wasn't good for business. This comment by Paul Levertoff sums up the situation well: "All down the ages the world has been refusing Jesus because it prefers its pigs."[45]

Though Matthew concludes the narrative after the clear demonstration of Jesus' authority over demons and the hostile human response, the Gospel of Mark reports the final outcome for at least one of the demoniacs. When the people of the village came to see what had happened, they saw the demon-possessed man "clothed and in his right mind" (Mark 5:15). As Jesus and the disciples were getting into the boat to go home, the man understandably wanted to join them (Mark 5:18). However, Jesus urged him, "Go home to your people and report to them what great things the Lord has done for you, and how He had mercy on you" (Mark 5:19). This man, once bound by spiritual darkness but now filled with light, indeed began proclaiming throughout the Decapolis "what great things Jesus had done for him" (Mark 5:20).

APPLICATION: MATTHEW 8:28-34

Standing against Demonic Power

Though it's important to know the basics about demons, their nature, and their power, from a practical perspective it's best to focus on God, His character, and His power in our lives. After all, through Him we have victory over the forces of wickedness. To understand the divine protection we have through Christ by the power of the Spirit, let me share four vital principles from the Bible's principal passage on spiritual warfare, Ephesians 6:10-18.

First, *expect struggles with unseen forces.* Ephesians 6:10-12 says, "Finally, be strong in the Lord and in the strength of His might. . . . For our struggle is not against flesh and blood, but against the rulers, against the powers, against the world forces of this darkness, against the spiritual forces of wickedness in the heavenly places." Beyond the world of our five senses, an unseen world exists, where spirits of wickedness are strategizing under the direction of Satan. As children of God and servants of Christ, we are engaged in battles against evil whether we know it or not. It's important for us to realize that our primary enemies are not in the realm of what we can touch, see, and hear. Rather, our primary enemies are those who stand behind the forces of temptation, deception, persecution, immorality, and injustice.

Second, *stand firm in the full armor of God.* Ephesians 6:11-13 says, "Put on the full armor of God, so that you will be able to stand firm against the schemes of the devil. . . . Take up the full armor of God, so that you will be able to resist in the evil day, and having done everything, to stand firm." Wear the equipment God gives you with confidence. Acknowledge that the power and resources you have in your own strength could not enable you to do battle against demons and their schemes. Without God's provision, you will fail. His armor includes truth, righteousness, the good news of peace, faith, the gift of salvation, and the word of God (Eph. 6:14-17).

Third, *hold up the shield of faith and pray in the Spirit.* Ephesians 6:16-18 says, "In addition to all, [take] up the shield of faith with which you will be able to extinguish all the flaming arrows of the evil one. . . . With all prayer and petition pray at all times in the Spirit." When you feel attacked and are in the presence of a great temptation, deception, or affliction that Satan is using to torment you, stand strong in faith and pray. Ask the Lord God to take control of the situation and send the forces of wickedness fleeing with a single word.

Fourth, *never forget that you're on the winning side.* In the end, God will win the victory. Revelation 20:10 is worth memorizing: "And the devil who deceived them was thrown into the lake of fire and brimstone, where the beast and the false prophet are also; and they will be tormented day and night forever and ever." In the meantime, remember that we can have victory over the spirits of wickedness and the schemes of the devil because of the power of the Holy Spirit within us, as 1 John 4:4 says: "You are from God, little children, and have overcome them; because greater is He who is in you than he who is in the world."

Critics on Patrol
MATTHEW 9:1-17

NASB

¹Getting into a boat, Jesus crossed over *the sea* and came to His own city. ²And they brought to Him a paralytic lying on a bed. Seeing their faith, Jesus said to the paralytic, "Take courage, ªson; your sins are forgiven." ³And some of the scribes said ªto themselves, "This *fellow* blasphemes." ⁴And Jesus knowing their thoughts said, "Why are you thinking evil in your hearts? ⁵Which is easier, to say, 'Your sins are forgiven,' or to say, 'Get up, and walk'? ⁶But so that you may know that the Son of Man has authority on earth to forgive sins"—then He said to the paralytic, "Get up, pick up your bed and go home." ⁷And he got up and ªwent home. ⁸But when the crowds saw *this,* they were ªawestruck, and glorified God, who had given such authority to men.

⁹As Jesus went on from there, He saw a man called Matthew, sitting in the tax collector's booth; and He said to him, "Follow Me!" And he got up and followed Him.

¹⁰Then it happened that as ªJesus was reclining *at the table* in the house, behold, many tax collectors and ᵇsinners came and were dining with Jesus and His disciples. ¹¹When the Pharisees saw *this,* they said to His disciples, "Why is your Teacher eating with the tax collectors and sinners?" ¹²But when Jesus heard *this,* He said, "*It is* not those who are healthy who need a physician, but those who are sick. ¹³But go and learn ªwhat this means: 'I DESIRE ᵇCOMPASSION, ᶜAND NOT SACRIFICE,'

NLT

¹Jesus climbed into a boat and went back across the lake to his own town. ²Some people brought to him a paralyzed man on a mat. Seeing their faith, Jesus said to the paralyzed man, "Be encouraged, my child! Your sins are forgiven."

³But some of the teachers of religious law said to themselves, "That's blasphemy! Does he think he's God?"

⁴Jesus knew* what they were thinking, so he asked them, "Why do you have such evil thoughts in your hearts? ⁵Is it easier to say 'Your sins are forgiven,' or 'Stand up and walk'? ⁶So I will prove to you that the Son of Man* has the authority on earth to forgive sins." Then Jesus turned to the paralyzed man and said, "Stand up, pick up your mat, and go home!"

⁷And the man jumped up and went home! ⁸Fear swept through the crowd as they saw this happen. And they praised God for giving humans such authority.

⁹As Jesus was walking along, he saw a man named Matthew sitting at his tax collector's booth. "Follow me and be my disciple," Jesus said to him. So Matthew got up and followed him.

¹⁰Later, Matthew invited Jesus and his disciples to his home as dinner guests, along with many tax collectors and other disreputable sinners. ¹¹But when the Pharisees saw this, they asked his disciples, "Why does your teacher eat with such scum?*"

¹²When Jesus heard this, he said, "Healthy people don't need a doctor—sick people do." ¹³Then he added, "Now go and learn the meaning of this Scripture: 'I want you to show mercy, not offer sacrifices.'* For I have come to call not those who

NASB

for I did not come to call the righteous, but sinners."

14Then the disciples of John came to Him, asking, "Why do we and the Pharisees fast, but Your disciples do not fast?" 15And Jesus said to them, "The aattendants of the bridegroom cannot mourn as long as the bridegroom is with them, can they? But the days will come when the bridegroom is taken away from them, and then they will fast. 16But no one puts aa patch of unshrunk cloth on an old garment; for bthe patch pulls away from the garment, and a worse tear results. 17Nor do *people* put new wine into old wineskins; otherwise the wineskins burst, and wine pours out and the wineskins are ruined; but they put new wine into fresh wineskins, and both are preserved."

9:2 aLit *child*   9:3 aLit *among*   9:7 aOr *departed*
9:8 aLit *afraid*   9:10 aLit *He*   bI.e. irreligious
Jews   9:13 aLit *what is*   bOr *mercy*   cI.e. more than
9:15 aLit *sons of the wedding place*   9:16 aLit *that
which is put on*   bLit *that which fills up*

NLT

think they are righteous, but those who know they are sinners."

14One day the disciples of John the Baptist came to Jesus and asked him, "Why don't your disciples fast* like we do and the Pharisees do?"

15Jesus replied, "Do wedding guests mourn while celebrating with the groom? Of course not. But someday the groom will be taken away from them, and then they will fast.

16"Besides, who would patch old clothing with new cloth? For the new patch would shrink and rip away from the old cloth, leaving an even bigger tear than before.

17"And no one puts new wine into old wineskins. For the old skins would burst from the pressure, spilling the wine and ruining the skins. New wine is stored in new wineskins so that both are preserved."

9:4 Some manuscripts read *saw.*   9:6 "Son of
Man" is a title Jesus used for himself.   9:11 Greek
with tax collectors and sinners?   9:13 Hos 6:6
(Greek version).   9:14 Some manuscripts read
fast often.

Even a casual reading of Matthew's Gospel gives me the feeling of walking right next to Jesus. As He climbs into a boat to sail back across the Sea of Galilee (9:1), I can almost catch the twinkling of the sunlight bouncing off the lake and feel droplets of cool water spraying on my face. As we come ashore, I feel the sensation of finding my land legs after swaying back and forth on a boat for hours. As I follow the disciples through the crowd gathered in Capernaum, I experience the murmurs and whispers, the scent of fresh fish, and the odors of heavy labor; I see the expectant faces wondering what Jesus is going to do or say next.

As we work through this next section, we witness a strange phenomenon, already foreshadowed back on the other side of the lake in the response of the Gadarene pig herders. Some people's reaction to Jesus' miraculous power was negative: They didn't want Jesus around, disrupting their everyday "normal," as mundane as it was. They preferred the status quo to bowing to the intrusive power of the Lord God.

When we travel with Jesus back to the other side of the lake, we see the same kind of simmering resentment by the "powers that be." As Jesus continues to perform miraculous healings, bring spiritual restoration, and provide deliverance from unrighteous living, some rejoice in the Savior, but others harbor feelings of jealousy and lash out in criticism. As those who presumed to have a monopoly on righteousness and a cornered market on spirituality, the scribes and Pharisees slowly begin turning against Jesus, seeing Him as a threat to their illegitimate claim on the hearts and minds of the people. At the same time, a group of disciples of John the Baptizer continue to hold onto the Pharisaic traditions of religious piety with a white-knuckle grip, criticizing Jesus' disciples for not following suit.

As we look at three episodes—the healing of a paralytic, the calling of a tax collector, and the discussion of fasting—look into your own heart and ask yourself these questions: *In which category do I belong? Am I among those who think they are righteous and don't really need Jesus? Or do I fit among those who know they are sinners and desperately need the Lord?*

— 9:1-8 —

For the second time that day, Jesus and the disciples loaded into a boat. Perhaps the disciples had originally thought they were going to continue into the city of Gadara southeast of the lake, then on to other cities in the Decapolis deeper inland. But the rejection by the locals got them back in the boat and headed on a return trip across the Sea of Galilee. They landed back at Jesus' "own city" of Capernaum (9:1).

Most likely the events described after 9:1 occurred sometime in the days following their return. Though Matthew doesn't give us enough details to decipher *when* these events took place, we do know *where*, thanks to the version recorded in Mark 2:1-12. There we're told that Jesus was indoors, perhaps in Peter's home, teaching a large crowd that had gathered there (Mark 2:2). Four men carrying a paralytic man on a pallet tried to get to Jesus, but the house was too crowded. In an act of desperation and faith, in the middle of Jesus' teaching they removed parts of the roof and lowered the man down so Jesus could heal him (Mark 2:3-4).

Matthew picks up the account with Jesus "seeing their faith" (Matt. 9:2), expressed through the lengths they went to in bringing the man to the Master. Had they entertained a halfhearted, double-minded belief in Jesus, they surely wouldn't have gone through all the trouble they did in lugging the man to the house, climbing to the flat roof, and lowering him carefully through the hole. It was a bold, risky move that required absolute confidence that Jesus could, in fact, do something about the man's condition.

When Jesus saw the man, He made a bold pronouncement: "Take courage, son; your sins are forgiven." Not quite what they had shown up for, was it? Some have taken this statement to suggest that all sicknesses and diseases are punishments for specific sins. In fact, many people in Jesus' day believed in a sort of karma in which good deeds were rewarded with health and wealth in this life while sins were punished with sickness and poverty. But that is patently false. Jesus rejected this kind of thinking (John 9:1-3). Yes, sometimes pain and suffering come as a natural consequence of sin or as an act of discipline by God toward His children (see Heb. 12:4-11; Jas. 5:14-15; 1 Jn. 5:16-17). But certainly not all ailments can be seen in this light.

Nevertheless, Jesus' words of forgiveness would have been a great reassurance to the paralytic that his condition was not necessarily the result of some kind of curse, and even if it were, he had been brought to the right place! Jesus not only has authority over physical sickness, but He also has authority over the spiritual sickness of the soul. Notice Christ's focus here: He wasn't concerned merely with the external, temporal condition of the man's body; He was concerned with the eternal, spiritual condition of the man's soul.

Not everyone in the room was convinced. We've already seen a scribe—a highbrow scholar of the Law—who had gotten close to Jesus but had sought enrollment as a disciple only on certain conditions (see commentary on Matt. 8:19-20). Now a small group of these academics heard Jesus' pronouncement of forgiveness and balked: "This fellow blasphemes" (9:3). If Jesus had been a mere man, as they believed, they would have been right; it would have been blasphemy to claim for oneself the authority to forgive sins. The Gospel of Mark adds the scribes' reasoning: "Who can forgive sins but God alone?" (Mark 2:7). Though they weren't wrong in their theological reasoning, they were wrong in their presupposition. Jesus was not a mere man. As the God-man, He does have the authority to forgive sin. But how would anybody in the room know that the pronouncement of pardon was anything more than just words?

Jesus didn't let the murmuring of these scribes get outside their small circle and corrupt the minds of His followers, thus spreading the baseless charge of blasphemy that day. Instead, with His divine knowledge of what they were thinking, He said, "Why are you thinking evil in your hearts? Which is easier, to say, 'Your sins are forgiven,' or to say, 'Get up, and walk'?" (Matt. 9:4-5). Maybe He paused to let that question sink in. As far as making hollow claims goes, it would be easier to declare forgiveness of sins than to command a person to be instantly healed.

The former is unverifiable, because the spiritual condition of a person's soul is invisible to all but God. But if somebody were to tell a paralyzed person to get up and walk, and that person didn't do so, the one making the claim would be exposed as a false prophet or charlatan.

What happened next was sure to send a shock through the crowd. Loudly and clearly, so all could hear, Jesus said, "But so that you may know that the Son of Man has authority on earth to forgive sins"—a brief pause followed as He turned to the paralytic—"Get up, pick up your bed and go home" (9:6). This high-tension moment could have ended badly for Jesus and gloriously for the scoffing scribes. Had the man on the cot simply moaned and groaned, Jesus would have been outed as a fake. But that didn't happen. Instead, the man "got up and went home" (9:7), not only healed physically but also assured that his sins had been forgiven.

The response of the crowd was understandable. They were "awe-struck," and they "glorified God" (9:8). I can imagine there being clapping, laughing, singing, and dancing. In their midst was a man like no other, with authority granted to heal both body and soul. No doubt the skeptical critics lurking in the corner slipped out the back door, increasingly unnerved that their attempts at discrediting Jesus to protect their own power were being undermined at every turn.

— 9:9-10 —

Jesus wasn't finished irritating the religious authorities that day. As He left the home where He had been teaching, He came upon a man named Matthew. Yes, *that* Matthew—the author of this very Gospel account, who was also called "Levi the son of Alphaeus" (Mark 2:14; see also Luke 5:27). I can picture the rest of Jesus' entourage either sneering at Matthew or steering far from him, because he was one of the most hated men in town. Matthew, we're told, was "sitting in the tax collector's booth" (Matt. 9:9)—not because he was benevolently helping somebody pay their taxes, but because he was a dreaded tax collector. In other words, he was a traitor to his people—a Jew who worked as an agent for the Roman government. He was likely banned from the synagogue, shunned by his countrymen, untrusted as a friend, and numbered with robbers and murderers. Nobody wanted anything to do with Matthew. Except Jesus.

When Jesus turned *toward* the tax collector's booth, I can imagine many of His disciples stood back. "Um, where are you going, Lord?" Can you picture it? Maybe as Jesus approached the man behind the

TAX COLLECTORS

MATTHEW 9:9

Of all the occupations in the New Testament era, tax collector was close to the bottom of the list of respectable professions. In the Roman imperial bureaucracy, there were actually two classes of tax collector: the "chief tax collector," like the short-statured Zaccheus (Luke 19:2), and the "publican," or street-level collector who worked face-to-face with the common taxpayers.[46] Matthew was the latter. As such, he probably would have had an earned reputation for extortion—charging beyond the amount required by his supervisor and pocketing the extra. Though this was illegal, it was a well-known practice, and it generated great dissatisfaction among the remote provinces, like Judea, where the rules of the empire were less strictly enforced.[47]

The Romans exacted two types of taxes on the populations under their control. The first was similar to our income or sales taxes—fixed rates connected to the amount of money earned or the price of goods bought. It was difficult for tax officers to find wiggle room with those fixed percentages. Everybody would know if they were inflating rates or fudging on numbers.

However, the second type of tax related to customs, imports, and exports. These areas gave corrupt officials plenty of opportunity to reap serious coin. Michael Green explains how Matthew would have made a killing collecting taxes: "There was limitless opportunity for the bribery and extortion that made the *publicani* so hated. Matthew had his tax office at Capernaum, on the main road from Damascus to Egypt, which passed through Samaria and Galilee. He was working under the direct employ of Herod Antipas, who, in turn, had to make massive block tax disbursements to Rome. It was a very lucrative place in which to work."[48]

table, some of His followers took a few steps in, hoping to hear a tongue lashing from Jesus, the preacher of righteousness. Nobody deserved it more than Matthew, that scoundrel! But as they leaned in, the words they heard would have widened eyes and dropped jaws: "Follow Me!"

You probably could have heard a tiny copper coin drop as the crowd waited for Matthew's response. But apparently the wait wasn't long. Matthew himself reports, "And he got up and followed Him" (9:9). Without hesitation, the hated tax collector dropped everything and went with Jesus. No doubt Matthew had heard the stories about Jesus' words and deeds. No doubt the Spirit had already been prodding his conscience. But he still needed the call from the Lord. And the moment he got the call, he pushed himself from that table and followed.

Matthew's response to Jesus' call had surprising reverberations in what many pious and self-righteous persons of Capernaum would have considered the "slimeball" community. Matthew points out that "many tax collectors and sinners" gathered at his home that evening to dine with Jesus and the disciples (9:10). Mark's account adds the detail that "they were following Him" too (Mark 2:15). Luke mentions that the dinner was a "big reception" for Jesus (Luke 5:29). Clearly, Matthew's sudden conversion from crook to disciple had made a mark on the people in his immediate circle of influence. This conglomeration of outcasts, undesirables, and social misfits was at the table dining with Jesus!

— 9:11-13 —

Then *they* showed up. Like the scribes who had grumbled a few hours earlier when Jesus had declared the paralytic forgiven, the religious leaders also had a problem with Jesus' behavior that night. Mark identifies this group as "the scribes of the Pharisees" (Mark 2:16), indicating that these particular scholars were of the hyper-religious Pharisaic party. Maybe they were peeking through a side window or conducting an exit poll as guests left. In any case, these nitpicking hypocrites were on the hunt for anything that even smelled like an infraction of the Law—that is, their man-made interpretations and applications of the Law of Moses.

These self-righteous, ever-judging, grace-killing elitists couldn't see the redemption of lives that was taking place before their very eyes. Instead, they complained to the disciples of Jesus, "Why is your Teacher eating with the tax collectors and sinners?" (Matt. 9:11). Driven by jealousy over Jesus' sudden popularity and their loss of influence among the masses, they were probably trying to plant little seeds of doubt and discord among the disciples. They probably hoped that Jesus' followers would be ashamed of His new associations with the "scum of Capernaum" and would turn their backs on Him.

But Jesus was again one step ahead of them. He made three stinging points, aimed directly at the faultfinding Pharisees. First, He pointed out that physicians deal with people who are sick, not with the healthy (9:12). How could tax collectors and sinners ever get the spiritual therapy they needed if the One with the cure avoided them? It didn't take an expert in the Law to read between the lines: Jesus was calling Himself the true Physician, who cared enough to reach out to the sick with a cure—while the selfish and self-righteous Pharisees were avoiding the ones who most needed spiritual help!

Second, Jesus argued that, in terms of spiritual priorities, God demanded compassion shown through grace, mercy, and love far more than sacrifices—especially "sacrifices" that were man-made like the (flaunted) public purity of the Pharisees. Jesus turned the tables on the Pharisees, who were the renowned teachers of the Law, by quoting Hosea 6:6 and sending them away to do their homework—"Go and learn what this means: 'I desire compassion, and not sacrifice'" (Matt. 9:13). There, in front of everybody, Jesus schooled them in Bible 101! How humiliating and offensive it would have been to the Pharisees to be given homework assignments from Jesus—who seemed to be just a common carpenter.

Finally, Jesus showed that His mission stands in contrast to the actions of the Pharisees. Rather than seeking to cozy up with the so-called righteous as a member of the "Holy Club," Jesus' mission is to reach out to sinners and call them to repentance. Jesus' heart went out to the outcasts—those who lived in the muck and mire of shame and disgrace. He stepped into their lives to extend forgiveness and grace so that they could start over on a new path of faith and righteousness.

— 9:14-17 —

I'm convinced that Jesus' disciples didn't entertain the Pharisees' hairbrained hypocrisy even for a second. At least not the true disciples. They had heard and seen enough to convince them that Jesus' style of grace and mercy, love and compassion, truth and goodness, was the pattern to follow. Even though they may not have understood everything Jesus said and did, they knew Jesus—and they knew that everything He said was true and that everything He did was right.

However, at this point, another group poked their heads into Jesus' busy day of asserting His divine mission—not scribes and Pharisees this time, but a group of John the Baptizer's disciples. We often get the impression that when Jesus began His ministry and John was imprisoned by Herod, all of John's disciples simply transferred allegiance to the One to whom John had been pointing—the Lamb of God. Not so. For whatever reason, some disciples were still loyal to John, unwilling or unready to turn to Jesus. In fact, such a group seems to have endured even into the apostolic church (Acts 18:24–19:7).

Though these disciples of the Baptizer were not themselves close-knit associates of the Pharisees, they shared the same weekly regimen of fasts the Pharisees had developed by oral tradition over the centuries. They had apparently watched Jesus' ministry from a distance over

Ardo Beltz/Wikimedia

A natural wineskin

the previous few days and realized that He and His disciples didn't follow those man-made rules. I have to commend John's disciples for going directly to Jesus to find out why this was, unlike the Pharisees, who mumbled to each other or tried to spread venomous gossip among Jesus' followers. At least they had the integrity to go to the source and ask, "Why do we and the Pharisees fast, but Your disciples do not fast?" (Matt. 9:14).

Jesus' answer was steeped in profound imagery as well as prophetic mystery. Fasting was incompatible with the joy His disciples had in being with Him. Like time wedding guests spend in the presence of the bridegroom, this time at the feet of the Messiah called for celebration, not somber mourning or solemn commemorating. Only when the bridegroom was taken away (a veiled reference to His death) would the wedding guests mourn (9:15).

Then Jesus went further with two more analogies—patching an old garment with unshrunk cloth, causing the garment to tear again, and putting new wine into old wineskins, causing the wineskins to burst (9:16-17).

The skins of animals were sewn together to form a kind of flexible bottle to store wine. New wine that had not fully fermented could only be placed in new, fresh wineskins, which had enough natural elasticity to handle the expansion caused by the buildup of gas in the fermentation process. Old wineskins would burst under the pressure.[49]

How did these analogies answer the question of John the Baptizer's disciples? R. T. France explains, "Jesus has brought something new, and the rituals and traditions of official Judaism cannot contain it. The explosive exuberance of the new era . . . must break out of the confines of legalism and asceticism."[50] In other words, not only was it inappropriate for the disciples to fast—a somber, solemn sign of repentance and mourning—in the presence of the King, but the Pharisees' man-made rituals associated with fasting would never have a fixed place in the new, dynamic work of the Spirit in the age to come.

Stan Toussaint sums up the rhetorical power of Jesus' words to the disciples of John the Baptizer: "John belonged to the old age; Jesus was the One who was bringing a new dispensation. They should therefore leave the forerunner and join themselves to the King. Unless they did, they could not partake of any new dispensation which Jesus might bring."[51]

APPLICATION: MATTHEW 9:1-17
Sticking Close to Jesus

Like the desperate paralytic who needed forgiveness and healing (9:1-8) and the underhanded tax collector who needed redemption and restoration (9:9-13), Jesus' true followers know that they are terminally infected with sin and guilt and can only be healed by the Great Physician. The Pharisees and scribes, however, operated under the gross misconception that they were just fine. And the disciples of John the Baptizer, holding on to their traditions-of-men approach to religion, were little better.

Imagine you're sitting there at either of those tables in either of those homes—the home in which Jesus supposedly transgressed a theological code by forgiving sin on His own authority or the home of Matthew the tax collector, surrounded by a crowd of former extortionists desiring to learn what it meant to follow Jesus. Would you embrace the discomfort of radical grace and mercy embodied by Jesus, or would you look for a way out of that hot spot and opt for a cooler, more comfortable set of doctrines and practices, like scheduled fasts and other familiar traditions?

And what about today? When Christians want to reach outside the bubble of your ethnic, cultural, racial, or generational demographic, do you retreat to your corner and criticize, or do you roll up your sleeves and embrace the discomfort of showing compassion even when it hurts? When people who have special needs, who are debilitated, or who are physically, mentally, or emotionally challenged appear in your midst, do you stand in judgment over them, or do you step forward to help, even if it will cost you your coziness? If we approach life and ministry with the acknowledgment that we're all dirty, rotten sinners in need of a Savior, we can inoculate ourselves against the disease of self-righteous Pharisaism and fall into the healing hands of the Great Physician.

Nonstop Daze of Miracles
MATTHEW 9:18-38

NASB

18While He was saying these things to them, ᵃa *synagogue* ᵇofficial came and ᶜbowed down before Him, and said, "My daughter has just died; but come and lay Your hand on her, and she will live." 19Jesus got up and *began* to follow him, and *so did* His disciples.

20And a woman who had been suffering from a hemorrhage for twelve years, came up behind Him and touched the ᵃfringe of His ᵇcloak; 21for she was saying ᵃto herself, "If I only touch His garment, I will ᵇget well." 22But Jesus turning and seeing her said, "Daughter, take courage; your faith has ᵃmade you well." ᵇAt once the woman was ᶜmade well.

23When Jesus came into the ᵃofficial's house, and saw the flute-players and the crowd in noisy disorder, 24He said, "Leave; for the girl has not died, but is asleep." And they *began* laughing at Him. 25But when the crowd had been sent out, He entered and took her by the hand, and the girl ᵃgot up. 26This news spread throughout all that land.

27As Jesus went on from there, two

NLT

18As Jesus was saying this, the leader of a synagogue came and knelt before him. "My daughter has just died," he said, "but you can bring her back to life again if you just come and lay your hand on her."

19So Jesus and his disciples got up and went with him. 20Just then a woman who had suffered for twelve years with constant bleeding came up behind him. She touched the fringe of his robe, 21for she thought, "If I can just touch his robe, I will be healed."

22Jesus turned around, and when he saw her he said, "Daughter, be encouraged! Your faith has made you well." And the woman was healed at that moment.

23When Jesus arrived at the official's home, he saw the noisy crowd and heard the funeral music. 24"Get out!" he told them. "The girl isn't dead; she's only asleep." But the crowd laughed at him. 25After the crowd was put outside, however, Jesus went in and took the girl by the hand, and she stood up! 26The report of this miracle swept through the entire countryside.

27After Jesus left the girl's home,

NASB

blind men followed Him, crying out, "Have mercy on us, Son of David!" 28When He entered the house, the blind men came up to Him, and Jesus said to them, "Do you believe that I am able to do this?" They said to Him, "Yes, Lord." 29Then He touched their eyes, saying, "ªIt shall be done to you according to your faith." 30And their eyes were opened. And Jesus sternly warned them: "See that no one knows *about this!*" 31But they went out and spread the news about Him throughout all that land.

32As they were going out, a mute, demon-possessed man ªwas brought to Him. 33After the demon was cast out, the mute man spoke; and the crowds were amazed, *and were* saying, "Nothing like this has ªever been seen in Israel." 34But the Pharisees were saying, "He casts out the demons by the ruler of the demons."

35Jesus was going through all the cities and villages, teaching in their synagogues and proclaiming the gospel of the kingdom, and healing every kind of disease and every kind of sickness.

36Seeing the ªpeople, He felt compassion for them, because they were ᵇdistressed and ᶜdispirited like sheep ᵈwithout a shepherd. 37Then He said to His disciples, "The harvest is plentiful, but the workers are few. 38Therefore beseech the Lord of the harvest to send out workers into His harvest."

9:18 ªOr *one* ᵇLit *ruler* ᶜOr *worshiped* 9:20 ªI.e. tassel fringe with a blue cord ᵇOr *outer garment* 9:21 ªLit *in herself* ᵇLit *be saved* 9:22 ªLit *saved you* ᵇLit *from that hour* ᶜLit *saved* 9:23 ªLit *ruler's* 9:25 ªOr *was raised up* 9:29 ªOr *Let it be done;* Gr command 9:32 ªLit *they brought* 9:33 ªLit *ever appeared* 9:36 ªLit *crowds* ᵇOr *harassed* ᶜLit *thrown down* ᵈLit *not having*

NLT

two blind men followed along behind him, shouting, "Son of David, have mercy on us!"

28They went right into the house where he was staying, and Jesus asked them, "Do you believe I can make you see?"

"Yes, Lord," they told him, "we do."

29Then he touched their eyes and said, "Because of your faith, it will happen." 30Then their eyes were opened, and they could see! Jesus sternly warned them, "Don't tell anyone about this." 31But instead, they went out and spread his fame all over the region.

32When they left, a demon-possessed man who couldn't speak was brought to Jesus. 33So Jesus cast out the demon, and then the man began to speak. The crowds were amazed. "Nothing like this has ever happened in Israel!" they exclaimed.

34But the Pharisees said, "He can cast out demons because he is empowered by the prince of demons."

35Jesus traveled through all the towns and villages of that area, teaching in the synagogues and announcing the Good News about the Kingdom. And he healed every kind of disease and illness. 36When he saw the crowds, he had compassion on them because they were confused and helpless, like sheep without a shepherd. 37He said to his disciples, "The harvest is great, but the workers are few. 38So pray to the Lord who is in charge of the harvest; ask him to send more workers into his fields."

Think of your busiest day. Maybe it included a wedding, the birth of a child, a graduation, a holiday, a vacation, or a funeral. Maybe it was a particularly stressful day on the job, or a family crisis or emergency that drained you in body and mind. Nonstop, fast-paced, barely-treading-water busy. You know the feeling? It's the kind of day that causes you to stumble into bed in a daze and sleep like a log.

Chances are good that you've known several days like that. We often use the image of "putting out fires" to describe such times. A significant, maybe even life-changing, event or serious problem emerged, and you had to pour your whole self out to extinguish it. And while in the midst of putting out that fire, another one erupted into a blaze. You hardly had the chance to get that first flame snuffed before yet another burst on the scene—and then another. Sometimes the flames from one day ignite the next, and the crisis spans the better part of a week.

Jesus faced this sort of busyness in the midst of His Galilean ministry. It seemed there was no end to the lines of needy people, no pause in their groaned requests for help, no break in the demonic attacks or the cries for mercy. He knew what it was like to be constantly "on," living His life entirely for others. There was a difference, however, between our busiest days and those that Jesus faced. The situations He had to deal with always contained an element of the *impossible*. Nobody has ever asked of me the things they were bringing to Jesus. Instantaneous deliverance over those troubles was in the hands of only one man in history.

Beyond the work Jesus did to get His message out and draw people to Himself, He also faced the sneers and jeers of the religious elite standing nearby, taking issue with what He said and did. These weren't simply misguided men who failed to understand. They were increasingly positioning themselves as His enemies, who were there for out-and-out evil purposes—finding fault, casting blame, and questioning motives. As Jesus heaped up overwhelming evidence that He was, in fact, the King, Israel's long-awaited Messiah, many of those who had been eagerly longing for the Messiah were building a case that Jesus was a servant of the devil himself!

— 9:18-22 —

In 9:18, we're dropped right into the middle of the action. With no chance to even catch His breath, Jesus was approached by a leader of the synagogue of Capernaum. The man bowed before Him and with deep emotion begged Jesus to come to his home, lay His hand on his daughter who had just died, and restore her to life. Imagine what some of the critics of Jesus may have thought about their colleague turning traitor on them and appealing to Jesus in his hour of desperation. He would pay a price for just talking to Jesus. But in this moment, that didn't matter, and he bowed down in absolute humility and reverence. Jesus responded as we would expect: He began following the official to his home (9:19).

While on His way through the crowd of people toward the official's home, Jesus was interrupted by a woman who had been hemorrhaging for twelve years (9:20). The Gospel of Mark adds the detail that she "had endured much at the hands of many physicians, and had spent all that she had and was not helped at all, but rather had grown worse" (Mark 5:26). Having heard the news of Jesus' power, the woman reasoned that if she could just touch His garment, she would be healed (Matt. 9:21).

What the woman did would have been regarded by many as a severe breach of propriety. According to Jewish purity laws, her condition rendered her perpetually unclean. Leviticus 15:25-27 says that any woman with a discharge of blood would be in a state of ritual impurity, and "whoever touches [anything that such a woman has sat on or laid upon] shall be unclean and shall wash his clothes and bathe in water and be unclean until evening." Thus, the woman undoubtedly thought she couldn't ask Jesus to heal her by touch, as the synagogue ruler had requested for his daughter.

Matthew's account specifies that the woman actually touched the "fringe of His cloak" (Matt. 9:20). In those days, devout Jews wore an outer tunic that had four tassels, called *tsitsiyōt* (singular *tsitsit* [H6734]), that hung from the hem. This was done in obedience to the Lord's commands in Numbers 15:37-40 and Deuteronomy 22:12. By reaching out and touching just the tassel on the hem of the outer cloak that hung loosely on Jesus' body—without His knowledge—she would be able to keep Him from becoming ritually impure.

No doubt many of the hypersensitive, legalistic Pharisees would have seen no difference between Jesus reaching out and touching the unclean woman and the woman reaching out and touching the fringe of Jesus' outer garment—especially since they were already looking for some kind of basis to accuse Him of breaking the Law. But a literal reading and application of the Law would have shown that Jesus remained ritually pure. The woman's act of reaching out to touch the fringe of His garment not only demonstrated sincere faith in Jesus but also revealed a deep level of respect for Him and for God's Law.

Mark includes the detail that Jesus perceived "power proceeding from Him" when she touched His cloak (Mark 5:30). The irony of this

The *tsitsiyōt* are still worn on the outermost garments of observant Jews today.

miraculous touch shouldn't be missed: Whereas the scribes would have believed that the woman's discreet touch of Jesus' garment imparted to Him ritual impurity, the opposite was true; the touch imparted to the woman Jesus' cleansing power! We shouldn't see this episode as a case of magic. God didn't capitulate to the woman's superstition. In fact, Jesus turned to the woman and said, "Daughter, take courage; your faith has made you well" (Matt. 9:22).

Notice that Jesus addressed the woman gently as "daughter," similar to the way He had addressed the paralytic as "son" (9:2). And just as with the paralytic, He encouraged this woman to "take courage" (Greek *tharseō* [2293]). Note that Jesus isn't merely in the business of imparting physical healings; He is also interested in relating to people personally, ministering to them emotionally, and restoring them spiritually. He is concerned with their *whole being*.

— 9:23-26 —

After continuing to wind His way through the crowded streets of Capernaum, Jesus finally made it to the official's home, where He stepped into chaos. You can imagine the weeping and wailing at the death of a twelve-year-old girl (see Luke 8:42, 52). When Jesus entered the house with Peter, James, John, and the girl's parents (see Luke 8:51), He said to the mourners, "Leave; for the girl has not died, but is asleep" (Matt. 9:24). The fact that professional mourners with funeral music were already present indicates that everybody knew the girl was really dead. When we read of those who laughed at Jesus, we shouldn't picture the actual family members of the girl scoffing at Him, but non-family mourners who had been hired (see Jer. 9:17).[52]

Jesus knew the girl was dead, but by saying that she was only asleep, He boldly affirmed that her condition was temporary. In a moment, He would awaken her from death. In the quietness following the departure of the tumultuous crowd, Jesus took the girl by the hand and lifted her from the bed, very much alive (Matt. 9:25). And though the room had been cleared of people, news of this miracle spread everywhere (9:26).

— 9:27-31 —

As we recall the packed itinerary thus far in Matthew 9, I can imagine Jesus and His disciples were exhausted:

- the paralytic lying on the bed—healed (9:2-8)
- Matthew the tax collector—redeemed (9:9-13)
- the woman with incurable bleeding—cured (9:20-22)
- the daughter who had died—resurrected (9:23-26)

If anybody had earned a breather, it was Jesus. But as He made His way back to where He was staying—likely Peter's home—two blind men followed Him, crying out, "Have mercy on us, Son of David!" (9:27).

For some reason, Jesus wanted to keep the eyewitnesses of His miracles to a small number. He didn't gather crowds, stand on a high platform, and draw attention to Himself prior to healing. Rather, He tended to heal behind closed doors, with just a handful of people present. This explains why Jesus waited until He entered the house where He was staying before acknowledging the cries of the blind men. When Jesus went in, the men didn't bother to knock—they walked right in behind Him. The dialogue Matthew reports was brief. Just a simple affirmation of their faith in His ability to heal them was all it took for Him to give them what they so desperately longed for—He touched their eyes, and they were instantly healed (9:28-30). And the first thing they saw when light broke through their darkened eyes was the face of Jesus!

Again, even though Jesus tried to keep His miraculous healings quiet, the men couldn't contain themselves—they spread the news about Jesus throughout the region (9:31). He might as well have hung a sign outside the door to the house saying, "The Healer Is In" or set up a receptionist in the street shouting, "Next!"

MIRACLES IN HISTORY . . . AND TODAY

MATTHEW 9:35

It's obvious that miracles don't happen every day. A colleague of mine once noted, "If they did, we'd call them 'regulars.'" Even though they seem to be commonplace in the Bible, if we take a closer look, we realize that they're actually quite rare. In fact, God seemed to cluster miracles around bursts of new revelation or during epochal transitions in how He interacted with His people. We can discern three relatively short, extremely remarkable eras during which miracles were particularly concentrated and astonishing:

1. *The Exodus from Egypt, Wilderness Wanderings, and Conquest of Israel.* After four hundred years of silence, God astonished the Egyptians—and the Hebrews—with a series of miraculous events as He freed His covenant people from slavery in Egypt, guided them through the wilderness, and then settled them in the Promised Land.

2. *The Prophetic Ministries of Elijah and Elisha.* In the days of the Israelite kings, after many decades of repeated warnings, God sent these two prophets to turn His people from idolatry. He used miracles to validate that their messages had a divine origin.

3. *The Foundational Ministries of Jesus Christ and the Apostles.* After another four hundred years of silence, God sent His Son with the ability to accomplish miraculous feats that surpassed the miracles of the Old Testament. God then produced miracles through the apostles to validate their message about Jesus Christ, God's Son.

Truly miraculous works of God are rare, having occurred infrequently throughout history. When they have occurred, the purpose of the miracles has usually been to draw attention to God's work in the world or to authenticate the activity or words of His special prophets or apostles.

— 9:32-38 —

The next in line was a man afflicted by a demon that had rendered him unable to speak (9:32). Discerning that the man's problem was spiritual, not physical, Jesus cast the demon out, thus restoring the man's ability to talk (9:33). Here was yet another display of Jesus' divine authority demonstrating that He was, in fact, the long-awaited Messiah. And, of course, here was yet another mouth eager to spread the news that a miraculous healer had taken up residence in Capernaum!

In light of the nonstop daze of miracles, wave after wave of reports was flowing from the epicenter. As soon as one story made its way to the market or living room, another story was heading to the highways and synagogues. The city and region were quickly buzzing with amazement: "Nothing like this has ever been seen in Israel" (9:33).

Because of Jesus' great compassion for the people who were "distressed and dispirited like sheep without a shepherd" (9:36), and because of the overwhelming magnitude of the mission with so few laborers (9:37-38), Jesus launched what might be called the first evangelistic crusade. Matthew says that He traveled "through all the cities and villages, teaching in their synagogues and proclaiming the gospel of the kingdom, and healing every kind of disease and every kind of sickness" (9:35).

But not everybody was on board. Some met Jesus' ministry and message with negative reactions. The sarcastic laughter from the hired mourners and paid flute players can be excused; the girl was, after all, dead, and saying she was just asleep sounded ludicrous (see 9:24). But the caustic conclusion and radical reaction of the hard-hearted Pharisees was inexcusable. In the face of obvious miraculous power—exercised in love and compassion—the likes of which only God could perform, the Pharisees claimed, "He casts out the demons by the ruler of the demons" (9:34). Because they could no longer doubt the existence of His supernatural power, all they could do to avoid bowing to His authority and accepting Him as their King and long-awaited Messiah was to call into question the *source* of His power. In a striking, tragic move, they attributed the power of the God-man to Satan himself!

APPLICATION: MATTHEW 9:18-38
Lord, Liar, or Lunatic?

If you had been standing in the crowd of onlookers in Capernaum during that nonstop day of miracles, you would have been presented with an intellectual dilemma that would call for a decision of your will. Whatever choice you made that day would have a lasting impact on your life. The choice facing first-century eyewitnesses of the Lord's words and works has been classically summed up by C. S. Lewis's "trilemma." Eric Metaxas puts it this way:

C. S. Lewis rather famously said that when it came to deciding who Jesus Christ was, we really only had three choices. First, we could say he was a liar, that all of the things he said were simply lies. Second, we could say he was not a liar but a lunatic, so he couldn't be held responsible for saying the things he said. And third, we could say he was actually who he said he was, the Lord of Heaven and Earth.[53]

If they had their heads on straight, every Jacob, Reuben, Miriam, or Sarah standing anywhere near Jesus that day could have come to the rational conclusion. Jesus couldn't have been insane or a deceiver—how could a madman or a mesmerizer perform those miracles? They weren't simple sleights of hand or entertaining parlor tricks. Jesus wasn't pulling coins out of children's ears or making handkerchiefs disappear. He was healing paralytics, restoring sight to the blind, conquering conditions that medical doctors had only made worse, casting out demons, and raising the dead! All the while, He was claiming to have authority to forgive sins, was demonstrating an ability to see into people's hearts and minds, and was answering to the messianic titles "Son of David" and "Son of God."

But these facts didn't stop the hardheaded and hard-hearted Pharisees from claiming that Jesus' ability to do miracles came directly from Satan himself. This was a spiritual problem, not an intellectual problem. And it's a problem people still have today. In spite of the evidence, people deny the existence of God. And in spite of the compelling claims of Christ, they willfully reject Him as their Savior and Lord. The solution to this spiritual blindness, then, is not another book that presents the evidence or another verbal bludgeoning that tries to argue people into the kingdom. The only One who can soften hearts and break down wills is the Holy Spirit.

Do you ever encounter lost scoffers who laugh about the faith? Pray for the Spirit to cut through their folly and open their eyes both to the seriousness of their condition and to the fittingness of the person and work of Christ. Are you faced with Pharisees who call Jesus a liar, a lunatic, or a legend, who come up with any explanation for the facts except the truth that Jesus is the Lord? Bring their names to God, who alone can shine His light through the darkness of unbelief and clear away the fog of deception.

Listen Well, Think Right, Talk Straight, Travel Light
MATTHEW 10:1-15

NASB

¹Jesus summoned His twelve disciples and gave them authority over unclean spirits, to cast them out, and to heal every kind of disease and every kind of sickness.

²Now the names of the twelve apostles are these: The first, Simon, who is called Peter, and Andrew his brother; and ªJames the son of Zebedee, and ᵇJohn his brother; ³Philip and ªBartholomew; Thomas and Matthew the tax collector; ᵇJames the son of Alphaeus, and Thaddaeus; ⁴Simon the ªZealot, and Judas Iscariot, the one who betrayed Him.

⁵These twelve Jesus sent out after instructing them: "Do not ªgo ᵇin *the* way of *the* Gentiles, and do not enter *any* city of the Samaritans; ⁶but rather go to the lost sheep of the house of Israel. ⁷And as you go, ªpreach, saying, 'The kingdom of heaven ᵇis at hand.' ⁸Heal *the* sick, raise *the* dead, cleanse *the* lepers, cast out demons. Freely you received, freely give. ⁹Do not acquire gold, or silver, or copper for your money belts, ¹⁰or a ªbag for *your* journey, or even two ᵇcoats, or sandals, or a staff; for the worker is worthy of his ᶜsupport. ¹¹And whatever city or village you enter, inquire who is worthy in it, and stay ªat his house until you leave *that city.* ¹²As you enter the ªhouse, give it your ᵇgreeting. ¹³If the house is worthy, ªgive it your *blessing of* peace. But if it is not worthy, ᵇtake

NLT

¹Jesus called his twelve disciples together and gave them authority to cast out evil* spirits and to heal every kind of disease and illness. ²Here are the names of the twelve apostles:

first, Simon (also called Peter),
then Andrew (Peter's brother),
James (son of Zebedee),
John (James's brother),
³ Philip,
Bartholomew,
Thomas,
Matthew (the tax collector),
James (son of Alphaeus),
Thaddaeus,*
⁴ Simon (the zealot*),
Judas Iscariot (who later betrayed him).

⁵Jesus sent out the twelve apostles with these instructions: "Don't go to the Gentiles or the Samaritans, ⁶but only to the people of Israel—God's lost sheep. ⁷Go and announce to them that the Kingdom of Heaven is near.* ⁸Heal the sick, raise the dead, cure those with leprosy, and cast out demons. Give as freely as you have received!

⁹"Don't take any money in your money belts—no gold, silver, or even copper coins. ¹⁰Don't carry a traveler's bag with a change of clothes and sandals or even a walking stick. Don't hesitate to accept hospitality, because those who work deserve to be fed.

¹¹"Whenever you enter a city or village, search for a worthy person and stay in his home until you leave town. ¹²When you enter the home, give it your blessing. ¹³If it turns out to be a worthy home, let your blessing stand; if it is not, take back the

back your *blessing of* peace. ¹⁴Whoever does not receive you, nor heed your words, as you go out of that house or that city, shake the dust off your feet. ¹⁵Truly I say to you, it will be more tolerable for *the* land of Sodom and Gomorrah in the day of judgment than for that city.

10:2 ªOr *Jacob;* James is the Eng form of Jacob ᵇGr *Joannes,* Heb *Johanan* 10:3 ªI.e. son of Talmai (Aram) ᵇOr *Jacob* 10:4 ªOr *Cananaean* 10:5 ªOr *go off* ᵇOr *on the road of* (Gr *hodos: way* or *road*) 10:7 ªOr *proclaim* ᵇLit *has come near* 10:10 ªOr *knapsack,* or *beggar's bag* ᵇOr *inner garments* ᶜLit *nourishment* 10:11 ªLit *there until* 10:12 ªOr *household* ᵇI.e. the familiar Heb blessing, "Peace be to this house!" 10:13 ªLit *your peace is to come upon it* ᵇLit *your peace is to return to you*

blessing. ¹⁴If any household or town refuses to welcome you or listen to your message, shake its dust from your feet as you leave. ¹⁵I tell you the truth, the wicked cities of Sodom and Gomorrah will be better off than such a town on the judgment day.

10:1 Greek *unclean.* 10:3 Other manuscripts read *Lebbaeus;* still others read *Lebbaeus who is called Thaddaeus.* 10:4 Greek *the Cananean,* an Aramaic term for Jewish nationalists. 10:7 Or *has come,* or *is coming soon.*

As we watch Jesus' ministry of powerful miracles and profound messages unfold before our eyes, it's easy to forget a very important priority He had while on earth: the training of the Twelve. After all, He would soon be gone and would leave the work He had begun in their hands.

It's also easy to forget that the Twelve were often nearby, partly because their presence isn't always obvious in Matthew's narrative. They were by Jesus' side throughout His earthly ministry, always watching, frequently learning, occasionally responding. Their training remained at the forefront of His agenda, even though He didn't frequently call attention to it. At times, however, He paused to address them and pass along specific information they were expected not only to remember but also to put into practice after He left them.

The time had come for the disciples to step up and move out into the real world, to face settings similar to those Jesus had been facing and to engage in a ministry similar to that of their Master. Like baby birds being coaxed out of their nest, it was time for the Twelve to spread their wings and face their own struggles in ministry. Next we'll see Jesus delegate authority and empower His handpicked ministry team (10:1-4). He'll prepare them with vital information before sending them out and set forth specific instructions regarding what they could expect and how to accomplish their mission (10:5-15). Though the authority and specific mission of the Twelve was unique and is distinct from ours in the twenty-first century, we can still gain some important principles and insights regarding our own calling and mission today.

— 10:1-4 —

In the immediate context of the sending of the Twelve, Matthew records that Jesus was "going through all the cities and villages, teaching in their synagogues and proclaiming the gospel of the kingdom, and healing every kind of disease and every kind of sickness" (9:35). We've seen how rapidly the ministry was expanding and can envision how exhausting the nonstop activity must have been as Jesus felt compassion for the masses of people and stepped in to relieve their distress (9:36).

As Jesus surveyed the people, who were "like sheep without a shepherd" (9:36), He turned to His disciples and said, "The harvest is plentiful, but the workers are few. Therefore beseech the Lord of the harvest to send out workers into His harvest" (9:37-38). And as is often the case, the ones praying become themselves the answer to the prayer! Until then, the Twelve had been observers of Jesus' ministry. All of a sudden, they were equipped to be engaged in that ministry.

Jesus gathered His team together and extended His divine authority to them, granting them the ability to cast out unclean spirits and to heal sickness and disease—in short, to exercise the kind of miraculous power they had thought could only belong to Jesus (10:1). We need to remember, though, that the only reason the disciples had this ability was because it had been granted to them by the Lord. It was rightfully

THE TWELVE			
MATTHEW 10:2-4	**MARK** 3:16-19	**LUKE** 6:14-16	**ACTS** 1:13
Simon (Peter)	Simon (Peter)	Simon (Peter)	Peter
Andrew James (son of Zebedee) John	James (son of Zebedee) John Andrew	Andrew James (son of Zebedee) John	John James (son of Zebedee) Andrew
Philip	Philip	Philip	Philip
Bartholomew Thomas Matthew	Bartholomew Matthew Thomas	Bartholomew Matthew Thomas	Thomas Bartholomew Matthew
James (son of Alphaeus)	James (son of Alphaeus)	James (son of Alphaeus)	James (son of Alphaeus)
Thaddaeus Simon (the Zealot) Judas Iscariot	Thaddaeus Simon (the Zealot) Judas Iscariot	Simon (the Zealot) Judas (son of James) Judas Iscariot	Simon (the Zealot) Judas (son of James) ----

WERE MATTHEW AND JAMES BROTHERS?

MATTHEW 10:3

Both Matthew and James (not the brother of John) are said to be the "son of Alphaeus" (10:3; Mark 2:14). Hence, some commentators have suggested that Matthew and James were brothers. For example, Michael Green writes,

> It is possible that James the son of Alphaeus shared the fierce, nationalistic patriotism of the Zealots. Most of the common people of Israel did in those days. But his brother, Matthew or Levi, was totally different. He farmed taxes for Herod Antipas. He cooperated with the occupying power that his brother seems to have been set on seeking to overthrow with bloody revolution. The quisling and the freedom fighter were brothers in the same family![54]

However, we can't be sure of this relationship. It may be just a coincidence that these two men on opposite ends of the political spectrum had fathers with the same name. However, it's also possible that Jesus chose two previously estranged brothers—Levi and James—to demonstrate that following Christ can mend broken relationships. Let's imagine this situation in modern terms: One brother is a radical right-winger of the anti-government type . . . the other is a radical, left-wing liberal who works for the IRS! Then one day they both experience the grace of Jesus Christ, abandon their worldly priorities, and find themselves serving the Lord side by side.

Only God knows whether Matthew and James were actual blood brothers or were purely spiritual brothers in Christ. But one thing is certain: Only Christ could change the hearts of people like Matthew and James and call them to minister side by side.

His, but as He called and sent His disciples into ministry, He also supernaturally equipped them.

As if to underscore the fact that these were normal, everyday men who had been granted supernatural authority to carry out their mission, Matthew lists the names of the Twelve in 10:2-4. There's not a single Hercules or Apollo, not a Jason or Achilles, not an Odysseus or Perseus. Not a single demigod, celebrity, or mythical Greek hero in the lot. Rather, there are some blue-collar workers named Simon and Andrew, James and John, Philip and Bartholomew. Then there are the skeptical Thomas and the despicable Matthew—a tax collector, of all things! Add to this James the son of Alphaeus and Thaddaeus, both of whom we know virtually nothing about. Finally, there's another Simon, who has radical tendencies, and the infamous traitor, Judas Iscariot.

What strikes me is the completely unremarkable character of this selection of interns lined up to serve as future leaders. I love how Robert Coleman puts it:

> None of them occupied prominent places in the Synagogue, nor did any of them belong to the Levitical priesthood. For the most part they were common laboring men, probably having no professional training beyond the rudiments of knowledge necessary for their vocation. . . . None of them could have been considered wealthy. They had no academic degrees in the arts and philosophies of their day. . . . By any standard of sophisticated culture then and now they would surely be considered as a rather ragged aggregation of souls.[55]

Let's never forget that this dirty dozen were mere men—with the human faults and failings that characterize all our lives. They were selected not because of what they were, but because of what they were to become by God's empowering grace. We need to be realistic, not romantic, when we envision Jesus' disciples. They were no different from you or me. Therefore, any of us and all of us can roll up our sleeves and get involved as Jesus' harvest workers.

— 10:5-10 —

From 10:5 all the way to the end of the chapter (10:42), Matthew recounts the instructions Jesus gave the disciples prior to sending them out. This includes both positive instructions ("Do this!") and negative commands ("Don't do this!").

First, He told them where to go and where not to go (10:5-6). They were to go only to the Jews—"the lost sheep of the house of Israel"—not to the Gentiles or Samaritans. This first wave of missionary work was focused on the people they knew best—their own kinsmen according to the flesh. They knew their language, their religion, and their culture. For this very first missionary endeavor, Jesus was keeping it simple.

Second, Jesus told them what to say (10:7). We shouldn't be surprised that the essence of their message was the same as Jesus'—"The kingdom of heaven is at hand." This was probably shorthand for a fuller message similar to what Jesus had been teaching in greater detail, perhaps including the call to repent in anticipation of the coming messianic age and to respond with water baptism (see John 3:22; 4:1). The disciples were to present a true extension of Jesus' own preaching ministry, repeating His message and not coming up with their own.

Third, Jesus equipped them to minister to those in great need (Matt.

10:8). By virtue of His own divine authority, Jesus gave them power to do the kinds of miracles that He had been doing up until that point. They were to heal the sick, raise the dead, cleanse lepers, and cast out demons—freely, without the thought of charging for their miraculous acts of mercy. These signs and wonders would be proof that their message was true—the kingdom of the Messiah was imminent!

Fourth, Jesus instructed them to travel lightly, depending on God's provision for their journey (10:9-10). They could have spent days—even weeks—planning, strategizing, outfitting, and fund-raising for the mission. But that would have squelched the urgency and bogged down the disciples. Instead of taking money with them or weighing themselves down with extra supplies, they would have their needs supplied by God through others' generosity.

Now, before going any farther, I need to clarify something. From Jesus' instructions throughout Matthew 10, we learn some important principles we can apply to our own callings and ministries today. However, not everything Jesus said to His disciples applies to us. Two significant differences between the first-century context of the original disciples and our twenty-first-century context need to be underscored.

First, those original disciples had unique apostolic authority (10:1). Jesus gave them special power over unclean spirits and the ability to heal diseases, to raise the dead, and to cleanse lepers (10:8). The Gospel of Luke tells us that at the same time Jesus also extended this same kind of authority to seventy others (Luke 10:1-20). The apostle Paul indicated that he was the "last" and "least" of the apostles (1 Cor. 15:8-9), given special authority to perform "the signs of a true apostle . . . by signs and wonders and miracles" (2 Cor. 12:12).

Second, the mission of those original disciples had a unique scope. They were given a temporary itinerant ministry specifically and exclusively to Jews, not to Samaritans or Gentiles (Matt. 10:5-6). The itinerant nature and limited scope of their mission thus involved elements that appear extreme to us today. They went out with nothing—no planning, no preparation, no supplies, no money (10:9-10). But after Jesus' death and resurrection, the scope of the mission changed for the disciples. Immediately prior to His ascension, Jesus said, "You shall be My witnesses both in Jerusalem, and in all Judea and Samaria, and even to the remotest part of the earth" (Acts 1:8).

So, although we can gain some principles from Jesus' instructions to those original, first-century disciples, we need to recognize that He wasn't speaking directly to us. We must carefully think through the implications and applications of this passage for our twenty-first-century context.

— 10:11-15 —

After selecting the Twelve (10:2-4), Jesus gave them an urgent message (10:7), empowered them with unique authority to do miraculous signs and wonders (10:1, 8), and sent them out with no resources for the journey (10:9-10). As we look at the next set of instructions for their itinerant preaching ministry, we realize that Jesus was teaching them not permanent ministry methods but important lessons about trusting in God's provision.

Just as He would provide them with support from those among whom they ministered (10:10), God would providentially arrange a place for them to stay when they entered each city or village. However, in the case of their lodging, they still needed to be discerning. They were to inquire about "who is worthy" (10:11). R. T. France notes, "They [were] to look for someone able and willing to accommodate them, and this would normally be someone open to their message, though not necessarily already committed to their cause."[56] For the disciples-on-mission to find such "worthy" accommodations in remote cities and villages suggests that God would go ahead of them and prepare the hearts and minds of people on their behalf. They just had to trust the Lord and take Him at His word.

At times, the disciples would be tested. Not everybody would turn out to be as they first appeared. Some would prove to be worthy of the presence of the disciples and receive their blessing (10:12-13), but others would prove to be unworthy of the message, perhaps turning against the disciples or feigning fidelity to the cause. Those who rejected the disciples were actually rejecting the message with which they had been entrusted. In such cases the disciples were to "shake the dust off" their feet as a sign of their rejection of that home, village, or city (10:14). One commentator explains the significance of this act: "Shaking the dust off their feet as they left an inhospitable place symbolized their rejection of the Jewish city as if it were a despised Gentile city, whose very dust was unwanted."[57]

Because the message the disciples were bringing related to the coming kingdom of heaven, Jesus warned of severe consequences for rejecting it and spoke of the need for preparation and repentance. He said, "It will be more tolerable for the land of Sodom and Gomorrah in the day of judgment than for that city" (10:15).

APPLICATION: MATTHEW 10:1-15
Not Apostles, but Still Sent Out

The Greek word *apostolos* [652] literally means "one sent out." Though none of us today can claim to be directly commissioned as an "apostle" like Jesus' original disciples—with their specific mission and special, miraculous abilities—each of us is sent out to engage the world with the message of the gospel of Jesus Christ. How do we apply the very specific sending in Matthew 10 to our own twenty-first-century context?

First, *remember that we have similar motives and methods.* Like Jesus and the disciples, we are to be moved by compassion for the lost and to pray to the Lord of the harvest (9:36-38). At the same time, we need to recognize that, like the disciples, we may become the answers to those prayers. When we realize this, we get motivated to step out and reach out to others.

Second, *remember that the reaping of the harvest is done by all believers.* There are those who are called to be "goers" and those who are called to be "givers." The goers need the givers. If you're not called to be one of the workers of the field in the form of vocational Christian service, then you can give of your resources, just like those unnamed supporters of the disciples' ministry who contributed to the cause (10:9-12).

Third, *remember what we're to model—the character and commitment of Christ.* We need to reflect His authenticity, simplicity, and integrity. We're to be real, not phony—free from hypocrisy, suffering hardship without complaining, and serving with pure motives. That's authenticity. Beyond this, we should live simple lives. We shouldn't engage in ministry for the money or the fame or the pride. We shouldn't pursue an agenda. Finally, we should be men and women of integrity as we're going and serving. Trustworthiness, unselfishness, morality and ethics—these are the things of integrity.

May we be moved by compassion to pray that the Lord will send people into the harvest. May we constantly seek His will for how He wants us to be involved in the project—either as a goer or a giver. And may we always emulate Jesus in authenticity, simplicity, and integrity in everything we do for the advancement of His kingdom.

Sheep among Wolves:
What to Expect
MATTHEW 10:16-31

16 "Behold, I send you out as sheep in the midst of wolves; so ªbe shrewd as serpents and innocent as doves. 17 But beware of men, for they will hand you over to *the* courts and scourge you in their synagogues; 18 and you will even be brought before governors and kings for My sake, as a testimony to them and to the Gentiles. 19 But when they hand you over, do not worry about how or what you are to say; for it will be given you in that hour what you are to say. 20 For it is not you who speak, but *it is* the Spirit of your Father who speaks in you.

21 "Brother will betray brother to death, and a father *his* child; and children will rise up against parents and ªcause them to be put to death. 22 You will be hated by all because of My name, but it is the one who has endured to the end who will be saved.

23 "But whenever they persecute you in ªone city, flee to ᵇthe next; for truly I say to you, you will not finish *going through* the cities of Israel until the Son of Man comes.

24 "A ªdisciple is not above his teacher, nor a slave above his master. 25 It is enough for the disciple that he become like his teacher, and the slave like his master. If they have called the head of the house ªBeelzebul, how much more *will they malign* the members of his household!

26 "Therefore do not fear them, for there is nothing concealed that will not be revealed, or hidden that will not be known. 27 What I tell you in

16 "Look, I am sending you out as sheep among wolves. So be as shrewd as snakes and harmless as doves. 17 But beware! For you will be handed over to the courts and will be flogged with whips in the synagogues. 18 You will stand trial before governors and kings because you are my followers. But this will be your opportunity to tell the rulers and other unbelievers about me.* 19 When you are arrested, don't worry about how to respond or what to say. God will give you the right words at the right time. 20 For it is not you who will be speaking—it will be the Spirit of your Father speaking through you.

21 "A brother will betray his brother to death, a father will betray his own child, and children will rebel against their parents and cause them to be killed. 22 And all nations will hate you because you are my followers.* But everyone who endures to the end will be saved. 23 When you are persecuted in one town, flee to the next. I tell you the truth, the Son of Man* will return before you have reached all the towns of Israel.

24 "Students* are not greater than their teacher, and slaves are not greater than their master. 25 Students are to be like their teacher, and slaves are to be like their master. And since I, the master of the household, have been called the prince of demons,* the members of my household will be called by even worse names!

26 "But don't be afraid of those who threaten you. For the time is coming when everything that is covered will be revealed, and all that is secret will be made known to all. 27 What I tell you now in the darkness, shout

the darkness, speak in the light; and what you hear *whispered* in *your* ear, proclaim upon the housetops. 28 Do not fear those who kill the body but are unable to kill the soul; but rather fear Him who is able to destroy both soul and body in ªhell. 29 Are not two sparrows sold for a ªcent? And *yet* not one of them will fall to the ground apart from your Father. 30 But the very hairs of your head are all numbered. 31 So do not fear; you are more valuable than many sparrows.

10:16 ªOr *show yourselves to be*   10:21 ªLit *put them to death*   10:23 ªLit *this* ᵇLit *the other* 10:24 ªOr *student*   10:25 ªOr *Beezebul:* ruler of demons   10:28 ªGr *Gehenna*   10:29 ªGr *assarion,* the smallest copper coin

abroad when daybreak comes. What I whisper in your ear, shout from the housetops for all to hear!
28 "Don't be afraid of those who want to kill your body; they cannot touch your soul. Fear only God, who can destroy both soul and body in hell.* 29 What is the price of two sparrows—one copper coin*? But not a single sparrow can fall to the ground without your Father knowing it. 30 And the very hairs on your head are all numbered. 31 So don't be afraid; you are more valuable to God than a whole flock of sparrows.

10:18 Or *But this will be your testimony against the rulers and other unbelievers.*   10:22 Greek *on account of my name.*   10:23 "Son of Man" is a title Jesus used for himself.   10:24 Or *Disciples.* 10:25 Greek *Beelzeboul;* other manuscripts read *Beezeboul;* Latin version reads *Beelzebub.* 10:28 Greek *Gehenna.*   10:29 Greek *one assarion* [i.e., one "as," a Roman coin equal to ¹⁄₁₆ of a denarius].

Until the mini-commission and "sending out" of the disciples recorded in Matthew 10, the Twelve listed in 10:2-4 remained, for the most part, behind the scenes. They watched their Master while standing back in security. They were protected from spiritual evil and physical disaster by His loving care and concern. As He taught, they listened in safety; as He dealt with criticism, they never felt threatened. As He healed the sick, cast out demons, and raised the dead, their confidence in His unquestioned authority over all things gave them comfort and confidence.

No longer.

It was time for them to step up and move out into the real world and to face similar settings to those Jesus had been facing. Though their initial assignment would not last long, they would at least get their first taste of real-world ministry, no longer as observers or followers, but as doers and leaders. To give them a realistic understanding of what was soon to happen—as well as what would take place after He departed and left the mission in their hands—Jesus prepared them by outlining the obstacles they would encounter.

He didn't hold back when explaining what lay ahead for them. He told His disciples clearly, up front, that He was sending them out "as sheep in the midst of wolves" (10:16). He then spelled out in vivid terms more specifics about their future. While this information was specifically for the twelve apostles—and the seventy others sent out around the same time—it also relays important practical truths for all of us who are "ones sent out" today.

— 10:16 —

Jesus cared deeply about His disciples. So, like a loving father or mother who prepares a son or daughter to face the world, Jesus shot straight with the Twelve. He knew what they didn't. He saw their eagerness, zeal, and excitement, but also their potential naiveté, imprudence, and recklessness. In the eyes of the Shepherd, the disciples looked like little sheep dancing around in the safety of the pen, unaware of the dangers that lurked just outside the fence and untrained in how to deal with them.

I love how Jesus began His stern warning: "Behold!" (10:16). It's the equivalent of "Listen up!" or "Look here!" He needed their full attention for the serious and sobering warning: "I send you out as sheep in the midst of wolves." Normally, shepherds worried about wolves breaking into their sheep pens and attacking the sheep. Jesus' approach to mission was completely the opposite: He sent the sheep out of the pen and into the world, where wolves were on the loose. He knew sheep are vulnerable, defenseless, easily frightened, and clueless most of the time. Meanwhile, wolves are aggressive, vicious, cunning, unafraid, and ravenous. It was a dangerous mission! But while the disciples may have been like sheep among wolves, Jesus was their defense. On their own, they could never have taken on a single wolf—much less a pack of wolves. But Christ was their ever-present help, extending His power and authority to them to carry out their mission.

Jesus then gave them advice on their demeanor and manner as they went about their mission: They were to be "shrewd as serpents and innocent as doves." The Greek word translated "shrewd" is *phronimos* [5429]. It means "sensible, thoughtful, prudent, wise."[58] Though in the Bible the serpent is often associated with evil, its abilities to slip past predators, hide from sight, and slither away undetected are cast in this context as positive aspects of its nature. However, Jesus balanced this image with the picture of the gentle, innocent dove, often a symbol of peace and purity. A. T. Robertson explains, "The serpent was the emblem of wisdom or shrewdness, intellectual keenness (Ge 3:1; Ps 58:5), the dove of simplicity (Ho 7:11). It was a proverb, this combination, but one difficult of realization. Either without the other is bad (rascality or gullibility)."[59]

Only a balance between the two would serve as protection in the enemy-infested mission field to which the disciples were being sent. It is neither brave nor wise to be abrasive, coarse, retaliatory, inconsiderate, belligerent, or blunt. Verbal abuse is still abuse. Believers are to remain gentle in their tone, gracious in their responses, and disarming in their charm—even in the midst of slavering wolves. At the heart of Jesus' words is the all-important value of inner character, which must be present in the midst of wolves, lest the sheep be torn to shreds in the blink of an eye.

SHREWD AS SERPENTS	INNOCENT AS DOVES
Alert	Gentle
Sharp-minded	Pure
Relevant	Honest
Cautious	Winsome
Discerning	Peaceful

How easy it would have been for the Twelve to think that people in the world would be waiting for them with open arms! Jesus popped that idealistic balloon in Matthew 10:17-31, going into detail about the kind of "wolves" they'd face in their ministry—both during the short-term mission on which they were being sent and throughout their lives. In fact, the three categories of opposition that Jesus outlined are the same as those we face today: religious persecution (10:17), governmental persecution (10:18-20), and domestic, cultural persecution (10:21-31).

— 10:17 —

First, Jesus described the religious persecution His disciples would face. The first place where they would experience backlash was the place of worship and religious instruction—the synagogue. When Jesus mentioned "courts," He was talking about the local Jewish courts connected with the synagogues, not those of the secular government at the time. John Peter Lange notes, "The councils, or Sanhedrim, were the spiritual judicatories connected with the synagogues of the country, where the sentence of scourging pronounced upon heretics was executed."[60] Even under the jurisdiction of the Roman Empire, the Jews had some limited control over their own matters—especially religious matters.

As the Twelve preached and ministered in the name of Jesus among fellow Jews (see 10:6), they would have had every reason to expect their countrymen to accept the miraculous signs and the message of the coming messianic kingdom. But Jesus warned that, for the most part, the opposite would occur. Those in charge would have them arrested, drag them before the religious courts, try them for heresy and blasphemy, and punish them severely.

The Twelve faced this kind of religious persecution throughout the New Testament period, and Christians throughout history have faced this same kind of persecution—frequently at the hands of so-called Christians. Paul warned the elders of Ephesus, "I know that after my departure savage wolves will come in among you, not sparing the flock; and from among your own selves men will arise, speaking perverse things, to draw away the disciples after them" (Acts 20:29-30). The "church" has often been the instigator of persecutions against reformers who, on the basis of the Word of God, pointed out wickedness, hypocrisy, and false teaching. Many have even been put to death because of their message. William Barclay aptly notes, "It has often been true that the man with a message from God has had to undergo the hatred and the enmity of a fossilized orthodoxy."[61]

— 10:18-20 —

Second, Jesus described the governmental persecution His disciples would endure. Not only would they be mistreated at the hands of their fellow Jews, but also "governors and kings" would persecute them (10:18). The term "governors" refers here to first-century Roman procurators like Pilate, Felix, and Festus (27:2; Acts 23:24; 24:27). In later generations, and in our own day, this reference to governmental leadership can be applied to any government official, from a justice of the peace to a city-council member to a judge—anybody who exercises power and enforces policy on behalf of the secular government.

"Kings" would have referred to high officials like the Agrippas, Herod Antipas, or the emperor. The modern equivalent might be a president or dictator, a supreme court, a congress, or a parliament. These institutions exercise great control over the establishment and enforcement of laws, which could be either a boon or a burden for believers.

Notice the reason for the persecution: "for My sake" (Matt. 10:18)—that is, "because you are my followers" (NLT). Christians should not be getting persecuted because they are mean, subversive, or wicked. In fact, Christians should be innocent as doves (10:16). The world will hate Christians because the world hates the Lord Jesus Christ, whom Christians love, worship, and obey (John 15:18-21).

Just when His disciples may have begun to tremble in their sandals, Jesus offered them timely words of encouragement. He highlighted the promise that He wasn't sending them *away* but sending them *out* in His power. He would still be with them. He assured the disciples that even when they were handed over to testify before hostile political powers, God would provide them with the right words to say. In fact, God's Spirit would speak His words through them (Matt. 10:19-20). This promise applied in a particular way to the disciples, who spoke with unique prophetic and apostolic authority—an authority not replicated in any other age. When they opened their mouths, God's infallible words would come forth and would boldly testify concerning Christ. Nonetheless, this promise still has application for us today: The Spirit continues to give us boldness, confidence, and effectiveness as we speak the saving message of Jesus Christ recorded in the inspired Scriptures.

— 10:21-31 —

Third, Jesus described the domestic and cultural persecution His disciples would experience. This warning supplied perhaps the most disheartening news of them all. It was already disappointing that leaders of the disciples' own religious community—the synagogues—would turn against them and their message. Now the warning hit home . . . literally. In 10:21, Jesus tells the disciples that members of their own families would turn against them! Those close relatives would not just ridicule and berate them, disowning or shunning them; they would seethe with such anger that they would betray their believing brothers, children, or parents *to death*!

Jesus again relayed the reason why all this persecution would come their way. The disciples' communities—and society itself—would turn on them and hate them because they claimed the name of Jesus. Amid these somber warnings, Jesus encouraged His followers to persevere when facing even the harshest and deadliest attacks, saying, "It is the one who has endured to the end who will be saved" (10:22). On the other side of death, they would receive a reward for their faithfulness. Some might mistakenly take this to suggest that those who fail to endure persecution will lose their eternal salvation. However, these words were meant to be an encouragement, not a warning. Jesus wasn't saying, "If you just hold out to the end, I'll save you." Rather, the sense is, "Keep persevering even when it seems unbearable, knowing that even if they kill the body, your soul is eternally saved!" As such, it foreshadows Jesus' words in Revelation 2:10: "Be faithful until death, and I will give you the crown of life." It is a statement of fact to bring hope, not an offer of salvation in exchange for good works.

Now, disciples shouldn't intentionally set themselves up for persecution or actively seek it. There's nothing commendable about having a "martyr complex." Jesus advised the Twelve that if they were persecuted in one city and could flee to a different city, then they should do it (Matt. 10:23). This idea reinforces the instructions given a few moments earlier, when Jesus told the disciples to leave places that rejected them, shaking the dust off their feet (10:13-15).

The last clause of 10:23 looks forward to the future coming of the Son of Man. Commentators have gone back and forth on what Jesus meant by the statement "You will not finish going through the cities of Israel until the Son of Man comes." In the limited scope of the disciples' mission here, they did not complete a total canvasing of the cities of Judea. And even after Pentecost, when the early Christians began preaching throughout Judea, the persecution they met with led to their scattering (Acts 8:1-4).

In any case, Jesus' basic point was that there would be a continual and enduring hardening of Jews against the gospel—all the way up to the Second Coming. This fits with Paul's teaching articulated in Romans: "I do not want you, brethren, to be uninformed of this mystery—so that you will not be wise in your own estimation—that a partial hardening has happened to Israel until the fullness of the Gentiles has come in" (Rom. 11:25). It seems, then, that the return of Jesus is connected with the final conversion of Israel, when hard hearts will be softened and the mission to the Jewish people will be met with success (see Rom. 11:15, 26-27). But even though the cities of Israel will continue to pit themselves against the preaching of the gospel until the end, this doesn't mean that the mission should be abandoned. It means that the mission will always be in effect, including in the midst of persecution.

Next, Jesus used a typical Jewish rhetorical device, arguing from the greater to the lesser (Matt. 10:24-25). Because servants or students are not "greater" (in a more privileged position) than their master or teacher, the disciples of Jesus should expect to receive the same kind of treatment that Jesus was receiving. The disciples had already witnessed the criticisms from Jesus' detractors, who claimed, "He casts out the demons by the ruler of the demons" (9:34). Jesus returned to that blasphemous charge and reasoned, "If they have called the head of the house Beelzebul, how much more will they malign the members of his household!" (10:25). In essence, Jesus was saying, "When it comes to persecution for the sake of the good news, *welcome to My world!*"

How easy it would have been for the disciples to just opt out at this point. Persecution? Suffering? Rejection? Scourging? Death? No way! Knowing the human tendency toward fear rather than faith, Jesus ministered to His disciples with encouraging words. Three times He told them, "Do not fear" (10:26, 28, 31). Why not fear in this mission of being sheep among wolves? Jesus gave three main reasons. First, God wants His message revealed, not concealed (10:26-27). Therefore, He would see to it that they were protected and that His word would be proclaimed. Second, even if the enemies of the gospel succeeded at putting His witnesses to death, they would continue on to eternal life (10:28). It is the persecutors who should be afraid—of God's eternal judgment! Third, God never ceases to love and care for His disciples even in the midst of great trials and tribulations. God is sovereign and providentially cares for even the sparrows (10:29). God is omniscient and knows even the number of hairs on a person's head (10:30). Because of God's omnipotence, omniscience, and benevolence, the disciples could have confidence that He will never abandon or forsake His own (10:31).

APPLICATION: MATTHEW 10:16-31

Sent Out, but Not Sent Away

Sometimes when Jesus sends us out into foreign—even hostile—territory, we can feel like we're being sent away to fend for ourselves. Nothing could be further from the truth. Yes, all of us are being sent *out*, but none of us are being sent *away*. With this truth as a backdrop, what practical principles can we glean from this passage? I can think of two important reminders.

First, *we can expect treatment similar to that of the initial disciples.* In 2 Timothy 3:11-12, Paul says, "What persecutions I endured, and out of them all the Lord rescued me! Indeed, all who desire to live godly in Christ Jesus will be persecuted." Don't be surprised when it happens. Perhaps it will be mild—rejection from family and friends, or insults from neighbors and co-workers. Perhaps it will be severe—official repression or persecution from a local or national government. In any case, know that you're in good company. Jesus was persecuted at every level, and so were His initial followers. We have no reason to expect different treatment. Be grateful during times of relief from mistreatment, but when persecution comes, don't be surprised.

Second, *we don't have to be afraid.* Remember, we aren't being sent *away* but sent *out.* When we're given the orders to roll out and cast off into whatever mission field Christ has for us, we're not sent away with nothing. In fact, we're given everything we need; Jesus' promise still stands: "All authority has been given to Me in heaven and on earth. Go therefore and make disciples of all the nations, baptizing them in the name of the Father and the Son and the Holy Spirit, teaching them to observe all that I commanded you; and lo, I am with you always, even to the end of the age" (Matt. 28:18-20). In Hebrews 13:5, God says, "I will never desert you, nor will I ever forsake you." We can count on the fact that even though we're sent out as "sheep in the midst of wolves" (Matt. 10:16), Christ is at our side to strengthen us, encourage us, and bind our wounds when the world treats us poorly.

A Serious Checklist for Disciples
MATTHEW 10:32-42

NASB

32 "Therefore everyone who ᵃconfesses Me before men, I will also confess ᵇhim before My Father who is in heaven. 33 But whoever ᵃdenies Me before men, I will also deny him before My Father who is in heaven.

34 "Do not think that I came to ᵃbring peace on the earth; I did not come to bring peace, but a sword. 35 For I came to SET A MAN AGAINST HIS FATHER, AND A DAUGHTER AGAINST HER MOTHER, AND A DAUGHTER-IN-LAW AGAINST HER MOTHER-IN-LAW; 36 and A MAN'S ENEMIES WILL BE THE MEMBERS OF HIS HOUSEHOLD.

37 "He who loves father or mother more than Me is not worthy of Me; and he who loves son or daughter more than Me is not worthy of Me. 38 And he who does not take his cross and follow after Me is not worthy of Me. 39 He who has found his ᵃlife will

NLT

32 "Everyone who acknowledges me publicly here on earth, I will also acknowledge before my Father in heaven. 33 But everyone who denies me here on earth, I will also deny before my Father in heaven.

34 "Don't imagine that I came to bring peace to the earth! I came not to bring peace, but a sword.

35 'I have come to set a man against his father,
a daughter against her mother,
and a daughter-in-law against her mother-in-law.
36   Your enemies will be right in your own household!'*

37 "If you love your father or mother more than you love me, you are not worthy of being mine; or if you love your son or daughter more than me, you are not worthy of being mine. 38 If you refuse to take up your cross and follow me, you are not worthy of being mine. 39 If you cling to your

lose it, and he who has lost his ªlife for My sake will find it.

⁴⁰ "He who receives you receives Me, and he who receives Me receives Him who sent Me. ⁴¹ He who receives a prophet in *the* name of a prophet shall receive a prophet's reward; and he who receives a righteous man in the name of a righteous man shall receive a righteous man's reward. ⁴² And whoever in the name of a disciple gives to one of these ªlittle ones even a cup of cold water to drink, truly I say to you, he shall not lose his reward."

10:32 ªLit *will confess in Me* ᵇLit *in him*
10:33 ªLit *will deny*   10:34 ªLit *cast*   10:39 ªOr *soul*   10:42 ªI.e. humble

life, you will lose it; but if you give up your life for me, you will find it.

⁴⁰ "Anyone who receives you receives me, and anyone who receives me receives the Father who sent me. ⁴¹ If you receive a prophet as one who speaks for God,* you will be given the same reward as a prophet. And if you receive righteous people because of their righteousness, you will be given a reward like theirs. ⁴² And if you give even a cup of cold water to one of the least of my followers, you will surely be rewarded."

10:35-36 Mic 7:6.   10:41 Greek *receive a prophet in the name of a prophet.*

Throughout our lives, we face different levels of problems, from simple things like changing a tire to difficult challenges like completing a degree to exceedingly complex challenges like raising children. In all these cases, though, checklists can help. Checklists break down problems and tasks into specific steps to take toward their resolution or completion. They remove the need to rely on our memories or intuition. They force us to keep the essentials in mind and to keep our eyes on the goal. And they increase the likelihood of success. Of course, a checklist doesn't guarantee the desired outcome, but it can definitely keep us moving in the right direction.

When Jesus prepared to send the Twelve on their first assignment to minister without Him, He knew they would face challenges. Each of the disciples was unique. None had ever done anything like this before. And the general public didn't know them and wouldn't trust them. Since they were inexperienced and unknown, the obstacles they would face and the persecution they would endure would likely be demoralizing. So to soften the blow of the "ministry shock" they were about to experience, Jesus gave them a kind of checklist.

Two words describe the checklist Jesus gave to His disciples: *painfully honest*. Anyone hearing this checklist would have all doubt removed regarding the seriousness of representing the Master before a watching world. It would not be easy. In fact, it would be exacting. As we work our own way through the checklist, it would be a good time for us to pause and ask ourselves the questions Isaac Watts asked in one of his hymns:

Am I a soldier of the cross?
A foll'wer of the Lamb?
And shall I fear to own His cause
Or blush to speak His name?[62]

Jesus was like a commander preparing His platoon for spiritual combat. There was no room for "making them feel good" about their situation. They needed to think realistically about it. In helping them do this, Jesus pointed to four vital qualities of a loyal disciple enlisted in the Master's service. The four principles given here are essential for claiming victory on the battlefield.

— 10:32-33 —

The first item on the checklist: *Loyal disciples openly acknowledge Christ before the world.* The faithful soldier isn't ashamed to identify with Christ or hesitant to confess Him as Savior and Lord. The Greek term translated "confess" in Matthew 10:32 is *homologeō* [3670], which means to "acknowledge" or "agree."[63] Some people incorrectly define "confessing" as merely assenting to something verbally. But the language used here to communicate the idea of acknowledging Christ is stronger than this. James 2:19 addresses those with a false, paper-thin confession: "You believe that God is one. You do well; the demons also believe, and shudder." The demons believe in the fact of God's existence without doubt. But instead of loving Him and acknowledging His lordship, they simply tremble in fear.

In the New Testament, confessing Christ is closely associated with believing in Him unto salvation. Romans 10:9-10 says, "If you confess with your mouth Jesus as Lord, and believe in your heart that God raised Him from the dead, you will be saved; for with the heart a person believes, resulting in righteousness, and with the mouth he confesses, resulting in salvation." Thus, confessing Christ in Matthew 10:32-33 means more than just giving an objective nod to the fact of His existence. True confession of Christ means fully identifying with Him in word and action—the fruit of true salvation by grace alone through genuine faith alone in Christ alone.

So, in Jesus' first checklist item, He urged His disciples, who were His representatives, to acknowledge Him before others and to persuade others to acknowledge Him as Savior and Lord. They were to leave no doubt in people's minds about where they stood. Nobody should wonder, *Is Matthew (or Peter, or John) really a follower of Jesus?* To emphasize the importance of maintaining consistency between faith and confession of that faith, Jesus flipped the urging into a warning: "Whoever denies Me before men, I will also deny him before My Father who is in heaven" (10:33). People deny Christ by their words (denouncing Him before others), by their actions (living as if Jesus isn't Lord of their lives), or by their silence (refusing to speak up when they could share the gospel).

Whenever we make our faith known, we are entering battle. That was true in Jesus' day, and it's true in ours. People often don't want to see or hear anything about our faith. It's not considered politically correct or culturally appropriate to preach the gospel. In fact, we can set off a firestorm of controversy just by saying "in Jesus' name" after a public prayer. The very real prospect of opposition may be why Jesus immediately transitioned into a discussion of the social and family conflict that erupts when we consistently and boldly confess Christ in our words and actions.

— 10:34-36 —

Now we move on to the second item on Jesus' checklist: *Loyal disciples willingly accept rejection, even from their own families.* When we openly acknowledge our identity as Christ followers through words and actions (10:32-33), we shouldn't be surprised when social conflict ensues. When Christ returns and sets everything right, peace will reign across the globe. All nations will acknowledge the kingship of Jesus. But until then, our expressed commitment to Christ will not result in increasing peace and harmony. Instead, it will bring division, disharmony, misunderstanding, and the harshest kinds of rejection and persecution. In His first coming, Christ did not come to immediately usher in the messianic age of peace and prosperity (10:34). Rather, during His time on earth—and during the subsequent age of the church—spiritual warfare would ensue, manifested in godless cultures and in conflict among those in even the closest relationships.

Christians shouldn't deliberately seek conflict with family members. In fact, Paul says, "If possible, so far as it depends on you, be at peace with all men" (Rom. 12:18). But even those words suggest that it won't always be possible. We must willingly accept conflict with friends and family if it occurs. And it does. I've often heard of parents turning against their sons or daughters because of their strong commitment to Christ. Sometimes the opposition is mild: "Believe what you want, just don't become a fanatic." The problem is, "fanatic" in their minds often means going to church frequently, reading the Bible, praying, and sharing Christ with others—the things a normal Christian should do. At other times, the family of a committed believer might be downright hostile: "You're dead to us!" I've heard of parents disowning children, breaking off contact with them, or constantly making malicious, ugly comments about their faith. And in some parts of the world, conversion to Christianity is tantamount to treason against one's country and is considered the worst kind of betrayal of one's people. In those cases, physical harm or even death might result.

Jesus wasn't sugarcoating the life of discipleship. He was preparing His followers for what was ahead. Faithfulness to Jesus Christ can set family members at variance. This isn't because the gospel is wicked, intrusive, hateful, or intolerant. In fact, just the opposite! In Matthew 10:35-36, Jesus paraphrased Micah 7:6, a Scripture that presents a general picture of the wickedness of the world, which has turned its back on God and rejected His prophets (see Mic. 7:1-6). Conflict arises because of the invasion of truth and righteousness into a world of falsehood and wickedness. We are called to seek peace with family, friends, and our communities whenever possible (see, for example, Exod. 20:12; Eph. 6:1-3; Heb. 12:14). But division will inevitably occur between those who embrace the lordship of Christ and those who don't.

This regrettable state of strained and broken relationships due to our confession of Christ as Savior and Lord leads to Jesus' next exhortation.

— 10:37-39 —

The third item on Christ's checklist is this: *Loyal disciples sacrificially choose their essential priorities.* Fidelity to Christ will be neither easy nor popular. In Matthew 10:37-39, we see that it calls for a complete reversal of the world's priorities, passions, and pursuits. The world tells us to be concerned about ourselves, our own lives, our own interests, our own identities, our own families, our own peace and security, and our own possessions. The world feeds the insatiable beast of *self*. But the call of Christ puts Jesus alone on the throne of our lives.

This doesn't mean that we should hate everything else in life. Jesus is not suggesting that we shouldn't love our parents and our children. But we're not to love them more than we love Christ. In the present context, this applies to situations in which our non-Christian parents or unbelieving children may be hostile toward our faith in Christ and demand

CARRYING YOUR CROSS

MATTHEW 10:38

Though crucifixion had been common in the ancient Near East for some time prior to the first century, the Romans took particular advantage of this horrific form of torturous execution in order to provide a deterrent against crime, especially against insurrection. To do this, they made crucifixion into a spectacle by parading the condemned through densely populated parts of the city, carrying their own implement of torture—the crossbeam (Latin *patibulum*) that would be affixed to the permanent stake (Latin *stipes*) at the site of public execution (see 27:32; John 19:17).[64]

By telling His disciples that a worthy follower had to "take his cross and follow after" Him (Matt. 10:38), Jesus made it clear that the kingdom of heaven and righteousness that He was bringing would not be understood by the authorities as a boon for the kingdoms of this world. One commentator notes, "If Jesus and his followers were to be taken for revolutionaries and arrested by the Romans, this kind of death was possible."[65] Yet even with the possibility of being mistaken for violent zealots—and suffering the customary punishment—they were not to change their countercultural message.

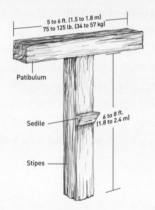

5 to 6 ft. (1.5 to 1.8 m)
75 to 125 lb. (34 to 57 kg)

Patibulum

Sedile

6 to 8 ft.
(1.8 to 2.4 m)

Stipes

Robert Gaither

Illustration of a Cross. The *patibulum* (crossbeam), which would be carried by the victim, was attached to the *stipes* (vertical member) at the site of crucifixion with a mortise-and-tenon joint, which allowed the Romans to dismantle the cross for the next victim more easily. Sometimes, to delay death and to prolong the victim's agony, the executioner attached a *sedile* (seat) between the victim's legs.

Even if the disciples' self-sacrificial service did not end in actual arrest and crucifixion, Jesus' words would have still carried the general sense that they should be willing to bear the burden of suffering "the cares and troubles of life"—up to and including the cross.[66] In other words, this can be seen as an example of arguing from the greater to the lesser: If you're willing to suffer crucifixion for Christ, you should be willing to suffer any lesser hardship or discomfort.

that we set it aside for the sake of the family. As tragic as that situation is, the response of the loyal disciple is clear: Faithfulness to Christ calls for a commitment to Him that supersedes all other commitments.

Jesus drew on a vivid image that would have been all too familiar in the minds of His first-century hearers: taking up a cross (10:38). Remember, when Jesus uttered those words, He was probably still a couple of years away from His own crucifixion. How would His original disciples have understood this comment? R. T. France explains, "Crucifixion itself was not an uncommon sight in Roman Palestine; 'cross-bearing' language would have a clear enough meaning, even before they realized how literally he himself was to exemplify it."[67]

Even without knowing about the coming crucifixion and death that Christ would endure for the sins of the world, the disciples knew that Jesus was calling for a willingness to give up *everything*. Even their own lives. *Even through the most excruciating, humiliating suffering of their day.* John Peter Lange elaborates: "Crucifixion was the worst kind of punishment then known; hence the phrase, *to take his cross*, signifies the voluntary readiness to suffer the utmost in this world for Christ."[68]

Yet Jesus didn't just leave them with the prospect of dragging a cross to their own crucifixions. Instead, He reminded them that if they lost their lives for the sake of the kingdom, they would gain eternal rewards (10:39). A. B. Bruce puts it this way: "Crucifixion, death ignominious, as a criminal—horrible; but horrible though it be it means salvation. This paradox is one of Christ's great, deep, yet ever true words."[69]

Self-denial is a discipline that never comes easily and is never fully understood by others. If you take it up, though you appear to others to be walking through life as a constant loser, in the end, *you win!* I love how Douglas O'Donnell puts it:

> If you are doing everything in your power "to make it"—to get the perfect spouse, the lucrative job, the big house, and all the right connections, guess what? You lose. The biggest gainers are the biggest losers. But if you are willing to come to Jesus as King and give him your life . . . then (and this is the beautiful irony of the kingdom life) you will find life, true life in this life and true life (and reward) in the life to come.[70]

— 10:40-42 —

There is one final item on Christ's checklist in this passage: *Loyal disciples experience the blessing of union with Christ.* How valuable it is to remember that Christ indwells His people! He doesn't forsake them when He sends them on their mission. He's with them, among them, within them. In fact, whenever someone receives a disciple and/or their message, it is as though they are receiving Christ Himself—and, by association, God the Father (10:40).

As the disciples worked their way into remote villages, those who received them, who showed hospitality and benevolence toward Jesus' prophetic messengers of righteousness, would receive blessings similar to those the messengers themselves would receive (10:41-42). Hebrews 6:10 echoes this teaching: "God is not unjust so as to forget your work and the love which you have shown toward His name, in having ministered and in still ministering to the saints."

These final statements hearken back to Jesus' remarks about the welcome the disciples would receive (or not receive) upon entering various cities and villages (Matt. 10:11-15). While in the earlier passage Jesus commented specifically on the judgment that awaits the inhospitable, here He reflected on the rewards for those who do receive His messengers.

APPLICATION: MATTHEW 10:32-42
Reward Awaits You!

Though Jesus covered some pretty rough territory in His serious checklist for disciples, He also alluded a couple of times to the glorious promise of irrevocable reward (10:32, 40-42). What great news for those engaged in the raging spiritual battle!

Your courage to acknowledge Jesus publicly (10:32-33) will be rewarded. Your willingness to accept rejection even from family members (10:34-36) will be rewarded. Your self-denial and self-sacrificial living, even when it could mean suffering and death (10:37-39), will be rewarded. And your generosity, hospitality, and benevolence toward other messengers of Christ (10:40-42) will be rewarded. By the grace of God, awards await us for our loyalty in serving as Christ's willing disciples.

The implication and application is clear: *Press on!* Get over rejection from strangers, friends, and family members. You'll receive a reward! Sacrifice your own passions, priorities, and pursuits. You'll receive a reward! Take time for the "least" among you who are neglected, suffering, oppressed, and downtrodden. You'll receive a reward! It may not be revealed exactly what the eternal reward will look like, but we can be sure of one thing: It will make everything we endure in this life worth it. As Paul said in Romans 8:18, "I consider that the sufferings of this present time are not worthy to be compared with the glory that is to be revealed to us."

The Juxtaposing of Jesus and John
MATTHEW 11:1-19

NASB

[1] When Jesus had finished [a]giving instructions to His twelve disciples, He departed from there to teach and [b]preach in their cities.

[2] Now when John, [a]while imprisoned, heard of the works of Christ, he sent *word* by his disciples [3] and said to Him, "Are You the [a]Expected One, or shall we look for someone else?" [4] Jesus answered and said to them, "Go and report to John what you hear and see: [5] *the* BLIND RECEIVE SIGHT and *the* lame walk, *the* lepers are cleansed and *the* deaf hear, *the* dead are raised up, and *the* POOR HAVE THE [a]GOSPEL PREACHED TO THEM. [6] And blessed is he [a]who does not [b]take offense at Me."

[7] As these men were going *away*, Jesus began to speak to the crowds about John, "What did you go out into the wilderness to see? A reed shaken by the wind? [8] [a]But what did you go out to see? A man dressed in soft *clothing*? Those who wear soft *clothing* are in kings' [b]palaces! [9] [a]But what did you go out to see? A prophet? Yes, I tell you, and one who is more than a prophet. [10] This is the one about whom it [a]is written,

NLT

[1] When Jesus had finished giving these instructions to his twelve disciples, he went out to teach and preach in towns throughout the region.

[2] John the Baptist, who was in prison, heard about all the things the Messiah was doing. So he sent his disciples to ask Jesus, [3] "Are you the Messiah we've been expecting,* or should we keep looking for someone else?"

[4] Jesus told them, "Go back to John and tell him what you have heard and seen—[5] the blind see, the lame walk, those with leprosy are cured, the deaf hear, the dead are raised to life, and the Good News is being preached to the poor." [6] And he added, "God blesses those who do not fall away because of me.*"

[7] As John's disciples were leaving, Jesus began talking about him to the crowds. "What kind of man did you go into the wilderness to see? Was he a weak reed, swayed by every breath of wind? [8] Or were you expecting to see a man dressed in expensive clothes? No, people with expensive clothes live in palaces. [9] Were you looking for a prophet? Yes, and he is more than a prophet. [10] John is the man to whom the Scriptures refer when they say,

'BEHOLD, I SEND MY MESSENGER
ᵇAHEAD OF YOU,
WHO WILL PREPARE YOUR WAY
BEFORE YOU.'

¹¹Truly I say to you, among those born of women there has not arisen *anyone* greater than John the Baptist! Yet the one who is ᵃleast in the kingdom of heaven is greater than he. ¹²From the days of John the Baptist until now the kingdom of heaven ᵃsuffers violence, and violent men ᵇtake it by force. ¹³For all the prophets and the Law prophesied until John. ¹⁴And if you are willing to accept *it,* John himself is Elijah who ᵃwas to come. ¹⁵He who has ears to hear, ᵃlet him hear.

¹⁶"But to what shall I compare this generation? It is like children sitting in the market places, who call out to the other *children,* ¹⁷and say, 'We played the flute for you, and you did not dance; we sang a dirge, and you did not ᵃmourn.' ¹⁸For John came neither eating nor drinking, and they say, 'He has a demon!' ¹⁹The Son of Man came eating and drinking, and they say, 'Behold, a gluttonous man and a ᵃdrunkard, a friend of tax collectors and ᵇsinners!' Yet wisdom is vindicated by her deeds."

11:1 ᵃOr *commanding* ᵇOr *proclaim* 11:2 ᵃLit *in prison* 11:3 ᵃLit *Coming One* 11:5 ᵃOr *good news* 11:6 ᵃLit *whoever* ᵇOr *stumble over Me* 11:8 ᵃOr *Well then,* ᵇLit *houses* 11:9 ᵃOr *Well then,* 11:10 ᵃLit *has been written* ᵇLit *before your face* 11:11 ᵃOr *less* 11:12 ᵃOr *is forcibly entered* ᵇOr *seize it for themselves* 11:14 ᵃOr *is going to come* 11:15 ᵃOr *hear!* Or *listen!* 11:17 ᵃLit *beat the breast* 11:19 ᵃOr *wine-drinker* ᵇI.e. irreligious Jews

'Look, I am sending my messenger ahead of you, and he will prepare your way before you.'*

¹¹"I tell you the truth, of all who have ever lived, none is greater than John the Baptist. Yet even the least person in the Kingdom of Heaven is greater than he is! ¹²And from the time John the Baptist began preaching until now, the Kingdom of Heaven has been forcefully advancing,* and violent people are attacking it. ¹³For before John came, all the prophets and the law of Moses looked forward to this present time. ¹⁴And if you are willing to accept what I say, he is Elijah, the one the prophets said would come.* ¹⁵Anyone with ears to hear should listen and understand!

¹⁶"To what can I compare this generation? It is like children playing a game in the public square. They complain to their friends,

¹⁷ 'We played wedding songs,
   and you didn't dance,
so we played funeral songs,
   and you didn't mourn.'

¹⁸For John didn't spend his time eating and drinking, and you say, 'He's possessed by a demon.' ¹⁹The Son of Man,* on the other hand, feasts and drinks, and you say, 'He's a glutton and a drunkard, and a friend of tax collectors and other sinners!' But wisdom is shown to be right by its results."

11:3 Greek *Are you the one who is coming?* 11:6 Or *who are not offended by me.* 11:10 Mal 3:1. 11:12 Or *the Kingdom of Heaven has suffered from violence.* 11:14 See Mal 4:5. 11:19 "Son of Man" is a title Jesus used for himself.

There's an all-too-familiar syndrome that poisons our expectations, leading to disappointment and doubt. It goes like this: We set our hearts on something we long for and think will occur. Perhaps we trust somebody to do something, to be something, or to say something. As we turn it over in our minds, we mentally see it playing out just as we hope. Our anticipation grows into confident expectation. In fact, we become so sure that it's going to happen, nothing can dissuade us. It's only a matter of time before the imagined scenario comes to pass.

But that's a vulnerable place to be. Instead of mentally tapping the brakes and recalculating our perception, we allow our emotions free rein, which fuels further expectations. Finally, imagination gives way to reality. And things almost *never* turn out the way we expect once we have built them up in our minds. Those high expectations often crash and burn, leaving us under a cloud of disappointment. And if that cloud of disappointment hangs over us long enough, disillusionment sets in, which swings open the door to doubt. We've all been there, haven't we?

As Jesus' disciples were sent out to preach, perform miracles, and proclaim the coming kingdom, the fame of the coming King spread far and wide. Yet the way the kingdom was advancing—with at least as much rejection as acceptance—led some of the most stalwart early supporters to begin doubting whether Jesus was really the long-expected Messiah. Such disappointment and doubt would have been understandable among the ruling elite, who had every reason to despise somebody whose very existence was a threat to their own power. But when the disillusionment affected even John the Baptizer and his disciples, that's a little more difficult to understand. We'll see how Jesus responded to John's doubts, which will give us insight into how He responds to our doubts today.

— 11:1-3 —

The Bible tells the truth about its heroes and spiritual leaders—including some not-so-glorious aspects. This makes sense, because no one moves from earth to heaven without struggling against the flesh. And nobody embraces the life of faith without occasional doubts.

Doubts never just drop in from nowhere. Rather, a set of circumstances leads us to begin to question things we thought we knew and the reasons we thought we knew them. This happened to John the Baptizer and his disciples just as Jesus' ministry was really taking off.

Recall the context: Jesus has just given sobering instructions to His disciples prior to sending them out to preach to the people of Israel that "the kingdom of heaven is at hand" (10:7). He gave them authority over wicked spirits, the ability to heal diseases, and even the power to raise the dead—all on His behalf (10:1, 8). Now, as Matthew 11:1 says, "When

Jesus had finished giving instructions to His twelve disciples, He departed from there to teach and preach in their cities." Jesus and His disciples split up temporarily. Mark 6:30 records that they later regathered and the disciples reported "all that they had done and taught." But during their mission He traveled to "their cities"—probably referring to the cities in the area of Capernaum where most of the disciples had grown up.

While this was going on, John the Baptizer was still sitting in prison. John's career as the forerunner of the Messiah had come to a sudden end. You may recall the events leading up to John's unjust imprisonment. Herod Antipas had seduced and married his own brother's wife after divorcing his original wife. For this immoral action, John the Baptizer had justly rebuked Herod—publicly. In response, Herod had John arrested and thrown into a dungeon (Matt. 4:12; see 14:1-5). There he languished, possibly expecting each day to wake up to the news that the Messiah had finally overthrown not only the wicked Herod but also all the kingdoms of this godless world. John knew one thing for sure: When the Messiah's long-awaited kingdom arrived, the prison doors would be flung open and the oppressed would go free!

In that dank hole of a prison, John's own disciples reported some of the things they had seen and heard about Jesus (11:2). Because the information was secondhand, the picture John had would have been a little sketchy. Yes, he heard of the miracles, healings, exorcisms, preaching, and teaching . . . but he probably also heard about the controversy, conflict, and rejection that had already beset Jesus' ministry. So the reports John heard were likely a mixed bag.

John's ministry had been one of preparation for the coming of the Messiah. If Jesus was the long-expected Messiah, the King of Israel, why did it seem like the kingdom hadn't begun? Why did the ministry of Jesus and the disciples look a lot like John the Baptizer's ministry of preparation? R. V. G. Tasker characterizes John's outlook well: "He was becoming impatient and beginning to wonder why Jesus was not asserting His messianic claims more forcibly and more openly. He was perhaps also expecting that if Jesus was the Messiah, He would secure his release from prison."[71]

John sat alone with his thoughts and remembered what he himself had preached about the Messiah—baptism with fire, righting wrongs, turning the world right-side up. But his situation, which never improved, told a different story. And he got to wondering, *Is Jesus just another forerunner like me? Is Jesus' ministry just an extension of the "voice of one crying in the wilderness"?* With thoughts like these running through his head, John sent his own disciples to Jesus with a question: "Are You the Expected One, or shall we look for someone else?" (11:3).

When the expectations that had built up in his imagination were failing, John slipped into disillusionment and doubt.

— 11:4-11 —

John the Baptizer's bout with doubt wasn't born of a disdain for Jesus and His ministry or a hard-hearted rejection of His messianic claims. No, his doubts came when his genuine faith in Jesus faced circumstances that were at odds with his expectations of what it meant for Jesus to be the Messiah. Because John's doubt arose in the context of faith, Jesus responded gently. His response had two components, one directed toward John's disciples and one directed toward the crowd.

First, Jesus responded by answering John's questions with evidence (11:4-6). The Gospel of Luke makes it clear that Jesus performed astonishing miracles at the "very time" the followers of John the Baptizer came to Him with John's question (Luke 7:21). Jesus was proving a point. Anybody could claim to be anything. How easy it would be for a charlatan or a lunatic to say, "I'm the Messiah." In fact, in the first and second centuries, several people claimed to be the Messiah. But Jesus backed up the claim with the works of the Messiah. He instructed the disciples of John to return to the dungeon and report what they saw and heard with their own eyes and ears: "The blind receive sight and the lame walk, the lepers are cleansed and the deaf hear, the dead are raised up, and the poor have the gospel preached to them" (Matt. 11:5).

Yes, Jesus wasn't meeting John's expectations regarding the *timing* of the full advent of the messianic kingdom. But Jesus knew things John didn't. He knew of His impending atoning death and miraculous resurrection. He knew of His commissioning of the apostles and His ascension to the right hand of the Father. He knew of the coming of the Holy Spirit at Pentecost, the establishment of the church, and the preaching of the gospel throughout the church age. He knew about the mission to the Gentiles and the conversion of believers in the centuries to come—including you and me. He knew of His second coming, when He would finally bring about the perfect kingdom John the Baptizer and all the Jews of the first century were hoping for. John wasn't wrong in his picture of what the messianic age would look like; he was just wrong about the timing of the events.

Notice what Jesus didn't do in response to John's doubts. He didn't blame or shame John for doubting. He didn't rebuke him for voicing his concerns and asking his question. He didn't lecture him in a condescending tone, pull a "you don't know what you're talking about" attitude, or remind him of who was in charge of the timing and who wasn't. Rather, He simply sent the messengers back to report what they had seen and heard.

EXCURSUS: PROPHETIC TELESCOPING

MATTHEW 11:4-11

John the Baptizer wasn't alone in expecting the immediate advent of the messianic kingdom on earth. His perspective was similar to that of the Old Testament prophets, who didn't have a clear picture of God's full plan. The prophets saw, as it were, two mountain peaks, which in retrospect we might call Mount Golgotha and Mount Olivet. On Golgotha the Messiah would die in humility and disgrace (see Mark 15:22-25); on Olivet He would return in glory and power (Zech. 14:4). They saw the peaks, but from their vantage point they couldn't see the great valley that stretched between the two mountains. This valley represents the present age of the church.

The Old Testament believers were also at a disadvantage in that they didn't have the permanent indwelling of the Holy Spirit as we do today. The Spirit of God spoke through the prophets, igniting their message, but they had not experienced spiritual baptism into the body of Christ (1 Cor. 12:12-13; Eph. 3:4-6). Today the Spirit works to empower us with faith and hope as in no other era. With the cross behind us and the crown of glory before us, we are encouraged to press on.

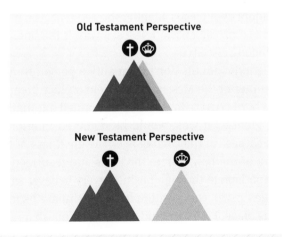

Old Testament Perspective

New Testament Perspective

Jesus also extended to John an "extra beatitude." I call this one "Blessed are the unoffended" (see 11:6). This might include those who can accept unfair suffering, who can continue in spite of unanswered questions, or who can exercise patient endurance when God doesn't act on a man-made timetable. Those unoffended by such things are, in Jesus' estimation, blessed. Jesus doesn't live according to our unrealistic expectations. He lives according to the Father's eternal plan. If John would just hold on and continue to trust Christ even if it meant suffering and death, he would be blessed!

The second aspect of Jesus' response, which was directed toward the crowd, was an affirmation of John's noble character (11:7-11). Without a doubt some in the crowd had heard the disciples of John the Baptizer asking their worrisome question about the identity of Jesus. Perhaps their estimation of John would have begun to wane in their minds. Instead of rolling His eyes at John's flakiness or trashing John for faltering in his faith, Jesus heaped praise on John with eloquent and lofty words. Even though John struggled, doubted, and questioned, Jesus lifted John up, exalted him, and honored him. And Jesus wasn't simply flattering John in front of the Baptizer's disciples. They were gone by the time He sang John's praises. Rather, Jesus affirmed John before the crowd of onlookers.

Jesus referred to John as a man of strong convictions. John knew what he believed and wasn't hesitant or afraid to make those beliefs known. Every generation could use men and women of such strength. John was also a man of genuine self-denial. He cared nothing about making a good impression or being well thought of (11:8). He cared only about staying true to his calling. He was the forerunner with the mission of pointing people to the Messiah (11:9-10). Think about it. John's question of doubt about Jesus' identity showed that even in prison John was still focused on his mission. If Jesus wasn't the one, John would "look for someone else" (11:3)!

Clearly, periodic doubts don't disqualify a person from greatness. As the forerunner of the Messiah, John held a place greater than any other person born (11:11). However, Jesus pointed out that even John's ministry, as great as it was, would be rendered inferior by the unparalleled greatness of the coming age. The greatness of the Baptizer in the old era of the Law, before the cross and resurrection of Jesus, fades in comparison to the high position every believer will have after Pentecost (see Acts 2). Our position in Christ situates us in an exceedingly glorious place. Paul expounds on this in Ephesians 2:4-7:

But God, being rich in mercy, because of His great love with which He loved us, even when we were dead in our transgressions, made us alive together with Christ (by grace you have been saved), and raised us up with Him, and seated us with Him in the heavenly places in Christ Jesus, so that in the ages to come He might show the surpassing riches of His grace in kindness toward us in Christ Jesus.

— 11:12-19 —

Jesus dealt with John the Baptizer's doubts with a gentle hand. He challenged others with direct confrontation, however. The difference was that John *wanted* to believe but wavered because of external circumstances that didn't make sense. The enemies and critics of Jesus, meanwhile, wanted to remain in their unbelief, and they built up numerous vacuous arguments against Him.

Jesus addressed the unbelief, rejection, and spiritual conflict encountered in His own ministry as well as in those of the people He had sent out to preach. He clarified that though He did, in fact, bear all the marks of the coming Messiah through His miraculous works, they were still living in the period of time leading up to and anticipating the full realization of the messianic kingdom. With Jesus' coming to earth, this new era was being announced and inaugurated, but it would not be consummated until a future time. As He and His disciples traveled from city to city, the offer of the kingdom of heaven was intended to generate the response of repentance and faith, not a violent coup. This message of repentance and faith was the same as that preached originally by John the Baptizer. But the wicked leaders among the Jews wanted nothing to do with it. In fact, they attacked it violently and instead desired a kingdom they could take by force in a worldly manner (11:12).[72]

For those doubters who were motivated by worldly priorities, pride, and stubborn unbelief, Jesus had some choice words. Here He exposed the responses of those who had rejected Him as Messiah and looked with skepticism on His works (11:12-19). First, He looked to the time when John had begun proclaiming the message of repentance and salvation. The antagonists had responded with violence and vicious attacks (11:12). This was nothing new—the prophets prior to John, who had also prophesied about the coming kingdom (11:13), had likewise been treated with violence (see 23:37). This past violence also serves as a warning of the inevitability of violence yet to come against those who preach and live the truth.

Jesus also said that if the doubters and scoffers had accepted the truth that He was the long-awaited Messiah, the coming King of Israel—"if you are willing to accept it" (11:14)—then the coming of John the Baptizer would have fulfilled their expectation of a prophet coming in the spirit and power of Elijah.[73] Stan Toussaint explains, "There is scarcely a passage in Scripture which shows more clearly that the kingdom was being offered to Israel at this time. Its coming was contingent upon one thing: Israel's receiving it by genuine repentance. . . . John is the forerunner of the King. He could be Elijah if Israel would but respond correctly."[74] This teaching about the contingent nature of the genuine offer of the kingdom to Israel, as well as its anticipated rejection in the plan and purpose of God, are hard concepts to wrap our minds around. Perhaps this is why Jesus said, "He who has ears to hear, let him hear" (11:15).

Jesus then castigated "this generation" (11:16)—the generation of Jews who rejected the preaching of John and were beginning to reject the preaching of Jesus and His disciples. He compared them to pouting, petulant children who always want to have their own way when playing games—"Let's play wedding! Let's play funeral!" (see 11:17). In other words, the Jewish leaders wanted John and Jesus to meet *their* expectations, to dance to *their* tune, and to march to the beat of *their* drums. But that's backward—just as backward as children bossing around their parents. John was the great prophet; Jesus is the King! If anybody should be choreographing the dance or conducting the music, it should be the forerunner and the Messiah!

If you've ever watched children play a game where somebody's making up the rules as they go, you'll understand Matthew 11:18-19. When you play a game by somebody else's ever-changing rules, you can't win! If you do something right, they come up with a rule to make it wrong. Jesus pointed out that when John came with an ascetic lifestyle, eating locusts and honey and dressing in ragged clothes, his scoffing opponents said, "He has a demon!" (11:18). But when Jesus came eating and drinking, attending social gatherings and dinners with guests—things that normal people do every day—His enemies called Him "a gluttonous man and a drunkard" who hung out with tax collectors and sinners (11:19).

The signs and wonders that Jesus and His disciples were doing would have no effect on those with such unreasonable doubt. They simply didn't want to believe. Neither miracle nor message could penetrate the hardness of their hearts. Only an inner work of the Spirit could persuade them.

The proverbial statement that closes this section—"Wisdom is vindicated by her deeds" (11:19)—indicates that, while John and Jesus would be rejected by many, their actions would ultimately be justified. These two wise messengers of God didn't have to answer to the worldly critics and cynics; their mission had been directed by God. Similarly, the wisdom of accepting the message of John the Baptizer and Jesus will ultimately be vindicated. When the dust settles from the conflict of worldviews and religions ancient and modern, time will reveal who has believed and lived correctly.

APPLICATION: MATTHEW 11:1-19
Reasonable (and Unreasonable) Doubt

If, in the first century, John the Baptizer's seaworthy faith could be tossed to and fro by waves of doubt, we believers in the twenty-first century can certainly lose our bearings and drift into doubt as well. And if first-century eyewitnesses of Jesus' miracles could anchor their resistance in the depths of coldhearted doubt, we shouldn't be surprised when we encounter enemies of Christ who shipwreck their lives on the jagged reefs of error rather than finding shelter in the harbors of truth. As we live in this age between the first and second comings of Jesus, called to walk by faith and not by sight, what do we need to know about the doubts that inevitably come *our* way?

First, *doubt will arise because we're only human*. Because of our finiteness, we're naturally oriented to the things around us, having a limited understanding of the big picture. And because we and the world around us are fallen and frail, it's easy to succumb to the domino effect of doubt, whereby idealistic anticipation and unrealistic expectation lead to disillusionment, disappointment, and—ultimately—doubt. Many times throughout our lives we'll find ourselves heading down that path.

Second, *doubts may temporarily disturb a person's relationship with the Lord, but they don't permanently destroy it*. Jesus didn't criticize or rebuke John when he expressed his doubts. He didn't conclude that John had gone off the deep end and abandoned the faith entirely. Instead, Jesus responded with gentleness and clarity in a way that would have provided John with assurance. As we endure seasons of doubt, we can expect a similar kind of assurance, which can lead to a strengthening of our faith.

Third, *we can push through periodic doubts by exposing them to the light.* In the midst of our doubts, we may find ourselves surrounded by those who have turned doubt into a science, who direct constant ridicule toward faith in Christ. But such doubts—ours and others'—need not derail us. Instead of feeding our doubts in the darkness, expose them to the light of God's Word, offer them to God in prayer, and talk about them with other believers. When you do, you'll experience a new depth of blessing that will drive out cynicism and restore the peace and joy of your relationship with God.

Bad for the Wicked . . .
Good for the Weary
MATTHEW 11:20-30

NASB

20 Then He began to denounce the cities in which most of His ᵃmiracles were done, because they did not repent. 21 "Woe to you, Chorazin! Woe to you, Bethsaida! For if the ᵃmiracles had occurred in Tyre and Sidon which occurred in you, they would have repented long ago in ᵇsackcloth and ashes. 22 Nevertheless I say to you, it will be more tolerable for Tyre and Sidon in *the* day of judgment than for you. 23 And you, Capernaum, will not be exalted to heaven, will you? You will descend to Hades; for if the ᵃmiracles had occurred in Sodom which occurred in you, it would have remained to this day. 24 Nevertheless I say to you that it will be more tolerable for the land of Sodom in *the* day of judgment, than for you."

25 At that ᵃtime Jesus said, "I praise You, Father, Lord of heaven and earth, that You have hidden these

NLT

20 Then Jesus began to denounce the towns where he had done so many of his miracles, because they hadn't repented of their sins and turned to God. 21 "What sorrow awaits you, Korazin and Bethsaida! For if the miracles I did in you had been done in wicked Tyre and Sidon, their people would have repented of their sins long ago, clothing themselves in burlap and throwing ashes on their heads to show their remorse. 22 I tell you, Tyre and Sidon will be better off on judgment day than you.

23 "And you people of Capernaum, will you be honored in heaven? No, you will go down to the place of the dead.* For if the miracles I did for you had been done in wicked Sodom, it would still be here today. 24 I tell you, even Sodom will be better off on judgment day than you."

25 At that time Jesus prayed this prayer: "O Father, Lord of heaven and earth, thank you for hiding these things from those who think

things from *the* wise and intelligent and have revealed them to infants. [26]Yes, Father, for this way was well-pleasing in Your sight. [27]All things have been handed over to Me by My Father; and no one knows the Son except the Father; nor does anyone know the Father except the Son, and anyone to whom the Son wills to reveal *Him.*

[28]"Come to Me, all [a]who are weary and heavy-laden, and I will give you rest. [29]Take My yoke upon you and learn from Me, for I am gentle and humble in heart, and YOU WILL FIND REST FOR YOUR SOULS. [30]For My yoke is [a]easy and My burden is light."

11:20 [a]Or *works of power* 11:21 [a]Or *works of power* [b]I.e. symbols of mourning 11:23 [a]Or *works of power* 11:25 [a]Or *occasion* 11:28 [a]Or *who work to exhaustion* 11:30 [a]Or *comfortable, or pleasant*

themselves wise and clever, and for revealing them to the childlike. [26]Yes, Father, it pleased you to do it this way!

[27]"My Father has entrusted everything to me. No one truly knows the Son except the Father, and no one truly knows the Father except the Son and those to whom the Son chooses to reveal him."

[28]Then Jesus said, "Come to me, all of you who are weary and carry heavy burdens, and I will give you rest. [29]Take my yoke upon you. Let me teach you, because I am humble and gentle at heart, and you will find rest for your souls. [30]For my yoke is easy to bear, and the burden I give you is light."

11:23 Greek *to Hades.*

When people hear the message of Jesus, they have a choice—either accept it and go on to have their lives transformed or follow the majority and reject it altogether. Such rejection is expressed in one of two ways: active resistance or passive indifference. Those who are active in their resistance aggressively—sometimes loudly and violently—stand against it. The rest express their indifference by completely ignoring Jesus' message. This dual response was evidenced in the first century, when Jesus preached the coming kingdom, and it remains operative today.

People heard Jesus' words and witnessed His works firsthand. His normal method of ministry was to speak truth and then underscore it with acts that authenticated His message as divine. This included miracles designed to convince others that He was, in fact, the promised Messiah, the King of Israel. But even then, among most who heard Him speak and saw Him perform signs and wonders, there was either active resistance or passive indifference.

Periodically, Jesus paused and addressed those who rejected Him. At times, He offered a mild and gentle statement of reproof. But as the rejection and ridicule intensified, Jesus turned up the heat on His senseless critics and called them out for their hypocrisy. In these instances, Jesus adopted apocalyptic imagery as He warned those who rejected Him of the coming judgment. After all, Jesus came to baptize with fire

(3:11)—to test the authenticity of people's faith and rid the world of wickedness and rebellion. In Matthew 11:20-30, we'll see how Jesus addressed those who turned a blind eye to their Messiah, as well as how He comforted the faithful remnant who had forsaken all to follow Him.

— 11:20-24 —

After mentioning the irreverent and irrational mocking of the critics who had rejected His preaching and miracles (11:16-19), Jesus decided it was time to denounce the passivity of those places that had received maximum exposure to the words and works of the Messiah. They were without excuse. The three cities He explicitly mentioned were Chorazin, Bethsaida, and Capernaum—His own ministry base. Though we aren't given any specific details of Jesus' ministry in the first two cities mentioned, we can assume these were included among the cities where Jesus preached after departing from Capernaum (11:1). While the disciples made longer and farther trips in their preaching mission, Jesus likely stayed closer to His home base. Evidently, the reception of His message had been lukewarm to downright chilly in those cities (11:20).

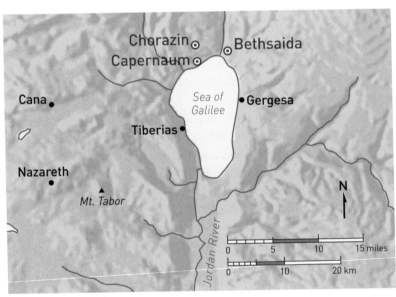

The three towns of Chorazin, Bethsaida, and Capernaum were censured by Jesus because they displayed a lack of faith in Him despite having witnessed many of His miracles.

Jesus first took aim at Chorazin and Bethsaida, pronouncing woes upon them. In the first century, "Woe to you!" was a powerful phrase of sorrowful anguish. Jesus didn't delight in condemning these cities for their stubborn unbelief. He took no joy in prophesying judgment against them. Rather, it pained His heart to do so. He had privileged these cities with a great number of astonishing miracles, but they still refused to repent. In His condemnation, then, He likened them to Tyre and Sidon (11:21). Those ancient port cities near the northern border of Israel epitomized pagan, Gentile corruption, being known for their immorality and godless deeds.[75] In other words, He was bringing shame upon His hearers by comparing them to those wicked, Gentile cities. If Jesus had done the same kinds of signs and wonders in Tyre and Sidon, the people there would have repented with sackcloth and ashes . . . even though they were Gentiles, not Jews! Because of what Chorazin and Bethsaida had seen and heard with their own eyes and ears, they would be held to a more severe standard in the day of judgment (11:22).

Then Jesus similarly condemned the privileged city of His own temporary residence, Capernaum. More of His miraculous deeds are recorded as having occurred in Capernaum than in any other single city. But the people there rejected Christ too. Instead of being exalted to heaven, then, that city would be brought down to Hades in the day of judgment (11:23). Jesus likened Capernaum to a city even more explicitly wicked in His listeners' minds than Tyre and Sidon—Sodom. Nobody would scratch their heads and wonder what Jesus was saying through this analogy. So serious was Capernaum's passive rejection of Jesus' words and works that they had become worse than the worst— even Sodom would have repented if they had seen the miracles Jesus did at Capernaum (11:23-24).

— 11:25-27 —

The crowd that stood before Jesus—men and women from Capernaum, Chorazin, and Bethsaida—must have been shocked to hear such strong woes pronounced against them and their neighboring cities. Some "got it," of course, but I suspect that most didn't have a clue . . . and didn't even care. Then, without announcement, Jesus lifted His head toward heaven, raised His palms upward and His chest high, and began to pray loudly enough for everybody to hear.

The content of His prayer is at the same time theologically profound and practically perplexing. Jesus praised God the Father for hiding the truths of the kingdom of God from the wise and intelligent people and instead revealing them to "infants." In fact, such a plan was "well-pleasing" in God's sight (11:25-26). What an unexpected thing to pray! We would instead expect Jesus to ask the Father to open the eyes of all the spiritually blind so they would believe. It's difficult to wrap our minds around the idea that God might have bigger plans that involve leaving people in their self-condemning unbelief and rebellion. However, Jesus was echoing a prophecy in Isaiah 29:13-14, which states,

> Because this people draw near with their words
> And honor Me with their lip service,
> But they remove their hearts far from Me,
> And their reverence for Me consists of tradition learned
>   by rote,
> Therefore behold, I will once again deal marvelously with
>   this people, wondrously marvelous;
> And the wisdom of their wise men will perish,
> And the discernment of their discerning men will be
>   concealed.

Paul also picked up on this prophecy when he wrote, "The word of the cross is foolishness to those who are perishing, but to us who are being saved it is the power of God. For it is written, 'I will destroy the wisdom of the wise, and the cleverness of the clever I will set aside'" (1 Cor. 1:18-19).

R. T. France puts into perspective the important doctrine of the sovereign grace of God taught in this passage: "Spiritual understanding does not depend on human equipment or status. It is the gift of God, and so is given to those in whom he is well pleased. . . . It depends on the sovereign purpose of the *Lord of heaven and earth*, and his choice falls on those the world would never expect."[76] The apostle Paul underscored this point when he urged the Corinthians,

> Consider your calling, brethren, that there were not many wise according to the flesh, not many mighty, not many noble; but God has chosen the foolish things of the world to shame the wise, and God has chosen the weak things of the world to shame the things which are strong, and the base things of the world and the despised God has chosen, the things that are not, so that He may nullify the things that are, so that no man may boast before God. (1 Cor. 1:26-29)

In the end, salvation is entirely of the Lord, not of ourselves (Eph. 2:8-9). And there is no alternate path to God except through the Son. Jesus Himself makes this clear in Matthew 11:27. God the Father has handed all authority over to the Son. The Son and the Father are intimately related—nobody truly knows the Father or the Son like they know each other. (Here we see veiled glimpses of the eternal relationship of the Father and Son shining through.) In order for anybody to truly know God in a saving relationship, that person must be invited into such a relationship through the Son.

This inner life of the Father and Son appears more frequently in the Gospel of John:

- "For not even the Father judges anyone, but He has given all judgment to the Son." (John 5:22)
- "He who does not honor the Son does not honor the Father who sent Him." (John 5:23)
- "Just as the Father has life in Himself, even so He gave to the Son also to have life in Himself." (John 5:26)
- "The Father knows Me and I know the Father." (John 10:15)

It has sometimes been said that the Gospel of John—written about thirty years after the Gospel of Matthew—contains a much "higher" view of Jesus as the eternal Son of God with a special relationship to the Father than the Gospel of Matthew. In fact, some misguided scholars allege that the synoptic Gospels (Matthew, Mark, and Luke) present Jesus simply as an exalted human being. Jesus' words in Matthew 11:27 are like a torpedo fired at that faulty view. Jesus knew He was the Messiah, the Son of David and Son of God. He knew He had a special, eternal, divine relationship with God the Father. Though He didn't flaunt it, He gave enough clues in His words and works that anybody whose heart was opened to the Spirit's work would be able to see who Jesus really was.

— 11:28-30 —

Of all the words Jesus said during His earthly ministry, these are among the most beloved. Many Christians can probably quote the last three verses of Matthew 11 from memory. Often, we learn Bible verses like these and even quote them to others without being aware of the context of the words when they were originally spoken. Most of us would guess this familiar and much-loved offer from Jesus was said to His committed followers, those who had already trusted in Him and accepted His offer of salvation. As it turns out, these words conclude His great call to all those who have become worn out as a result of spending their lives under the heavy burden of sin and its consequences.

As Solomon once wrote, "The way of the treacherous is hard" (Prov. 13:15). Looking at those around Him who were overwhelmed with

THE YOKE

MATTHEW 11:29

Literally, a yoke was "a bar of wood so constructed as to unite two animals, usually oxen, enabling them to work in the fields."[77] We can't be sure that Jesus made yokes as a carpenter, but we can be sure He was quite familiar with how they were made. And His hearers would have understood the reference immediately: As a pair of oxen were brought together by a yoke, Jesus Himself would be bound with the person who took on the yoke.

Anna from Eagle, WI, USA/Wikimedia

A pair of oxen yoked together

Beyond the literal sense, rabbis at this time referred positively to the Law and its commandments as a "yoke."[78] However, in addition to the straightforward commands of the Law of Moses, the Pharisees had piled on countless legalistic demands and traditions and had made the observance of all these rules and regulations, dos and don'ts, and rites and rituals virtually impossible for everyday people. Instead of being a joy and protector, the Law as taught by the Pharisees had become a burdensome yoke and even a demoralizing killer.

The apocryphal Jewish writing Sirach (also known as Ecclesiasticus), well known during the time of Jesus, supplies additional background on the notion of a yoke. Sirach invites the uneducated to acquire wisdom through instruction: "Draw near to me, you who are uneducated, and lodge in the house of instruction. . . . Acquire wisdom for yourselves without money. Put your neck under [wisdom's] yoke, and let your souls receive instruction" (Sirach 51:23-26).[79] Echoing the sentiments of the book of Proverbs, Sirach suggests that people who put themselves under the tutelage of wisdom will have peace and joy.

In light of these historical uses of the image of the yoke, we can see that Jesus was intentionally pitting His own words of wisdom against the increasingly complex and difficult instructions of the rabbis, with their countless traditions and stifling regulations. To come under Jesus' yoke of instruction was to be liberated from the bondage of the Pharisees' legalism and enabled by a partnership with the Lord to accomplish the true spirit of the Law.

guilt and shame—even the hard-hearted unbelievers from the cities of Chorazin, Bethsaida, and Capernaum—Jesus urged them to come to Him, to trade their rebellion for submission, their burdens for belief, their heavy yoke of sin and guilt for His light yoke of peace and joy. Jesus ended His harsh condemnation of the unbelieving Jews with an open invitation to *come!*

This is Jesus' message to a crowd of people who knew nothing of grace and who knew nothing of resting in God's provision of salvation rather than working to earn their own way. I find five categories of words used by Jesus here: words that invite, words that expose, words that describe, words that promise, and words that relieve.

The first set of words *invites*: "come," "take," and "learn" (Matt. 11:28-29). Let's not complicate Jesus' first invitation, to *come*. I can almost picture Jesus with open arms, welcoming anybody at all to simply step forward and accept His eternal embrace. We don't come to a creed, a church, a priest, or a pastor. *We come to Jesus Himself.* And we come by believing, trusting, and receiving Him by grace alone through faith alone.

The second invitation is to *take* Jesus' "yoke" upon us and in that way to *learn* from Him. Barclay notes, "The Jews used the phrase *the yoke* for *entering into submission to.*"[80] The word "yoke" had also slipped into descriptions of the world of education in ancient days. A student was often spoken of as being "under the yoke" of his teacher. Thus, Jesus connected "take My yoke upon you" with "learn from Me." Unlike the overly burdensome and impossibly complex yoke of the Pharisees' legalism, Jesus' teaching was liberating. To accept Jesus' invitation to come and be fitted with His custom-made yoke would mean to begin a lifetime of learning from Him and growing with Him in a side-by-side relationship of discipleship.

The second set of words *exposes*: "weary and heavy-laden" (11:28).

One of the great benefits of learning from Jesus is facing the truth about ourselves. We are often "weary and heavy-laden." This was a perfect description of those burdened to the point of breaking by the legalistic demands of the Law as taught by the scribes and Pharisees. How great was that burden! Constantly trying to please God. Trying to impress others. Trying to follow an ever-growing code of commands and satisfy an enlarging body of traditions. People in Jesus' day were overloaded by obligations, guilt, shame, and requirements that left them exhausted!

The third set of words *describes*: Jesus is "gentle and humble in heart" (11:29). Before entering a permanent relationship, such as a marriage, you need to know the one to whom you're committing. If you're going to "yoke up" and share with someone both the direction and pace of life, you need to know that person's character, convictions, personality, and passions. Hence, Jesus offers a description of Himself—"gentle and humble in heart." The Greek term *praus* [4239], translated "gentle," is the same term used in the beatitude of Matthew 5:5—"Blessed are the gentle, for they shall inherit the earth." It carries the sense of "humble" or "considerate."[81] Now, we shouldn't picture somebody who's wimpy and weak, easy to push around and pick on. Rather, we should imagine a fair-minded, careful, thoughtful, considerate, and unassuming figure. As people came to Jesus, He was tender and loving, patient and kind—not harsh, touchy, or easily incensed.

This term conveying humility implies that Jesus put the needs of others before His own needs. Even though as Lord of heaven and earth He had every right to demand absolute and instant obedience from every creature in the universe, He instead chose to rule by invitation, instruction, training, and transformation. When you come to Christ, slip into His yoke, and walk with Him through life, you learn real gentleness and humility along the way.

The fourth set of words *promises*: "I will give you rest" and "You will find rest for your souls" (11:28-29). The verb in the first statement, *anapauō* [373], means "to cause someone to gain relief from toil."[82] It's the same term used of those who "rest" from their earthly labors when they die "in the Lord" (Rev. 14:13). When one experiences this rest in the present life of discipleship, the result is refreshment and renewal. The noun form used in Matthew 11:29, *anapausis* [372], refers to "cessation from wearisome activity."[83] Here Jesus quoted from Jeremiah 6:16: "Thus says the LORD, 'Stand by the ways and see and ask for the ancient paths, where the good way is, and walk in it; and you will find rest for your souls.'" By coming to Christ, disciples would cut through the

Take Time

MATTHEW 11:28

Years ago, my oldest son and I were lingering in a local gift shop. Our eyes fell upon a row of large posters framed and stacked together. We laughed at some of the nutty ones, nodded at some of the serious ones, and then meditated on one of them. When my son Curt found it, he said nothing at first. Then moments later he whispered quietly, "Wow, Dad—that's good!"

It was a picture of a misty morning on a calm lake. In a little skiff were a father and his son looking at the two corks floating at the ends of their fishing lines. The sun was tipping its hat over the mountains in the distance. Stretching across the scene were peace, refreshment, and easygoing small talk. Two wistful words beneath the border of the image appropriately summed up a message everybody needs to hear today:

TAKE TIME.

In my younger years, I would have been irritated by that message. Like many young people gearing up to make their mark on the world, I would have preferred the image of a speedboat cutting through the waves at 80 miles per hour. My preferred caption would have been

DON'T WASTE YOUR TIME!

At the same time, I would have been nagged by the seemingly incomprehensible words of that old, well-worn hymn by William Longstaff:

> Take time to be holy,
> Speak oft with thy Lord. . . .
> Take time to be holy,
> The world rushes on.[84]

Now, decades later, with children, grandchildren, great-grandchildren, and many miles and mistakes behind me, those words of Longstaff make a lot of sense. Through years of striving to rush through life at my own fast pace, I began to understand the chastening whisper of the Lord in Psalm 46:10: "Cease striving and know that I am God." Likewise, Jesus' counsel in Matthew 11:28 makes so much sense after having tried to outpace the One with whom I am yoked: "Come to Me . . . and I will give you rest."

accumulated trash of human tradition that had obscured the beauty and freedom of a relationship with God. Christ's preaching and teaching was in a real sense a retrieval and reformation of that relationship.

The final set of words *relieves*: "My yoke is easy and My burden is light" (Matt. 11:30). At first, this might sound like an oxymoron. How could a yoke that fit a pair of oxen for the arduous labor of hauling a load or plowing a field be "easy" and "light"? But in contrast to the works righteousness of the Pharisees, in which a person's relationship with God and with the covenant community of Israel supposedly depended entirely on his or her own efforts, Christ's yoke offered something revolutionary: *grace!* The finished work of Christ on the cross and His miraculous resurrection and ascension would mean no more debt to sin and guilt, no more threat of eternal damnation, no more fretting over whether one has done enough to please God. The restoration of our vertical relationship with God is an accomplished fact because of salvation by grace alone through faith alone in Christ alone. And our horizontal relationships with others are also transformed through the unifying bond of the Spirit and the ongoing grace of His enabling power. Not for a moment are we left alone to bear the burden on our own. In fact, Christ accomplishes everything, and we are simply attached to Him and His awesome strength. It's like a father who allows his toddler son or daughter to "help" him carry a heavy burden. All the work is done by the dad, but the child participates in the task and grows in his or her personal relationship with the father through the process.

APPLICATION: MATTHEW 11:20-30

Rest for the Weary

Though Jesus offered true rest from their labor and release from their guilt and shame, the people of Chorazin, Bethsaida, and Capernaum preferred to bear their own sin and labor under the legalism of the Pharisees. Why? Because of pride. Even in the light of obvious, miraculous signs confirming the truthfulness of Jesus' identity and power and the validity of His offer of salvation and rest, they preferred to surrender *nothing* to His lordship. To do so would mean somebody other than themselves was in charge of their lives.

But to those whose eyes have been opened to the truth, the invitation stands. Exchange your unfruitful, constant activity for all that Christ wants to do in your life. Come to Him, take His yoke, learn from Him, receive His promises, and bask in His peace. To the broken, bruised, downtrodden, oppressed, failed, fallen, ashamed, rejected, brutalized, and bullied, Jesus' invitation comes like a gasp of air to a drowning person.

By surrendering control, we lose nothing and gain everything. And by daily reminding ourselves that we're under His yoke, we can rest in His protection, His provision, His perfect timing, and His constant guidance. Tied to Him, we can be confident that we're not running ahead or lagging behind in danger. We can be sure that we're accomplishing the task He wants accomplished through us. And we don't have to worry about where our ability and sufficiency might come from. He provides both.

How do we do all this? By offering ourselves to Him in prayer. By learning from Him through His Word. By learning His works and ways through a community of fellow disciples in the church. By actively participating in the work He's given us to do, while relying on nothing but His strength to accomplish it. And all of this takes faith, which comes to us by *grace*. In light of the enabling grace of Jesus Christ, resting in His easy yoke and submitting to His light burden make perfect sense.

Legalists vs. Lord of the Sabbath
MATTHEW 12:1-14

NASB

[1] At that [a] time Jesus went through the grainfields on the Sabbath, and His disciples became hungry and began to pick the heads *of grain* and eat. [2] But when the Pharisees saw *this*, they said to Him, "Look, Your disciples do what is not lawful to do on a Sabbath." [3] But He said to them, "Have you not read what David did when he became hungry, he and his companions, [4] how he entered the house of God, and they ate the [a] consecrated bread, which was not lawful for him to eat nor for those

NLT

[1] At about that time Jesus was walking through some grainfields on the Sabbath. His disciples were hungry, so they began breaking off some heads of grain and eating them. [2] But some Pharisees saw them do it and protested, "Look, your disciples are breaking the law by harvesting grain on the Sabbath."

[3] Jesus said to them, "Haven't you read in the Scriptures what David did when he and his companions were hungry? [4] He went into the house of God, and he and his companions broke the law by eating the sacred

229

with him, but for the priests alone? 5Or have you not read in the Law, that on the Sabbath the priests in the temple ªbreak the Sabbath and are innocent? 6But I say to you that something greater than the temple is here. 7But if you had known what this ªmeans, 'I DESIRE ᵇCOMPASSION, AND NOT A SACRIFICE,' you would not have condemned the innocent.

8For the Son of Man is Lord of the Sabbath."

9Departing from there, He went into their synagogue. 10And a man *was there* whose hand was withered. And they questioned ªJesus, asking, "Is it lawful to heal on the Sabbath?"—so that they might accuse Him. 11And He said to them, "What man ªis there among you who ᵇhas a sheep, and if it falls into a pit on the Sabbath, will he not take hold of it and lift it out? 12How much more valuable then is a man than a sheep! So then, it is lawful to do ªgood on the Sabbath." 13Then He said to the man, "Stretch out your hand!" He stretched it out, and it was restored to ªnormal, like the other. 14But the Pharisees went out and ªconspired against Him, *as to* how they might destroy Him.

12:1 ªOr *occasion* 12:4 ªOr *showbread;* lit *loaves of presentation* 12:5 ªOr *profane* 12:7 ªLit *is* ᵇOr *mercy* 12:10 ªLit *Him* 12:11 ªLit *will be from you* ᵇLit *will have* 12:12 ªLit *well* 12:13 ªLit *health* 12:14 ªLit *took counsel*

loaves of bread that only the priests are allowed to eat. 5And haven't you read in the law of Moses that the priests on duty in the Temple may work on the Sabbath? 6I tell you, there is one here who is even greater than the Temple! 7But you would not have condemned my innocent disciples if you knew the meaning of this Scripture: 'I want you to show mercy, not offer sacrifices.'* 8For the Son of Man* is Lord, even over the Sabbath!"

9Then Jesus went over to their synagogue, 10where he noticed a man with a deformed hand. The Pharisees asked Jesus, "Does the law permit a person to work by healing on the Sabbath?" (They were hoping he would say yes, so they could bring charges against him.)

11And he answered, "If you had a sheep that fell into a well on the Sabbath, wouldn't you work to pull it out? Of course you would. 12And how much more valuable is a person than a sheep! Yes, the law permits a person to do good on the Sabbath."

13Then he said to the man, "Hold out your hand." So the man held out his hand, and it was restored, just like the other one! 14Then the Pharisees called a meeting to plot how to kill Jesus.

12:7 Hos 6:6 (Greek version). 12:8 "Son of Man" is a title Jesus used for himself.

Without dismissing Jesus' principle that peacemakers are blessed and will be called "sons of God" (5:9) or Paul's exhortation to be at peace with all men as far as it depends on us (Rom. 12:18), there are times when it's right to fight. While Jesus was never looking for an argument, He never ran away from one if there was a significant principle at stake. Whenever wrong thinking was attempting to smother the truth, Jesus refused to shrug it off and look the other way. Instead, He stood His ground and set the record straight.

Matthew 12 includes a series of such moments in the life and ministry of Jesus. This series of conflicts occurred between Jesus and the Pharisees, the ultraorthodox religious leaders of His day. These decisive moments also represent a turning point in the reaction of the religious leaders toward Him. No longer satisfied simply to argue with Jesus, they came to an official decision that nothing short of His complete elimination would be the solution. This hostility is clearly conveyed in 12:14, where we read, "The Pharisees called a meeting to plot how to kill Jesus" (NLT). Make no mistake regarding their ongoing arguments: This was not just a series of disagreements. From here on, a murderous plot was being hatched.

— 12:1-8 —

Jesus consistently, repeatedly, and intentionally failed at one thing over and over again: living up to the legalistic expectations of the scribes and Pharisees. Legalism isn't the same as faithfully observing God's laws or avoiding what God explicitly forbids. When we obey God with sincere hearts and humble spirits, wanting to please Him out of love, that's a liberating observance of His Word, which is good for us and others. So what is legalism? Charles Ryrie defines it as "a fleshly attitude which conforms to a code for the purpose of exalting self."[85] The code is man-made, often part of a system of traditional practices going back several generations.

When it came to keeping all those man-made traditions and fulfilling the expectations of the Pharisees, Jesus was a complete disappointment to the religious bullies of His day. He broke the mold of what it looked like to be a righteous Jew. The Pharisees found Jesus shocking, even revolting. What began as mere suspicion eventually led to investigation, then to open hostility, and ultimately to a determination to eliminate Jesus entirely! What really pushed the Pharisees over the edge was Jesus' apparent lack of respect for their rules and regulations regarding the Sabbath.

We must understand that the Mosaic Law as originally given on Mount Sinai (Exod. 19–24) and repeated on the eve of entering the Promised Land (see the book of Deuteronomy) simply required that no work be done on the Sabbath. One of the Ten Commandments states, "Remember the sabbath day, to keep it holy. Six days you shall labor and do all your work, but the seventh day is a sabbath of the LORD your God; in it you shall not do any work, you or your son or your daughter, your male or your female servant or your cattle or your sojourner who stays with you" (Exod. 20:8-10). However, as Jewish history unfolded, the laws and traditions governing the Sabbath grew in complexity. One scholar explains,

> During the period between Ezra and the Christian era the scribes formulated innumerable legal restrictions for the conduct of life under the law. Two whole treatises in the Talmud are devoted to the details of Sabbath observance. One of these, the *Shabbath*, enumerates the following thirty-nine principal classes of prohibited actions: sowing, plowing, reaping, gathering into sheaves, threshing, winnowing, cleansing, grinding, sifting, kneading, baking; shearing wool, washing it, beating it, dyeing it, spinning it, making a warp of it; making two cords, weaving two threads, separating two threads, making a knot, untying a knot, sewing two stitches, tearing to sew two stitches; catching a deer, killing, skinning, salting it, preparing its hide, scraping off its hair, cutting it up; writing two letters, blotting out for the purpose of writing two letters, building, pulling down, extinguishing, lighting a fire, beating with a hammer, and carrying from one property to another. Each of these chief enactments was further discussed and elaborated, so that actually there were several hundred things a conscientious, law-abiding Jew could not do on the Sabbath.[86]

All these man-made rules served as a kind of "oral law" or "case law" added to God's inspired Word. As a result, the Sabbath became anything but a time of rest. Rather, it led to frustration and anxiety as faithful Jews fretted over whether they had walked too far, carried too much, or exerted enough energy for it to count as "labor" and place them under the curse of the Law. To make matters worse, people lived under not only the man-made traditions but also the watchful eyes of religious nitpickers, ready to pounce the moment they saw an infraction of their exaggerated and unbiblical Sabbath rules.

Jesus and His disciples found themselves in that situation one Sabbath. As they were wandering through fields of grain, the disciples got hungry and spontaneously made fists around the stalks as they walked by. They let the long stems of the grain run through their closed fingers, and when they pulled the heads of the stalks through their fists, a few kernels of grain would gather in their palms—just enough for a snack. They would then rub their hands together to remove the berries from the hulls and pop the soft kernels into their mouths (Matt 12:1; Luke 6:1).

At first glance, this might make it seem like the disciples were guilty of stealing somebody else's grain. But Deuteronomy 23:25 says, "When you enter your neighbor's standing grain, then you may pluck the heads with your hand, but you shall not wield a sickle in your neighbor's standing grain." In other words, a person could snatch a modest snack on their way through a field without being guilty of stealing, but they couldn't do any actual harvesting.

The problem wasn't plucking and eating the grain. In the minds of the Pharisees, the problem was doing it on the Sabbath. Remember, the oral tradition of the rabbis made it a breach of the Sabbath to "reap" grain. Had the disciples grabbed some sickles and started reaping, gathering the stalks of grain into sheaves, and hauling them off the field to process, they would have not only been guilty of breaking the Sabbath, but they also would have been thieves. But the Law made a clear distinction between actual reaping and grabbing a snack—one was labor, the other was leisure!

The strangest thing about this account, though, is that the Pharisees were watching. Think about how close they had to be to see those tiny kernels going from the disciples' hands to their mouths. They were spying on Jesus, just longing for a glimpse of even a minor infraction of their man-made laws! As soon as they saw the disciples snacking, they pounced: "Look, Your disciples do what is not lawful to do on a Sabbath" (Matt. 12:2). The way the statement is phrased in Greek gives the impression that they were standing right there, pointing at something the disciples were doing at that very instant. How bizarre! But how typical of legalists!

It's interesting that the disciples didn't even think twice about what they were doing. They didn't ask permission from Jesus, nor did Jesus give any indication that the disciples might want to refrain from snacking so as not to offend the sensitive Pharisees. The disciples had been around Jesus long enough and had heard enough of His teachings to know the difference between the Mosaic Law and man-made traditions. They knew they weren't breaking the Sabbath. But in the Pharisees' exhaustive explication of the Law, to pluck the grain was the same as reaping, and to roll the grain between their hands was the same as threshing.[87] How absurd! But how typical of legalists!

Simply put, if we understand the Sabbath according to the broad, general principles of the inspired Word of God, there was nothing wrong with what the disciples were doing. But if we understand the Sabbath according to the man-made, meticulous rules and regulations of the legalistic Pharisees, the disciples had broken one of the Ten Commandments, and Jesus was doing nothing to stop them!

In fact, instead of dissuading the disciples, Jesus was defending them with Scripture. Dipping back into Jewish history, He reminded the Pharisees of what David and his men had done when they were hungry while fleeing from the wrath of King Saul. To feed themselves, David and his soldiers ate the consecrated bread from the tabernacle, which, according to the Law, was only supposed to be eaten by the priests (12:3-4). Clearly David wasn't considered to have broken the Law, because the hunger of his men and lack of any other food created a special circumstance that superseded the ceremonial laws.

Jesus also pointed out the fact that the Sabbath itself wasn't as inviolably sacrosanct as the Pharisees had made it. While they were nitpicking about plucking a handful of grain and asserting that this constituted harvesting, the priests in the temple didn't cease carrying out their duties of offering sacrifices just because it was the Sabbath (12:5). Clearly, God Himself had established the Sabbath with built-in exceptions.

Jesus then argued from the lesser to the greater: His presence on earth was greater than the temple and the ministry going on there (12:6). The ministry Jesus did on the Sabbath therefore took precedence over anything that occurred at the temple. Stan Toussaint notes, "If the ministry of the temple superseded Sabbath rules, how much more does the work of the Messiah overrule the Sabbath!"[88]

In the end, Jesus didn't grant the legalistic Pharisees their premise that His disciples were doing work on the Sabbath. Rather, Jesus said the Pharisees had "condemned the innocent" because they had never taken to heart the vital principle of Hosea 6:6—"I desire compassion, and not a sacrifice" (Matt. 12:7). When legalistic dos and don'ts that have no basis in Scripture lead to the self-righteous condemnation of innocent people who fail to live up to those man-made traditions, something is severely wrong. *The Pharisees were the sinners, not the disciples.*

Of course, the Pharisees could have stood tall and proud and insisted, "*We* are the experts in the Law. *We* get to decide what counts as reaping and threshing. And if there are exceptions to Sabbath observance in certain circumstances, *we* are the ones who determine what those exceptions are." As if anticipating their thoughts, Jesus asserted His superior authority over the proper interpretation and application of Sabbath laws: "For the Son of Man is Lord of the Sabbath" (12:8).

Defending against Legalism

MATTHEW 12:1-7

In 1976, Cynthia and I traveled to Washington, DC, for a United States Bicentennial tour. With others in our group, we wandered through the center of the majestic Thomas Jefferson Memorial. It took our breath away! Yet more moving than his memorial are the words Jefferson wrote in a letter to William S. Smith in 1787: "The tree of liberty must be refreshed from time to time, with the blood of patriots and tyrants."[89] In other words, maintaining the freedoms we enjoy in our country sometimes requires taking a stand and being willing to sacrifice our own comfort and contentment.

The same can be said of maintaining our spiritual liberty from the tyranny of legalists. The tree of Christian liberty must be upheld and defended—not with literal violence and bloodshed, but by taking a stand with spiritual weapons of warfare. "Our struggle is not against flesh and blood, but against the rulers, against the powers, against the world forces of this darkness, against the spiritual forces of wickedness in the heavenly places" (Eph. 6:12). Make no mistake: The fight against legalism is a spiritual battle.

Many Christians in Bible-believing churches have lost touch with the things that are worth fighting for. That is not to say that we've lost our knack for fighting. Oh, we have plenty of fight left in us! It's just that we nag, nitpick, and wrangle over things that aren't worth the effort, while at the same time we succumb to things we ought to stand firmly against. One of those things to stand against is the same thing Jesus frequently faced in His earthly ministry: a religion of legalistic dos and don'ts that have no basis at all in Scripture.

Jesus' words in 12:6 and 12:8 together would have landed like a one-two punch in the minds of the Pharisees: Jesus' ministry was superior to the ministry of the temple. Ouch! And Jesus Himself—not the Pharisees or the long-standing tradition of the rabbis—was Lord of the Sabbath. Yikes!

— 12:9-13 —

In the next episode, immediately following the confrontation in the grainfield, it seems that the Pharisees were intentionally trying to provoke Jesus in order to find a basis for condemning Him in front of everybody—fellow Pharisees, elders of the synagogue, and others in attendance. However, by the time the episode is over, Jesus will have forced everybody to consider the absurdity of their legalistic approach to the day of rest.

Jesus and the disciples had left the grainfield and entered the synagogue (12:9). Now they were in the Pharisees' home territory. In attendance that day was a man with a withered hand, who suddenly found himself the center of attention. The frowning Pharisees walked over to the man and asked Jesus, "Is it lawful to heal on the Sabbath?" (12:10). This was not a sincere question for which they sought an answer. They asked it only to catch Jesus teaching something contrary to their interpretation of the Sabbath laws. All they needed was for Jesus to answer yes, and He would be guilty according to their senseless understanding of the Law. Just one tiny word in Aramaic—*heh*—would have done the trick.

But Jesus didn't step into their trap. Instead, He sprung it. He responded to their yes-or-no question with a question of His own, a sort of poll to see how the crowd would respond to a real-life scenario: "What man is there among you who has a sheep, and if it falls into a pit on the Sabbath, will he not take hold of it and lift it out?" (12:11). I doubt any hands went up. They knew it was a rhetorical question. And there wasn't a man among them who would let the poor sheep bleat all night and all day waiting to be rescued. Compassion toward the sheep and the valuing of its life would compel them to action. The rescuing of a sheep from danger wouldn't have been considered *labor* for the sake of profit but *action* for the sake of life. Surely that wouldn't be a violation of the Sabbath, would it?

Perhaps the indecisive ones in the crowd, having been bullied for years by the nitpicking Pharisees, turned to their religious experts to see how they would respond. Of course, their teachers didn't answer.

So Jesus went on, arguing from the lesser to the greater: "How much more valuable then is a man than a sheep! So then, it is lawful to do good on the Sabbath" (12:12). The logic was unimpeachable. If it was permissible to save a lamb from a bad situation on the Sabbath, then surely it would be permissible, if possible, to save a person from a bad situation that was robbing them of truly living. If someone was actually able to heal a man with a withered hand, and that someone encountered the man with a withered hand on the Sabbath, then wouldn't it be lawful to do good to that man that day, even though it was the Sabbath?

The Pharisees had their opinion of the right interpretation of the Law. Jesus had His opinion. The Pharisees claimed higher authority as trained experts in the Law. Jesus claimed to be Lord of the Sabbath. They couldn't both be right. But there they stood in that synagogue, face-to-face, toe-to-toe, in a sort of stalemate . . . until Jesus turned the theoretical into the practical. He turned to the man with the withered hand and said, "Stretch out your hand!" Instantly the man's hand was restored (12:13).

Think about it. With those four words, Jesus won the debate. The legalistic quibbling about the Sabbath that had spanned generations was tossed to the trash heap when the Lord of the Sabbath proved that He and He alone had the final authority in all matters of doctrine and practice. The rabbis could reason their way into condemning anybody who disagreed with them and could claim to be enforcing God's laws, but when the Author of Scripture Himself stepped into history and corrected their flawed interpretation, all arguments were over.

— 12:14 —

When Jesus proved His divine authority by healing the man, the Pharisees should have raised the white flag of surrender then and there. It should have taken them two seconds to reason, *If He can heal instantly, then He has divine authority; if He has divine authority, then His teaching carries divine authority; if His teaching carries divine authority, then He knows better than we do about how to interpret the Sabbath laws.*

But they didn't. Instead, they seethed. It was bad enough that He had exposed the stupidity of their man-made rules and humiliated them in public. But He had underscored it by healing a man with a withered hand—certainly a man well known to the members of the synagogue. There was no hiding the fact that Jesus had miraculous power, a power unparalleled by any of the Pharisees.

In response to the embarrassing situation, the Pharisees hightailed it out of the synagogue, put their heads together, and came up with a solution: "destroy Him" (12:14). Thus began the conspiracy against Jesus to take Him out. Talk about hardness of heart! Here we witness the sad truth of unrepentant legalism. The Pharisees were so proud that instead of admitting they were wrong in the face of obvious proof, they sought to destroy the one who had corrected their stunning error. How horrifying! But how typical of legalists!

Jesus' reaction? He left them to plot and scheme, departing from the synagogue and, not surprisingly, gaining more followers than He had before (see 12:15). Jesus knew it wasn't time for Him to be arrested. He had much more to teach and to do among His disciples to prepare them for the life of ministry ahead of them.

APPLICATION: MATTHEW 12:1-14

Realigning Your Allegiance from Legalism to Lordship

As an application of this pivotal portion of Scripture, I want to ask four questions designed to make you think. Maybe they'll make you squirm. Ponder them deeply. Answer them honestly. Use them to probe your own attitudes toward both Christ's lordship and man-made legalism.

First, *do you allow legalists to control you?* Many people are so desperate to avoid conflict that they just let legalists get their way. But this is never a good policy. It's not good for you, for the church, or even for the legalist. The truth is that you can never fully please a legalist. As an old proverb says, if you give them an inch, they'll take a mile. And if legalists get used to getting their own way, they'll create an entire culture around their man-made list of rules and regulations.

Second, *has your spiritual maturity been stunted by legalism . . . and are you stifling the growth of others in the same way?* My heart goes out to you if you were raised in a legalistic home or grew up in a legalistic church. Many people I've spoken with in my own generation were raised in homes filled with rules and requirements that had nothing to do with the Bible or true Christian morality. These made-up rules were enforced by parents or churches as if they had come down from Sinai itself. Parents and Christian leaders often thought that by creating rules for every situation, they would protect their children and church members from going astray. But that approach fails to teach self-control, wisdom, and how to walk in the Spirit. Legalism actually stunts true spiritual growth. One of the marks of spiritual maturity is working through "gray" issues. And it's important to know when you're taking something too far. As you grow up in the Lord, you develop that sense of knowing what's best without needing to be told by some authority figure or consulting some noninspired set of dos and don'ts.

Third, *can you discern between God's instructions and others' expectations?* The Christian faith isn't without its imperatives and mandates. Jesus issued commands to His disciples, and the Bible is filled with lists of things to embrace and things to avoid. Those are lists worth following because they are *God-breathed!* But then there are other instructions that come from people's preferences, opinions, and personal experiences, with only a contrived relationship to the principles of God's Word. As you grow in the Lord, you need to be able to tell the difference. When you do, you'll be liberated from the carnal constraints of legalism and freed to live by the spiritual principles of the Lord: "If you continue in My word, then you are truly disciples of Mine; and you will know the truth, and the truth will make you free" (John 8:31-32).

Finally, *are you becoming an agent of grace?* As a true disciple, set free by God's grace to live according to divine wisdom and righteousness, you are to broadcast messages of grace as often as you can—both in your words and in your actions. Here's a way to tell if you're an agent of grace: Are you resisting the tendency to control others? Start with your own older children if you have them. Are you still trying to control them, or do you release them? They're on their own now. Are you releasing others from various forms of probation, or do you hold people back for a period of time until they prove themselves? Do you look for opportunities to affirm others? Do you offer encouragement to at least one person every day? Are you breaking the habits of shame and blame? If so, you're an agent of grace.

Many believers who have been bullied by legalists or who have become legalists themselves need to realign their allegiance. They have been under the thumb of legalism for too long. Instead of passing that unholy tradition down to the next generation, they need to break free from legalism and submit instead to the lordship of Christ.

God's Servant or Satan's Pawn?
MATTHEW 12:15-30

NASB

15 But Jesus, ᵃaware of *this*, withdrew from there. Many followed Him, and He healed them all, 16 and warned them not to ᵃtell who He was. 17 *This was* to fulfill what was spoken through Isaiah the prophet:

18 "BEHOLD, MY ᵃSERVANT WHOM I
ᵇHAVE CHOSEN;
MY BELOVED IN WHOM MY SOUL
ᶜis WELL-PLEASED;
I WILL PUT MY SPIRIT UPON HIM,
AND HE SHALL PROCLAIM ᵈJUSTICE
TO THE ᵉGENTILES.
19 "HE WILL NOT QUARREL, NOR CRY
OUT;
NOR WILL ANYONE HEAR HIS
VOICE IN THE STREETS.
20 "A BATTERED REED HE WILL NOT
BREAK OFF,
AND A SMOLDERING WICK HE WILL
NOT PUT OUT,
UNTIL HE ᵃLEADS ᵇJUSTICE TO
VICTORY.
21 "AND IN HIS NAME THE ᵃGENTILES
WILL HOPE."

22 Then a demon-possessed man *who was* blind and mute was brought to ᵃJesus, and He healed him, so that the mute man spoke and saw. 23 All the crowds were amazed, and were saying, "This man cannot be the Son of David, can he?" 24 But when the Pharisees heard *this*, they said, "This man casts out demons only by ᵃBeelzebul the ruler of the demons." 25 And knowing their thoughts Jesus said to them, "ᵃAny kingdom divided against itself is laid waste; and ᵃany city or house divided against itself will not stand. 26 If Satan casts out Satan, he ᵃis divided against himself; how then will his kingdom stand? 27 If I by ᵃBeelzebul cast out demons, by whom do your

NLT

15 But Jesus knew what they were planning. So he left that area, and many people followed him. He healed all the sick among them, 16 but he warned them not to reveal who he was. 17 This fulfilled the prophecy of Isaiah concerning him:

18 "Look at my Servant, whom I
have chosen.
He is my Beloved, who
pleases me.
I will put my Spirit upon him,
and he will proclaim justice
to the nations.
19 He will not fight or shout
or raise his voice in public.
20 He will not crush the weakest
reed
or put out a flickering candle.
Finally he will cause justice
to be victorious.
21 And his name will be the hope
of all the world."*

22 Then a demon-possessed man, who was blind and couldn't speak, was brought to Jesus. He healed the man so that he could both speak and see. 23 The crowd was amazed and asked, "Could it be that Jesus is the Son of David, the Messiah?" 24 But when the Pharisees heard about the miracle, they said, "No wonder he can cast out demons. He gets his power from Satan,* the prince of demons." 25 Jesus knew their thoughts and replied, "Any kingdom divided by civil war is doomed. A town or family splintered by feuding will fall apart. 26 And if Satan is casting out Satan, he is divided and fighting against himself. His own kingdom will not survive. 27 And if I am empowered by Satan, what about your own exorcists? They cast out demons, too, so

sons cast *them* out? For this reason they will be your judges. ²⁸But if I cast out demons by the Spirit of God, then the kingdom of God has come upon you. ²⁹Or how can anyone enter the strong man's house and carry off his property, unless he first binds the strong *man?* And then he will plunder his house.

³⁰He who is not with Me is against Me; and he who does not gather with Me scatters.

12:15 ªLit *knowing* **12:16** ªLit *make Him known* **12:18** ªLit *Child* ᵇLit *chose* ᶜOr *took pleasure* ᵈOr *judgment* ᵉOr *nations* **12:20** ªOr *puts forth* ᵇOr *judgment* **12:21** ªOr *nations* **12:22** ªLit *Him* **12:24** ªOr *Beezebul;* i.e. ruler of demons **12:25** ªLit *Every* **12:26** ªLit *was* **12:27** ªV 24, note 1

they will condemn you for what you have said. ²⁸But if I am casting out demons by the Spirit of God, then the Kingdom of God has arrived among you. ²⁹For who is powerful enough to enter the house of a strong man and plunder his goods? Only someone even stronger—someone who could tie him up and then plunder his house.

³⁰"Anyone who isn't with me opposes me, and anyone who isn't working with me is actually working against me.

12:18-21 Isa 42:1-4 (Greek version for 42:4). **12:24** Greek *Beelzeboul;* also in 12:27. Other manuscripts read *Beezeboul;* Latin version reads *Beelzebub.*

How do you respond when you know that others are working against you? If you're like most, you look for ways to cut them off at the pass, to hit them before they hit you! Or you retaliate, hitting them harder so they'll think twice about coming at you again. Preemptive action, retaliation, and revenge—I can't think of any reactions more common to human nature than those.

If anybody had reason to strike back with overwhelming force, it was Jesus. Think about how difficult the Pharisees made His life—day to day, minute by minute. In their deep suspicion, they started following Him around and began concocting false charges. When they were unable to stop Him and unwilling to believe in Him, they began conspiring to kill Him (12:14)!

Yet Jesus was unfazed by the cruel conniving of the Pharisees. Instead, He called their bluff and demonstrated publicly how profoundly wrong they were (12:9-13). Jesus was unalarmed by their increasingly desperate attempts at silencing Him, even when they began to plot His physical demise. Instead, Jesus continued with business as usual, preaching and teaching, healing and delivering—all the while aware that the Pharisees continued to plot and lay traps for Him.

Observing how Jesus responded to His nemeses will give us insight into how we can respond to critics of Christ and enemies of the cross in our own day.

— 12:15-21 —

Aware of the Pharisees' plotting and scheming, Jesus did a couple of remarkable things. First, He slipped away without one word—not even a whisper, a shake of the fist, a knowing grin, or a cluck of the tongue (12:15). When He departed, He didn't head for the hills or find shelter in a cave. Instead, He stayed focused on His mission, gathering followers and healing the masses—the very things that had led to the Pharisees' jealousy and rage.

He also continued to downplay His identity as the Messiah (12:16). Why would He do that? Think about it. There were a lot more followers of Jesus than credentialed scribes and committed Pharisees. Aware that many in the crowd had in their minds a false image of a battle-ready Messiah, Jesus knew that too much talk of His legitimate kingship in the wrong way or at the wrong time could have incited the crowd to band together against the establishment and revolt.

What would have happened if Jesus had stood up one day and shouted, "Those Pharisees are plotting to kill Me! Something needs to be done!"? It would have been like tossing a grenade into a munitions facility. The result would have been a catastrophe. His work of calling a people to Himself would have come to an end. The true nature of the kingdom of God as distinct from the world would have been distorted by the world's methods of gaining and maintaining power by force. His teachings about love, peace, grace, and mercy would have been undone. And His training of the disciples would have come to a screeching halt. Jesus wanted to exemplify for His followers how to handle situations like this by letting God work.

Matthew quotes from the messianic prophecy of Isaiah 42:1-4, written about seven centuries earlier, to again explain Jesus' mission and to clarify His methods. This is the longest quote from the Old Testament in Matthew's Gospel. As the prophesied chosen Servant endowed with the Spirit of God, well-pleasing to the Father (Matt. 12:18), Jesus, in His messianic mission, was involved not only in the proclamation of His kingship to Israel but also in the proclamation of justice to the Gentiles, who would hope in His name (12:18, 21).

Isaiah's prophecy, and Matthew's quotation of it, clearly stated that the Messiah would Himself be a preacher of righteousness to the nations beyond Israel. Yet up to this point, the vast majority of those to whom Jesus had been preaching and teaching had been Jews. In fact, when Jesus had sent out the twelve (as well as the seventy) disciples to preach and do miracles in His name, He had sent them just to the people of Israel, not to the Gentiles or even to the Samaritans (10:5-6). By quoting this prophecy, Matthew made it clear that Jesus' messianic mission had only just begun. Rushing to establish the kingdom of Israel immediately would have been forsaking the mission to the Gentiles.

Matthew's quotation also explains Jesus' ministry methods. Instead of engaging His adversaries with swords, He engaged them with words. And His words were well chosen, terse, and few. This, too, was in keeping with the messianic prophecy of Isaiah. The mission of the chosen Servant was to be

- well-pleasing to God (12:18)
- accomplished through proclamation (12:18)
- free from quarreling or crying out (12:19)
- without ruckus or riot (12:19)
- considerate of the weak and vulnerable (12:20)
- focused on the goal of justice (12:20)[90]

One last implication of Matthew's quotation of Isaiah 42 needs to be mentioned. It's a theme already materializing in the background of Matthew's Gospel and that is about to be moved to center stage: Israel's rejection of their Messiah. Notice the double reference to the Messiah's mission to the Gentiles. Not only would Jesus "proclaim justice [or righteousness] to the Gentiles" (Matt. 12:18), but they would actually hope in His name (12:21). When Matthew wrote his Gospel sometime in the AD 60s, it was a well-known fact that the leaders of Israel had rejected Jesus as the Messiah. Most of the religious leaders were also rejecting the subsequent proclamation of the apostles, while many Gentiles, on the other hand, were trusting in Jesus as their Savior. In the next few scenes, Matthew points out how these developments began in Jesus' ministry when the Jewish leaders who refused to bow to King Jesus were actually making it possible for the gospel to go forth to the Gentiles. Ironically, by trying to destroy the Messiah's mission, the Pharisees were, in fact, promoting it!

— 12:22-24 —

Matthew presents a specific example of how the Pharisees were continuing to increase the public slandering and smear campaign against Jesus. It began with the deliverance of a demonized man who had been afflicted with the inability to see and speak (12:22). While this feat was astonishing and miraculous, by this point in Jesus' ministry such healings had become common. Matthew simply presents this event as a fact. The story turns bizarre, however, with the response of the Pharisees.

The crowds marveled and discussed whether Jesus could be the long-awaited Son of David, the King of Israel (12:23). That was the most obvious conclusion. Yet the way Matthew words the people's question suggests that while the crowds really wanted it to be true, they were for some reason doubtful and reluctant to fully embrace Jesus as the Messiah.[91] Perhaps this was partly due to Jesus' own hesitance to broadcast His true identity.

However, there was another reason the people of the crowd couldn't fully bring themselves to accept Jesus as their Messiah: the pressure of the Pharisees. These religious leaders were always there, working the crowd, planting seeds of doubt and poisoning the people's minds. This occasion was no different. In the presence of obvious power to instantly heal a demonized man, the Pharisees stepped in with their own ridiculous explanation: "This man casts out demons only by Beelzebul the ruler of the demons" (12:24). The name Beelzebul is likely another name for the Philistine god Baal-Zebub, which can be translated as "Lord of the Flies."[92] The term *baal* simply meant "lord," but in ancient Canaanite religion, *Baal* had become a proper name for the chief deity over their many gods. To the Jews, the term had become a kind of slang for Satan, the prince of demons.

The Pharisees couldn't deny the supernatural power Jesus had at His disposal. But they could use the lawyerly strategy of "pleading in the alternative." Having failed to argue that Jesus was some quack or charlatan claiming to do things He couldn't do, they acknowledged that He was performing miraculous wonders. But instead of admitting that God was working through Him (which would have been tantamount to accepting Him as the Messiah), the Pharisees argued that the supernatural power to cast out demons was coming from the chief of the demons—Satan himself!

What a desperate attempt to avoid the obvious! But what else could they say? To maintain their anti-Jesus stance, the Pharisees had to resort to attributing the work of God Almighty to the devil. Such blasphemy was unconscionable . . . and unpardonable.

— 12:25-30 —

Jesus wasted no time in responding to the Pharisees' murmured charge that His divine power actually came from Satan. He hadn't heard the accusation directly from the Pharisees themselves, but Jesus knew their thoughts and responded appropriately (12:25). He didn't need a couple of days to formulate an argument or gather His evidence. He addressed their serious charge head-on. Their blasphemy was an attack on Jesus' divine authority, an attack on the Spirit of God's miraculous works, and thus an attack on the divine nature itself! He gave three crushing arguments to explain that He couldn't have been operating under the influence of Satan's power.

First, if Jesus were casting out demons by Satan's power, then Satan would be working against himself (12:26). Why would Satan allow Jesus to free people from his own demonic control? Why would the outcome of these cases be so positive? The blind saw. The deaf could hear. The mute could speak. The lame could walk. The possessed were restored to normalcy. The self-destructive were given peace. The wicked were made righteous. If Satan's endgame was death and destruction, why would he bring about life and restoration day after day? No kingdom can last very long if its army fights against itself.

Second, if Jesus were casting out demons by Beelzebul, what about the Pharisees' own exorcists (12:27)? By what power or authority did they cast them out? To fully appreciate the force of Jesus' argument here, we need to realize that the *quality* of Jesus' authority over demonic forces was remarkably greater than that of other known Jewish exorcists (see Acts 19:13-16). The Jewish historian Josephus mentions a legend that Solomon himself had bequeathed the skill of expelling demons, which was "useful and sanative to men."[93] And in one of the apocryphal books well known by first-century Jews, we can read a story of a man named Tobias who drove off a demon by the pungent stench of a smoldering liver and heart of a fish (Tobit 8:2-3). Historical sources suggest that the first-century Jewish remedy for demon possession "was closer to a magic art than an irruption of divine power."[94]

If the Pharisees were to answer that their own exorcisms were performed by divine power, not by human or demonic power, then the next question would be "Why, then, are they *less* effective over demons than Jesus' are?" If the Pharisees continued to suggest that Jesus cast out demons by the prince of demons, then the argument would cut in the other direction: The Jewish exorcists must have been working with an even lesser power than Beelzebul—either some lower demonic power or natural human magic. Clearly, the best explanation, requiring less fiddling with facts, would be the simplest: Jesus cast out demons not by another evil spirit but by the Spirit of God. But then that would mean that Jesus was, in fact, the personal representative of the kingdom of God—the Messiah (Matt. 12:28).

Third, by driving out demons, Jesus proved that He was stronger than the demonic forces (12:29). He was able to step into the "strong man's house" (this demon-infested domain) and "carry off his property" (those possessed by demons). To do this, the strong man himself had to have been bound first. For the strong man (Satan) to plunder his own domain is implausible. And for some demon lesser than Satan to plunder Satan's domain is impossible. Only God has the power to plunder the kingdom of Satan and free his enslaved victims.

I can picture the crowd, who had earlier heard the outrageous murmurs of the Pharisees, turning from Jesus to their astute rabbis to hear their rejoinder. But instead of a bold refutation, a well-reasoned objection, or even a probing question, they had nothing. Literally nothing. The silence of the Pharisees spoke volumes. You probably could have heard their hearts pounding as beads of sweat formed on their red faces. Then the crowd may have turned again to Jesus, who proclaimed, "He who is not with Me is against Me; and he who does not gather with Me scatters" (12:30).

These were powerful words of reproof for His Pharisaic opponents. But Jesus wasn't done with them yet.

APPLICATION: MATTHEW 12:15-30

With or Against?

There would have been no question regarding what Jesus was talking about when He said, "He who is not with Me is against Me" (12:30). That day Jesus drew a line in the sand and said to the wavering crowd, essentially, "Now it's time to choose. You've seen the miracles. You've heard the excuses of the Pharisees. You've heard My teaching. You've heard their senseless explanations. There's no neutral ground. You're either with Me or against Me."

We face the same question—first and ultimately in our initial conversion to following Christ and our acceptance of Him as Savior and Lord: Are you with Him or against Him? We need to embrace the truth of who He is and what He has done. He's the God-man who died for our sins and rose from the dead. He's the Messiah, the King of Israel. He's the long-awaited Savior and Lord.

But we also have to answer this question every day after that initial decision. We can't waver in indecision about whether we will "gather" with Him or "scatter" with His enemies.

That crowd of hangers-on had seen and heard astonishing things. Yet they wavered. Think about what must have been going through their heads: *Hmm. It sure looks like He's the Messiah and all, but, well, it's really awkward, because those Pharisees with their curled lips and furrowed brows sure make it hard to think straight. Do I accept the obvious and get pummeled by the pious prudes . . . or do I just ignore all the evidence and avoid conflict? Such a tough decision!*

No, it's not a tough decision! The arguments and evidence have never changed. The claims of Christ have withstood two millennia of skeptics, scoffers, doubters, deceivers, opponents, apostates, critics,

EXCURSUS: GOD VS. SATAN?

MATTHEW 12:29

People often think that Satan is the opposite of God—that he is God's eternal enemy and that the forces of good and evil have battled each other for eons. However, this picture is not accurate according to the biblical view of God and Satan.

The religion of Zoroastrianism, the chief religion of ancient Persia, has a dualistic concept of God—that two equally powerful gods, one good and one evil, stand in opposition to each other. Similar to the Eastern concept of the yin and yang, light and dark, and positive and negative, these two gods are engaged in immortal combat with each other over the obedience of humans.[95]

This ancient, dualistic notion of the spiritual realm has influenced many pagan religions and has often worked its way into popular art and culture. Various ancient heresies advanced a dualistic view of the world that split divinity into balancing forces of good and evil. Numerous superstitious Christians of the medieval period viewed God and Satan as having equal influence in the world—for good and evil, respectively. Today, certain films have popularized the idea of a balanced "force" with a light and a dark side.[96]

But the Bible teaches that Satan is an angelic creature made by God (see Ezek. 28:12-16) who can do nothing apart from God's control or permission (see Job 1:6-12; Luke 22:31). He is not an "equal but opposite" counterpart of God but is more an opposite of the archangel Michael (Jude 1:9; Rev. 12:7). Yet he is also the enemy and accuser of humans (Zech. 3:1-2; 1 Pet. 5:8). While we must not deny that Satan has power to attack and ensnare us (Eph. 4:27; 6:11; 1 Tim. 3:7), we must also guard against attributing to Satan more power than he actually has.

heretics, debunkers, myth busters, and truth twisters. Through it all, the truth of Jesus Christ has never been defeated. It's *not* a tough decision. But it *is* a decision. This is spiritual combat between the kingdom of God and the kingdom of Satan. It's an either-or matter. There's no middle ground. You're either with Him or against Him.

Severe Warnings Everyone Must Remember
MATTHEW 12:31-37

NASB

31 "Therefore I say to you, any sin and blasphemy shall be forgiven people, but blasphemy against the Spirit shall not be forgiven. 32 Whoever ªspeaks a word against the Son of Man, it shall be forgiven him; but whoever ªspeaks against the Holy Spirit, it shall not be forgiven him, either in this age or in the *age* to come.

33 "Either make the tree good and its fruit good, or make the tree bad and its fruit bad; for the tree is known by its fruit. 34 You brood of vipers, how can you, being evil, speak ªwhat is good? For the mouth speaks out of that which fills the heart. 35 The good man brings out of *his* good treasure ªwhat is good; and the evil man brings out of *his* evil treasure ᵇwhat is evil. 36 But I tell you that every ªcareless word that people ᵇspeak, they shall give an accounting for it in the day of judgment. 37 For ªby your words you will be justified, and ªby your words you will be condemned."

12:32 ªLit *will speak*   12:34 ªLit *good things*
12:35 ªLit *good things* ᵇLit *evil things*   12:36 ªOr *useless* ᵇLit *will speak*   12:37 ªOr *in accordance with*

NLT

31 "So I tell you, every sin and blasphemy can be forgiven—except blasphemy against the Holy Spirit, which will never be forgiven. 32 Anyone who speaks against the Son of Man can be forgiven, but anyone who speaks against the Holy Spirit will never be forgiven, either in this world or in the world to come.

33 "A tree is identified by its fruit. If a tree is good, its fruit will be good. If a tree is bad, its fruit will be bad. 34 You brood of snakes! How could evil men like you speak what is good and right? For whatever is in your heart determines what you say. 35 A good person produces good things from the treasury of a good heart, and an evil person produces evil things from the treasury of an evil heart. 36 And I tell you this, you must give an account on judgment day for every idle word you speak. 37 The words you say will either acquit you or condemn you."

Two words describe the situation at this stage in Jesus' earthly ministry: *growing hostility*. When news first reached the official religious authorities—the Pharisees and scribes—telling them of His ever-enlarging following, they began to check Jesus out, probably motivated initially by mere curiosity. Whenever they were in His presence, though, they heard His bold exposé of their hypocrisy and witnessed His amazing and undeniable miracles. As a result, their curiosity turned to suspicion.

At that point, they began to stalk Him, looking for opportunities to criticize Him, to question His motives, and to disprove both His words and works. By then, they had become His implacable enemies, determined to portray Him as untrustworthy and then to condemn Him as an impostor unworthy of respect—in fact, as an agent of Satan. When they found themselves unable to silence Him or prove that He was a dangerous leader, their animosity turned to rage. This prompted them to meet in secret and lay out a plan to kill Him. Jesus, fully aware of their plot, intensified His instructions and warnings—warnings for the Pharisees, yes, but also warnings for anyone else who would harden their hearts to the Messiah.

— 12:31-32 —

As we reenter the unfolding scene in Matthew 12, we find that the Pharisees were beginning to see another side of Jesus they had not expected and for which they were unprepared. A. T. Robertson describes the atmosphere: "They now find out what a powerful opponent Jesus is. By parables, . . . by sarcasm, by rhetorical question, by merciless logic, he lays bare their hollow insincerity and the futility of their arguments."[97] This had begun in His response to their baseless and senseless charge that He had been casting out demons by the power of the prince of demons (12:25-29).

Jesus had also issued an ultimatum for decisive discipleship: "He who is not with Me is against Me; and he who does not gather with Me scatters" (12:30). With those words, Jesus threw down the gauntlet. He wasn't being unkind, just uncompromising. Robertson again pictures the situation vividly: "Christ is the magnet of the ages. He draws or drives away."[98] Those in the crowd had to decide yea or nay. There was no option for an abstention, no motion to table, no filibustering to delay the decision.

At this point in Jesus' ministry, the sides were forming, the crowds were dividing, and the true character of His detractors was coming to light. Those who were being driven further and further away from faith in Christ began to act out in a shocking way. They attributed the works of the Spirit of God to the power of Satan ("Beelzebul"; 12:24). They were essentially calling the eternal, divine Son of God a tool of the devil!

I like to imagine Jesus looking directly into the faces of His accusers when He declared, "Therefore I say to you, any sin and blasphemy shall be forgiven people, but blasphemy against the Spirit shall not be forgiven" (12:31). He went on to clarify this general pronouncement in 12:32. If a person speaks a word against the Son of Man, it can be forgiven. Rejecting the claims of Christ is not enough to commit this unpardonable sin. Think about it. Some of the most amazing testimonies come from those who were once doubters and skeptics, scoffers and critics, persecutors and blasphemers. We only need to think of the apostle Paul, who described his former life as a rabid rabbinical devotee: "I was formerly a blasphemer and a persecutor and a violent aggressor. Yet I was shown mercy because I acted ignorantly in unbelief" (1 Tim. 1:13). If Paul could be forgiven for blasphemy against Christ, anybody can be.

However, Jesus described a different category of blasphemous sin—one that His Pharisaic opponents were dangerously close to committing, if they hadn't already gone over the edge: "Whoever speaks against the Holy Spirit, it shall not be forgiven him, either in this age or in the age to come" (Matt. 12:32). What exactly is this blasphemy against the Spirit? And who is it that commits it? Is it possible somebody reading this has already crossed that line?

In the immediate context of this statement, we see the kind of deep-seated, inexcusable, hard-hearted, spiteful act that Jesus describes as an unpardonable sin. The Pharisees were attributing to Satan what can only be accomplished by the power of the Spirit of God. Note that this is a combination of *irrefutable proof*—of Christ's identity and the Spirit's power—and *intentional rejection*. The Pharisees acknowledged that God exists, but in the face of clear and convincing proof of the Holy Spirit's miraculous work through Christ, they attributed that work to Satan and dismissed Jesus, God's Messiah, as Satan's messenger.

By contrast, Paul's unbelief was a result of acting "ignorantly" (1 Tim. 1:13). He had not seen the miracles, had not heard the messages, had not come face-to-face with the work of the Holy Spirit in the life and ministry of Jesus. But when Jesus Himself met him on the road to Damascus, Paul's immediate response was not "Get away from me, you devil!" but "Who are You, Lord?" (Acts 9:5). And when presented with the true identity of Jesus in that miraculous encounter and through the words of Ananias in Damascus (Acts 9:17), Paul "got up and was baptized" (Acts 9:18). How vastly different from the response of the Pharisees, who witnessed astonishing miracles day after day but responded with anger, hate, and violent rejection of Jesus!

Snakes in Suits

MATTHEW 12:34

One of the most fascinating books in my library is titled Snakes in Suits. The cover is chilling. It's a man dressed in a tailored suit ready for business. White shirt, well pressed, sharp looking, but instead of a necktie around his collar, there is a snake coiled around his neck. The subtitle says it all: When Psychopaths Go to Work. Written by two PhDs in psychology, the book explores the world of psychopaths in the workplace.

The authors describe psychopaths this way: "This group . . . displays a personality disorder rooted in lying, manipulation, deceit, egocentricity, callousness, and other potentially destructive traits."[99] Psychopaths are found in every realm of life, including politics, the workplace, the home, and, yes, even churches and ministries. I'm not a psychologist, but after reading this book, I'm sure I've run into some people in ministry who would fit comfortably in this category.

Such people have no sign of an active conscience. They have no loyalty except to themselves. They love to be the center of attention in public and are master manipulators behind the scenes. They are incorrigible and always believe they're right, and they respond to confrontation or correction with bullying, blasting, or bludgeoning. Not only are they ruinous to themselves, but they will also almost always destroy the churches or ministries of which they are members.

Jesus dealt with such individuals during His earthly ministry, except that instead of wearing suits, they were vipers in religious robes—the scribes and Pharisees. And though the clothing has changed through the centuries, the same snakelike psychopaths have slithered their way into the church throughout history. As I close my eyes, I can picture a long parade of these men and women whom I've encountered throughout my own life and ministry. At first, they seem harmless. They may come across in an initial interview as the long-awaited gift to the ministry. But then they start to wrap themselves

(continued on next page)

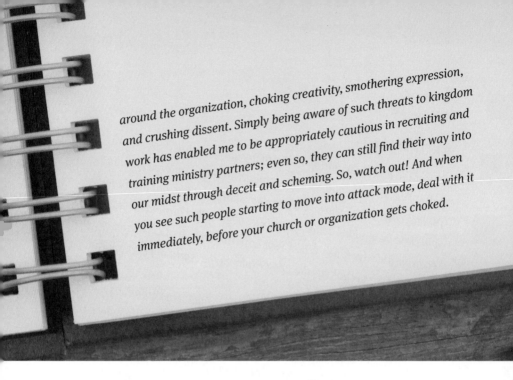

around the organization, choking creativity, smothering expression, and crushing dissent. Simply being aware of such threats to kingdom work has enabled me to be appropriately cautious in recruiting and training ministry partners; even so, they can still find their way into our midst through deceit and scheming. So, watch out! And when you see such people starting to move into attack mode, deal with it immediately, before your church or organization gets choked.

So the prospect of this unpardonable sin, from which there was no opportunity for repentance, was unique to the eyewitnesses of Jesus' miracles and message—those who rejected it knowingly, willingly, and persistently. In that narrow sense, such blasphemy against the Holy Spirit is no longer possible because Jesus' earthly ministry is over. However, in a more general sense, the sin for which there is no hope today would be to persist in the rejection of Christ throughout one's life and then die in that state of rejection. There is no biblical support for the idea of a second chance after death. *But until that moment,* anybody can believe and be saved.

This means, of course, that the unpardonable sin can't be committed by a believer indwelled by the Spirit. A believer is "in Christ" (see 1 Cor. 1:30). Once someone has given his or her heart to the Lord Jesus, that relationship is secure throughout eternity. But a person who chooses to reject Christ, who stays with that rejection and continues in hardness and callousness, becomes like Pharaoh, who subjected himself to wrath before God. I've had people ask, "Is it possible that I have committed the unpardonable sin?" My response: "Not so long as you're concerned about it." In other words, the very fact that you care at all is proof that you haven't. Those Pharisees who were guilty of blasphemy against the Holy Spirit delighted in their rejection of Jesus.

So, on top of His statement against neutrality regarding His identity (Matt. 12:30), Christ added this severe warning that it's incorrect to think you can't go too far in your rejection of Him and the Spirit operative in Him (12:31-32). The Pharisees had done it. And anyone who rejects Christ repeatedly, increasingly, and intentionally all the way to the end of his or her life is in an equally hopeless state.

— 12:33-37 —

Up to this point, Jesus had been addressing the visible manifestation of deep depravity, not its invisible source. He confronted the results, not the causes; the actions, not the reasons. However, as a follow-up to His strong warning about blasphemy against the Holy Spirit, He dug deeper to the core of the problem. When we understand the root of a problem, we'll better understand the nature of its solution.

Jesus was still directly addressing the Pharisees, now focusing on the source of their wickedness. This wasn't just a superficial, easily changeable faux pas they had committed. They didn't misstep or experience a slip of the tongue. They didn't momentarily lose their tempers and lapse into a temporary fit. Their problem was deep-seated. As fruit is to a tree, their actions were to the condition of their eternal souls. If the fruit of a tree is bad, it means the tree itself is diseased. And if the fruit of a tree is good, then the tree itself is healthy: "The tree is known by its fruit" (12:33).

By their external words and actions, then, the Pharisees revealed their true inner natures. They were a "brood of vipers" who, being evil, could only speak what came from their hearts—evil (12:34-35). The results of their lives were reliable indicators of the inner condition of their souls. By contrast, the "good man" produces good things from the treasure of his heart. The contrast in the immediate context was between Jesus Himself and the Pharisees. His words and works promoted and resulted in nothing but good—healing, deliverance from wickedness, repentance, good works, and righteousness. But if people followed the dictates of the Pharisees, the results would be wickedness, oppression, division, dissension, and, yes, even murderous plots against an innocent man!

The truth is, the heart is like a well of values, priorities, thoughts, and attitudes deep within us. The tongue is like the bucket that draws from that well. Until others actually drink from that invisible well, they won't know whether the water is good or bad, life-giving or toxic. The Pharisees' hidden well of wickedness had been revealed by their words of blasphemy. Jesus' warning to them was severe: "Every careless word that people speak, they shall give an accounting for it in the day of judgment" (12:36).

There are consequences for our words and actions. And while some people are justified by their right words, which manifest true, believing hearts, so, too, will some be condemned by their wicked words, which reveal sinful, unrepentant hearts (12:37). As Paul said, "If you confess with your mouth Jesus as Lord, and believe in your heart that God raised Him from the dead, you will be saved; for with the heart a person believes, resulting in righteousness, and with the mouth he confesses, resulting in salvation" (Rom. 10:9-10).

Clearly, the Pharisees had neither believed in their hearts nor confessed with their mouths that Jesus was Lord. Rather, they believed in their hearts and confessed with their mouths that He was worse than a liar or lunatic; He was, they said, the devil! And now they had to face a terrible truth: Nobody attributes the works of God to the power of the devil and gets away with it. Having failed to heed the first severe warning—not to make the wrong decision "with" or "against" Him (Matt. 12:30)—they then failed to heed the second severe warning: not to knowingly, intentionally, callously, and maliciously reject Him (12:31-32). Finally, they failed to heed the last severe warning: not to seal their fate with words that would one day come back and stand in judgment over them for all eternity (12:33-37).

APPLICATION: MATTHEW 12:31-37
Honest Evaluation of Personal Hypocrisy

None of us are Pharisees. None of us have lived in the first century. None of us were eyewitnesses of the miracles of Jesus Himself, obviously wrought by the unquestionable power of the Holy Spirit. But any of us could be hard-hearted hypocrites in our own twenty-first-century context. We may not blaspheme against the Holy Spirit, but we can grieve the Spirit (Eph. 4:30) and quench the Spirit (1 Thes. 5:19). Therefore, we need to occasionally make realistic evaluations of where we are spiritually.

First, *do you see yourself portrayed among those who are teetering on neutrality, believing you're safe in your indecision regarding Christ?* Are you sitting on the fence of indecision? Are you attempting the impossible—trying to remain neutral when Jesus Himself said that you're either *with Him* or *against Him* (Matt. 12:30)? Many people raised in church have tried to navigate between the conclusive yes and no of a decision regarding Christ. They know who He is and what He's done. They've heard the gospel all their lives but keep telling themselves, "I'll deal with Jesus another day." Today is the day. The middle ground doesn't exist. If you're not all in, you're all out.

Second, *would you have to admit that you have gotten callous regarding spiritual things?* Has overexposure desensitized you to the promptings of the Spirit? Do you zone out when the preacher is exhorting you from the Word? Do you zonk out when you read Scripture or pray? Hopefully, you've not gone so far that you're grieving or quenching the Spirit or intentionally turning away from the truth. Today would be the perfect time for you to step back and remember your need for Christ and your submission to the Spirit. Put an end to cynicism and walk into His arms.

Third, *are you beginning to realize that your words are not only careless but also reflect a toxic, unrepentant heart?* Have you let things into the depths of your heart that ought not to be there and are now coming out in the damaging use of your tongue? Ask Christ to cleanse your heart today, to enable you to break the habit. Clear things from your life that are polluting your mind, dirtying your heart, and poisoning your soul. Turn to Christ alone to cleanse you of those impurities by His Spirit.

Miraculous Signs, Evil Spirits, Startling Statements
MATTHEW 12:38-50

NASB

38 Then some of the scribes and Pharisees said to Him, "Teacher, we want to see a ᵃsign from You." 39 But He answered and said to them, "An evil and adulterous generation craves for a ᵃsign; and *yet* no ᵃsign will be given to it but the ᵃsign of Jonah the prophet; 40 for just as JONAH WAS THREE DAYS AND THREE NIGHTS IN THE BELLY OF THE SEA MONSTER, SO

NLT

38 One day some teachers of religious law and Pharisees came to Jesus and said, "Teacher, we want you to show us a miraculous sign to prove your authority."

39 But Jesus replied, "Only an evil, adulterous generation would demand a miraculous sign; but the only sign I will give them is the sign of the prophet Jonah. 40 For as Jonah was in the belly of the great fish for three days and three nights, so will

NASB

will the Son of Man be three days and three nights in the heart of the earth. ⁴¹The men of Nineveh will stand up with this generation at the judgment, and will condemn it because they repented at the preaching of Jonah; and behold, something greater than Jonah is here. ⁴²The Queen of *the* South will rise up with this generation at the judgment and will condemn it, because she came from the ends of the earth to hear the wisdom of Solomon; and behold, something greater than Solomon is here.

⁴³"Now when the unclean spirit goes out of a man, it passes through waterless places seeking rest, and does not find *it*. ⁴⁴Then it says, 'I will return to my house from which I came'; and when it comes, it finds *it* unoccupied, swept, and put in order. ⁴⁵Then it goes and takes along with it seven other spirits more wicked than itself, and they go in and live there; and the last state of that man becomes worse than the first. That is the way it will also be with this evil generation."

⁴⁶While He was still speaking to the crowds, behold, His mother and brothers were standing outside, seeking to speak to Him. ⁴⁷Someone said to Him, "Behold, Your mother and Your brothers are standing outside seeking to speak to You."ᵃ ⁴⁸But ᵃJesus answered the one who was telling Him and said, "Who is My mother and who are My brothers?" ⁴⁹And stretching out His hand toward His disciples, He said, "Behold My mother and My brothers! ⁵⁰For whoever does the will of My Father who is in heaven, he is My brother and sister and mother."

12:38 ᵃI.e. attesting miracle   12:39 ᵃI.e. attesting miracle   12:47 ᵃThis verse is not found in early mss   12:48 ᵃLit *He*

NLT

the Son of Man be in the heart of the earth for three days and three nights.

⁴¹"The people of Nineveh will stand up against this generation on judgment day and condemn it, for they repented of their sins at the preaching of Jonah. Now someone greater than Jonah is here—but you refuse to repent. ⁴²The queen of Sheba* will also stand up against this generation on judgment day and condemn it, for she came from a distant land to hear the wisdom of Solomon. Now someone greater than Solomon is here—but you refuse to listen.

⁴³"When an evil* spirit leaves a person, it goes into the desert, seeking rest but finding none. ⁴⁴Then it says, 'I will return to the person I came from.' So it returns and finds its former home empty, swept, and in order. ⁴⁵Then the spirit finds seven other spirits more evil than itself, and they all enter the person and live there. And so that person is worse off than before. That will be the experience of this evil generation."

⁴⁶As Jesus was speaking to the crowd, his mother and brothers stood outside, asking to speak to him. ⁴⁷Someone told Jesus, "Your mother and your brothers are standing outside, and they want to speak to you."*

⁴⁸Jesus asked, "Who is my mother? Who are my brothers?" ⁴⁹Then he pointed to his disciples and said, "Look, these are my mother and brothers. ⁵⁰Anyone who does the will of my Father in heaven is my brother and sister and mother!"

12:42 Greek *The queen of the south.*
12:43 Greek *unclean.*   12:47 Some manuscripts do not include verse 47. Compare Mark 3:32 and Luke 8:20.

As we read the narratives of the Gospels, it's easy to forget that these are accounts of people, places, and events that actually happened. These aren't simply bedtime stories of fictional characters told to convey nice morals to sleepy children. And they aren't myths or legends drawn from the foggy memories of distant relatives who may or may not have been there. These are narratives based on eyewitness accounts—written either by the eyewitnesses themselves (Matthew and John) or by those with access to numerous eyewitnesses (Mark and Luke).

As we read Matthew's recounting of the words and deeds of Jesus, we should try to envision an on-the-ground reality because these things took place in the real world. Admittedly, this is difficult to do, even for historians immersed in first-century language, culture, and geography. As the biblical narrative runs its course, it flows through unfamiliar places among people we've never met who lived in a first-century, Middle Eastern culture altogether different from our twenty-first-century world.

As we read brief snippets of conversations that involved more details than what's preserved in the summary accounts, we often have to fill in the gaps with some knowledge of the context and world around the events. The interactions recorded in Matthew 12:38-50 between Jesus and both the Pharisees and His family are great examples of dialogues that require careful thought in determining how they fit in the overarching plot of the Gospel. If we had an audio recording of these dialogues and could understand Aramaic—what was likely the street language of the day—we would certainly hear a tone of voice from Jesus' conversers that would help us make better sense of the conversations. So, we'll apply a little "sanctified imagination" as we place ourselves in the crowd of onlookers to hear Jesus' surprising and startling statements.

— 12:38-42 —

The first snippet of conversation in this section involves a strange request from the scribes and Pharisees: "Teacher, we want to see a sign from You" (12:38). What strikes me as odd about this is the source: the scribes and Pharisees who had just condemned Jesus for being an emissary of Satan (12:24). In their hypocrisy, the religious leaders were feigning honor for Jesus in front of the crowd. They reinforced this ruse by addressing Jesus with the seemingly respectful title "Teacher," which in Aramaic would have been *Rabbi*. But as A. B. Bruce notes, we readers should realize what's really going on: Their demand for a sign "was impudent, hypocritical, insulting."[100]

Why would they ask for a sign, then? Maybe the Pharisees thought that if they could just get Jesus to do enough of His "signs," which they regarded as fake, they would be able to figure out how He *really* did them. It would be like telling a magician, "Do it again . . . do it again . . . do it again" in order to expose the sleight of hand. In any case, we know Jesus' opponents weren't coaxing Him to do more signs so that more of the crowd would believe, though that's what would inevitably happen. Nor were they interested in the healing benefits of the miracles; after all, they had not cared enough about people to allow a man to be healed on the Sabbath. No, the scribes and Pharisees wanted to set Jesus up as a phony. They had already made up their minds that Jesus was a tool of the devil; now they just wanted to see exactly what it was about His "signs" that would give Him away.

Jesus, knowing their hypocrisy, didn't capitulate. Instead, He called the sign seekers "an evil and adulterous generation" (12:39). Paul would later castigate Jews in general for their insatiable desire for "signs" in order to believe the Word of God (1 Cor. 1:22). The ironic thing about Jesus' rebuke is that He had been performing great signs, wonders, and miracles since launching His ministry. He had even done many of these amazing signs before the very eyes of the scribes and Pharisees. Why wouldn't He do just one more for them on demand? Because He knew their motives, the hardness of their hearts, and the increased wickedness that would result if He were to cater to their every whim. Jesus knew even better than His opponents that miracles would do them no good. In fact, since miracles would only increase the amount of clear and convincing proof of His identity, their rejection of further evidence would render the Pharisees even more guilty before God.

Jesus said that they would only be privy to one more sign: "the sign of Jonah the prophet" (Matt. 12:39). Just as Jonah was three days and three nights in the belly of the fish and survived, the Son of Man would be three days and three nights in the heart of the earth and then rise again (12:40). Of course, the Pharisees would have had no idea Jesus was talking about His own death, burial, and resurrection.

However, knowing the future, Jesus was well aware of the fact that, for the most part, the Jewish leadership and the nation of Israel would not respond even to the miracle of the Resurrection. This is where the similarities between Jonah's miraculous deliverance from the belly of the fish and Jesus' future miraculous resurrection from the dead stop. When Jonah appeared three days after his death-like immersion in the sea, preaching in Nineveh while smelling of fish and having acid-bleached skin, the people of Nineveh repented (12:41). Those people who responded to God's word and His works would later be in a position to condemn the "evil and adulterous generation" (12:39) that had rejected the Messiah. Jesus was clearly "greater than Jonah" (12:41).

Jesus was not just the greatest prophet; He was also the greatest king. As such, He was also greater than Solomon, who had been regarded as the wisest king of Israel. So greatly had Solomon been renowned for his wisdom that even the "Queen of the South" had traveled

EXCURSUS: THREE DAYS AND THREE NIGHTS

MATTHEW 12:40

According to Matthew's account of the death, burial, and resurrection of Jesus later in his Gospel, Jesus died on a Friday afternoon sometime after three o'clock (27:45), and He was buried shortly before the sun went down and the Sabbath began, probably by about six o'clock. (27:57-61; see also Mark 15:42-47). Jesus' body lay in the ground throughout the Sabbath, and then He rose again by dawn on Sunday morning, probably sometime before six o'clock. (Matt. 28:1). All told, Jesus' body was in the tomb for about thirty-six hours. So, by our usual reckoning of time, Jesus was only in the earth for a day and a half. Yet Matthew records Jesus as saying He would be "three days and three nights in the heart of the earth" (12:40). How do we solve this apparent contradiction?

We can start with the assumption that Matthew wasn't perjuring himself, either purposely or accidentally. The timeline of the death, burial, and resurrection of Jesus would have been familiar to many. So, clearly, Jesus' words must be understood in light of the well-known facts that He was buried on Friday before sundown, lay in a tomb all day Saturday, and rose Sunday morning before sunrise. How, then, do we make sense of Jesus' words?

The key to interpreting Jesus' words relates to recognizing the way first-century Jews would have understood the expression He used. The phrase "three days and three nights" was a figurative idiom at the time, not a literal designation of twenty-four-hour periods.[101] The same phrase is used in 1 Samuel 30:12, describing an Egyptian servant who "had not eaten bread or drunk water for three days and three nights." In the next verse, the servant notes that he had fallen sick "three days ago" (1 Sam. 30:13). The Hebrew expression there, *hayōm shelōshah* [H3117 + H7969], refers to the exact same period of time as Jesus' time in the tomb, involving two nights, a whole day, and parts of two days at the beginning and end.

So, Matthew doesn't contradict himself, nor are we left wondering whether Jesus was buried for three (at least partial) days and two nights (as the account in Matthew 27 presents) or three days and three nights (as Jesus' parallel with Jonah suggests in Matthew 12). In first-century Jewish parlance, "three days and three nights" was a figure of speech describing a known period of time.

far to seek an audience with him to "test him with difficult questions" (1 Kgs. 10:1). When she perceived his wisdom and greatness, as well as the greatness of his kingdom, she observed, "Behold, the half was not told me. You exceed in wisdom and prosperity the report which I heard" (1 Kgs. 10:7). By contrast, when the Pharisees stood in the presence of one "greater than Solomon" (Matt. 12:42), instead of recognizing His wisdom and greatness, they rejected Him as a fool and a fraud. In that, the queen of Sheba would, as it were, stand in condemnation of them on the day of judgment.

Jesus' interaction with the hard-hearted Pharisees proves that it's possible to be exposed to truth but not allow it to enter and transform our lives.

— 12:43-45 —

At first glance, Jesus' story of the "unclean spirit" seems out of place. Here's the parable: A demon departs from a man and tries to find a different place to dwell. The implication is that while in the body of his host, the wicked spirit had been tormented, perhaps by an exorcism, and it needs "rest" (12:43). However, its quest for a better place to dwell is in vain. The demon then decides to return to the original man it had possessed, perhaps thinking the source of its earlier discomfort was over. When the spirit returns, it finds the man's body "unoccupied, swept, and put in order" (12:44). This implies that the man has "turned over a new leaf" and cleaned up his life. However, he's done so by external reform alone. Finally, finding such a spacious, clean vessel, the demon finds seven other spirits even worse than itself, and they all possess the man, resulting in an even worse condition than before (12:45).

What does this parable have to do with the hard-hearted scribes and Pharisees? The comparison is subtle but clear. The Pharisees had attempted a superficial reformation through strict religious observances, by external legislation and enforcement, and perhaps even by casting out demons through rites and rituals common in their day. They were law-abiding but unconverted. The resulting condition was worse than before because with their self-help approach to righteousness, they had deceived themselves into thinking they were actually clean and holy. This false righteousness brought self-deception and opened the door for an even more wicked state. It set them up for committing the unpardonable sin: the rejection of the Messiah and blasphemy against the Holy Spirit.

The truth is, it's much easier to deal with a person who's an out-and-out sinner and knows it than a self-righteous moralist who won't acknowledge his or her own need for salvation. The latter state marked the Jewish leaders in Jesus' day. Just as the man in the parable fell into a worse condition after his attempts at self-reformation without the indwelling Spirit, "it will also be with this evil generation" (12:45).

— 12:46-50 —

Finally, as things were heating up between Jesus and the Pharisees, an unexpected party showed up: "His mother and brothers were standing outside, seeking to speak to Him" (12:46). We aren't told what they wanted. The fact that Jesus' mother *and* brothers appeared suggests they weren't just stopping by to say *shalom*. They had intentionally made their way from Nazareth to Capernaum. The situation looked more like an intervention.

It appears that Jesus' earthly father, Joseph, had died by this time. After Jesus was born, Mary and Joseph had four other sons as well as some daughters (13:55-56). We are told that during Jesus' earthly ministry "not even His brothers were believing in Him" (John 7:5). In fact, some of His own people in His hometown—perhaps even His family— were saying, "He has lost His senses" (Mark 3:20-21).

A messenger went into the house where Jesus had been teaching and told Jesus that His mother and brothers had come to speak with Him (Matt. 12:47). Perhaps they wanted to "rescue" Jesus from Himself. A. T. Robertson's explanation seems reasonable: "It was natural for Mary to want to take him home for rest and refreshment."[102]

Jesus' response sounds harsh: "Who is My mother and who are My brothers?" (12:48). What a startling answer! Had He forgotten His own family? Had He genuinely lost His mind? Then, with a dramatic wave of His hand toward His dear disciples who were sticking close to Him even in the midst of blasphemous charges and dangerous opposition, He said, "Behold My mother and My brothers! For whoever does the will of My Father who is in heaven, he is My brother and sister and mother" (12:49-50).

We need to understand a few things. Jesus wasn't utterly rejecting His earthly family. He wasn't being dismissive or disrespectful. He was, rather, practicing what He preached. Just as He had taught His disciples that the kingdom of heaven took precedence over earthly family relationships (10:37), Jesus was looking at things through spiritual eyes and wanted His listeners to understand that there is no deeper relationship than one that is founded on faith in Christ. Even His own mother and siblings needed to have that kind of relationship with Him as their Savior and Lord. As John Peter Lange notes, "Jesus here places spiritual above carnal ties. His relatives are set aside, in as far as, for the moment, they had turned from the obedience of discipleship."[103]

It's comforting to know what the original readers of Matthew's Gospel already knew when they read this account in the AD 60s: Mary and Jesus' brothers eventually came around. Sometime between Jesus' resurrection and the coming of the Spirit at Pentecost, Jesus' natural family was folded into His larger—and more eternally significant—spiritual family. Acts 1:14 says, "These [disciples] all with one mind were continually devoting themselves to prayer, along with the women, and Mary the mother of Jesus, and with His brothers." How wonderful it is to see that Jesus' family became "charter members" of the church in Jerusalem.

APPLICATION: MATTHEW 12:38-50
Three Crucial Questions

These snippets of the growing controversy surrounding Jesus' teachings cover a lot of territory. A disingenuous request for a sign stemming from deep unbelief . . . a parable about evil spirits and the dangers of self-styled reform . . . a startling contrast between Jesus' earthly family and His spiritual family. These episodes from Jesus' ministry lead me to three crucial questions we ought to consider.

First, related to the Pharisees' hypocritical request for a sign: *Am I becoming a cynic?* This is a chief sign of Pharisaism. Let me tell you why I want you to ask yourself this question. Sunday after Sunday, week after week, month after month, class after class, sermon after sermon, Bible study after Bible study, you may be constantly exposed to God's Word. For many people, these moments are continually transformative. However, others begin to become desensitized to all of it. They're like a rock in a stream; the water can flow around it for ages but never penetrate its surface. Ask yourself, *Have I changed over the last year because I've sat under the ministry of the Word? Am I more patient? More kind? Gentler or more loving? Am I more forgiving? Or have I developed such a calloused heart that I want God to make Himself real to me through something other than His Word ministered by the Spirit?* Only you can answer these questions.

Second, related to the deep-seated moralism and self-reform of the Pharisees, illustrated by the self-scrubbed demoniac: *Am I relying on the Spirit's work in my life to change my mind and heart from the inside, or am I engaging in mere behavior modification to conform to external standards?* If you feel you're a pretty good person, have it all together, don't sin much, and pretty much avoid temptation, then you're in trouble. Chances are good that you've slipped into old-fashioned moralism. You need to instead acknowledge that you're a sinner who needs a Savior. You need Him not just at the beginning of the Christian life, to save you from damnation, but you also need Him throughout your life, to save you from a sinful lifestyle and to grant forgiveness when you go astray. May God deliver us all from religiosity and self-help and make us deeply aware that we're flawed and in need of His truth and grace.

Third, related to prioritizing our relationship with Christ: *Am I placing Christ first in my life, even above my earthly family?* If Christ were to call you from your current job to something more pivotal and strategic for His kingdom, would you go, even if it meant a little hardship for your family? Would you or your family move to a part of the country—or the world—that was far away from extended family, like parents, grandparents, brothers, and sisters? Or do you make all life and ministry decisions with family considerations as priority number one? Now, don't mishear me. I'm not talking about neglecting, abusing, or failing to provide for your family. Those of us who have a spouse or children have very serious and crucial ministries at home. But how easy it can be to allow family to take the throne of our lives and dictate every decision and every action.

In light of Christ's teachings and His example, we can more positively answer these three crucial questions, avoiding cynicism, moralism, and a loss of focus on Jesus Christ. But we can only do this through a right relationship with Him and by depending on the power of the Holy Spirit.

A Story for the Hard of Listening
MATTHEW 13:1-23

NASB

1 That day Jesus went out of the house and was sitting by the sea. 2 And a large crowds gathered to Him, so He got into a boat and sat down,

NLT

1 Later that same day Jesus left the house and sat beside the lake. 2 A large crowd soon gathered around him, so he got into a boat. Then he

NASB

and the whole crowd was standing on the beach. ³And He spoke many things to them in parables, saying, "Behold, the sower went out to sow; ⁴and as he sowed, some *seeds* fell beside the road, and the birds came and ate them up. ⁵Others fell on the rocky places, where they did not have much soil; and immediately they sprang up, because they had no depth of soil. ⁶But when the sun had risen, they were scorched; and because they had no root, they withered away. ⁷Others fell ᵃamong the thorns, and the thorns came up and choked them out. ⁸And others fell on the good soil and yielded a crop, some a hundredfold, some sixty, and some thirty. ⁹He who has ears, ᵃlet him hear."

¹⁰And the disciples came and said to Him, "Why do You speak to them in parables?" ¹¹ᵃJesus answered them, "To you it has been granted to know the mysteries of the kingdom of heaven, but to them it has not been granted. ¹²For whoever has, to him *more* shall be given, and he will have an abundance; but whoever does not have, even what he has shall be taken away from him. ¹³Therefore I speak to them in parables; because while seeing they do not see, and while hearing they do not hear, nor do they understand. ¹⁴ᵃIn their case the prophecy of Isaiah is being fulfilled, which says,

"ᵇYOU WILL KEEP ON HEARING,
　ᶜBUT WILL NOT UNDERSTAND;
ᵈYOU WILL KEEP ON SEEING, BUT
　WILL NOT PERCEIVE;
¹⁵ FOR THE HEART OF THIS PEOPLE
　HAS BECOME DULL,
WITH THEIR EARS THEY SCARCELY
　HEAR,

NLT

sat there and taught as the people stood on the shore. ³He told many stories in the form of parables, such as this one:

"Listen! A farmer went out to plant some seeds. ⁴As he scattered them across his field, some seeds fell on a footpath, and the birds came and ate them. ⁵Other seeds fell on shallow soil with underlying rock. The seeds sprouted quickly because the soil was shallow. ⁶But the plants soon wilted under the hot sun, and since they didn't have deep roots, they died. ⁷Other seeds fell among thorns that grew up and choked out the tender plants. ⁸Still other seeds fell on fertile soil, and they produced a crop that was thirty, sixty, and even a hundred times as much as had been planted! ⁹Anyone with ears to hear should listen and understand."

¹⁰His disciples came and asked him, "Why do you use parables when you talk to the people?"

¹¹He replied, "You are permitted to understand the secrets* of the Kingdom of Heaven, but others are not. ¹²To those who listen to my teaching, more understanding will be given, and they will have an abundance of knowledge. But for those who are not listening, even what little understanding they have will be taken away from them. ¹³That is why I use these parables,

For they look, but they don't
　really see.
They hear, but they don't really
　listen or understand.

¹⁴This fulfills the prophecy of Isaiah that says,

'When you hear what I say,
　you will not understand.
When you see what I do,
　you will not comprehend.
¹⁵ For the hearts of these people are
　hardened,
　and their ears cannot hear,

AND THEY HAVE CLOSED THEIR
  EYES,
OTHERWISE THEY WOULD SEE
  WITH THEIR EYES,
HEAR WITH THEIR EARS,
AND UNDERSTAND WITH THEIR
  HEART AND RETURN,
AND I WOULD HEAL THEM.'

¹⁶ But blessed are your eyes, because they see; and your ears, because they hear. ¹⁷ For truly I say to you that many prophets and righteous men desired to see what you see, and did not see *it*, and to hear what you hear, and did not hear *it*.

¹⁸ "Hear then the parable of the sower. ¹⁹ When anyone hears the ªword of the kingdom and does not understand it, the evil *one* comes and snatches away what has been sown in his heart. This is the one on whom seed was sown beside the road. ²⁰ The one on whom seed was sown on the rocky places, this is the man who hears the word and immediately receives it with joy; ²¹ yet he has no *firm* root in himself, but is *only* temporary, and when affliction or persecution arises because of the ªword, immediately he ᵇfalls away. ²² And the one on whom seed was sown among the thorns, this is the man who hears the word, and the worry of the ªworld and the deceitfulness of wealth choke the word, and it becomes unfruitful. ²³ And the one on whom seed was sown on the good soil, this is the man who hears the word and understands it; who indeed bears fruit and brings forth, some a hundredfold, some sixty, and some thirty."

13:2 ªLit *Many* 13:7 ªLit *upon* 13:9 ªOr *hear!* Or *listen!* 13:11 ªLit *He* 13:14 ªLit *For them* ᵇLit *With a hearing you will hear* ᶜLit *and* ᵈLit *Seeing you will see* 13:19 ªI.e. message 13:21 ªI.e. message ᵇLit *is caused to stumble* 13:22 ªOr *age*

and they have closed their eyes—
so their eyes cannot see,
and their ears cannot hear,
and their hearts cannot
  understand,
and they cannot turn to me
and let me heal them.'*

¹⁶ "But blessed are your eyes, because they see; and your ears, because they hear. ¹⁷ I tell you the truth, many prophets and righteous people longed to see what you see, but they didn't see it. And they longed to hear what you hear, but they didn't hear it.

¹⁸ "Now listen to the explanation of the parable about the farmer planting seeds: ¹⁹ The seed that fell on the footpath represents those who hear the message about the Kingdom and don't understand it. Then the evil one comes and snatches away the seed that was planted in their hearts. ²⁰ The seed on the rocky soil represents those who hear the message and immediately receive it with joy. ²¹ But since they don't have deep roots, they don't last long. They fall away as soon as they have problems or are persecuted for believing God's word. ²² The seed that fell among the thorns represents those who hear God's word, but all too quickly the message is crowded out by the worries of this life and the lure of wealth, so no fruit is produced. ²³ The seed that fell on good soil represents those who truly hear and understand God's word and produce a harvest of thirty, sixty, or even a hundred times as much as had been planted!"

13:11 Greek *the mysteries.* 13:14-15 Isa 6:9-10 (Greek version).

Anyone reading through the Gospel of Matthew realizes something has changed when they cross the threshold from chapter 12 to chapter 13. Before, Jesus spoke openly and freely. He offered Himself without restraint, demonstrating by His words and works that He was, in fact, the long-awaited Messiah, the King of Israel. One miracle after another grabbed the attention of all who followed Him, which prompted Him to communicate clearly and boldly the teachings of the kingdom of God and true righteousness. He offered stunning proof that He was a prophet and king like no one had ever seen; in fact, He was the "Son of Man" with divine authority over sin, sickness, and Satan.

But not everybody was responding positively to Jesus' messages. Cold curiosity characterized the religious leaders' initial reaction: *What could some previously unknown, roaming preacher from Nazareth say that's worth hearing?* And the more He taught, the more He exposed their hypocrisy, which led them to feel resentment and ultimately plot to kill Him!

At that point, Jesus went "underground." He changed His tactic from that of an open forum to an oblique form of communication. He started to intentionally veil His message so only the spiritually alert and committed could "get it." He began employing cryptic parables that required proper interpretation.

And not everybody who heard the messages was going to listen.

— 13:1-2 —

Jesus must have been exhausted!

Back on the Sabbath, He'd had to defend His disciples from the nitpicky Pharisees who had accused them of harvesting grain when they were doing no such thing (12:1-7). The same day, those legalists found fault with Jesus for healing a man's withered hand (12:10). The same group responded to Jesus' biblical defense of His actions with a plot to kill Him (12:14). Aware of that scheme, Jesus escaped, but the crowds kept growing and He kept healing the sick (12:15). Then He encountered a demonized man who was blind and mute and delivered him (12:22). In response to that, the Pharisees accused Jesus of operating by the power of Satan (12:24). His opponents pushed harder, trying to set Him up by finding some kind of flaw in His miracles (12:38-45). In the midst of all this cat-and-mouse commotion, Jesus' family showed up from Nazareth, probably to take Him home, and possibly thinking He'd lost His mind (12:46-50).

I've had busy days, but the harried and high-stress events of

A Little R & R

MATTHEW 13:1

When I read about Jesus' hectic ministry schedule in Matthew 12 and His desire to get out of the house and sit by the sea in Matthew 13:1, I can't help but smile. It reminds me of an occasion in my own life many years ago when all my children were small. I had plowed through one of those nonstop periods of "always on" ministry—not just a day or two, but months. After my family had labored long to keep life together, I realized that we all needed to get away. Cynthia and I made plans to escape to our favorite island among the Hawaiian chain, the island of Kauai. We couldn't get much farther away from our ministry obligations than that. It would be the perfect retreat for a little R & R. Nobody there would know us.

Early one morning, the boys and I went fishing. We headed to the North Shore, long before daylight. We got into a boat and ended up catching a bunch of fish. It was a terrific day. We put them on a stringer and headed back. As I waded ashore, flanked on my right and left by my two sons, we looked up and saw a gathering of people walking toward us. One of the boys said under his breath, "They're coming for you, Dad. We're out of here."

"No, no, no," I said. "Nobody even knows we're here."

But the boys were gone. They headed for the car, leaving me with that string of fish and a crowd of Hawaiians. To my amazement, the members of the crowd got their Bibles ready and said, "Brother Swindoll, we heard you were on our island, and we've come for you to teach us." Part of me wanted to stage a miracle: "You close your eyes, count to forty-five, and I'll disappear." But I didn't. That would have been unkind toward them.

But I didn't teach them either. That would have been unkind to my family. I was able to dismiss the crowd by letting them know that I had plans with my family to have some greatly needed peace and quiet.

(continued on next page)

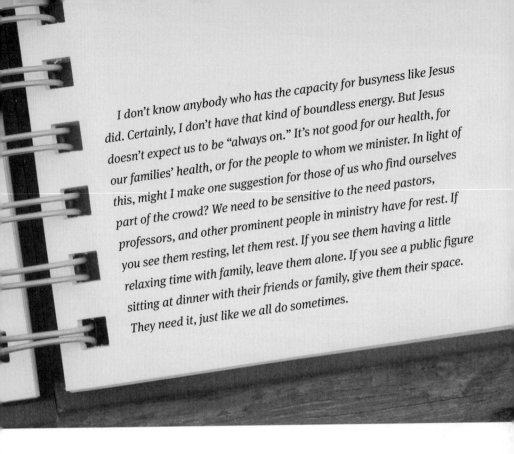

I don't know anybody who has the capacity for busyness like Jesus did. Certainly, I don't have that kind of boundless energy. But Jesus doesn't expect us to be "always on." It's not good for our health, for our families' health, or for the people to whom we minister. In light of this, might I make one suggestion for those of us who find ourselves part of the crowd? We need to be sensitive to the need pastors, professors, and other prominent people in ministry have for rest. If you see them resting, let them rest. If you see them having a little relaxing time with family, leave them alone. If you see a public figure sitting at dinner with their friends or family, give them their space. They need it, just like we all do sometimes.

Matthew 12 seem over the top. It's no wonder that chapter 13 begins, "That day Jesus went out of the house and was sitting by the sea" (13:1). He had to get away and catch His breath, taking in the fresh air. If He closed His eyes, He would absorb the sweet scent of wildflowers, the sound of birds chirping, the waves lapping against the shore, and . . . the crowd gathering around Him to see and hear what He would do or say next (13:2)! We don't know how long Jesus was able to rest before it was back to business. His break was over!

We can surmise the most likely location of His teaching here. About a mile southwest from Capernaum on the Sea of Galilee, a semicircular inlet forms a natural theater. Its bowl-shaped landscape provides ideal acoustics, enabling a speaker to be heard by a large crowd assembled on the gradually sloping land.[104] But there's a slight problem—not impossible to overcome, but a little inconvenient. The teacher or preacher has to be in the water facing the shore! As the sound of a voice is deflected off the surface of the water, it can be carried to the ears of thousands of listeners on land. This is why Jesus got into a boat, positioning Himself in the center of the semicircle. From a seated position, He began to teach "in parables" (13:3).

The **"Cove of the Sower,"** or "Bay of Parables," thought by scholars to be the likely location of Jesus' teaching from the boat.

— 13:3-9 —

I've often heard it said that Jesus taught with parables in order to make His teachings understandable to the common person. By using stories and illustrations drawn from everyday life, He could make complicated concepts simple and difficult truths easier to accept. As nice as that sounds, it's grossly inaccurate. As we'll see, when opposition to His ministry began heating up, Jesus began teaching in parables to *conceal* truth from those who denied Him as much as He wanted to *reveal* truth to those who desired Him. As such, the main truth of each parable wasn't easy, obvious, or accessible to everyone like the low-hanging fruit of a tree. It required the hearer to *listen*—to open both heart and mind with the interpretive key, which was Jesus Himself.

The first story in this series of stories by the sea introduces a now-iconic image that would have been very familiar in Jesus' day. In the previous chapter we saw Jesus walking with His disciples through a field of cultivated grain (12:1). Everybody knew how that grain got there. A farmer—the owner or manager of the field—would have tossed the seeds onto the soil. In those days, farmers didn't plant grain in perfect rows to accommodate harvesting machines. They first broke the ground and softened the soil of the field with a plow or other handheld instrument; then, with bags of seeds tied around their waists, sowers would broadcast the seed by hand.

PARABLES

MATTHEW 13:3

Of all the teaching tools at Jesus' fingertips, none had greater power to convey deep spiritual truths than the parable. Yet the parable was a double-edged sword. Not only could it reveal . . . it could also conceal. This is why Jesus preferred using parables when teaching a mixed audience of disciples and detractors. In fact, parables comprise more than one-third of Jesus' recorded sayings.[105] This unique form of illustrative storytelling accomplished two important objectives: It repelled hostile skeptics and equipped serious disciples.

The term "parable" is essentially a transliteration of the Greek word *parabolē* [3850]. This word connotes the idea of being "set alongside"—that is, drawing an instructive parallel between the story and the lesson or principle the teacher is trying to communicate.[106] We might call it an illustration, but a parable is always told in the form of a narrative, either brief or long. Unlike an allegory, in which the figurative elements have direct, literal counterparts, a parable is intentionally less precise, focusing on a single big idea. Therefore, when interpreting parables, we need to guard against two errors: missing what's of central importance in the illustrated truth and overanalyzing every detail. The first error would occur if somebody took the story as if it were a historical narrative, a record of actual events. The second would occur if somebody were to treat the story like an allegory, in which every detail has a direct connection to something literal.

In parables, a teacher uses common, everyday circumstances to communicate things that are unfamiliar or even supernatural. Parables appear to communicate something simple and obvious, but they invite the listener to think more deeply in order to really hear the truths being conveyed. Two factors make correct interpretation possible for the hearer.

First, *a willingness to understand*. An unteachable spirit will find it easy to twist a parable into nonsense and then reject the teacher as a fool. Hence, those who wanted to reject Jesus found more than enough justification—in their minds—to do so in His parables. They were confused or offended by what appeared to be either pointless meandering or shallow, folksy yarn spinning.

Second, *spiritual discernment*. The parables of Jesus reveal truths that exist beyond the present, natural realm. They may be heavenly truths or future, prophetic truths. His lessons can't be accessed through scientific research. They must be revealed by someone able to transcend the natural world to comprehend the supernatural. Therefore, the listener must have the aid of the Holy Spirit and an interpretive key to understand the parables of Jesus. Fortunately, the Lord has promised to teach anyone willing to learn—those who have accepted Him for who He really is and thus have received the Holy Spirit as their Guide.

Usually, a field would be bounded by some kind of obstruction, like a wall or a paved path formed by stones pulled from the field. Sometimes thorny bushes were allowed to grow to mark the edges of a farmer's lot. The quality of the soil itself might vary in a given field. Some parts might be deep and rich, others shallow and unfertile. Inevitably, some seeds would end up in places where they couldn't actually grow.

This familiar scene was the background of Jesus' Parable of the Sower, the Soil, and the Seed. In this parable, Jesus named four different types of terrain upon which the sower's seed could potentially fall: the road, or footpath (13:4); shallow, rocky soil (13:5-6); thornbushes (13:7); or good, fertile soil (13:8). Let's look at each of these in turn.

The footpath (13:4). A road, or footpath, is one of the "paths along the edge of a ploughed field or even across it where the seed lies upon the beaten track."[107] These areas would often be hard, packed down by farmers walking on them, sometimes solid as pavement. Picture a well-trod path through the middle of a lawn, where not even grass will grow because of the foot traffic. When seeds of grain land on those areas, the birds will inevitably snatch them up.

Shallow soil (13:5-6). Jesus referred to these areas as "rocky places," where the depth of the topsoil might be just a couple of inches. From the outside, it may appear to be good, rich soil worthy of seeding, but as soon as a farmer scrapes it with a hoe, he will hit impenetrable rock. The result is that the planted seed does germinate and its stalk springs up, but because it has no root to nourish it, the sun will quickly burn the grain to a crisp.

Thorny soil (13:7). This could refer to soil that is close to large thornbushes, like those that may be found on the edges of fields. Another way of interpreting this image is to picture the soil as containing seeds from thornbushes, like earth ridden with weeds, but unperceivable to the farmer. As the grain germinates, so do the thorn plants, which grow up much more quickly.[108] Either way, the end result is the same: As the thorny weeds grow, they rob sunlight from surrounding plants and steal nutrients from the soil, thus choking out the grain.

Good soil (13:8). The good soil, of course, refers to deep, rich soil, not contaminated by weeds, smothered by thorns, trampled by feet, invaded by birds, scorched by heat, or ridden with rocks. From such ideal soil, a crop of grain will grow—sometimes producing as much as thirty-, sixty-, or a hundredfold what was planted. The idea is a bountiful multiplication.

With this, the parable ends. The story has been told. All that's necessary now is for those willing to "hear" its truth to ponder the parable (13:9). Of course, everybody gathered around the little cove on the Sea of Galilee that day could hear what Jesus was saying. However, having ears to hear didn't necessarily mean they were truly *listening*. The audience would have completely missed the point if they all nodded their heads in agreement and thought, *Nice agricultural lesson. I'll have to remember to be careful where I plant seeds next spring.* Those who were truly listening would have realized that Jesus was pointing to a deeper, spiritual meaning through the story.

— 13:10-17 —

So markedly different was this style of teaching from what had come before that Jesus' disciples came to Him privately and said, "Why do You speak to them in parables?" (13:10). Jesus' answer explained more thoroughly why He was employing this new method. It wasn't to place lofty concepts on the bottom shelf. It wasn't to grab the attention of a crowd. And it wasn't to simply add variety to His teaching style. (I've heard Bible teachers suggest all these things.) Rather, Jesus used parables to separate the mere *hearers* from the true *listeners*.

In 13:11-13, Jesus described two kinds of people—those, like His disciples, to whom had been granted by God "to know the mysteries of the kingdom of heaven" and those, like the Pharisees and other unbelievers, to whom such knowledge "has not been granted" (13:11). The term translated "mysteries" (*mystērion* [3466]) refers to "secret teaching," "private counsel of God," or something that "transcends normal understanding."[109] In this case Jesus was referring to things of God that can only be known by special revelation, which itself can only be understood by the illuminating work of the Spirit.

Jesus then noted that some people who have understanding and who respond to that knowledge will be given even deeper understanding (13:12). This was a veiled reference to the disciples themselves, who may not have understood everything about who Jesus was and what He had come to accomplish but who understood enough to accept Him, to trust Him, and to continue to learn deeper and deeper truths about God's mysteries. By accepting Jesus, they had the interpretive key for understanding the parables.

By contrast, however, those who are stubborn and unbelieving will lose even the little they have if they don't respond to it (13:12). The hardhearted Pharisees, who had been exposed to so much truth but had rejected it (see Matthew 12), were now in a condition of increasing denial and compounding guilt. They'd had their chance to respond with faith but had instead rebelled.

In this way, Jesus spelled out the two different types of responses to His parables. He began using this method of teaching precisely because not all had eyes to really see what His miraculous works meant or ears to hear the deeper significance of His teaching. That is, they didn't really understand who Jesus was, and if they didn't get that basic truth, nothing else would make any sense (13:13).

In this state of hard-hearted rebellion, in which even the simplest spiritual truths were inaccessible to them, the Jewish leaders were responding to God's word just as their ancestors had done seven centuries before during the time of Isaiah the prophet. Sadly, through the centuries, nothing had changed about human nature. Jesus drew a few lines from Isaiah 6:9-10 that give us insight into the deep heart condition of His opponents. Though they would be constantly "hearing" and "seeing," they would neither "understand" nor "perceive" the reality of what was before them (Matt. 13:14). Why? Because "the heart of this people has become dull," resulting in a stubborn closing of their eyes and blocking of their ears. As such, true repentance was far from them, and with it, true healing (13:15).

The religious leaders in Jesus' day were like the rebellious nation of Isaiah's day. So firm had been Israel's rebellion that it resulted in the destruction of the nation and exile of the people. Ultimately, the problem wasn't with their ears, eyes, or even minds. The problem was a problem of the heart—a *spiritual* problem.

Jesus ended His diatribe against the spiritually deaf and blind by commending His disciples who *had* embraced His identity as Messiah and thus had the key to unlock the deeper spiritual truths (13:16). They had this knowledge not by their own power but by the blessing of God. What the disciples of Jesus were able to understand and perceive with their hearts was nothing less than the hopes of the Old Testament prophets and righteous people of old—the coming of the King, Israel's long-awaited Messiah (13:17).

— 13:18-23 —

Because of their special relationship with Him, the center and source of all truth, Jesus shared with the disciples the interpretation of the Parable of the Sower, the Soil, and the Seed (13:18). The main idea of the parable applied directly to the hard-heartedness of His opponents.

In the parable, the condition of the soil represents the condition of the heart, which determines a person's receptivity to the truth. Everybody in the crowd could hear the message regarding the kingdom, but many did not understand it (13:19). These people, we know, lacked understanding because of the hardness of their hearts and their subsequent blindness to spiritual truths (13:13-15). They had not had their understanding illumined or their eyes and ears opened to receive the truth.

Thus, in the explanation of the parable, the road represents the hard heart (13:19). Such a heart leads to the person's mind being shut and their eyes blinded to the truth. Such people are utterly unteachable because they refuse to listen and accept anything the Teacher says and does. Their blindness is voluntary, flowing from a hard, rebellious heart. Therefore, what little understanding they have is snatched away by Satan, the "evil one." The seed—that is, the message—has done them no good.

The rocky places represent the shallow heart, ultimately hardened to the truth but in a different way (13:20-21). Such people have a burst of emotion after hearing the message, but they fail to think things through. They're quick to grab each new fad, follow the excitement of the crowd, even jump in and get involved. But their hasty start has no follow-through or endurance. Driven by a burst of emotion, they lack a firm commitment of the heart and mind. Their rootless "faith" can't withstand affliction, much less persecution, and they fold at the first sign of hardship or conflict.

The thorns represent the crowded heart (13:22). Worldly interests, pursuits, desires, and goals have rendered such hearts unresponsive to heavenly things. The soil of these hearts is poisoned by the worries of the world and the deceitfulness of riches, which ultimately yield an unfruitful life. All this crowds out the seeds of the truth and never gives them a chance to germinate.

Finally, the good soil represents the heart open to the truth (13:23). This heart is softened and rendered teachable, having been prepared in humility by the Holy Spirit. When the message comes to people with this kind of heart, they receive it with understanding. Such a man or woman hears the word, sees the truth, listens, and understands. This translates into faith and obedience, which result in a life that bears great fruit.

At this point, a question often comes up: In Jesus' parable, which are the truly saved? Clearly, the last example—the good soil—represents genuine disciples who are saved from their sin through faith. And, just as clearly, the first example—the hard footpath—depicts people who are not saved, because of their rebellious resistance to the word of God. Regarding the two middle examples, though, theologians have debated for generations the eternal fate of the "rocky soil" and "thorny soil" people.

Does the initial faith represented in these two examples indicate genuine, eternal salvation, with the stumbling or smothering of the resultant plants referring simply to an unfruitful life? If so, then the warning of 1 Corinthians 3:12-15 would apply—that is, these people would still have eternal life in heaven, but because they would have nothing to show for their lives on earth, they would lose their reward ("He will suffer loss; but he himself will be saved").

Others have understood the second and third types of soil to represent those who genuinely believe but who lose their salvation because their faith turns out to be only temporary. This view rejects the concept of eternal security, which I see as clearly taught in many passages of Scripture (e.g., Rom. 8:37-39; Jude 1:24). Jesus promised, "My sheep hear My voice, and I know them, and they follow Me; and I give eternal life to them, and they will never perish; and no one will snatch them out of My hand" (John 10:27-28).

Still others would see the kind of "faith" in the rocky and thorny soils as "feigned faith" or "fake faith." From the outside, these phony believers appear to be genuine, but eventually they are exposed for what they really are. If this is the case, then the description of the apostates in 1 John 2:19 would apply: "They went out from us, but they were not really of us; for if they had been of us, they would have remained with us; but they went out, so that it would be shown that they all are not of us."

The issue has generated debate because Jesus isn't completely clear. The point of the parable, though, wasn't to solve all the mysteries of eternal salvation. It was to illustrate different observable responses to the message of the kingdom. Jesus commended only the "good soil," so we should too. We shouldn't ask, "What's the bare minimum of responsiveness needed to get into heaven?" but "What kind of response to the preaching of the Word is Jesus looking for in my life?"

APPLICATION: MATTHEW 13:1-23
Testing Your Soil

It seems pretty clear that the first three types of "soil" are not what Jesus was looking for as responses to the word of God. Only the last response—the soft, receptive "good soil"—receives the favorable commendation of the Master. Only those plants grow to produce thirty-, sixty-, or a hundredfold fruitfulness. Those of us who are believers in Christ, who have received God's word of the gospel of salvation by grace alone through faith alone in Christ alone, are still faced with the day-to-day decision of hearing, receiving, and living God's word. Jesus' Parable of the Sower, the Soil, and the Seed thus has application for us today. Take a moment to test your own soil by asking four questions.

First, *are you faithful and fruitful?* Do you keep your heart well watered by prayer, by reading and studying Scripture, and by fellow-shiping with a body of believers? Do you keep your soil soft and receptive by keeping short accounts with God, seeking forgiveness for your shortcomings, and reconciling with brothers and sisters in Christ when relationships are strained? Continue to nurture a healthy heart by maintaining intimacy with God through dependence on Christ and a life yielded to the Holy Spirit.

Second, *are you worried and worldly?* Is your heart constantly distracted by the worries of this world—the pursuit of wealth and material things or the preservation of comforts, luxuries, and privileged positions? How high on your list is your pursuit of Christ, His kingdom, and His righteousness? Do you easily forsake the gathering of the church for work, for recreation, or for personal rest and relaxation? This kind of condition isn't healthy for a believer, and it will prevent unbelievers from truly embracing the word of God.

Third, *are you shallow and shaky?* Churches are filled with believers who have shallow faith—thick on emotion and sentimentalism but thin on real substance and weak on commitment and perseverance. Such rootless religion won't be able to withstand the normal trials of life, much less endure direct attacks on the Christian faith by critics. Contrary to popular belief, it isn't enough to just "follow your heart" and "do what you feel is right." If you're a believer, you need to deepen your knowledge of God through meditation on and application of His Word, through fellowship with His people, and through a rejection of superficiality.

Fourth, *are you faithless and stubborn?* This category in the parable is the only one that describes a person who clearly and unquestionably rejects the truth and doesn't have a saving relationship with Christ. If this describes you, it's not too late to "plow up the hard ground of your hearts" (Jer. 4:3, NLT) and receive the saving gospel of the person and work of Christ. He died for you and rose again, and by faith alone you can receive eternal life and the illumination of the Holy Spirit.

A World Full of Wheat, Weeds, and Mustard Seeds
MATTHEW 13:24-43

NASB

24Jesus presented another parable to them, saying, "The kingdom of heaven ᵃmay be compared to a man who sowed good seed in his field. 25But while his men were sleeping, his enemy came and sowed ᵃtares among the wheat, and went away. 26But when the ᵃwheat sprouted and bore grain, then the tares became evident also. 27The slaves of the landowner came and said to him, 'Sir, did you not sow good seed in your field? ᵃHow then does it have tares?' 28And he said to them, 'An ᵃenemy has done this!' The slaves said to him, 'Do you want us, then, to go and gather them up?' 29But he said, 'No; for while you are gathering up the tares, you may uproot the wheat with them. 30Allow both to grow together until the harvest; and in the time of the harvest I will say to the reapers, "First gather up the tares and bind them in bundles to burn them up; but gather the wheat into my barn."'"

31He presented another parable to them, saying, "The kingdom of heaven is like a mustard seed, which a man took and sowed in his field; 32and this is smaller than all *other* seeds, but when it is full grown, it is larger than the garden plants and becomes a tree, so that THE BIRDS

NLT

24Here is another story Jesus told: "The Kingdom of Heaven is like a farmer who planted good seed in his field. 25But that night as the workers slept, his enemy came and planted weeds among the wheat, then slipped away. 26When the crop began to grow and produce grain, the weeds also grew.

27"The farmer's workers went to him and said, 'Sir, the field where you planted that good seed is full of weeds! Where did they come from?'

28"'An enemy has done this!' the farmer exclaimed.

"'Should we pull out the weeds?' they asked.

29"'No,' he replied, 'you'll uproot the wheat if you do. 30Let both grow together until the harvest. Then I will tell the harvesters to sort out the weeds, tie them into bundles, and burn them, and to put the wheat in the barn.'"

31Here is another illustration Jesus used: "The Kingdom of Heaven is like a mustard seed planted in a field. 32It is the smallest of all seeds, but it becomes the largest of garden plants;

OF THE ªAIR come and NEST IN ITS BRANCHES."

³³He spoke another parable to them, "The kingdom of heaven is like leaven, which a woman took and hid in three ªpecks of flour until it was all leavened."

³⁴All these things Jesus spoke to the crowds in parables, and He did not speak to them without a parable. ³⁵This was to fulfill what was spoken through the prophet:

"I WILL OPEN MY MOUTH IN PARABLES;

I WILL UTTER THINGS HIDDEN SINCE THE FOUNDATION OF THE WORLD."

³⁶Then He left the crowds and went into the house. And His disciples came to Him and said, "Explain to us the parable of the ªtares of the field." ³⁷And He said, "The one who sows the good seed is the Son of Man, ³⁸and the field is the world; and as for the good seed, these are the sons of the kingdom; and the tares are the sons of the evil one; ³⁹and the enemy who sowed them is the devil, and the harvest is the ªend of the age; and the reapers are angels. ⁴⁰So just as the tares are gathered up and burned with fire, so shall it be at the ªend of the age. ⁴¹The Son of Man will send forth His angels, and they will gather out of His kingdom ªall stumbling blocks, and those who commit lawlessness, ⁴²and will throw them into the furnace of fire; in that place there will be weeping and gnashing of teeth. ⁴³Then THE RIGHTEOUS WILL SHINE FORTH AS THE SUN in the kingdom of their Father. He who has ears, ªlet him hear.

13:24 ªLit *was compared to*   13:25 ªOr *darnel,* a weed resembling wheat   13:26 ªLit *grass* 13:27 ªLit *From where*   13:28 ªLit *enemy man*   13:32 ªOr *sky*   13:33 ªGr *sata*   13:36 ªOr *darnel,* a weed resembling wheat   13:39 ªOr *consummation*   13:40 ªOr *consummation* 13:41 ªOr *everything that is offensive*   13:43 ªOr *hear! Or listen!*

it grows into a tree, and birds come and make nests in its branches."

³³Jesus also used this illustration: "The Kingdom of Heaven is like the yeast a woman used in making bread. Even though she put only a little yeast in three measures of flour, it permeated every part of the dough."

³⁴Jesus always used stories and illustrations like these when speaking to the crowds. In fact, he never spoke to them without using such parables. ³⁵This fulfilled what God had spoken through the prophet:

"I will speak to you in parables. I will explain things hidden since the creation of the world.*"

³⁶Then, leaving the crowds outside, Jesus went into the house. His disciples said, "Please explain to us the story of the weeds in the field."

³⁷Jesus replied, "The Son of Man* is the farmer who plants the good seed. ³⁸The field is the world, and the good seed represents the people of the Kingdom. The weeds are the people who belong to the evil one. ³⁹The enemy who planted the weeds among the wheat is the devil. The harvest is the end of the world,* and the harvesters are the angels.

⁴⁰"Just as the weeds are sorted out and burned in the fire, so it will be at the end of the world. ⁴¹The Son of Man will send his angels, and they will remove from his Kingdom everything that causes sin and all who do evil. ⁴²And the angels will throw them into the fiery furnace, where there will be weeping and gnashing of teeth. ⁴³Then the righteous will shine like the sun in their Father's Kingdom. Anyone with ears to hear should listen and understand!

13:35 Some manuscripts do not include *of the world.* Ps 78:2.   13:37 "Son of Man" is a title Jesus used for himself.   13:39 Or *the age;* also in 13:40, 49.

Ever wonder where God is when you really need Him? When you're surrounded by wrongdoers and justice seems far away, why doesn't God step in and take care of business? Doesn't He care about His people? If you haven't pondered questions like these, believe me, you will. It's natural that in this fallen world we experience seasons of disappointment and dissonance during which we wonder, *Where's God?*

In moments like these, we need to be reminded of who God is. We know that God is holy, loving, and wise. So, when God seems to hold back in the face of so much evil in the world—and hardship in our own lives—it isn't because He's wicked, unfair, or uncaring. Of course we long for our righteous Lord to step in and deal with evil sooner rather than later. *Now*, not *then*. But He doesn't do it—at least not usually. It's not uncommon for us to wait a long time for God to judge wrongdoing and to weed out the wrongdoers. Most often, we have to wait and wait . . . and wait some more.

This prompts us to ask again and again, *Why doesn't God DO something?* Christian leaders, Bible teachers, and pastors are frequently asked that question, perhaps more than any other. Tragedies happen. Horrific accidents devastate lives and fracture families. Tyrants take over. Bullies execute their hurtful plans on people, and instead of being stopped, they seem to get away with it! These unfair scenarios seem to repeat themselves day after day.

These questions take the front seat in the parables of Matthew 13:24-43. Jesus addresses other important matters here as well, but the problem of the ever-present wicked among the righteous is such a nagging issue that it dominates the landscape of these lessons. This is an obstacle that can't be overcome except by divine power.

— 13:24-30 —

As far as we know, Jesus was still sitting in the boat in the "Bay of Parables" when He presented the story commonly called the Parable of the Wheat and Tares. He seemed to pick up on the same image as in the previous story, the Parable of the Sower, the Soil, and the Seed (13:3-23). We might even consider this a kind of sequel to that parable. This time, instead of focusing on the different kinds of soil upon which seeds can fall, Jesus' attention shifted to the plants that grow up in the field.

In the parable, a farmer sowed good seeds in his field (13:24). But at night, when nobody was watching over the field, the farmer's enemy came and sowed tares among the wheat seeds (13:25). What are tares? One author describes the tare as a plant called the "bearded darnel" and notes, "It is difficult to distinguish domesticated grains from the wild darnel until their heads mature. At harvesttime the grain is fanned and put through a sieve. The smaller darnel seeds left after fanning pass through the sieve, leaving behind the desired fruit."[110] The greatest problem with the tares mixing with the wheat isn't the extra work it takes to separate them at harvesttime. The problem is that the bearded darnel hosts a kind of fungus—poisonous to humans—that could contaminate the good wheat and utterly ruin a farmer's crop. This is why "to sow darnel among wheat as an act of revenge was punishable in Roman law."[111] The act of the farmer's enemy in the parable was vicious and cruel.

Bluemoose/Wikimedia

A wheat plant

As would be expected, the wheat and tares grew up together and began to bear their distinctive grains (13:26). Quickly the farmer realized what had happened—an enemy had contaminated the wheat crop (13:27-28). Though the servants of the farmer dutifully offered to go through the wheat field and gather the tares from among the wheat, the farmer wisely warned them, "No; for while you are gathering up the tares, you may uproot the wheat with them" (13:28-29). Instead, the farmer instructed the laborers to let both grow together until the harvest, when it would be easier to separate the tares from the wheat. They could gather the bad grains to burn and store the good wheat in the barn (13:30).

In this parable, we see three periods of time. During the *time of planting*, the farmer plants good seed, but his enemy deviously infiltrates the field and plants dangerous, poisonous, look-alike seed. During the *time of waiting*, the farmer advises the workers to allow the bad grain to grow side by side with the good grain, patiently waiting and refraining from taking action. Throughout this in-between time, the workers are responsible for tending and protecting the wheat field. Then, at the *time of harvesting*, the farmer's harvesters—not the workers who tended the wheat—will carry out the task of separating the harmful and deceptive weeds from the healthy wheat.

— 13:31-35 —

As intriguing as this story was, Jesus left a lot of elements hanging. Who was the planter? Who were the helpers? Why the three periods of time—planting, waiting, harvesting? And, most importantly, why permit the tares to grow up among the wheat? Why not pull them out while the grains were growing? Why wait?

While the crowd was mulling over the Parable of the Wheat and Tares, Jesus told two smaller parables to illustrate the kingdom of God. In the first, He likened the kingdom of heaven to "a mustard seed" (13:31). I can imagine the analogy initially got a few chuckles from the audience. *The tiny mustard seed, of all things!* When Jesus said that the mustard seed was "smaller than all other seeds" (13:32), He wasn't giving a scientific lesson in botany or comparing this seed with all other seeds on the planet. He was referring to the cultivated seeds of "garden plants" in the region of Galilee, with which His audience was familiar. He was also clearly using the figure of speech called hyperbole, as evidenced when He said that the mustard plant that grows from such a small seed "becomes a tree." This language was no doubt informed by Jesus' allusions to Ezekiel 31:6 and Daniel 4:12, 20-22. The point is that, compared to the tiny size of the seed, the mustard plant grows quite large—often taller than the height of a person. Stan Toussaint explains that the incredible growth represented by the mustard seed "is a reference to the extraordinary spread and growth of the kingdom message in the age before the kingdom is established" and "the seemingly prosperous growth in number of those who should be heirs of the kingdom."[112] While the crowd of people able to hear Jesus' voice from the fishing boat was relatively small, Jesus' followers would one day encompass a massive, worldwide movement that would include even the Gentile nations!

Actual size

When planted, the small mustard seed (left) turns into a large, vibrant plant (right).

While the mustard-seed parable addressed the rapid and surprising positive growth of the kingdom from such a small start, the next parable drew parallels between the expansion of the kingdom and the spread of "leaven" (or yeast) throughout a measure of dough (Matt. 13:33). The Greek expression translated "three pecks of flour" indicates enough flour to make bread for a hundred people.[113] Because the previous parable referred positively to the rapid spread of the kingdom throughout the earth, many commentators have understood the Parable of the Leaven as a reference to the same thing: "Both these parables show how thoroughly Jesus was aware that great things grow from minute beginnings."[114]

That's a feasible interpretation. However, because leaven is often associated with evil (16:6, 11; 1 Cor. 5:6-8), other commentators (myself included) understand the spread of leaven to correspond to the spread of false teaching and wickedness among those who claim to be children of the kingdom.[115] In this case, the image would be similar to the presence of the tares among the wheat two parables earlier—the pervasive, inseparable presence of the wicked side by side with the righteous.

In 13:34-35, Matthew briefly steps out of the narrative to make an editorial aside. He informs his readers—which includes you and me—that Jesus was speaking to the crowds in parables in order to fulfill the words of Psalm 78:2, which says, "I will speak to you in a parable. I will teach you hidden lessons from our past" (NLT). Matthew's rendering of that passage ("I will open My mouth in parables; I will utter things hidden since the foundation of the world") intends to draw a parallel between what the psalmist was doing in his day and what Jesus was doing in the first century. Stan Toussaint explains the significance of Matthew's use of this passage: "Psalm 78 is a review of God's workings in connection with Israel's past history. In introducing his subject, Asaph, the writer of the Psalm, writes the verse which Matthew quotes. Christ 'establishes'... the meaning of this verse by His use of parables, for He is indicating God's workings in connection with the kingdom in the light of Israel's rejection of its King."[116]

— 13:36-43 —

If the working of the leaven through the entire batch of bread represents the permission of wickedness to spread throughout the church, and if the tares growing up beside the wheat represent the same thing, why would God allow this to happen to the kingdom between Christ's first coming and His second coming? Why does God permit the "mystery of lawlessness" to work its way through the church (2 Thes. 2:7)? Like the dutiful workers in the master's field (Matt. 13:28), we're understandably anxious to jerk out every one of the evildoers, confront every devious act, and put a stop to every attempt to thwart and harass the work of God. Yet the parables seem to suggest that such a spread of wickedness and deceit among the people of God is inevitable.

When Jesus finally got out of the boat, made His way through the crowd, and returned to the house in Capernaum where He was staying, His disciples came to Him and said, "Explain to us the parable of the tares of the field" (13:36). Notice that they didn't ask about the mustard seed or the leaven. They were troubled by the fact that God would tolerate the imperfection and impurity of the poisonous tares growing among the wheat.

In 13:37-43, then, Jesus explains the parable, but only to His close disciples. In almost bullet-point fashion, Jesus solves the puzzle:

- The one who sows = the Son of Man, Jesus (13:37)
- The field = the world (13:38)
- The good seed = the sons of the kingdom (the saved righteous) (13:38)
- The tares = the sons of the evil one (the unsaved wicked) (13:38)
- The enemy = the devil (13:39)
- The harvest = the end of the age (13:39)
- The reapers = angels (13:39)

At the end of the age, when Christ returns to purge the world of wickedness and fully establish His kingdom on earth, He will send His angels to gather those wicked plants of the devil and cast them into eternal fire (13:40-42). This will put an end to the mixture of the just and unjust, a mingling that has been seen in the church throughout its history. From that time forward, the kingdom of God will be characterized by purity and righteousness, and the righteous will shine like the sun (13:43).

In the end, it's the responsibility of Jesus Christ as Judge to separate the tares from the wheat—that is, the wicked from the righteous. In the meantime, we need tremendous patience and wisdom to know when to step up and wage an aggressive fight against wrong . . . and when to step back and fulfill other work God has called us to do, knowing that God Himself will deal with the wicked. If we rush in and try to purge every sinner and confront every sin, we'll inevitably uproot the true believers who fail to live up to our unreasonably high standards. But if we keep our eyes on Jesus and His teaching, we'll gain the insight to pursue the quest for purity without trespassing into God's domain of sowing and reaping.

APPLICATION: MATTHEW 13:24-43
Why, When, and What *Not* to Weed

Hostile powers are always at work in this world. They try to cause us to stumble, through harassment, creating barriers, causing conflicts, and promoting confusion. Those who engage in lawless behavior overtly and deliberately work against the good. Without a doubt, enemies of the truth are at work in the world, inspired by the "power of the evil one" (1 Jn. 5:19). Given this reality, we can look to Jesus' parables to provide us with a few important, practical points to consider in relation to the evil in the world.

First, *it's hard to distinguish the good from the bad—the wheat from the weeds.* False teaching isn't just something we might encounter "out there" beyond the walls of the church or the barriers of our Christian safe-zone. It sometimes arises in our midst, within the church itself. The apostle Paul warned the elders of the church in Ephesus, "I know that after my departure savage wolves will come in among you, not sparing the flock" (Acts 20:29). And his words in 2 Corinthians 11:13-15 should keep us alert: "Such men are false apostles, deceitful workers, disguising themselves as apostles of Christ. No wonder, for even Satan disguises himself as an angel of light. Therefore it is not surprising if his servants also disguise themselves as servants of righteousness, whose end will be according to their deeds." How chilling! We must be constantly on guard, attentive, and alert because we can't always tell the difference between the good and the bad.

Second, *our tendency will be to rush to extremes when dealing with wrong.* In Jesus' Parable of the Wheat and Tares, the farmer restrains his workers from rushing to judgment and pulling up weeds too hastily. We need patience and perseverance to live in this evil, mixed-up world. At times, direct confrontation is needed, but we have to make sure we don't jump to wrong conclusions based on limited or false information. Such hasty action will bring worse problems than it solves. When we think we see the attitudes and actions of weeds among the wheat, we must proceed carefully and tread lightly. If the case is clear and unquestionable, that's one thing. But in my experience of ministry, those instances are few and far between. Most of the time we are dealing with issues for which great wisdom is needed to determine when to act and how to respond.

Third, *God is just.* He knows that evil is on the rise, that charlatans are working behind the scenes to damage our churches, and that Satan has his minions making their debilitating marks on the body of Christ. Evil workers tend to gain a following, and the number of weeds thus multiplies. This is inevitable during the present evil age. However, this age isn't the last. The King is coming, and with Him the judgment. He will sort out the wheat from the weeds—perfectly, precisely, and swiftly. We need to trust Him to provide for and protect His people until the day of Christ's appearing.

Got It? Good!
MATTHEW 13:44-58

NASB

44 "The kingdom of heaven is like a treasure hidden in the field, which a man found and hid *again;* and from joy over it he goes and sells all that he has and buys that field.

45 "Again, the kingdom of heaven is

NLT

44 "The Kingdom of Heaven is like a treasure that a man discovered hidden in a field. In his excitement, he hid it again and sold everything he owned to get enough money to buy the field.

45 "Again, the Kingdom of Heaven

NASB

like a merchant seeking fine pearls, 46 and upon finding one pearl of great value, he went and sold all that he had and bought it.

47 "Again, the kingdom of heaven is like a dragnet cast into the sea, and gathering *fish* of every kind; 48 and when it was filled, they drew it up on the beach; and they sat down and gathered the good *fish* into containers, but the bad they threw away. 49 So it will be at the ªend of the age; the angels will come forth and ᵇtake out the wicked from among the righteous, 50 and will throw them into the furnace of fire; in that place there will be weeping and gnashing of teeth.

51 "Have you understood all these things?" They said to Him, "Yes." 52 And ªJesus said to them, "Therefore every scribe who has become a disciple of the kingdom of heaven is like a head of a household, who brings out of his treasure things new and old."

53 When Jesus had finished these parables, He departed from there. 54 He came to ªHis hometown and *began* teaching them in their synagogue, so that they were astonished, and said, "Where *did* this man *get* this wisdom and *these* ᵇmiraculous powers? 55 Is not this the carpenter's son? Is not His mother called Mary, and His brothers, James and Joseph and Simon and Judas? 56 And His sisters, are they not all with us? Where then *did* this man *get* all these things?" 57 And they took offense at Him. But Jesus said to them, "A prophet is not without honor except in his ªhometown and in his *own* household." 58 And He did not do many ªmiracles there because of their unbelief.

13:49 ªOr *consummation* ᵇOr *separate* **13:52** ªLit *He* **13:54** ªOr *His own part of the country* ᵇOr *miracles* **13:57** ªOr *own part of the country* **13:58** ªOr *works of power*

NLT

is like a merchant on the lookout for choice pearls. 46 When he discovered a pearl of great value, he sold everything he owned and bought it!

47 "Again, the Kingdom of Heaven is like a fishing net that was thrown into the water and caught fish of every kind. 48 When the net was full, they dragged it up onto the shore, sat down, and sorted the good fish into crates, but threw the bad ones away. 49 That is the way it will be at the end of the world. The angels will come and separate the wicked people from the righteous, 50 throwing the wicked into the fiery furnace, where there will be weeping and gnashing of teeth. 51 Do you understand all these things?"

"Yes," they said, "we do."

52 Then he added, "Every teacher of religious law who becomes a disciple in the Kingdom of Heaven is like a homeowner who brings from his storeroom new gems of truth as well as old."

53 When Jesus had finished telling these stories and illustrations, he left that part of the country. 54 He returned to Nazareth, his hometown. When he taught there in the synagogue, everyone was amazed and said, "Where does he get this wisdom and the power to do miracles?" 55 Then they scoffed, "He's just the carpenter's son, and we know Mary, his mother, and his brothers—James, Joseph,* Simon, and Judas. 56 All his sisters live right here among us. Where did he learn all these things?" 57 And they were deeply offended and refused to believe in him.

Then Jesus told them, "A prophet is honored everywhere except in his own hometown and among his own family." 58 And so he did only a few miracles there because of their unbelief.

13:55 Other manuscripts read *Joses;* still others read *John.*

Anybody who enjoys stories with hidden meaning would love the thirteenth chapter of Matthew. Here Jesus told one parable after another. He started from a boat, addressing a large gathering of people with various intentions—some who believed Him, others who hated Him. From the shoreline of the Sea of Galilee they heard His parables, trying to figure out what the stories meant.

Then He left that crowd of people and went into a house in Capernaum (13:36), probably the house of Peter. There He met with a much smaller group—His disciples. Though His audience had changed, His storytelling continued. He also shared interpretations of parables with His closest followers, giving them the keys necessary to unlock the rest. While alone with His disciples, He told several more short parables (13:44, 45-46, 47-50). Unlike before, He didn't explain the meanings of these short stories. And, interestingly, when He had finished telling those parables, which He had not explained, He asked His disciples, in effect, "Got it?" Having had their minds opened by the Spirit to hear and perceive Jesus' message, they had gotten it. But not everybody did. We'll see momentarily a startling contrast between the open-minded acceptance and understanding of the disciples and the closed-minded rejection of Jesus' own friends and relatives back home, who just didn't get it.

— 13:44-46 —

The parables Jesus told in Matthew 13 can be divided into two categories: those He taught publicly to the mixed crowds of disciples, opponents, and undecided and those He taught privately, behind closed doors, to the committed disciples. The first batch included the Parable of the Sower, the Soil, and the Seed (13:3-9); the Wheat and Tares (13:24-30); the Mustard Seed (13:31-32); and the Leaven (13:33). But then, as Jesus transitioned indoors, He taught His disciples only, giving them the explanation of the Wheat and Tares (13:36-43) and a number of additional parables: the Treasure in the Field (13:44), the Valuable Pearl (13:45-46), the Dragnet (13:47-50), and the Head of Household (13:52).

In each parable of this chapter, except for the Sower, the Soil, and the Seed, Jesus began with something to the effect of "The kingdom of heaven is like . . ." (see 13:24, 31, 33, 44, 45, 47, 52). Although Jesus' teaching concerning the kingdom of heaven ultimately pointed forward to the long-anticipated kingdom that will come with the return of the Messiah, the parables of Jesus began to explain, in a veiled manner, the idea of an interim form of the kingdom between the first and second comings of the Messiah. During this in-between time, those who have accepted Jesus as their Messiah and have experienced the new birth by grace through faith are to live by a different code in anticipation of the kingdom coming fully on earth. In this sense, the parables refer to one aspect of the kingdom as a saving and transforming relationship with God through Jesus Christ in the present. The good news (or gospel) of the kingdom, then, is about the person and work of Jesus Christ in both His first *and* His second coming.

The first couple of parables that Jesus taught to His disciples after explaining the wheat-and-tares story related to the unparalleled value of the kingdom of God compared to anything else this world has to offer. For many, entering "kingdom life" is like stumbling upon a treasure in a field (13:44). Notice that the man in this story wasn't looking for this treasure. He was probably a simple day laborer or a man making his way through a field that its owner had neglected and therefore become unfamiliar with. In any case, the man just happened to discover the treasure. So valuable was it that he reburied it until he could make sure it was secure. Though the man hadn't actually claimed the treasure or counted it, he could tell by one glance that it was worth anything he could give up in order to possess it. Realizing its value, he sold everything he had in order to purchase the very land where the treasure had been buried.

It's an interesting side note that whoever owned the field and sold it to the man didn't realize the vast treasure he had been sitting on, something that suggests neglect of the field by this deed holder and/or heir. At this point, the disciples may have wondered if the indifference of the original owner of the field in the story was meant to symbolize the kind of negligence increasingly shown by the scribes, Pharisees, and other leaders of Israel. These religious leaders had been "entrusted with the oracles of God" (see Rom. 3:2) but did not recognize the hidden treasure of the gospel of the person and work of Christ and relinquished it to those who did.

The second parable told at this point presents a similar picture of the unequaled value of the kingdom of heaven. This time, Jesus spoke of a merchant seeking fine pearls (Matt. 13:45-46). The details are different from those of the Parable of the Treasure in the Field, particularly in that in this story the man was actively seeking the thing of value; he didn't simply happen upon it. When the man finds one pearl of particularly outstanding quality, he sells all he has in order to buy it. In that regard, the Parable of the Treasure in the Field and the Parable of the Valuable Pearl are identical.

During Jesus' life and ministry, many people sought out His help—His healing touch or His transformative teaching—like the merchant seeking an exquisite pearl. They had been on the lookout for the coming Messiah, and Jesus' presence satisfied their longing in an immeasurable way. Philip is a good example of this kind of person, as shown in what he said to his first convert, Nathanael: "We have found Him of whom Moses in the Law and also the Prophets wrote—Jesus of Nazareth, the son of Joseph" (John 1:45). Such people passionately embraced the gospel and were willing to go all in for the kingdom of heaven. Others, however, like the man finding the treasure in a neglected field, "happened upon" Jesus. Nathanael fit this bill: When Philip told him about Jesus, his response was cold—"Can any good thing come out of Nazareth?" (John 1:46). But quickly he recognized the priceless treasure that was before him (John 1:49).

Both of these parables would have been great encouragements to Jesus' disciples. They saw the religious rulers rejecting Jesus and the heat of persecution increasing against Him and His followers. These two parables would have reminded them of the thrill they had experienced when they had recognized Jesus for who He really is. And the stories would have underscored Jesus' assertion that whatever the disciples gave up for the kingdom of heaven was worth it. The benefits of the gospel of the kingdom are of inestimable worth.

The nineteenth-century Scottish preacher Thomas Guthrie wrote, "The Gospel alters both our character and condition—making the rude gentle, the coarse refined, the impure holy, the selfish generous—working a greater transformation than if a felon of the prison were to change into a courtier of the palace, or the once ragged boy who had been educated to crime on the streets were to wear a star on his manly breast and stand in the brilliant circle that surrounds a throne."[117] Without doubt, the blessing of being a child of God through faith in Christ is utterly and absolutely priceless. Only the gospel guarantees an inheritance imperishable and undefiled (1 Pet. 1:4)—"discovered" free of charge, but compelling enough for its possessors to give up everything to experience it.

— 13:47-50 —

The next parable presents the kingdom of God from a different angle and illuminates another facet of it as it is manifested in the present age, between the first and second comings of Christ. Jesus likened the kingdom of God to a giant fishing net, or dragnet. As a net like this drags through the water, all kinds of fish wind up caught in it—some "keepers," some "tossers" (13:47-48). This would have been a familiar image to Jesus' disciples, even to those who were not professional fishermen. Nets and fish, sorting and tossing back—even a tax collector like Matthew would have seen these activities frequently, especially given the fishing industry in Capernaum and the neighboring villages.

The theme of this parable is similar to what Jesus presented in the earlier Parable of the Wheat and Tares: The good wheat and the bad tares would grow together until the "end of the age," when the angels would gather the unsaved wicked and consign them to eternal fire, while the righteous would "shine forth as the sun" in the kingdom (13:40-43). In this case, the emphasis is on the process of gathering. Jesus had called His disciples to become "fishers of men" (4:19). Now He was encouraging them to cast the net wide and not fret about sorting out the keepers at the front end. "At the end of the age," Jesus said, "the angels will come forth and take out the wicked from among the righteous" (13:49). Ultimately, God will judge between the true and the false, the good and the bad. Those itty-bitty fish that have no real saving faith will eventually be sorted out. The preachers of the gospel are not responsible for determining the genuineness of a person's faith in response to the gospel; they simply cast the net.

— 13:51-52 —

At the conclusion of this string of parables, Jesus didn't just drop the mic and walk off the stage, as it were. He cared that His disciples understood what He had been teaching them. In fact, Matthew 13:51-52 could be paraphrased, "Get it?" "Got it!" "Good." Remember, Jesus was still in the house with His disciples. They were the ones who had heard the parables about the treasure in the field, the priceless pearl, and the dragnet. He wanted to make sure they "understood all these things" (13:51). A great teacher always gets feedback from His students to make sure they've "got it." They had.

In 13:52, then, Jesus envisions His disciples as "scribes" who had become disciples, real learners, unlike the frauds who were in cahoots with the Pharisees. These faithful followers of the kingdom of heaven were likened to a "head of household" responsible for the nurturing, nourishment, and health of those under his roof. How does the head of household manage this? By providing "things new and old" from his treasure. What does this mean? Tasker puts it well:

Seining for Shrimp

MATTHEW 13:47-48

Most of us have probably experienced fishing with a rod, reel, hook, and bait. We can remember—or at least imagine—what it's like to pull in a single fish after a long wait, size it up when we've landed it, and then either toss it back or keep it. However, few of us have ever fished with nets like the fishermen on the Sea of Galilee—gathering in a large quantity of fish, then sorting through dozens or even hundreds at a time.

When I was a little boy, our family would go to my grandfather's bay cottage on the coast of the Gulf of Mexico. We used to fish in the little bay near the cottage. But we needed live bait to catch anything. Little shrimp were the best. Now, we could have gone to the bait shop and bought some, but Dad had us work for ours. And that meant we seined for bait.

We had a long net, maybe about twenty yards. On each end was a pole, like a broom handle. Picture a giant scroll, but instead of paper between the rods there was a screen for catching small fish. Along the bottom of the net were lead weights to hold it against the bottom so nothing could escape underneath. With one of us on each pole, we would drag the net around the shallow waters, gather whatever was caught in it, and then bring it in to shore. That's when the sorting began.

But as a kid, I was interested in everything except the bait. I was hoping to find a baby shark or a crab. But you don't fish with sharks and crabs. You fish with shrimp. So, while I was playing around with everything else, my dad would constantly remind me, "Pick out the shrimp. We're looking for bait. Pick out the shrimp. Get rid of everything else. All we want is the bait."

I think of that experience when I read Jesus' Parable of the Dragnet and the sorting of fish. While God calls people of every kind by the gospel, people respond in various ways. The net swings widely—through personal evangelism, radio, television, literature, preaching, and proclaiming. But, of course, not everybody who is swept up by the message is a keeper. There are sharks and crabs among us. I've known some of them personally! But God knows His own, and He'll sort them out in His own time.

NAZARETH

MATTHEW 13:54

The name Nazareth most likely derives from one of two Hebrew terms. *Netser* [H5342] is the Hebrew word for "branch" or "shoot," and it forms a wordplay for Matthew (2:23) in relation to Isaiah 11:1. But just as likely as a background for this term is the Hebrew verb *natsar* [H5341], which means "to watch." Though modern Nazareth rests in a bowl-shaped depression, ancient Nazareth was situated farther up the hill. This made it a perfect place to keep watch over the vast Jezreel Valley (which included the Plain of Esdraelon, or the valley of Megiddo, also known as Armageddon), roughly 1,000 feet below.

The fact that the city's inhabitants only had access to one spring for fresh water[118] would have kept the ancient population rather low—perhaps numbering in the hundreds, not thousands. Because Nazareth was "off the beaten path," with no direct access to major highways or trade routes, its people lived simple lives by farming the land and raising cattle. In fact, so small and insignificant was this village that it is not mentioned by name in the Old Testament, the Apocrypha, the other Jewish literature of the intertestamental period, or even the writings of the historian Josephus.[119] This would have given the inhabitants a rather negative reputation of being "backward." To be associated with Nazareth would have been like calling someone a "hillbilly" today.

The reputation of the Nazarenes was one of little account. When the would-be disciple Nathanael heard that Jesus had grown up in Nazareth, he curled his lip and muttered, "Can any good thing come out of Nazareth?" (John 1:46).

Barry Beitzel

Nazareth Ridge. The village of Nazareth sat atop the mountain range overlooking the Jezreel Valley.

The reference would appear to be to the disciple of Jesus who has learned the truths of the kingdom of heaven . . . about which Jesus has been giving instruction. Such a "scribe" as a teacher of "the law of Christ" has a rich store of knowledge from which he can draw truth which can be described as both *new and old*. It is *new* in the sense that only with the coming of the Messiah has it been clearly revealed; it is *old* because it is concerned with *mysteries* that have been present in the mind of God but *kept secret from the foundation of the world.*[120]

— 13:53-58 —

When Jesus finished the set of parables reserved for His dedicated disciples, He decided to depart from Capernaum and take a short trip home to Nazareth. You may recall that not much earlier His mother and brothers had come to the home in Capernaum where He had been staying, desiring to speak with Him (12:46-50). Matthew doesn't tell us in that passage whether Jesus invited them in or stepped outside to see them, but I can't imagine that He would have snubbed His family, even if they were there for some kind of "intervention." It would have been dishonoring to His mother, whom He dearly honored, and offensive to His brothers, who probably looked up to Him. So, I suspect He had had at least a brief conversation with them that day in Capernaum, though I can't prove it. Regardless, it would make sense that His family in Nazareth was on His mind at this point.

It would also make sense for Jesus to be looking for a stopping point in His teaching ministry so that he could take a quick trip home. He needed a rest! Just a moment earlier He had confirmed that His disciples understood the significance of the parables and their import enough that they could carry out the work of "disciple-scribes" without Him (13:51-52). Perhaps His disciples all joined Him on His visit to Nazareth. Perhaps only a handful went along. Perhaps some of the disciples took the opportunity to have another shot at carrying on the missional work of teaching about the kingdom of heaven without their Master present.

Regardless, having wrapped up His teaching in parables, Jesus departed for Nazareth (13:53). The journey to Nazareth would have taken two full days on foot. And the trek would have taken Jesus southwest about 40 miles *uphill!* This was no quick trip to the market or jaunt to the next town. As He neared His old stomping ground, familiar places would have brought back memories of childhood, adolescence, and young adulthood. He walked past old trees He had climbed, gullies where He and His friends had played, and the homes of His father's customers, His friends, and His brothers and sisters who still lived in Nazareth. And, of course, the synagogue He had attended while growing up.

Eventually the familiar places gave way to familiar faces. However, not all the faces turned out to be friendly. On the following Sabbath, probably after a few days of lying low with His family and possibly gaining their confidence (or at least alleviating their panic), Jesus began teaching in the synagogue (13:54). The people were astonished not merely at His teaching and accompanying miracles but also because *they knew this guy!* Their response has a ring of cynicism or even ridicule about it—they said, in essence, "Who does this guy think He is?" As the saying goes, familiarity breeds contempt. The townspeople in Nazareth knew Jesus, knew Mary, knew His brothers, James, Joseph, Simon, and Judas, and knew His sisters . . . and had no idea where He could have gotten His training, His teaching, and His ability to do miracles (13:55-56)!

Strangely, instead of honoring Him in spite of His far-from-mysterious background, "they took offense at Him" (13:57). The words of A. T. Robertson bear repeating here: "What the people of Nazareth could not comprehend was how one with the origin and environment of Jesus here in Nazareth could possess the wisdom which he appeared to have in his teaching. . . . It was unpardonable for Jesus not to be commonplace like themselves."[121]

Not only did they scoff and sneer in their cynicism, but they also absolutely refused to believe in Him. As we would expect, Jesus responded with a stinging reproof: "A prophet is not without honor except in his hometown and in his own household" (13:57). Those last few words give us a glimpse into the situation "at home." Not only had the resentful neighbors rejected Jesus as a raving lunatic or worse, but apparently His own family had also written Him off as a lost cause. No wonder the apostle John would write sixty years later, "He came to his own people, and even they rejected him" (John 1:11, NLT).

As a result of their unbelief, Jesus did few miracles in Nazareth. On the one hand, we can look at this as an act of judgment—their rejection of Jesus would mean that their sick and oppressed would not receive the blessings of healing and deliverance. On the other hand, this withholding of miracles can be interpreted as an act of mercy toward the people of his hometown—the greater the revelation of Jesus' power and majesty, the greater the guilt for their rejection of Him as the long-awaited Messiah.

What a sad state! Just a dozen verses earlier, Jesus was speaking of the kingdom of heaven as a treasure or a pearl worth a person's entire net worth. Now His own townspeople were rejecting Him, considering Him a source of offense rather than a person of honor! Sadly, the people of Nazareth just didn't get it.

APPLICATION: MATTHEW 13:44-58
Scandalized or Impassioned?

For some of you reading this, the most difficult people to convince of your faith in Jesus are your own family members and close friends. You've discovered the "treasure hidden in the field" and found the "pearl of great value." Now you're trying to cast the net as far as you can as a "fisher of men." But sadly, those closest to you don't appreciate your passion, don't note the great change in your life, and don't understand how you can "waste your time with all that religious stuff." Sometimes parents even take it personally: "Are you saying we didn't raise you right?" Others are simply offended: "Who do you think you are?" Still others want the "old you" back. Your new, changed attitudes, words, and actions are strange to them . . . and convicting!

What do you do? Let me suggest two important approaches to maintaining your witness before those closest to you.

First, *retain your passion.* Don't budge from it. Don't let the scoffing and cynicism of your family members, relatives, close friends, or colleagues dim your enthusiasm for the things of the Lord. They'll be looking for chinks in your armor that can be exploited. They will want to drag you back into their ways of thinking and living because that would make them more comfortable. But if you passionately pursue Christ and His kingdom, maintain your walk and your witness, and retain the joy you experienced when you discovered the treasure in the field or the perfect pearl, eventually some will see that what you've found really is worth something. Those closest to you may start to see the joy they lack, the meaning they secretly long for, or the passion for life they've never had. Of course, some will simply write you off as a mindless fanatic. That's okay. You're in good company. Retain your passion.

Second, *continue to grow.* Sometimes when you're around friends or family who are unbelievers, you'll be tempted to behave in ways that look more like your old self—what they were used to. You might do this to reassure them that you're still the same person you were before, that they have nothing to worry about, and that you haven't been "lost" to some cult. While such an approach might make them more comfortable and reduce the amount of friction at social gatherings, it sends the wrong message. When you discovered the gospel of the kingdom—the saving message of the person and work of Jesus Christ—it was meant to transform you. It didn't just give you a new name; it set you on the path of growing into a new identity. Rather than dimming the light of your growth in Christ, turn it up. Let those closest to you see the fruit of the Spirit that you lacked before coming to know Christ (see Gal. 5:22-23). Only by letting our light shine before others will they see the change in us, leading some—not all, but *some*—to "glorify your Father who is in heaven" (Matt. 5:16).

The Strangest of All Gifts
MATTHEW 14:1-13

NASB

[1] At that [a]time Herod the tetrarch heard the news about Jesus, [2] and said to his servants, "This is John the Baptist; [a]he has risen from the dead, and that is why miraculous powers are at work in him."

[3] For when Herod had John arrested, he bound him and put him in prison because of Herodias, the wife of his brother Philip. [4] For John had been saying to him, "It is not lawful for you to have her." [5] Although Herod wanted to put him to death, he feared the crowd, because they regarded [a]John as a prophet.

[6] But when Herod's birthday came, the daughter of Herodias danced [a]before *them* and pleased Herod, [7] so *much* that he promised with an oath to give her whatever she asked. [8] Having been prompted by her mother, she said, "Give me here on a

NLT

[1] When Herod Antipas, the ruler of Galilee,* heard about Jesus, [2] he said to his advisers, "This must be John the Baptist raised from the dead! That is why he can do such miracles."

[3] For Herod had arrested and imprisoned John as a favor to his wife Herodias (the former wife of Herod's brother Philip). [4] John had been telling Herod, "It is against God's law for you to marry her." [5] Herod wanted to kill John, but he was afraid of a riot, because all the people believed John was a prophet.

[6] But at a birthday party for Herod, Herodias's daughter performed a dance that greatly pleased him, [7] so he promised with a vow to give her anything she wanted. [8] At her mother's urging, the girl said, "I

platter the head of John the Baptist." ⁹Although he was grieved, the king commanded *it* to be given because of his oaths, and because of ªhis dinner guests. ¹⁰He sent and had John beheaded in the prison. ¹¹And his head was brought on a platter and given to the girl, and she brought it to her mother. ¹²His disciples came and took away the body and buried ªit; and they went and reported to Jesus.

¹³Now when Jesus heard *about John,* He withdrew from there in a boat to a secluded place by Himself; and when the ªpeople heard *of this,* they followed Him on foot from the cities.

14:1 ªOr *occasion* 14:2 ªOr *he, himself* 14:5 ªLit *him* 14:6 ªLit *in the midst* 14:9 ªLit *those who reclined* at the table *with him* 14:12 ªLit *him* 14:13 ªLit *the crowds*

want the head of John the Baptist on a tray!" ⁹Then the king regretted what he had said; but because of the vow he had made in front of his guests, he issued the necessary orders. ¹⁰So John was beheaded in the prison, ¹¹and his head was brought on a tray and given to the girl, who took it to her mother. ¹²Later, John's disciples came for his body and buried it. Then they went and told Jesus what had happened.

¹³As soon as Jesus heard the news, he left in a boat to a remote area to be alone. But the crowds heard where he was headed and followed on foot from many towns.

14:1 Greek *Herod the tetrarch*. Herod Antipas was a son of King Herod and was ruler over Galilee.

In life and in ministry, I sometimes find myself shaking my head and saying, "You just can't make this stuff up." If anybody finds life drab, dull, or boring, they're not quite living. And if someone finds ministry humdrum and unexciting, they've probably disengaged from real ministry!

The Bible serves as a perfect mirror for the real world. Its narratives present life in all its varied, vivid colors—some brilliant and exhilarating, others dark and disturbing; some with sharp contrasts, others with nuanced blends. The stories of the Bible aren't made-to-order tales meant to delight or entertain. They're accounts of real life for real people in the real world.

This explains why some of the episodes in the life of Christ are, frankly, bizarre. Some are so sordid, so twisted, and so shocking that they lead us to conclude that it's highly unlikely that anybody would have made these things up. Matthew 14 begins with such a story. It appears suddenly and unexpectedly in the flow of Jesus' ministry of preaching, teaching, telling parables, and performing miracles. If the Gospel of Matthew were a movie, we'd probably see the words "Meanwhile, in the palace of Herod Antipas . . ." appear at the bottom of the frame. Oh—and this particular scene would probably earn the film an R rating. It's just that raw and real.

The story begins with a birthday party, involves a sexually provocative dance, turns on the strangest of all birthday gifts, and ends with the senseless beheading of a godly prophet by order of a lustful, creepy king. From the prominent figures in this story we can learn some valuable lessons about folly and sin—and their terrible consequences.

— 14:1-2 —

The adulterous, lustful Herod Antipas and his sadistic, hateful wife, Herodias, would have qualified as the Bonnie and Clyde of the New Testament. They personified evil in every way, the depth of which is exposed in the first part of Matthew 14. One expositor puts it this way:

> This true account is more incredible than the most bizarre soap opera. It is a story of infidelity, divorce, remarriage, incest, political intrigue, jealousy, spite, revenge, lewdness, lust, cold-heartedness, cruelty, brutality, violence, ungodly remorse, and godly mourning. But above all, it is the story of godless fear and the power of such fear to confuse, deceive, corrupt, destroy, and damn.[122]

What a bleak picture! But it's not an exaggeration. The setting of Matthew 14 takes us to the inner workings of the Judean mafia of the day: the despicable Herod family. The roots of that family tree were fed by the blood of those its members had murdered. The original "Godfather" of that family, Herod the Great (see the feature on page 35), gave new meaning to the phrase "human depravity." Married no fewer than ten times, Herod only added to his life of deception, cruelty, and crime with each new marriage. He had several of his wives murdered, as well as some of his sons. One of the lucky sons who escaped the bloodthirsty jealousy of his father was Herod Antipas, who came to rule over territory west of the Sea of Galilee and east of the Jordan River and Dead Sea during Christ's ministry.

As the scene opens in Matthew 14:1, we find Herod keeping tabs on the ministry of Jesus in the vicinity of his territory. The similarity of His message to John's, the rumors of miraculous signs, and his own superstition and guilt had driven him to conclude that John the Baptizer had risen from the dead (14:2). This seems to have been the only explanation Herod could come up with for how the man named Jesus could have such amazing power.

But wait! Matthew's last mention of John the Baptizer had him in Herod's prison. He had been arrested early on in Jesus' ministry (4:12).

Later, he had sent messengers from prison to inquire whether Jesus really was the long-awaited Messiah (11:2-3). How had John died in prison? At this point, Matthew presses the pause button on his narrative and presents his readers with a flashback to catch us up on how John had lost his life in the custody of Herod Antipas.

— 14:3-5 —

As we saw already in our discussion of John's arrest mentioned in Matthew 4:12, the Baptizer's preaching—particularly his criticism of Herod Antipas's illegitimate marriage to Herodias—had gotten him into trouble. John had been publicly proclaiming, "It is not lawful for you to have her" (14:4). You may recall that Herod Antipas had fallen in love with his niece and sister-in-law Herodias, who was a granddaughter of Herod the Great, the daughter of Antipas's half-brother Aristobulus, and also the wife of Antipas's brother Philip (who was also Herodias's uncle)! Like I said in the beginning: *You can't make this stuff up!* No wonder John the Baptizer had spoken out against the exploits of their king!

The Twisted Relationships of Herodias

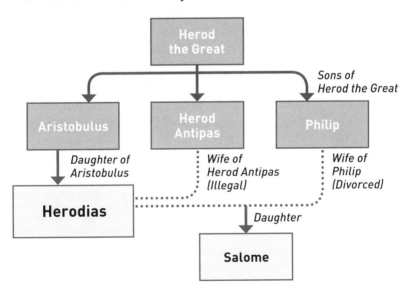

Matthew tells us that Herod had wanted to execute John but feared the public outcry because so many believed John to be a prophet (14:5). Besides this, Herod himself knew that John was a "righteous and holy man" and used to enjoy listening to his preaching (Mark 6:20). It could be that deep down inside, Herod knew that John's preaching against his sin was right; if so, Herod would have had a sense that he was in the wrong, so executing John would have been the epitome of injustice and wickedness. Herod Antipas had resolved, then, to just let John remain in prison, where the prophet was being kept safe (Mark 6:20). However, Herod's illegitimate wife, Herodias, couldn't let the matter go. She appears to have lacked a single ounce of morality and carried no tinge of guilt. She bore a bitter grudge against John and wanted him put to death (Mark 6:19). Naturally, such a wicked, scheming woman was waiting breathlessly for a chance to exact her revenge on John.

Herod stood in an awkward dilemma, considering John's popularity before the people, his own burdened conscience regarding John's treatment, and his wife's strong desire to murder John. Clearly, Herod found himself caught in a sticky web from which he couldn't extract himself.

— 14:6-13 —

Herodias's opportunity to get John the Baptizer put to death came in an unexpected way. On his birthday, Herod threw a large banquet for "lords and military commanders and the leading men of Galilee" (Mark 6:21). These guests were the bigwigs of the government, and Herod would have done anything to impress them. Herodias took advantage of Herod's unparalleled pride and unquenchable lust. She arranged for her daughter, Salome, to dance for Herod and the guests at his birthday bash.[123]

When Matthew tells us that Salome "danced before them and pleased Herod" (Matt. 14:6), we shouldn't picture a little girl in a pink tutu putting on a cute performance for daddy and his friends. This wasn't a few ballet moves—a couple of pliés and lively sautés topped off with a well-rehearsed pirouette. No, Salome, the daughter of Herodias through her first marriage with Philip, was no innocent child but a blossoming adolescent who danced in such a way that she "pleased" Herod and his guests. This doesn't mean they raised "perfect 10s" on scorecards to judge her performance. Rather, they were consumed with lust over the girl! A. T. Robertson describes the scene: "It was a shameful exhibition of lewd dancing prearranged by Herodias to compass her purpose for John's death. Salome had stooped to the level of an *almeh*, or common dancer."[124]

Then, in front of all his high-society guests, the inebriated Herod, engulfed in lust for his stepdaughter, blurted out a stupid promise to give her almost anything she asked for in payment for her dancing, sealing the pledge with an oath (Matt. 14:7). Mark provides additional details, noting that Herod made the public promise not once, but twice: "Ask me for whatever you want and I will give it to you. . . . Whatever you ask of me, I will give it to you; up to half of my kingdom" (Mark 6:22-23). As soon as those words left his mouth, he was bound to make good on his foolish oath. All the highest dignitaries of the region were present, waiting to hear Salome's request and witness Herod's actions.

This was the moment Herodias had been waiting for. When Salome whispered in her mother's ear, "What shall I ask for?" Herodias pounced: "The head of John the Baptist" (Mark 6:24). So, loudly and clearly, such that everybody in the banquet hall could hear her request, Salome announced, "Give me here on a platter the head of John the Baptist" (Matt. 14:8).

At that very moment, Herod Antipas "was grieved" (14:9). Perhaps the shock of the request afforded Herod a moment of lucidity, and he realized that Herodias had cunningly choreographed the entire evening to get what she wanted. But as he panned the hall of expectant faces of rulers, military leaders, and high government officials, he could do nothing but make good on his word. Against his conscience, he issued the order that John the Baptizer's head be brought up on a platter, in fulfillment of his stepdaughter's wicked request (14:10).

As ordered, the executioner delivered John's head on a platter and presented it to Salome, who in turn brought it to her mother (14:11). If anybody had been in doubt about who was really behind the plot, that action would have made it crystal clear. What would have made a moral person gag in disgust made Herodias grin in pleasure. She had gotten what she had wanted for months: the head of the prophet who—in her mind—had done nothing but point out the sinfulness of her own actions.

When the disciples of John the Baptizer heard of his execution, they immediately collected his body to give it a proper burial. They then reported to Jesus what had occurred (14:12). In response to the news, Jesus "withdrew from there in a boat to a secluded place by Himself" (14:13). We can only assume He went to mourn in silence and solitude, to reflect on the life of John. He had lost the one who had proclaimed the coming of the Messiah, who had baptized Him to fulfill all righteousness, and who had faithfully and courageously proclaimed the message of repentance to all, even to the wicked King Herod and his even more wicked wife, Herodias.

These events had presumably happened long before the words of Herod Antipas reported in Matthew 14:2. We see that the execution of

John continued to haunt Herod well into the future. When he heard about this astonishing prophet and teacher, Jesus of Nazareth, Herod assumed that John the Baptizer had risen from the dead. These are the words of a man driven to mad superstition by a wounded conscience. I can imagine, to alleviate his fears, Herod asking his wife, Herodias, to fetch the head of John the Baptizer just to make sure he was still dead.

APPLICATION: MATTHEW 14:1-13

Four Hard Lessons on Sin

Some passages of Scripture are encouraging, providing beautiful examples of faith, hope, and love. Others are shocking, illustrating the depths of wickedness and depravity—and the consequences of sin. The account of the beheading of John the Baptizer is one of those latter passages. In fact, if you think about it too hard, the episode is so repulsive you might feel like taking a shower after you've read it. However, even such tragic accounts of some of the nastiest people in Scripture provide lessons for us today.

First, *Herodias teaches us how dangerous and disastrous it is to nurse a grudge and seek revenge.* In her case, it led her to dress her teenage daughter like an exotic dancer, manipulate her husband in public, and call for the unjust murder of an innocent man against whom she had seethed with anger for months. Her obsession with getting revenge for the public humiliation she had experienced had so seared her conscience that when John the Baptizer was murdered at her request, she didn't even flinch. The truth is, if somebody harbors spite and bitterness long enough, it will eat away at that person's soul. There will be no limit to what a person will do to get even or to get back at someone. Such a grudge is like an aggressive cancer eating away at the mind, emotions, and will. Instead of bitterly rejecting those who justly rebuke us, it would be better to accept the reproof, change our ways, and move on. And even if someone unjustly offends us, it's better to forgive and forget. Are you holding a grudge against someone? A former employer or co-worker? A parent? Your spouse? Let it go.

Second, *Herod Antipas teaches us about the power of peer pressure.* You know why he didn't go back on his foolish oath to Salome? Because he cared more about what the people around him thought of him than doing what was right. He didn't even consider his responsibility toward God or justice, or his ultimate legacy in the annals of history. Instead, he cared only about the here and now—how those faces in the banquet hall would view him. And clearly, Herod was not functioning with all his faculties of better judgment in place. He was probably drunk, unable to think clearly about the right course of action. His pride and bravado took over, and he has become a historic example of a fool. Are you living under the intimidation of peer pressure? Of what others at school or work may say or think regarding your faith in Christ or your convictions about moral issues? Do you find yourself caving in before a group of peers who don't have heaven's interests in mind? Wanting to show off in ways you think will impress them, even if deep down you know it's wrong? It's not worth it! Look instead to do what's right.

Third, *Salome teaches us about the treachery of rationalization.* Salome was probably not simply an innocent victim of her mommy's manipulation. She was likely a willing participant, which is how she ended up in this sordid affair. I imagine that she rationalized her behavior, convincing herself through a long, twisted thought process that it was okay for a princess to appear before Herod and his guests half naked and perform what was tantamount to a lewd striptease. And if anybody ever pointed out her poor judgment and its tragic results, Salome could just smugly respond, "I was only following orders." The power to rationalize evil is shocking. Those who do it can suddenly find themselves in places they would have never expected to be, doing things they would have never imagined themselves doing. Do you rationalize behavior you know is wrong? Do you appeal to the lame excuse "I'm just doing what I'm told"? Or do you imagine the categories of right and wrong don't apply in a given situation because "this is just too important"? Quit rationalizing evil . . . even in the little things. It will end in disaster.

Finally, *the whole story teaches us about the seductiveness and addictiveness of sin.* From Herod the Great all the way down through every member of his family, sin poisoned relationships. If it wasn't lust, it was greed; if it wasn't spite, it was murder; if it wasn't deception, it was blasphemy. The household of Herod was cursed by the cultivation and propagation of sin, sin, sin. Like an addiction passed down from generation to generation, the doses increased and the tragic effects grew. I have a little saying I wrote down and put on the copier in front of the computer in my home office. I look at it every day, and I'm constantly reminded of its wisdom. It goes like this: "Sin will take you farther than you want to go. Sin will keep you longer than you want to stay. Sin will cost you more than you want to pay." My constant prayer in response to this is *Lord God, keep me clean. Remind me to keep short accounts. Show me over and over how weak I am so that I'll lean hard on You and not bring shame to Your name or to my family or to the people to whom I minister.* Let this conviction and prayer be yours, too.

Eating a Miracle for Dinner
MATTHEW 14:14-21

NASB

¹⁴When He went ᵃashore, He saw a large crowd, and felt compassion for them and healed their sick.

¹⁵When it was evening, the disciples came to Him and said, "This place is desolate and the hour is already ᵃlate; so send the crowds away, that they may go into the villages and buy food for themselves." ¹⁶But Jesus said to them, "They do not need to go away; you give them *something* to eat!" ¹⁷They said to Him, "We have here only five loaves and two fish." ¹⁸And He said, "Bring them here to Me." ¹⁹Ordering the ᵃpeople to ᵇsit down on the grass, He took the five loaves and the two fish, and looking up toward heaven, He blessed *the food,* and breaking the loaves He gave them to the disciples, and the disciples *gave them* to the crowds, ²⁰and they all ate and were satisfied. They picked up what was left over of the broken pieces, twelve full baskets. ²¹There were about five thousand men who ate, besides women and children.

14:14 ᵃLit *out* 14:15 ᵃLit *past* 14:19 ᵃLit *crowds* ᵇLit *recline*

NLT

¹⁴Jesus saw the huge crowd as he stepped from the boat, and he had compassion on them and healed their sick.

¹⁵That evening the disciples came to him and said, "This is a remote place, and it's already getting late. Send the crowds away so they can go to the villages and buy food for themselves."

¹⁶But Jesus said, "That isn't necessary—you feed them."

¹⁷"But we have only five loaves of bread and two fish!" they answered.

¹⁸"Bring them here," he said. ¹⁹Then he told the people to sit down on the grass. Jesus took the five loaves and two fish, looked up toward heaven, and blessed them. Then, breaking the loaves into pieces, he gave the bread to the disciples, who distributed it to the people. ²⁰They all ate as much as they wanted, and afterward, the disciples picked up twelve baskets of leftovers. ²¹About 5,000 men were fed that day, in addition to all the women and children!

The feeding of the five thousand is the only miracle of Jesus recorded in all four Gospel accounts. Let that sink in. This points to its significance in the minds of the Gospel writers . . . as well as in the mind of God. However, because this story has become so familiar to us, we sometimes miss its importance and tend to diminish it in our own minds. We forget what a magnificent—and mysterious—event it was.

In fact, Jesus would later scold His disciples for failing to grasp the profound significance of the feeding of the five thousand—"Do you not yet understand or remember the five loaves of the five thousand, and how many baskets full you picked up?" (16:9). If we view the miracle simply as a supernatural way to feed hungry people—which, of course, is no trifling event in and of itself—we'll miss the spiritual meaning of the sign. The miracle of the loaves and fish was a sort of edible parable; while it had an immediate, physical impact on the hungry crowd being fed, it also has a spiritual purpose in communicating something about Jesus, about the kingdom, and about us.

Instead of shrugging at the familiar and moving on, we need to slow down and ponder its profundity. Let's give this miracle its due, seeing again that our God is the God of the impossible.

— 14:14 —

We live our lives surrounded by impossibilities—things that are completely out of our reach, situations we're unable to change, problems we're unable to solve. Maybe it's our failing health. Maybe it's a broken relationship. Maybe it's a tragic loss. Whatever it is, we simply have to label it "impossible" and struggle through it. The next event in Matthew's telling of Jesus' ministry pits five pieces of flatbread and two tiny fish against a hungry crowd of thousands of men, women, and children. Had we been there that day, we would have taken one look at the situation and pronounced it impossible. Nothing could be done to alleviate the people's need for food.

Before we examine the miracle itself, though, we need to remind ourselves that Jesus was still grieving the loss of His cousin John the Baptizer (14:12-13). Jesus had gotten into a boat to slip away to a remote place for some alone time. Yet in no time, the crowds of followers heard of His departure, figured out where He was going, and eventually found their way to what was supposed to be a "secluded place" (14:13). They showed up in droves from the cities, hoping to see the man about whom everybody was talking.

When Jesus got out of the boat, there was a crowd that could have been as large as twenty thousand people—about five thousand men as well as thousands more women and children (14:21). Matthew initially just calls the crowd "large" (14:14). Imagine the number of needs in that group. Think of the sick, the debilitated, the injured, and the spiritually oppressed! The suffering and pain of the people weighed on Jesus. And instead of showing irritation or frustration that His quiet time alone had been disturbed, He immediately rolled up His sleeves and got to work healing the sick. Why? Because He "felt compassion for them" (14:14).

As the clouds rolled across the sky and the sun made its way from east to west, Jesus worked His way through the crowd of people, healing one after another after another after another. No doubt His disciples were assisting Him in at least organizing the people, probably watching the sun slowly setting out of the corner of their eye as the crowd just seemed to swell. But Matthew's account gives no indication that Jesus slowed His pace for a moment.

— 14:15-17 —

Then, as twilight approached, the disciples had had enough. They were getting hungry and antsy. You know the feeling. You go so long without eating that you start feeling a little "hangry"—angry and irritable because of the lack of food. I'm sure most of the disciples were experiencing that, and so were the thousands of people in the crowd. Remember, there weren't just men but whole families. I don't care what century you're from—small children get mighty grumpy when they haven't eaten all day. Whatever provisions the people may have packed were certainly gone by now.

So the disciples pulled Jesus aside and said, essentially, "Look, enough is enough. The sun's going down, and we're in the middle of nowhere. Send all these people away so they can go to town and get something to eat" (see 14:15). Nothing about what the disciples said seemed unreasonable. From a strictly human point of view, it made perfect sense. Given the totality of the situation, "send them away" was the solution to the problem. What other options did they have except the impossible?

But the impossible was exactly what Jesus asked them to do.

"They do not need to go away," He said. "You give them something to eat!" (14:16). This may very well be one of the most preposterous things the disciples had heard from Jesus' lips—and they'd heard a lot. What Jesus was asking them to do was simply impossible. I'm sure they honored Jesus' command and ran through their options, striking a thick red line through each of them. First of all, they had almost no food. They made an explicit point of that—"We have here only five loaves and two fish" (14:17). When you think of these "loaves," you should probably picture small, flat pieces of cracker-like barley bread, each perhaps the size of an open hand. And for "fish," you should probably imagine something like dried, cured sardines, nothing more than an afternoon snack. John's account of the miracle tells us that these paltry provisions belonged to a small boy (John 6:9)! For all practical purposes, the disciples had no food. That was problem number one.

Second, they had no money. If Jesus pushed His mandate that the disciples feed the crowd, it would have required them to divvy up whatever money they had, go to nearby towns, and buy as much food as they could to feed as many people as possible. But it would have taken a small fortune to provide just a basic meal to the thousands of people gathered that evening. In fact, Philip quickly did the math and suggested that even a small snack for each person would cost "two hundred denarii" (John 6:7), which was about eight months of an average person's wages.[125] They simply didn't have the financial resources to do it.

Third, even if they'd had the money, they didn't have the time! It had taken Jesus all day to go through the crowd and heal those who were sick. The sun was setting. It would soon be time to sleep. Even if the disciples had a cartload of food at hand, and if they were to distribute the food in an orderly fashion so everybody got an equal amount, the process would take until morning! By then they'd have to start the breakfast round.

Finally, even if they'd had food and time, they didn't have the energy or the manpower to do it. The disciples were hungry and exhausted themselves!

From a purely human point of view, they could see no way around this problem. Jesus was demanding the impossible. John's account of this miracle fills us in on some insider information. Jesus told them to do what everybody knew was impossible in order to test them, "for He Himself knew what He was intending to do" (John 6:6).

Clearly, the disciples failed the test. In their objections, the disciples folded under the pressure of the natural, surrendered to the earthly, and capitulated to the rational. And in doing so, they had utterly forgotten that standing in front of them was *omnipotence personified*. Instead of saying, "We can't," they should have responded to Jesus the same way the prophet Jeremiah had toward God: "Behold, You have made the heavens and the earth by Your great power and by Your outstretched arm! Nothing is too difficult for You" (Jer. 32:17). But when our minds are riveted to the human perspective, our reason will be limited to human possibilities. All we can focus on is what *can't* be done. We forget that God is the God of the impossible, the One who said, "Behold, I am the LORD, the God of all flesh; is anything too difficult for Me?" (Jer. 32:27).

— 14:18-19—

Without showboating, without a loud announcement, without any profound declarations, Jesus carried out a stunning miracle like nothing that crowd had ever seen. How did He do it? With a simple prayer of thanksgiving. First, He had the disciples bring the five little loaves and two tiny fish (14:18). Did He really need them? No. The One who created everything out of nothing could have commanded a full meal into the lap of every member of the crowd. But He chose to take the seemingly insignificant offering of that nearby lad and multiply it. He ordered everybody to sit down where they were on the grass (14:19). Mark's Gospel adds the detail that they did this "in groups of hundreds and of fifties" (Mark 6:40). This made distribution much easier than if people had been running to and fro in the excitement.

With His eyes toward heaven—the normal posture of a person in prayer in those days—Jesus blessed the food and broke the bread. The typical Jewish blessing at the beginning of a meal was in our terms like saying, "Blessed art thou, O Lord our God, king of the world, who hast brought forth bread from the earth."[126] There would have been nothing unexpected with such a prayer. Those in the crowd closest to Jesus might have thought He and His disciples were going to have their own dinner together.

For the first few seconds, that's exactly what it looked like. Jesus broke the bread and divided the fish, then distributed the broken food to His disciples. They, in turn, gave bread to those nearest to them (Matt. 14:19). But then, emanating from Jesus in the center, wave after wave after wave after wave of an abundance of bread and fish flowed outward to the seated crowd.

— 14:20-21 —

Everybody ate bread and fish that evening, and all the people "were satisfied" (14:20). Here Matthew goes out of his way to point out that the "five thousand" numbered only the men. Besides them, women and children also ate (14:21). If there were as many women as men present, this would have increased the number of mouths to feed to ten thousand. If there were on average two children with every man, that would

The *kophinos* was a wicker basket, perhaps like the one pictured here.

have doubled the number to twenty thousand. In any case, what's clear is that whole families were blessed by the miracle of the loaves and fish.

And that's not all. Matthew mentions that "they picked up what was left over of the broken pieces, twelve full baskets" (14:20). The term translated "basket" here is *kophinos* [2894], a kind of wicker basket that could be carried in one's arms easily enough. Not only did Jesus provide what was needed—a feat thought impossible just hours earlier—but His miracle of multiplication produced an overabundance.

APPLICATION: MATTHEW 14:14-21

Impossible Situations, Great Opportunities

Through this unforgettable lesson, Jesus taught vital truths. Besides the demonstration that He is Lord of heaven *and earth*, of things spiritual *and physical*, of the possible *and impossible*, He underscored the fact that He deals not merely in the *sufficient* but also in the *abundant*. On another occasion, He would announce, "I came that they may have life, and have it abundantly" (John 10:10). And He "is able to do far more abundantly beyond all that we ask or think, according to the power that works within us," that is, the Holy Spirit (Eph. 3:20).

Are you facing a seemingly impossible situation today? Don't have enough money, time, or energy to go on? This is an opportunity for God to do the impossible. Those people who had been with Jesus all day needed food, so He provided it. While it was impossible for the disciples to meet the need, it was not impossible for the Lord. As long as we operate our lives from a horizontal point of view—focusing on the limitations of this physical world, with its inviolable laws of cause and effect—the only thing we'll see is the impossibilities. As long as we're stuck on that horizontal plane, looking only at the human side of things, we'll come up against walls over and over and over again. And our lives will be marked by the negative—what *can't* be done.

Yes, acknowledge that your situation is impossible. Your marriage problems? *Impossible.* Your teenager's rebellion? *Impossible.* Your employment situation? *Impossible.* Your medical diagnosis? *Impossible.* The legal battle you're going through? *Impossible.* The financial hardship? *Impossible.* The battle against temptation and sin? *Impossible.* Your emotional struggle? *Impossible.* Our political situation? *Impossible.*

Now pause. Yes, these and many more things are, from our horizontal perspective, impossible situations. But now look up. Thank the Lord in prayer, and let Him turn your impossible situation into a great opportunity to "supply all your needs according to His riches in glory in Christ Jesus" (Phil. 4:19). He knows what you need, and He knows when you need it. And the One who spoke this universe into existence isn't bound by our materialistic notions of "*if* this . . . *then* that."

From our limited viewpoint, we can't see the magnificent opportunities God sees. If we truly trust God, we need to accept this fact: Nothing is impossible with Him. To keep this truth ever present in the midst of your own impossible situations, take a moment to memorize these simple but profound verses:

- "Behold, I am the LORD, the God of all flesh; is anything too difficult for Me?" (Jer. 32:27)
- "Behold, You have made the heavens and the earth by Your great power and by Your outstretched arm! Nothing is too difficult for You." (Jer. 32:17)

What Brings Us to Our Knees?
MATTHEW 14:22-36

NASB

22Immediately He ᵃmade the disciples get into the boat and go ahead of Him to the other side, while He

NLT

22Immediately after this, Jesus insisted that his disciples get back into the boat and cross to the other side of the lake, while he sent the people sent the crowds away. ²³After He had sent the crowds away, He went up on the mountain by Himself to pray; and when it was evening, He was there alone. ²⁴But the boat was already ªa long distance from the land, ᵇbattered by the waves; for the wind was ᶜcontrary. ²⁵And in the ªfourth watch of the night He came to them, walking on the sea. ²⁶When the disciples saw Him walking on the sea, they were terrified, and said, "It is a ghost!" And they cried out ªin fear. ²⁷But immediately Jesus spoke to them, saying, "Take courage, it is I; do not be afraid."

²⁸Peter said to Him, "Lord, if it is You, command me to come to You on the water." ²⁹And He said, "Come!" And Peter got out of the boat, and walked on the water and came toward Jesus. ³⁰But seeing the wind, he became frightened, and beginning to sink, he cried out, "Lord, save me!" ³¹Immediately Jesus stretched out His hand and took hold of him, and said to him, "You of little faith, why did you doubt?" ³²When they got into the boat, the wind stopped. ³³And those who were in the boat worshiped Him, saying, "You are certainly God's Son!"

³⁴When they had crossed over, they came to land at Gennesaret. ³⁵And when the men of that place ªrecognized Him, they sent *word* into all that surrounding district and brought to Him all who were sick; ³⁶and they implored Him that they might just touch the fringe of His cloak; and as many as touched *it* were cured.

14:22 ªLit *compelled* **14:24** ªLit *many stadia from;* a stadion was about 600 feet or about 182 meters ᵇLit *tormented* ᶜOr *adverse* **14:25** ªI.e. 3-6 a.m. **14:26** ªLit *from* **14:35** ªOr *knew*

home. ²³After sending them home, he went up into the hills by himself to pray. Night fell while he was there alone.

²⁴Meanwhile, the disciples were in trouble far away from land, for a strong wind had risen, and they were fighting heavy waves. ²⁵About three o'clock in the morning* Jesus came toward them, walking on the water. ²⁶When the disciples saw him walking on the water, they were terrified. In their fear, they cried out, "It's a ghost!"

²⁷But Jesus spoke to them at once. "Don't be afraid," he said. "Take courage. I am here!*"

²⁸Then Peter called to him, "Lord, if it's really you, tell me to come to you, walking on the water."

²⁹"Yes, come," Jesus said.

So Peter went over the side of the boat and walked on the water toward Jesus. ³⁰But when he saw the strong* wind and the waves, he was terrified and began to sink. "Save me, Lord!" he shouted.

³¹Jesus immediately reached out and grabbed him. "You have so little faith," Jesus said. "Why did you doubt me?"

³²When they climbed back into the boat, the wind stopped. ³³Then the disciples worshiped him. "You really are the Son of God!" they exclaimed.

³⁴After they had crossed the lake, they landed at Gennesaret. ³⁵When the people recognized Jesus, the news of his arrival spread quickly throughout the whole area, and soon people were bringing all their sick to be healed. ³⁶They begged him to let the sick touch at least the fringe of his robe, and all who touched him were healed.

14:25 Greek *In the fourth watch of the night.* **14:27** Or *The 'I AM' is here;* Greek reads *I am.* See Exod 3:14. **14:30** Some manuscripts do not include *strong.*

All my life I've heard people talk about "walking with the Lord" after they "decided to follow Jesus" and "not turn back." But what if the Lord Jesus sends us onto a crowded fishing boat in the middle of the night to row in the dark? What if that boat faces a violent windstorm that threatens to capsize the vessel in the middle of the lake? What if Jesus beckons us to step out of the boat onto the raging surface of the water with the prospect of plummeting like a stone through the surface to the dark abyss below? It's one thing to promise to go wherever He leads and follow Him all of our days; it's another thing to go in the direction He points when it looks like He's sending us into harm's way.

As Matthew tells one story after another about what it's like to walk with Jesus wherever He goes, we're led into some unforgettable scenes with the disciples that should cause us to think long and hard about discipleship. If we use our imaginations and go where they went, see what they saw, and feel what they felt, it will have a profound impact on how seriously we take our commitment to follow Jesus where He leads and go where He sends.

The scene immediately following the late-evening feeding of the massive crowd of men, women, and children provides a powerful picture of the life of true discipleship. I'm sure the disciples would never forget that night on the sea. Its details would have been permanently etched in their minds . . . and its lessons of faith eternally impressed upon their hearts.

— 14:22-23 —

As the sun dropped behind the jagged horizon, clouds rolled in over Galilee, reducing the moonlight and starlight to an eerie glow. Some in the crowd had no doubt begun to disperse; others had probably found a soft patch of grass and begun to snooze. Surely some vigilant members of the throng were keeping their eyes on Jesus and the disciples to see what they might do next. Under the cover of night, Jesus led His disciples to the silver-lit eastern shoreline, had them load into the boat, and pointed northward across the water, directing them to go ahead to the other side toward Bethsaida (14:22; Mark 6:45).

As the crowds likely began to stir and ready themselves to follow Jesus to Bethsaida, He dismissed them, sending them to their homes while He finally took the opportunity to pray alone, ascending a nearby mountain (Matt. 14:22-23). It wouldn't be a mischaracterization to say that Jesus was intentionally trying to "ditch" the masses. John informs us at the end of his account of the feeding miracle, "Jesus, perceiving that they were intending to come and take Him by force to make Him king, withdrew again to the mountain by Himself alone" (John 6:15).

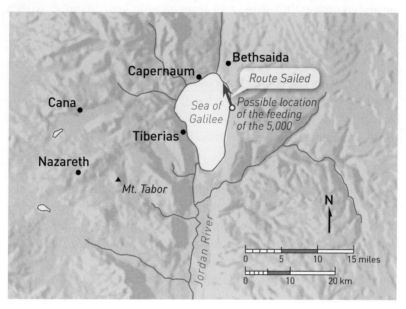

According to Mark's Gospel, Jesus sent the disciples by boat to Bethsaida after the feeding of the five thousand.

We need to notice a few things about this unusual scene. First, Jesus left the disciples alone. He didn't join them in the boat as He usually did. Perhaps for a few seconds they assumed He would be climbing in with them. That would have certainly made the prospect of sailing across the massive, dark body of water feel less daunting. After all, last time a near tragedy had struck the disciples on the Sea of Galilee in the form of a storm, Jesus had simply calmed it with a command (Matt. 8:24-26). But on this occasion, instead of boarding, He said, in effect, "You go on ahead. I'll join you later." Perhaps a wave of panic began to go over them as the bow began to cut through the dark waters, but as Jesus waved them on, they had no choice but to simply trust and obey Him.

Second, Jesus had sent them off into the dark. Of course, several of these men were seasoned fishermen, familiar with sailing on the Sea of Galilee in all kinds of conditions, day and night. But usually those expeditions would have only been back and forth from the shore to fishable water—at times and places they themselves had chosen. But here they were on a dark sea with no light in a boat probably nearing

313

capacity. And don't forget, it's possible they were also carrying at least some of the baskets of leftover bread and fish! The disciples had been ordered to go and do something they wouldn't have been entirely comfortable with, and Jesus simply sent them off with a "Bon voyage!"

Third, Jesus was finally getting a long-awaited quiet time alone. With the disciples heading across the northeastern quarter of the lake and the crowds dispersing, Jesus was able to slip away and climb one of the nearby hills in that secluded location. He was going to do what He had originally intended to do before the masses of people had swarmed Him—commune with His heavenly Father (see 14:13).

— 14:24-26 —

The scene suddenly cuts from Jesus praying on a mountain to the disciples laboring to cross to the north shore of the lake. The boat was literally "many stadia" from land (see the footnote on 14:24). A *stadion* [4712] was about 600 feet, which means the boat was precariously distant from the safety of the shore. What's worse, "the wind was contrary," and the boat was "battered by the waves" (14:24). Matthew describes the action of the waves with the word *basanizō* [928], a verb that means "to subject to severe distress, *torment, harass*."[127] Though the disciples had likely intended to hug the shoreline as they headed north, the wind and waves were pushing them farther and farther out to open water, away from their destination and toward certain calamity! It was after three o'clock in the morning, but not yet dawn—"the fourth watch of the night" (14:25).[128] In short, the disciples were in trouble, and as far as they knew, they were all alone.

Then, at the brink of exhaustion and the end of their hope, they saw Jesus coming toward them, walking on the surface of the water. At first, they didn't know it was Him. So unexpected and astonishing such a thing would have been that they assumed it was a ghost and began to panic (14:26). Admit it—you and I would have thought the same thing. Who could have imagined that Jesus would join the boat by walking across the water? The disciples were scared out of their wits. The Greek word translated "terrified" in 14:26 is a form of *tarassō* [5015], which means "to cause inward turmoil, *stir up, disturb, unsettle, throw into confusion*."[129] In such a moment, the last thing the disciples were doing was analyzing what they saw through the lens of a proper theology of bodies, spirits, ghosts, and phantoms. With tragedy impending, they had thrown their theology overboard.

— 14:27-33 —

Jesus rescued the disciples even from their bad theology. He immediately responded to their sudden, superstitious belief in ghosts: "Take courage, it is I; do not be afraid" (14:27). I see two specific parts to His reply—two complementary imperatives and one indicative. In the commands, Jesus essentially expressed one idea in two forms—positively ("take courage") and negatively ("do not be afraid"). The negative command "do not be afraid" addressed the disciples' panicked state in light of the dangerous situation they found themselves in. Meanwhile, the positive command "take courage" would inspire them to actively put a stop to their fear. The Greek verb translated "take courage," *tharseō* [2293], was used earlier in Matthew 9:2, when Jesus addressed the paralytic on his bed: "Take courage, son; your sins are forgiven." It was also used in 9:22, when He healed the woman with the twelve-year hemorrhage: "Daughter, take courage; your faith has made you well." The term means "to be firm or resolute in the face of danger or adverse circumstances."[130]

Between these two complementary imperatives, Jesus made a profound statement that would provide the basis for the disciples' confidence and strength: "It is I." Literally, Jesus' words were "I am"—perhaps a mysterious reference to His identity as the great "I AM" (Exod. 3:14; see also John 8:58). The One who had created that very body of water on which they were sailing decided to take an early morning stroll across it. His reassuring presence and encouraging words would have begun to calm their hearts. The memories of who Jesus was and what He had been able to do throughout His ministry would have begun to quiet their fear and trepidation even while the wind continued to blow and the waves continued to crash against the boat.

Those few words were all Peter needed to embolden him to take a literal leap of faith! In what looked like an impulsive move, Peter said, "Lord, if it is You, command me to come to You on the water" (Matt. 14:28). We could read this as Peter testing Jesus, but I prefer to read it as a bold act of faith. In any case, Jesus invited him out: "Come!" (14:29). Without hesitation, Peter climbed over the side of the rocking boat and plopped onto the water. Not *into . . . onto*. Step by step, he made his way toward Jesus as if he were walking through snow.

Everything seemed to be going fine as long as Peter kept his eyes on Jesus—the true source of courageous faith. But within a few seconds, Peter lost his focus on the Master of the elements and started examining the elements themselves: "Seeing the wind, he became frightened, and beginning to sink, he cried out" (14:30).

Yet even in his lapse into fear, Peter gave a sign of genuine faith. He didn't just cry out in horror. He cried out, "Lord, save me!" That simple prayer is all it took. Jesus reached out His hand, grabbed Peter, and lifted him out of the water with a few words of gentle but firm admonishment: "You of little faith, why did you doubt?" (14:31). The Greek word for "doubt" here is a rare one—*distazō* [1365]. In the whole New Testament it's found only here and in Matthew 28:17: "When they saw Him, they worshiped Him; but some were doubtful." In both places, the term is used in reference to people who do, in fact, believe in who Jesus is and what He's capable of but who at the same time harbor lingering doubts. This wasn't the kind of doubt that an unbeliever has, which is more like stubborn unbelief. It's the doubt that comes from living in a world filled with situations, circumstances, trials, and tribulations that cause strong believers to wonder about the goodness and mercy of God.

Finally, both Peter and Jesus climbed into the boat. Immediately the wind stopped and the waves ceased their tantrum. Everyone was safe and sound. A slick formed on the surface of the water. The boat was still rocking from the movement of the storm, but there was no wind or violent waves. Everything fell silent. The sea was suddenly smooth as glass.

Perhaps the first signs of daylight began to trickle over the eastern ridge such that the disciples could make out the edge of the shoreline. John's account tells us that "immediately the boat was at the land to which they were going" (John 6:21), indicating not only a miraculous deliverance from harm but also a miraculous delivery of the vessel to shore.

All this was too much for the disciples to take in. Matthew says they "worshiped Him, saying, 'You are certainly God's Son!'" (Matt. 14:33). Mark's Gospel gives us a different glimpse into the conclusion of the story: "They were utterly astonished, for they had not gained any insight from the incident of the loaves, but their heart was hardened" (Mark 6:51-52). Reeling from the events of the past twenty-four hours and faced with yet another sign of Jesus' identity, the disciples were still having trouble wrapping their heads and hearts around what it all meant. But don't be too hard on the disciples. They didn't have a complete understanding of the Incarnation. They could express the words "Son of God," but they couldn't fully grasp the idea that God the Son had become human—true God and true man in perfect unity in one person.

Nevertheless, slowly but surely the disciples were coming around.

— 14:34-36 —

The next few verses function as a transition. After the feeding of the thousands, the disciples eventually made their way to shore on the north side of the lake, in the area of the northern city of Bethsaida (Mark 6:45). The Gospel of John recounts that crowds of people, unsure of where Jesus and the disciples had gone, sailed around the next day looking for them (John 6:22-24). This suggests that Jesus and the disciples successfully "shook" the masses for a day to get some well-earned rest.

However, after Jesus and the disciples crossed over from the north side of the lake to the northwest coast near Gennesaret (Matt. 14:34), just south of Capernaum along the shore, a crowd began to gather. John tells us that the scrambling crowd, who had been seeking to find Jesus all day, had crossed the lake trying to locate Him (John 6:24-25). Matthew picks up the narrative with Jesus on the northwest side of the Sea of Galilee continuing His ministry to the suffering and sick (Matt. 14:35).

So powerful were His miracles that if people touched even the fringe of His cloak, they were cured of their diseases (14:36). That people entreated Jesus to let them touch His cloak for healing may suggest that they had heard the testimony of healing from the woman who had been cured of the twelve years of bleeding (see 9:20-22). If so, this gives us a good example of how word of Jesus' astonishing miracles had made an impact on the crowds.

APPLICATION: MATTHEW 14:22-36

Bringing Us to Our Knees

The story of Jesus walking on the water, calling Peter to walk with Him, and calming the storm with a command may feel like it's a world away and part of a remote past. But the truth is that all of us are, in a sense, in the same boat as the disciples. If we use our imaginations, we can relive that scene and understand the kind of test they went through. As I ponder the principles that emerge in this story, I can think of three connections with our own challenges in life—challenges that bring us to our knees in dependence on Christ.

First, we sometimes feel all alone when we experience dark nights, *but we're not.* We have Jesus, who takes up permanent residence in our lives. His Spirit indwells us to empower us, to remind us of His presence, and to enable us to endure whatever may come. He's there, even when the night is dark, even when the bottom seems to have dropped out of our lives and we see only a hopeless abyss. Maybe that's how you feel right now. You're running shy of hope and night is closing in. Loneliness is smothering you. Remember, you're never alone. He's there.

Second, the storms of life seem to last forever, *but they'll cease.* They're not too long to endure. No storm strikes us that's not known, permitted, or directed by the Lord our God. He's never taken by surprise by anything that transpires in our lives. Sometimes Cynthia and I will look at some event that occurs that sends our heads spinning, and in the swirl of confusion, think, *How long is this going to last?* Yet in those moments, we often say to each other, "This isn't an accident." It's important to remember that God knows what's going on. He knows what He's doing, and nothing is out of His control. The storms of life are never longer than they should be. Not only does God plan the depth of each test, but He plans the length of it as well. When it's time for the storm to come to an end, He'll stop it in an instant. It's helpful to remember that God is not *almost* sovereign.

Third, we sometimes experience dreadful moments when we think we'll drown, *but we don't.* Though we may initially take noble steps of faith and experience a boost of confidence, we often lose sight of our Lord, falter, and fall. But even when we begin to sink, we sink into His arms. I know there's nothing more horrifying than the feeling that we're drowning in the overwhelming floods of life. But instead of responding in panic and doubt, reach out to Him. Take His hand. Let Him strengthen and encourage you.

None of these tests are designed to finish us off—not the dark nights, not the raging storms, not even those moments when we think we'll drown. Rather, these experiences are designed to drive us to our knees in prayer and to lift our eyes to the Lord in worship. At these times, we need to see the unseen, to walk by faith. As we do, we will realize that there's more going on than what we see in the trial itself. God's bringing us to our knees . . . and to Himself.

Spiritual Blind Spots
MATTHEW 15:1-20

NASB

¹Then some Pharisees and scribes came to Jesus from Jerusalem and said, ²"Why do Your disciples break the tradition of the elders? For they do not wash their hands when they eat bread." ³And He answered and said to them, "Why do you yourselves transgress the commandment of God for the sake of your tradition? ⁴For God said, 'HONOR YOUR FATHER AND MOTHER,' and, 'HE WHO SPEAKS EVIL OF FATHER OR MOTHER IS TO ªBE PUT TO DEATH.' ⁵But you say, 'Whoever says to *his* father or mother, "Whatever I have that would help you has been ªgiven *to God*," ⁶he is not to honor his father or his motherª.' And *by this* you invalidated the word of God for the sake of your tradition. ⁷You hypocrites, rightly did Isaiah prophesy of you:

⁸ 'THIS PEOPLE HONORS ME WITH
    THEIR LIPS,
  BUT THEIR HEART IS FAR AWAY
    FROM ME.
⁹ 'BUT IN VAIN DO THEY WORSHIP
    ME,
  TEACHING AS DOCTRINES THE
    PRECEPTS OF MEN.'"

¹⁰After Jesus called the crowd to Him, He said to them, "Hear and understand. ¹¹*It is* not what enters into the mouth *that* defiles the man, but what proceeds out of the mouth, this defiles the man."

¹²Then the disciples came and said to Him, "Do You know that the Pharisees were ªoffended when they heard this statement?" ¹³But He answered and said, "Every plant which My heavenly Father did not plant shall be uprooted. ¹⁴Let them alone; they are blind guides ªof the blind.

NLT

¹Some Pharisees and teachers of religious law now arrived from Jerusalem to see Jesus. They asked him, ²"Why do your disciples disobey our age-old tradition? For they ignore our tradition of ceremonial hand washing before they eat."

³Jesus replied, "And why do you, by your traditions, violate the direct commandments of God? ⁴For instance, God says, 'Honor your father and mother,'* and 'Anyone who speaks disrespectfully of father or mother must be put to death.'* ⁵But you say it is all right for people to say to their parents, 'Sorry, I can't help you. For I have vowed to give to God what I would have given to you.' ⁶In this way, you say they don't need to honor their parents.* And so you cancel the word of God for the sake of your own tradition. ⁷You hypocrites! Isaiah was right when he prophesied about you, for he wrote,

⁸ 'These people honor me with
    their lips,
  but their hearts are far from
    me.
⁹ Their worship is a farce,
    for they teach man-made ideas
    as commands from God.'*"

¹⁰Then Jesus called to the crowd to come and hear. "Listen," he said, "and try to understand. ¹¹It's not what goes into your mouth that defiles you; you are defiled by the words that come out of your mouth."

¹²Then the disciples came to him and asked, "Do you realize you offended the Pharisees by what you just said?"

¹³Jesus replied, "Every plant not planted by my heavenly Father will be uprooted, ¹⁴so ignore them. They are blind guides leading the blind,

And if a blind man guides a blind man, both will fall into a pit."

¹⁵Peter ªsaid to Him, "Explain the parable to us." ¹⁶ªJesus said, "Are you still lacking in understanding also? ¹⁷Do you not understand that everything that goes into the mouth passes into the stomach, and is ªeliminated? ¹⁸But the things that proceed out of the mouth come from the heart, and those defile the man. ¹⁹For out of the heart come evil thoughts, murders, adulteries, ªfornications, thefts, false witness, slanders. ²⁰These are the things which defile the man; but to eat with unwashed hands does not defile the man."

15:4 ªLit *die the death*   15:5 ªLit *a gift;* i.e. an offering   15:6 ªI.e. by supporting them with it   15:12 ªLit *caused to stumble*   15:14 ªLater mss add *of the blind*   15:15 ªLit *answered and said*   15:16 ªLit *and He*   15:17 ªLit *thrown out into the latrine*   15:19 ªI.e. sexual immorality

and if one blind person guides another, they will both fall into a ditch."

¹⁵Then Peter said to Jesus, "Explain to us the parable that says people aren't defiled by what they eat."

¹⁶"Don't you understand yet?" Jesus asked. ¹⁷"Anything you eat passes through the stomach and then goes into the sewer. ¹⁸But the words you speak come from the heart—that's what defiles you. ¹⁹For from the heart come evil thoughts, murder, adultery, all sexual immorality, theft, lying, and slander. ²⁰These are what defile you. Eating with unwashed hands will never defile you."

15:4a Exod 20:12; Deut 5:16.   15:4b Exod 21:17 (Greek version); Lev 20:9 (Greek version).   15:6 Greek *their father;* other manuscripts read *their father or their mother.*   15:8-9 Isa 29:13 (Greek version).

In 2 Corinthians 4:3-4, the apostle Paul wrote, "Even if our gospel is veiled, it is veiled to those who are perishing, in whose case the god of this world has blinded the minds of the unbelieving so that they might not see the light of the gospel of the glory of Christ, who is the image of God."

Having struggled with some vision problems myself over the years, I have grown in my appreciation for the gift of sight. How frustrating and paralyzing blindness can be for those who are used to having light to guide them through life. Yet spiritual blindness—like the kind mentioned by Paul—has disastrous consequences *for eternity.* The spiritually blind are those whose minds have been paralyzed by unbelief through the deceptive workings of Satan—the so-called god of this world. Because of their blindness to spiritual truth, they're unable to see the light of the good news of Jesus Christ. What they need is a healing touch from the Holy Spirit to open their spiritual eyes to understand and accept Jesus as Savior.

Spiritual blindness has nothing to do with human intelligence, emotional stability, the ability to love one's family, or the capacity to learn and grow. Spiritual blindness can debilitate geniuses and average thinkers, rich and poor, famous and anonymous, moral and wicked.

The difference between the spiritually blind and those who "see" is how they respond to the life-changing gospel of the person and work of Jesus Christ. The spiritually blind don't see their sin or their need for a Savior. Their minds are veiled to the glories of who Jesus is—the God-man—and what He has done—died for their sins and risen from the dead as Lord of all.

When Jesus walked on this earth, He encountered religious leaders—namely, Pharisees and scribes—whom He identified as "blind guides leading the blind" (Matt. 15:14, NLT). He wasn't saying they lacked physical sight. What they lacked was the ability to see what should have been obvious—that He is the Light of the World. As a result, they were asking the wrong questions. And because of their spiritual blindness, Jesus often confronted them and warned His followers not to let these blind guides lead them astray.

— 15:1-9 —

Jesus and His disciples had arrived in the region of Gennesaret, where Jesus had immediately begun performing astonishing miracles among the crowd (14:34-36). While Jesus was performing these powerful signs demonstrating who He was and validating the divine authority of His teaching, the Pharisees and scribes showed up from Jerusalem (15:1). Had they come to seek healing? To ask Jesus to solve a nagging theological question? To be encouraged by His preaching? No, no, and no. Instead, they came with a completely wrong question: "Why do Your disciples break the tradition of the elders? For they do not wash their hands when they eat bread" (15:2). For non-Jewish readers, the Gospel of Mark gives a little background to this criticism:

> The Pharisees and all the Jews do not eat unless they carefully wash their hands, thus observing the traditions of the elders; and when they come from the market place, they do not eat unless they cleanse themselves; and there are many other things which they have received in order to observe, such as the washing of cups and pitchers and copper pots. (Mark 7:3-4)

I can imagine members of the crowd staring at the Pharisees in astonishment. "Can't you see what this guy's doing? And you're asking about handwashing?" Let me put this in modern terms. Imagine you're sharing the gospel with someone who's lost and spiritually blind. The person seems to be listening intently as you explain how Jesus has totally transformed your life—how your faith in who Jesus is and what He has done for you has made all the difference in the world. But during a pause, that person doesn't ask about your life before Christ, doesn't ask you to explain how Jesus' death could pay for sin, and doesn't ask how a person can accept Christ. Instead, you hear, "Did Jesus have a wife?" or "Are you pro-choice or pro-life?" or "Do you believe in evolution?" It's as if the spiritually blind carry around red herrings to toss whenever they feel threatened by an argument that has teeth or claws. Don't take the bait!

The religious elite had zero interest in who Jesus was and how He had such miraculous power. No, they wanted to know why His disciples' hygienic practices didn't measure up to their persnickety standards. Their rules and requirements prescribed the precise way to wash, when to wash, how often to wash, what to wash, and what dreadful consequences someone would face for not washing. Talk about a red herring!

But Jesus didn't take the bait. He had been breaking those unscriptural, contrived traditions since He began His ministry. If He wasn't touching unclean lepers, He was taking corpses by the hand and lifting them back to life. And when He wasn't fraternizing with scum-of-the-earth tax collectors, He had the audacity to heal people on the Sabbath! Knowing He was entirely in the right and they were in the wrong, Jesus answered the Pharisees' question with His own question, which exposed their hypocrisy and should have convicted them of their own need for a Savior.

Jesus' tone in this passage nears exasperation. He was fully aware of their man-made rules and regulations and couldn't have cared less about them. He'd been dealing with this Pharisaic nonsense for months now, and this was just the latest installment of an ongoing conflict with spiritually blind guides who were leading people astray. Enough was enough! Jesus confronted them head-on.

In His response, Jesus accused the scribes and Pharisees of breaking God's clear, biblical commandment to honor one's father and mother (Matt. 15:3-4; see Exod. 20:12; 21:17). They were doing so by fabricating a far-fetched exception: "Whoever says to his father or mother, 'Whatever I have that would help you has been given to God,' he is not to honor his father or his mother" (Matt. 15:5-6). In this way, the purportedly pious had "invalidated the word of God for the sake of . . . tradition." Jesus ingeniously quoted directly from Exodus 20:12 and 21:17—clear commands from the inspired, inerrant Word of God. And He cleverly demonstrated that the religious leaders' oral teachings actually invalidated God's Word and turned these men into hypocritical Law breakers.

So, in Jesus' day, the Pharisees had invented a way to shirk their responsibility to their aging parents. They claimed that people could dedicate all their possessions to God, devote themselves completely to God, and then excuse themselves from all other personal and financial responsibilities, such as caring for their family members according to the Law. The technical term for this practice was *Korban* (also spelled *Corban*) [H7133], which was a Hebrew word meaning "given [to God]"; John Peter Lange notes, "If a person *merely pronounced* the word 'Corban' over any possession or property, it was irrevocably dedicated to the temple. Thus it became a kind of interdict [official prohibition]."[131]

Yet Jesus asserted that the appeal to *Korban* had become a means of rationalizing disobedience to the spirit of the Law. R. T. France explains: "This convenient declaration apparently left the property actually still at the disposal of the one who made the vow, but deprived his parents of any right to it. . . . Such a pious fraud is in direct conflict with the will of God as expressed in the fifth commandment."[132]

Jesus didn't even give the scribes and Pharisees a chance to answer His rhetorical question. Anything they could have said in self-justification would have been senseless and hypocritical. Instead, He delivered a knockout punch, calling them hypocrites and applying to them a condemning passage of Scripture from Isaiah 29:13 (Matt. 15:7-9). In Isaiah's context, the Lord God was calling the people of Israel to task for offering mere lip service while their hearts were insincere. Such external worship without internal conviction manifested itself among the religious leaders of Jesus' day in their prioritization of the traditions of men over the true teachings of God.

The silence of the religious rulers is telling. They were mute in the face of Jesus' exposé. I can imagine them folding their arms, red-faced and fuming inside, but unable to talk their way out of the corner they had backed themselves into. As always for those who were spiritually unresponsive, the wisdom of God spoken from Jesus' lips fell on deaf ears. The light of truth only burns the eyes of the spiritually blind.

— 15:10-14 —

Jesus turned His attention to the people who had been listening to His exchange with the Pharisees (15:10). He returned to the issue of His disciples eating without washing their hands according to rabbinical standards. Those who followed such standards believed that a person who didn't wash thoroughly and properly before eating would be "unclean." Jesus shifted the focus from external and ritual cleanliness to internal and moral purity: "It is not what enters into the mouth that defiles the man, but what proceeds out of the mouth, this defiles the man" (15:11). With that, Jesus apparently withdrew from the crowd, leaving the Pharisees and scribes seething at His seemingly flippant dismissal of their complex purity regulations.

We can sense that the disciples were getting a little nervous about Jesus' confrontational tone with His opponents. Away from the public eye, they came to their Master and notified Him that He had offended the Pharisees with His assertion that it is not unclean food that defiles but unclean words (15:12). Jesus then made it clear that He was not in the business of yielding even one millimeter to Jerusalem's secret police of legalism. He compared those religious leaders to wild weeds that the Father hadn't planted, which needed to be uprooted and cast away (15:13). They were merely robbing the soil of the nutrients needed by the legitimate plants.

Jesus then took the opportunity to explain something the disciples needed to learn and never forget. He told them how to respond to people like the scribes and Pharisees who set themselves up as a sort of High Court of Holiness: "Let them alone" (15:14). The Greek verb that appears here (aphiēmi [863]) can be used to describe abandonment, giving up, or even divorce. Instead of obeying such bullies, the disciples were to ignore them or reject them. They were not to capitulate to them. Why? Because their ultimate doom was assured: When one blind man leads another blind man, eventually they will both end up falling into a pit. Because these religious leaders were spiritually blind, only others who were also spiritually blind would follow them. All the while, they would believe with all their hearts that they were in the right!

— 15:15-20 —

Jesus revealed the source of such blindness in His explanation of the "parable" for His disciples (15:15-16): Spiritual blindness isn't a matter of the mind; it's a matter of the heart. Jesus dismissed the issue of ritual uncleanness—which had so upset the Pharisees—as inconsequential to real spiritual maturity and purity. After all, whatever food enters the mouth eventually passes through (15:17). This natural function of the human body has no bearing on the purity of one's mind or heart, no effect on the state of the spirit or soul before God. How could it? The body itself filters out impurities, taking the good and rejecting the bad. To obsess over such things is ridiculous if one neglects the more important kind of defilement.

Knowing When to Leave

MATTHEW 15:14

Many years ago, early on in our marriage, Cynthia and I realized we were going to the wrong church. It was a long-standing tradition that we attend a church within a particular denomination—a tradition that created a sort of artificial loyalty to a name. But the longer we were there, the more we realized that legalism was being stuffed into every message. It wasn't subtle. It wasn't occasional. And it was getting worse and worse.

People were being intimidated to keep all the rules that the pastor laid down—not biblical rules, mind you; not the commands of Christ or the expectations of those called to walk in newness of life. These were man-made, legalistic requirements—silly taboos that had nothing to do with the Word of God: "You shouldn't do this. You can't do that. You aren't supposed to do those things. If you do them, you're going to answer for it." There was a lot of fearmongering, shaming, and power tripping going on.

Finally, we made the decision to leave. It was a hard decision, and not one that people should make hastily or lightly. But it was necessary. It turned out to be one of the best decisions we ever made. We pulled up roots and went to a place where we didn't know many people. Leaving those we had known for years was the hardest part. Many of them continued to be friends, but others who had been swept up with loyalty to a name or a pastor rather than to grace looked at us over the tops of their glasses and judged us for walking away from "the true way."

In speaking about extreme legalists, Jesus said, "Leave them" (15:14, NIV). If you stay under the authority of a legalist, you will suffer the consequences. You'll live in shame. You'll be chastised for no good reason. You'll be shunned and rejected for walking in freedom. Or you'll succumb to the disease of legalism yourself, trying to resolve the tension between man-made rules and the principles of Scripture.

The spiritually blind fail to realize that what defiles comes from the heart (15:18). Keeping your hands perfectly sanitized can do nothing for your soul. You can't wash away the deep-seated corruption of the fallen human heart by scrubbing dirt from your body. Jeremiah 17:9 says, "The heart is more deceitful than all else and is desperately sick; who can understand it?" The answer: Only God.

The words of our mouths demonstrate the content of our hearts. And in a spiritually sick, depraved, unsaved individual, nothing good can be found there. Jesus gave just a brief sample of the nastiness that flows from the hearts of the wicked: "evil thoughts, murders, adulteries, fornications, thefts, false witness, slanders" (Matt. 15:19). These things—not a little dirt under the fingernails or a smudge of ash on the wrist—defile a person (15:20). Even the filth of the sewer is not so great a defilement as that of a human heart not yet cleansed by the blood of Christ.

APPLICATION: MATTHEW 15:1-20
Between Jesus and the Pharisees

The crowd found themselves once again in an awkward place. On one side stood the scribes and Pharisees with their insistence on ritual purity according to their traditions. On the other side stood Jesus and the disciples with their bold rejection of the religious leaders' traditions and an insistence on deeper righteousness and spiritual sincerity. The Pharisees had generations of teachings on their side as well as their unquestioned standing of authority among the Jews. Jesus had His confident interpretation of the Word of God and His divine authority proven by miraculous signs and wonders. For the crowd, to lean toward the Pharisees would mean fitting in and maintaining the favor of the people in charge. To follow Jesus would make them outcasts, rebels, and infidels according to the "orthodox" religious standards of the day.

Now let's take it to the personal level. You—and you alone—must seek to know the true condition of your own heart. Where are you in all this? To answer that, you need to do some soul-searching. Consider these questions honestly.

Are you with Jesus and the disciples—willing to take an intrepid stand against legalistic action taken for the sake of man-made rules?

Do you refuse to capitulate to the traditionalists who want to maintain their stranglehold on the masses by whatever means necessary? Are you willing to ignore and abandon allegiance to them when they cross the line from simply ignorant to hypocritical and abusive? There will be a price to pay for taking a stand against legalism, but the reward will ultimately be worth it.

Are you with the confused crowd, living your life intimidated by the legalistic leaders who tell you to do this, do that, don't do this, don't say that? Do you crumble under the scolding gaze of certain influential members of your church? Do you avoid confronting things you know are wrong simply to keep the peace?

Or are you with the Pharisees and scribes themselves, nitpicking over inconsequential details of protocol, policy, and procedure in the face of weighty matters of eternal significance? Are you trusting in unscriptural beliefs and practices because some renowned teacher or text or tradition said so? Are you failing to realize that spiritual defilement has nothing to do with the neutral, external matters of life but the condition of the heart?

Wherever you find yourself today, do what you need to do to make the right decisions. If you're on the difficult, narrow path of discipleship, continue to follow Jesus. Don't be frightened or intimidated. If you're waffling and unsure whether you should cave in to the pressure of legalism, don't. Take a stand against it. And if you're part of the problem of unhealthy traditionalism, repent. Turn to trust the only One who can clean you from the inside out.

Compassion without Bounds
MATTHEW 15:21-39

NASB

21 Jesus went away from there, and withdrew into the district of Tyre and Sidon. 22 And a Canaanite woman from that region came out and *began* to cry out, saying, "Have mercy on me, Lord, Son of David; my daughter is cruelly demon-possessed." 23 But He did not answer her a word. And His disciples came and implored

NLT

21 Then Jesus left Galilee and went north to the region of Tyre and Sidon. 22 A Gentile* woman who lived there came to him, pleading, "Have mercy on me, O Lord, Son of David! For my daughter is possessed by a demon that torments her severely."

23 But Jesus gave her no reply, not even a word. Then his disciples urged him to send her away. "Tell her

NASB

Him, saying, "Send her away, because she keeps shouting ᵃat us." ²⁴But He answered and said, "I was sent only to the lost sheep of the house of Israel." ²⁵But she came and *began* ᵃto bow down before Him, saying, "Lord, help me!" ²⁶And He answered and said, "It is not ᵃgood to take the children's bread and throw it to the dogs." ²⁷But she said, "Yes, Lord; ᵃbut even the dogs feed on the crumbs which fall from their masters' table." ²⁸Then Jesus said to her, "O woman, your faith is great; it shall be done for you as you wish." And her daughter was healed ᵃat once.

²⁹Departing from there, Jesus went along by the Sea of Galilee, and having gone up on the mountain, He was sitting there. ³⁰And ᵃlarge crowds came to Him, bringing with them *those who were* lame, crippled, blind, mute, and many others, and they laid them down at His feet; and He healed them. ³¹So the crowd marveled as they saw the mute speaking, the crippled ᵃrestored, and the lame walking, and the blind seeing; and they glorified the God of Israel.

³²And Jesus called His disciples to Him, and said, "I feel compassion for the ᵃpeople, because they ᵇhave remained with Me now three days and have nothing to eat; and I do not want to send them away hungry, for they might faint on the way." ³³The disciples said to Him, "Where would we get so many loaves in *this* desolate place to satisfy such a large crowd?" ³⁴And Jesus said to them, "How many loaves do you have?" And they said, "Seven, and a few small fish." ³⁵And He directed the ᵃpeople to ᵇsit down on the ground; ³⁶and He took the seven loaves and the fish; and giving thanks, He

NLT

to go away," they said. "She is bothering us with all her begging."

²⁴Then Jesus said to the woman, "I was sent only to help God's lost sheep—the people of Israel."

²⁵But she came and worshiped him, pleading again, "Lord, help me!"

²⁶Jesus responded, "It isn't right to take food from the children and throw it to the dogs."

²⁷She replied, "That's true, Lord, but even dogs are allowed to eat the scraps that fall beneath their masters' table."

²⁸"Dear woman," Jesus said to her, "your faith is great. Your request is granted." And her daughter was instantly healed.

²⁹Jesus returned to the Sea of Galilee and climbed a hill and sat down. ³⁰A vast crowd brought to him people who were lame, blind, crippled, those who couldn't speak, and many others. They laid them before Jesus, and he healed them all. ³¹The crowd was amazed! Those who hadn't been able to speak were talking, the crippled were made well, the lame were walking, and the blind could see again! And they praised the God of Israel.

³²Then Jesus called his disciples and told them, "I feel sorry for these people. They have been here with me for three days, and they have nothing left to eat. I don't want to send them away hungry, or they will faint along the way."

³³The disciples replied, "Where would we get enough food here in the wilderness for such a huge crowd?"

³⁴Jesus asked, "How much bread do you have?"

They replied, "Seven loaves, and a few small fish."

³⁵So Jesus told all the people to sit down on the ground. ³⁶Then he took the seven loaves and the fish,

broke them and started giving them to the disciples, and the disciples *gave them* to the people. ³⁷ And they all ate and were satisfied, and they picked up what was left over of the broken pieces, seven large baskets full. ³⁸ And those who ate were four thousand men, besides women and children.

³⁹ And sending away the crowds, Jesus got into the boat and came to the region of Magadan.

15:23 ªLit *behind us*   15:25 ªOr *worshiped*
15:26 ªOr *proper*   15:27 ªLit *for*   15:28 ªLit *from that hour*   15:30 ªLit *many*   15:31 ªOr *healthy*
15:32 ªLit *crowd*   ᵇLit *are remaining*   15:35 ªLit *crowd*   ᵇLit *recline*

thanked God for them, and broke them into pieces. He gave them to the disciples, who distributed the food to the crowd.

³⁷ They all ate as much as they wanted. Afterward, the disciples picked up seven large baskets of left-over food. ³⁸ There were 4,000 men who were fed that day, in addition to all the women and children. ³⁹ Then Jesus sent the people home, and he got into a boat and crossed over to the region of Magadan.

15:22 Greek *Canaanite.*

Having compassion for others starts with actually *loving* others. It's a matter of the heart. When we see somebody in desperate need through the lens of loving compassion, our hearts break. And this heartache fuels our imaginations. We try to come up with ideas about how we can actually help the person. Then, when we've come up with a solution, we exercise the will and take steps to comfort the person in grief, relieve the person's suffering, provide for the person's need, or solve the person's problem.

One thing that attracts even unbelievers to the figure of Jesus Christ is His boundless compassion. Jesus demonstrated the unconditional, sacrificial nature of His compassion by giving it to even total strangers. Ultimately, He gave His own life—not for any personal gain, but for the sake of others. We are called to emulate His selfless, others-centered, loving attitudes and actions. The apostle John spelled this out in 1 John 3:17—"Whoever has the world's goods, and sees his brother in need and closes his heart against him, how does the love of God abide in him?" The question is rhetorical. The answer: It can't. The love of God that flows from our hearts into our lives is a *compassionate* love.

The three very diverse episodes we're going to explore in this section highlight different aspects of Christ's deep compassion. We'll see compassion without political or ethnic boundaries when He blesses an outsider—a Canaanite woman far removed from God's covenant people. We'll see compassion without personal boundaries when He once again forsakes His "alone time" for the sake of the masses of suffering people. And we'll see compassion without numerical boundaries when He feeds thousands more people in a manner mysteriously similar to the earlier feeding of the five thousand.

In all these scenes we become witnesses to the boundless compassion of Jesus Christ, a compassion each of His followers is expected to embrace and imitate.

— 15:21-28 —

By this point, the disciples knew better than to moan and groan about Jesus' next steps or to challenge the wisdom of His actions. They were at a high point in the ministry, having recently witnessed a number of astonishing miracles (14:13-36). And they had seen the genius of Jesus confounding the Pharisees and their legalistic teachings (15:1-20). So when Jesus said, "We're going to Phoenicia," the disciples simply followed. Still, I wonder if any of them murmured a little among themselves along the roughly 40-mile journey through mountainous territory, wondering, *Why here?*

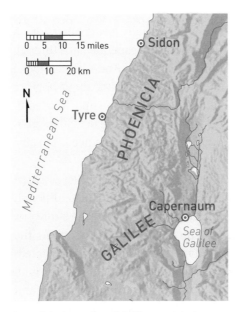

Matthew tells us that Jesus "withdrew into the district of Tyre and Sidon" (15:21). There's no indication that He actually went to those two specific cities. The region itself was called Phoenicia at the time. It had been annexed to the Roman province of Syria over a century earlier, and the two port cities of Tyre and Sidon would have been well known. In fact, the city of Tyre had been the object of some strong Old Testament condemnations (Isa. 23; Ezek. 26:1–28:19). In Jesus' day, the region was inhabited primarily by descendants of the Canaanite people who had remained when the Israelites had failed to drive them out of the land (Judg. 1–3). This largely Gentile area, far removed from the center of ethnic and religious purity in Jerusalem, would have been avoided by most pious Jews.

Jesus left the region of Galilee to visit the area of Tyre and Sidon, where He healed a Gentile woman's daughter who was possessed by a demon.

What was Jesus doing there? Mark's Gospel gives us a clue when it says that Jesus "entered a house" and "wanted no one to know of it" (Mark 7:24). It seems He wanted to get away for a spell from the frenzy of ministry in Galilee, to slip into a private residence and enjoy a retreat. Nothing wrong with that. Surely, He and His disciples had earned a breather before jumping back into the work. Yet it wasn't meant to be. Even in this remote region, where few Jews dared to go, Jesus' reputation preceded Him and He was found out. Mark continues, "He could not escape notice."

A Canaanite woman showed up and began crying out to Jesus (Matt. 15:22). Her non-Jewish ethnicity was clear to all—she was "a Gentile, of the Syrophoenician race" (Mark 7:26). Upon finding the famous miracle worker Jesus, she latched on in faith and hope . . . and wouldn't let go. She began by shouting, "Have mercy on me, Lord, Son of David; my daughter is cruelly demon-possessed" (Matt. 15:22). Everything about the situation had the makings of an awkward, puzzling, and even scandalous clash of cultures. First, in that context it was socially improper for a woman to be addressing a man in this way. Second, though the woman was a Gentile, she acknowledged Jesus as "Lord" and "Son of David"—a startling confession of faith in Jesus' messianic identity, especially in light of the fact that the Jewish religious leaders had rejected it. And third, to this point Jesus' preaching and ministry had been focused almost exclusively on Jews, on calling the house of Israel to repentance.

As the woman cried out, Jesus first behaved as the people might have expected: "He did not answer her a word" (15:23). This initial response sounds harsh, especially as we can imagine the sorrow and desperation the woman exhibited . . . and the risk she was taking in trying to approach Jesus. Why would Jesus take such a seemingly heartless, stoic stance in the face of her passionate plea for mercy? On top of this, the disciples took Jesus' apparent lack of interest in helping the woman to the next level, saying, "Send her away, because she keeps shouting at us." They were irritated! This woman was intruding on their quiet rest and relaxation. And they had probably read Jesus' silence as annoyance as well. We'll soon see that Jesus' choice to be unresponsive to the woman was not from a lack of concern but from a desire to draw out the woman's striking words of faith and to point out the hasty prejudice of the disciples.

Jesus explained the predicament, perhaps even giving voice to some of the thoughts in the minds of the disciples. He had been sent on a mission "to the lost sheep of the house of Israel" (15:24)—not to the Phoenician descendants of the Canaanites. *Especially* not to them! The Messiah was the Messiah of the Jews, right? Not the Savior of the Gentiles! Weren't they simply lost, the object of God's judgment and wrath? Certainly they weren't to be recipients of God's grace and mercy, were they?

Yet even in the face of this explanation of the limited scope of Jesus' mission, the woman was undeterred. Remember, she was desperate. Her daughter had been tormented and terrorized by that demon; she was a victim of the wicked spirit's whims and wiles. Like a kitten in the mouth of a ravenous wolf, the girl couldn't break free. Mom was entirely helpless, so she did the only thing she could do. She bowed down before Jesus in an act of total surrender and worship and cried out a simple prayer: "Lord, help me!" (15:25).

But Jesus pushed back again, clearly to test her unwavering faith. He explained to her, "It is not good to take the children's bread and throw it to the dogs" (15:26). Knowing Jesus—and knowing where He was leading this conversation and how it would unfold—we can imagine a twinkle in His eye and a softening tone. Everything He said was true, but His statement was intended to provoke the woman to demonstrate her persistence, not to crush her spirit. While it's quite true that parents who would take food from their children and use it instead to feed dogs would not be good and responsible parents, we should read Jesus' words with a remembrance of God's amazing grace.

It's also important to note Jesus' use of the word *kynarion* [2952], which means "little dog"[133] or "puppy." Jews frequently referred to Gentiles as "dogs," meaning the mangy, vicious canines that would roam the streets scavenging for food and attacking victims. Thus, while still playing off the common Jewish prejudice, using the diminutive form softens the language. Already we see evidence that Jesus was moving in an unexpected direction—at least unexpected to His disciples. R. T. France suggests, "It may be that Jesus was almost jocularly presenting her with the sort of language she might expect from a Jew in order to see how she would react. . . . The tone need not have been a humourless rudeness."[134] After Jesus' statement, the ball was again in her court.

From her humble place at His feet, the woman didn't miss a beat. She gently but confidently pushed back again, playing off Jesus' own illustration: "Yes, Lord; but even the dogs feed on the crumbs which fall from their masters' table" (15:27). I like to imagine the disciples gasping at her impudence but then turning to look at Jesus and seeing not a frown but a wide smile. He loved that response! In fact, it was exactly the one He was drawing out of her. In that moment, He not only gave the woman a perfect opportunity to demonstrate her faith but also exposed the flaws in the typical prejudices of the Jews, who regarded Gentiles as dogs. Even if they were to be so regarded, they were still part of the Master's household and thus valid recipients of the overflowing abundance of His provision. Though God, the creator of heaven and earth, has a special covenant relationship with Israel,

EXCURSUS: A BRIEF GLIMPSE OF THE MYSTERY

MATTHEW 15:21-28

Though the disciples didn't realize it at the time, Jesus' crossing into the region of Tyre and Sidon and healing the Canaanite woman's child provided a brief glimpse of the mystery that would be fully revealed later. That mystery involved the preaching of the gospel of salvation to Gentiles and the incorporation of both Jews and Gentiles into one body, the church.

In Ephesians 3:4-6, the apostle Paul wrote, "When you read you can understand my insight into the mystery of Christ, which in other generations was not made known to the sons of men, as it has now been revealed to His holy apostles and prophets in the Spirit; to be specific, that the Gentiles are fellow heirs and fellow members of the body, and fellow partakers of the promise in Christ Jesus through the gospel." Paul calls this new reality of Jews and Gentiles together a "mystery" (Greek *mystērion* [3466]). John Stott gives some insight into the meaning of this term:

> We need to realize that the English and Greek words do not have the same meaning. In English a "mystery" is something dark, obscure, secret, puzzling. What is "mysterious" is inexplicable, even incomprehensible.

The Greek word *mystērion* is different, however. Although still a "secret," it is no longer closely guarded but open. . . . The Christian "mysteries" are truths which, although beyond human discovery, have been revealed by God and so now belong openly to the whole church.[135]

Paul had been granted special insight into this "mystery of Christ" (Eph. 3:4). In fact, the revelation of this mystery was completely new, unheard of prior to its unveiling to the New Testament apostles and prophets (Eph. 3:5)—the participants in those foundational ministries established by Christ through the power of the Holy Spirit for the first generation of the church (see Eph. 2:20). Previous generations had been told of a coming Messiah, but they had assumed He would be a Messiah for the Jews only. They had no idea that the promised salvation through a Davidic king would be extended beyond the boundaries of Israel to be offered to the Gentiles as well. What's more surprising, this mystery involved an actual union of Jews and Gentiles into one body, with the Gentiles being rendered "fellow heirs," "fellow members," and "fellow partakers of the promise in Christ Jesus" (Eph. 3:6).

this doesn't change the fact that He is the God of all people. What a difference between this Gentile mother and the legalistic, judgmental Pharisees and scribes!

Next, after testing the woman, Jesus revealed His true heart: "O woman, your faith is great; it shall be done for you as you wish" (15:28). Immediately her daughter was healed. She didn't need Jesus to follow her home or to give her some kind of sign that He had done it. She trusted Him at His word, believing not only that He was *able* to heal from such a distance by a mere exercise of His will but that He was also *willing* to do it. She trusted in His power and His character. Mark 7:30 adds this lovely touch: "And going back to her home, she found the child lying on the bed, the demon having left."

— 15:29-31 —

Matthew went out of his way—literally—to include the interaction with the Canaanite woman in the region of Phoenicia. The very next scene has Jesus returning from there through the region of the Decapolis and back to the Sea of Galilee (15:29; see Mark 7:31). Again we see Him retreating from the inevitable crowds and climbing up a mountain. He was doubtless quite weary. He had just finished a long trip over rugged territory on foot and needed some quiet relief and relaxation away from the endless press of people.

But then the people returned in full force. Matthew describes the people as "large crowds" (Matt. 15:30)—perhaps suggesting numerous massive groups from different cities or geographical directions. They were all converging on Jesus with the "lame, crippled, blind, mute," and many others who needed healing. How easy it would have been for Jesus to send His disciples halfway down the hill to stop their ascent and say, "The Master is resting now. He's not taking any visitors. Go home." But Jesus did not have the disciples take on the role of bouncers or bodyguards . . . and neither did He start behaving like an unreachable superstar who could only be contacted through an agent.

Instead, Jesus showed that His compassion is not bound to a particular schedule. As the crowds made their way to where He was seated, they laid down the needy people at His feet, and He healed them. What a deliriously happy scene! Those who had been lame were made able to walk. Those who had been blind now saw clearly. Those who had been disabled now danced with joy. And those who had been speechless were now singing praises. In unanimity, the crowd "glorified the God of Israel" (15:31). The glory of God is the fruit of compassion.

— 15:32-39 —

How long did this relentless ministry to the needs of others continue? For three days! This is made clear when Jesus called His disciples to Himself and said, "I feel compassion for the people, because they have remained with Me now three days and have nothing to eat; and I do not want to send them away hungry, for they might faint on the way" (15:32). Jesus was very strategic in His articulation of the problem to the disciples. It was almost like a T-ball coach setting up the ball on a tee, helping a child hold the bat, and saying, "Swing!" He couldn't make this any easier for them. How difficult would it have been for the disciples to discern the genuine compassion in Jesus' voice, survey the situation of the thousands of hungry people, and spontaneously offer up the perfectly reasonable solution: "Lord, why don't You miraculously feed this crowd like You just did on the other side of the lake?"

What a missed opportunity to demonstrate that they were, in fact, getting it! Instead, the response of the disciples boggles the mind: "Where would we get so many loaves in this desolate place to satisfy such a large crowd?" (15:33). Everything in me wants to believe they were being sarcastic, saying those words with a smile, intonating their clear understanding that Jesus was willing and able to feed everyone. However, as Mark informs us, the disciples "had not gained any insight from the incident of the loaves, but their heart was hardened" (Mark 6:52). In what happened next, then, Jesus both demonstrated the disciples' hard-hearted forgetfulness of His power and purpose and began softening their hearts by once again teaching them the truth about His power.

The account of the feeding of the "four thousand men, besides women and children" (Matt. 15:38) mirrors the earlier miracle of the feeding of the five thousand men (plus women and children) in 14:13-21. The disciples articulated the impossibility of meeting the need (14:15-17; 15:33). The disciples then indicated the small amount of food they actually had on hand (14:17; 15:34). Jesus instructed the people to sit and organized them for distribution of food (14:19; 15:35). Then Jesus gave thanks, broke the bread, and distributed the food to all the people through His disciples (14:19; 15:36). In both cases the thousands of people were able to eat until they were satisfied, and in both cases a large amount of food was left over (14:20; 15:37).

Despite the similarities, this is clearly not just a flashback or a retelling of the same story. It's not as though Matthew forgot that he had happened to tell this story a little differently just a chapter earlier. The fact is that Matthew recorded two miraculous feedings of thousands of people because similar events took place on two separate occasions. This is reinforced by the differences between the very similar accounts. The sizes of the crowds were different, the quantities of original loaves and fish were different, the amounts of leftovers were different, and even the Greek words for the "baskets" were distinct, with the term in the second event indicating larger containers.

Somehow, in the busyness of ministry, in the weariness of their bodies and minds, and in the forgetfulness of their flesh, the disciples had failed to recall that Jesus was willing and able to provide for the people's needs. His power is infinite, His grace inexhaustible. It's also possible that, after three days of watching Jesus minister to people's needs, the disciples were burnt out on compassion. If so, Jesus' expression of love in another feeding miracle would have reinforced for them the boundless nature of His compassion. Regardless, another hungry crowd departed from Jesus with full bellies.

After Jesus sent the crowds away, He and His disciples got into a boat and headed to the region called Magadan (15:39), probably a variation of the name Magdala, which was located on the west coast of the Sea of Galilee. The crowds had dispersed, but they went away with full stomachs, full hearts, and full minds. They no doubt continued to share what the Lord had done for them with whomever would listen.

However, as Jesus' "fans" increased and His friends regrouped in Magdala, His foes were also on the move—plotting, scheming, and setting traps to catch Him in some kind of punishable crime. As the sun set over the Sea of Galilee, casting long shadows over the small village of Magdala, the hostility and resistance to Jesus' ministry was about to rise to a greater pitch of fury. Nevertheless, in the face of this growing resistance, Jesus would continue to teach and preach, to model compassion, and to prove to those with eyes to see and ears to hear that He really is the King, Israel's long-awaited Messiah.

APPLICATION: MATTHEW 15:21-39

Modeling Compassion

Even though many of us reading this passage have known the Lord Jesus for years—perhaps even decades—we may still fail to realize how faithful and powerful, how gracious and merciful, how loving and compassionate He is. How often has He stepped into our lives and met our needs? Yet how quickly we forget to trust Him. How powerfully has His great compassion been revealed to us in tangible ways? Yet how often we fail to extend that compassion to others. Let's consider a couple of lessons from the boundless compassion of Jesus as we seek to follow His model in our own lives.

First, *don't ever think there's a need too big for God.* Maybe you have been living with a need that's plaguing you, draining your energy, and causing you constant worry. Maybe it robs you of sleep at night and steals your joy during the day. Because it feels so huge, you can't imagine God reaching down in compassion and taking care of you in your need. Long distances and big numbers don't matter to God. God's compassion has no limits. The God of infinite love will never run short on grace. Unlike with insurance policies, there's no "lifetime maximum benefit" with God. "God will supply all your needs according to His riches in glory" (Phil. 4:19). And He is "able to do far more abundantly beyond all that we ask or think" (Eph. 3:20). No matter how huge your need may be, don't hesitate to take it to Him. Cry out repeatedly, passionately, and confidently before His throne of grace. And while you're reflecting on the limitless compassion of God, take a moment to consciously remove your own limits of compassion toward others. By walking in the power of the Spirit and following the model of Christ, you can meet opportunities to show love, grace, mercy, and compassion with an eager yes rather than a disappointing no. Don't let a daunting need paralyze you with inactivity or dissuade you from doing what you can for others.

Second, *don't forget the times He answers your prayers.* In America, the Thanksgiving holiday rolls around once a year. It's a time set aside to remember the faithfulness of God, with gratitude toward Him for His grace, mercy, and blessings in our lives. But this should be the believer's attitude every day. Think about Psalm 103:2: "Bless the LORD, O my soul, and forget none of His benefits." Make it a practice, more frequently than only once a year, to gather with family or friends to remember how the Lord has met your needs, provided for you in unexpected ways, and surprised you with His grace. Memorialize the compassion He's shown toward you. Never forget it.

ENDNOTES

INTRODUCTION

1. See comments in Charles R. Swindoll, *Mark*, Swindoll's Living Insights New Testament Commentary (Carol Stream, IL: Tyndale House Publishers, 2016), 362–63.
2. See Matt. 5:46; 9:10-11; 11:19; 18:17; 21:31-32; Mark 2:15-16; Luke 3:12; 5:29-30; 7:29, 34; 15:1; 18:9-14.
3. See R. T. France, *Matthew*, Tyndale New Testament Commentaries, ed. Leon Morris (Grand Rapids: Eerdmans, 1985), 167.
4. Michael Green, *The Message of Matthew: The Kingdom of Heaven*, The Bible Speaks Today (Downers Grove, IL: InterVarsity Press, 2000), 25.
5. William Barclay, *The Gospel of Matthew*, The New Daily Study Bible, rev. and updated (Louisville: Westminster John Knox Press, 2001), 1:6.
6. Papias, as quoted by Eusebius, *Church History* 3.39, in Philip Schaff, ed., *A Select Library of Nicene and Post-Nicene Fathers of the Christian Church*, series 2, vol. 1, *Eusebius: Church History, Life of Constantine the Great, and Oration in Praise of Constantine* (New York: The Christian Literature Publishing Company, 1890), 173.
7. Irenaeus, *Against Heresies* 3.1.1, in Alexander Roberts, James Donaldson, and A. Cleveland Coxe, eds., *The Ante-Nicene Fathers,* vol. 1, *The Apostolic Fathers with Justin Martyr and Irenaeus*, American ed. (New York: The Christian Literature Publishing Company, 1885), 414.
8. See John Peter Lange, *Commentary on the Holy Scriptures: Critical, Doctrinal and Homiletical*, vol. 8, *Matthew–Luke*, trans. Phillip Schaff, new ed. (Grand Rapids: Zondervan, 1976), 41–42.

ANNOUNCEMENT AND ARRIVAL OF THE KING (MATTHEW 1:1–4:25)

1. Walter Bauer, et al., *A Greek-English Lexicon of the New Testament and Other Early Christian Literature*, rev. and ed. Frederick William Danker (Chicago: University of Chicago Press, 2000), 543.
2. N. T. Wright, *Matthew for Everyone, Part 1: Chapters 1–15* (Louisville: Westminster John Knox Press, 2004), 2.
3. See France, *Matthew*, 74.
4. Myron S. Augsburger, *The Communicator's Commentary*, vol. 1, *Matthew*, ed. Lloyd J. Ogilvie (Waco, TX: Word, 1982), 26.
5. Stanley D. Toussaint, *Behold the King: A Study of Matthew* (Grand Rapids: Kregel, 1980), 40. See some possible explanations in Lange, *Matthew–Luke*, 48–49.
6. Toussaint, *Behold the King*, 40.
7. Bauer, et al., *Greek-English Lexicon*, 191–92.
8. See Alexander Balmain Bruce, "The Synoptic Gospels" in *The Expositor's Greek Testament*, ed. W. Robertson Nicoll (Grand Rapids: Eerdmans, 1951), 1:65.

9   Toussaint, *Behold the King*, 41.

10 Even as late as the second and third centuries, the church fathers continued to deal with this issue. See Origen, *Against Celsus* 1.32–35, in which Origen of Alexandria responds to concocted gossip spouted by a harsh critic of Christianity named Celsus, who said Jesus was born of an illicit affair between Mary and a Roman soldier named Panthera.

11 See Douglas Sean O'Donnell, *Matthew: All Authority in Heaven and on Earth*, Preaching the Word, ed. R. Kent Hughes (Wheaton: Crossway, 2013), 40–41.

12 "Marriage, Marriage Customs," in *Baker Encyclopedia of the Bible*, ed. Walter A. Elwell (Grand Rapids, MI: Baker, 1988), 1408–9.

13 Bauer, et al., *Greek-English Lexicon*, 336.

14 Gerard Van Groningen, *Messianic Revelation in the Old Testament* (Grand Rapids: Baker, 1990), 1:536.

15 Toussaint, *Behold the King*, 45–46.

16 Bauer, et al., *Greek-English Lexicon*, 608–9.

17 See Lange, *Matthew–Luke*, 56.

18 William Hendriksen, *New Testament Commentary: Exposition of the Gospel According to Matthew* (Grand Rapids: Baker, 1973), 150–51.

19 Josephus, *The Jewish War* i.6.2 [123]; cf. *Antiquities of the Jews* xiv.1.3 [9].

20 F. F. Bruce, *New Testament History* (New York: Doubleday, 1969), 13–14.

21 Macrobius, *The Saturnalia*, trans. Percival Vaughan Davies (New York: Columbia University Press, 1969), 171.

22 F. F. Bruce, *New Testament History*, 20–21.

23 John MacArthur, *Matthew 1–7*, The MacArthur New Testament Commentary (Chicago: Moody, 1985), 26.

24 Bauer, et al., *Greek-English Lexicon*, 882.

25 Lange, *Matthew–Luke*, 59.

26 Green, *The Message of Matthew*, 71.

27 Matt. 1:22; 2:15, 17, 23; 4:14; 8:17; 12:17; 13:14, 35; 21:4; 27:9.

28 Bauer, et al., *Greek-English Lexicon*, 827–29.

29 F. F. Bruce, *New Testament History*, 24.

30 Ibid., 27.

31 France, *Matthew*, 89.

32 Bauer, et al., *Greek-English Lexicon*, 640.

33 Louis A. Barbieri, Jr., "Matthew," in *The Bible Knowledge Commentary: New Testament Edition*, ed. John F. Walvoord and Roy B. Zuck (Wheaton: Victor, 1983), 24.

34 France, *Matthew*, 91.

35 There is some dispute among historians about whether the rabbinical sources describing "proselyte baptism" reflect a later, post-Christian development or a practice that was current at the time of Christ and the founding of the church. For a discussion on this issue, see Everett Ferguson, *Baptism in the Early Church: History, Theology, and Liturgy in the First Five Centuries* (Grand Rapids: Eerdmans, 2009), 76–82.

36 Clarence B. Bass, "Baptism," in *The New International Dictionary of the Bible*, pictorial ed., ed. J. D. Douglas and Merrill C. Tenney (Grand Rapids: Zondervan, 1987), 123.

37 Augsburger, *Matthew*, 42.

38 A. T. Robertson, *Word Pictures in the New Testament*, vol. 1, *The Gospel according to Matthew; The Gospel according to Mark* (Nashville: Broadman, 1930), 26.

39 Bauer, et al., *Greek-English Lexicon*, 1049.

40 F. F. Bruce, *New Testament History*, 72.

41 Ibid., 73.

42 Josephus, *Antiquities* 13.5.9.

43 See Merrill C. Tenney, *New Testament Times* (Grand Rapids: Eerdmans, 1965), 94–95.

44 One may notice that Mark identifies this quotation from Malachi as part of a prophecy of Isaiah. Rather than simply assuming that Mark was misquoting Scripture, the passage from Malachi can be viewed as a sort of preamble to the prophecy of Isaiah that immediately follows.

45 This list is taken from J. Scott Horrell, Nathan D. Holsteen, and Michael J. Svigel, "God in Three Persons: Father, Son and Holy Spirit," in *Exploring Christian Theology*, vol. 1, *Revelation, Scripture, and the Triune God*, ed. Nathan D. Holsteen and Michael J. Svigel (Minneapolis, MN: Bethany House, 2014), 130–31.

46 Benjamin B. Warfield, "Trinity," in *The International Standard Bible Encyclopedia*, ed. James Orr (Grand Rapids: Eerdmans, 1930), 5:3012.

47 Horrell, Holsteen, and Svigel, "God in Three Persons," 176, citing classic language from the Council of Chalcedon (AD 451).

48 See F. F. Bruce, *New Testament History*, 28.

49 LaMoine F. DeVries, *Cities of the Biblical World: An Introduction to the Archaeology, Geography, and History of Biblical Sites* (Peabody, MA; Hendrickson, 1997), 269.

50 See Steven Barabas, "Capernaum," in *New International Dictionary of the Bible*, 192.

51 MacArthur, *Matthew 1–7*, 108.

PROCLAMATION AND RECEPTION OF THE KING (MATTHEW 5:1–15:39)

1 John A. Martin, "Luke," in *The Bible Knowledge Commentary*, 220.

2 Robertson, *Word Pictures*, 101.

3 George A. Buttrick, "Exposition of the Gospel According to St. Matthew," in *The Interpreter's Bible: A Commentary in Twelve Volumes*, vol. 7, *New Testament Articles, Matthew, Mark* (Nashville: Abingdon, 1951), 279.

4 Augustus M. Toplady, "Rock of Ages," in *The Hymnal for Worship and Celebration* (Waco, TX: Word Music, 1986), no. 204.

5 Bauer, et al., *Greek-English Lexicon*, 795.

6 Ibid., 861.

7 Robertson, *Word Pictures*, 43.

8 John R. W. Stott, *The Message of the Sermon on the Mount (Matthew 5–7)*, The Bible Speaks Today (Downers Grove, IL: InterVarsity Press, 1978), 75.

9 France, *Matthew*, 122.

10 Josephus, *Antiquities of the Jews* 4.8, in William Whiston, ed., *The Works of Josephus: Complete and Unabridged* (Peabody: Hendrickson, 1987), 120.

11 See Charles R. Swindoll, *Matthew 16–28*, Swindoll's Living Insights New Testament Commentary (Carol Stream, IL: Tyndale House Publishers, forthcoming); see also Charles R. Swindoll, *1 & 2 Corinthians*, Swindoll's Living Insights New Testament Commentary (Carol Stream, IL: Tyndale House Publishers, 2017), 104–14.

12 Toussaint, *Behold the King*, 103.

13 Stott, *The Message of the Sermon on the Mount*, 108.

14 Augsburger, *Matthew*, 82.

15 Robert Robinson, "Come, Thou Fount of Every Blessing," in *The Hymnal for Worship and Celebration*, no. 2.

16 Toussaint, *Behold the King*, 111.

17 Bauer, et al., *Greek-English Lexicon*, 104.

18 R. V. G. Tasker, *The Gospel According to St. Matthew: An Introduction and Commentary*, Tyndale New Testament Commentaries (Grand Rapids: Eerdmans, 1961), 75.

19 Robertson, *Word Pictures*, 60.

20 Ibid.

21 France, *Matthew*, 144.

22 H. P. V. Nunn, *The Elements of New Testament Greek* (Cambridge: Cambridge University Press, 1923), 32.

23 "Dog," in *Holman Illustrated Bible Dictionary*, ed. Chad Brand, et al. (Nashville, TN: Holman Bible Publishers, 2003), 438.

24 Henry Chichester Hart, *The Animals Mentioned in the Bible* (London: The Religious Tract Society, 1888), 45.

25 Barclay, *Gospel of Matthew*, 1:314–15.

26 France, *Matthew*, 145.

27 Translation taken from *Holy Bible*, New Living Translation, Catholic Reader's Edition (Carol Stream, IL: Tyndale House Publishers, 2017).

28 Nathan D. Holsteen and Michael J. Svigel, eds., *Exploring Christian Theology*, vol. 2, *Creation, Fall, and Salvation* (Minneapolis, MN: Bethany House, 2015), 255.

29 C. S. Lewis, *Surprised by Joy: The Shape of My Early Life*, reissued ed. (San Francisco: HarperOne, 1955; reprint, 2017), 72.

30 Huub van de Sandt and David Flusser, *The Didache: Its Jewish Sources and its Place in Early Judaism and Christianity* (Minneapolis: Fortress, 2002), 147–55.

31 A. B. Bruce, "The Synoptic Gospels," 137.

32 Henry George Liddell, et al., *A Greek-English Lexicon* (Oxford: Clarendon Press, 1996), 1039.

33 Paul E. Adolph, "Diseases," in *New International Dictionary of the Bible*, 273.

34 See Lange, *Matthew–Luke*, 150.

35 France, *Matthew*, 152.

36 Barclay, *Gospel of Matthew*, 1:347.

37 F. F. Bruce, *New Testament History*, 70.

38 Buttrick, "Exposition of the Gospel According to St. Matthew," in *The Interpreter's Bible*, 343–44.

39 Bauer, et al., *Greek-English Lexicon*, 609–10.

40 Arthur M. Ross, "Gadara, Gadarenes," in *New International Dictionary of the Bible*, 365.

41 Robert Lightner, *Angels, Satan, and Demons*, Swindoll Leadership Library, ed. Charles R. Swindoll (Nashville: Thomas Nelson, 1998), 130–31.

42 Holsteen and Svigel, *Exploring Christian Theology*, 2:41.

43 Robertson, *Word Pictures*, 296.

44 Martin Luther, "A Mighty Fortress Is Our God," in *The Hymnal for Worship and Celebration*, no. 26.

45 Paul P. Levertoff, *St. Matthew*, rev. ed. (London: Thomas Murby, 1940), 26, as cited by France, *Matthew*, 164.

46 H. Paul Holdridge, "Occupations and Professions," in *New International Dictionary of the Bible*, 726.

47 Tenney, *New Testament Times*, 160.

48 Green, *The Message of Matthew*, 25.

49 See Arthur B. Fowler, "Bottle," in *New International Dictionary of the Bible*, 171.

50 France, *Matthew*, 169.

51 Toussaint, *Behold the King*, 131–32.

52 Robertson, *Word Pictures*, 74.

53 Eric Metaxas, *Miracles: What They Are, Why They Happen, and How They Can Change Your Life* (New York: Dutton, 2014), 115.

54 Green, *The Message of Matthew*, 24.

55 Robert E. Coleman, *The Master Plan of Evangelism* (Old Tappan, NJ: Revell, 1964), 22–23.

56 France, *Matthew*, 180–81.
57 Barbieri, "Matthew," in *The Bible Knowledge Commentary*, 42.
58 Bauer, et al., *Greek-English Lexicon*, 1066.
59 Robertson, *Word Pictures*, 80.
60 Lange, *Matthew–Luke*, 188.
61 Barclay, *Gospel of Matthew*, 1:434.
62 Isaac Watts, "Am I a Soldier of the Cross?" in *The Hymnal for Worship and Celebration*, no. 482.
63 Bauer, et al., *Greek-English Lexicon*, 708–9.
64 A. B. Bruce, "The Synoptic Gospels," 168.
65 Sherman E. Johnson, "Exegesis of the Gospel According to St. Matthew," in *The Interpreter's Bible*, 375.
66 John F. Gates, "Cross," in *New International Dictionary of the Bible*, 242.
67 France, *Matthew*, 189.
68 Lange, *Matthew–Luke*, 199.
69 A. B. Bruce, "The Synoptic Gospels," 168.
70 O'Donnell, *Matthew*, 289.
71 Tasker, *The Gospel According to St. Matthew*, 114.
72 See Barbieri, "Matthew," in *The Bible Knowledge Commentary*, 44.
73 For further explanation of the expectation of the coming of Elijah, see the comments on Matthew 17:9-13 in Swindoll, *Matthew 16–28*.
74 Toussaint, *Behold the King*, 153.
75 See DeVries, *Cities of the Biblical World*, 73–82.
76 France, *Matthew*, 199.
77 "Yoke," in *New International Dictionary of the Bible*, 1078.
78 Johnson, "Exegesis of the Gospel According to St. Matthew," in *The Interpreter's Bible*, 390.
79 Translation of Sirach taken from *Holy Bible*, New Revised Standard Version (Nashville: Thomas Nelson, 1989).
80 Barclay, *Gospel of Matthew*, 2:20.
81 Bauer, et al., *Greek-English Lexicon*, 861.
82 Ibid., 69.
83 Ibid.
84 William D. Longstaff, "Take Time to Be Holy," in *The Hymnal for Worship and Celebration*, no. 441.
85 Charles C. Ryrie, *Balancing the Christian Life* (Chicago: Moody, 1969), 159.
86 Steven Barabas, "Sabbath," in *New International Dictionary of the Bible*, 877.
87 See Robertson, *Word Pictures*, 93.
88 Toussaint, *Behold the King*, 159.
89 Thomas Jefferson, letter to Colonel William S. Smith, November 13, 1787, in *Letters and Addresses of Thomas Jefferson*, ed. William B. Parker and Jonas Viles (Buffalo, NY: National Jefferson Society, 1903), 65.
90 See France, *Matthew*, 206–7.
91 See D. A. Carson, "Matthew," in *The Expositor's Bible Commentary*, vol. 9, *Matthew–Mark*, rev. ed., ed. Tremper Longman III and David E. Garland (Grand Rapids, MI: Zondervan, 2010), 332.
92 See "Baal-Zebub," in *New International Dictionary of the Bible*, 115.
93 Josephus, *Antiquities* 8.2.5, in Whiston, *The Works of Josephus*, 176.
94 Eric Eve, *The Jewish Context of Jesus' Miracles*, Journal for the Study of the New Testament Supplement Series, vol. 231 (London; New York: Sheffield Academic Press, 2002), 378.
95 See Edwin M. Yamauchi, "Religions of the Biblical World: Persia," in *The International Standard Bible Encyclopedia*, ed. Geoffrey W. Bromiley, et al. (Grand Rapids: Eerdmans, 1988), 4:123–29.

96 See Robert P. Lightner, "Angels, Satan, and Demons: Invisible Beings that Inhabit the Spiritual World," in *Understanding Christian Theology*, ed. Charles R. Swindoll and Roy B. Zuck (Nashville: Thomas Nelson, 2003), 572–73.

97 Robertson, *Word Pictures*, 96.

98 Ibid.

99 Paul Babiak and Robert D. Hare, *Snakes in Suits: When Psychopaths Go to Work* (New York: HarperCollins, 2006), x.

100 A. B. Bruce, "The Synoptic Gospels," 191.

101 See. R. T. France, *Jesus and the Old Testament* (London: Tyndale Press, 1971; reprint, Grand Rapids: Baker, 1982), 81.

102 Robertson, *Word Pictures*, 98.

103 Lange, *Matthew–Luke*, 232.

104 B. C. Crisler, "The Acoustics and Crowd Capacity of Natural Theaters in Palestine," *Biblical Archaeologist* 39, no. 4 (1976): 128–41.

105 Robert R. Stein, *An Introduction to the Parables of Jesus* (Philadelphia: Westminster Press, 1981), 15.

106 Robertson, *Word Pictures*, 101.

107 Ibid., 102.

108 A. B. Bruce, "The Synoptic Gospels," 194.

109 Bauer, et al., *Greek-English Lexicon*, 661–62.

110 John L. Leedy, "Plants," in *New International Dictionary of the Bible*, 805.

111 France, *Matthew*, 225.

112 Toussaint, *Behold the King*, 181.

113 France, *Matthew*, 227.

114 See A. B. Bruce, "The Synoptic Gospels," 201.

115 Toussaint, *Behold the King*, 182.

116 Ibid., 170.

117 Thomas Guthrie, *The Parables Read in the Light of the Present Day* (London: Alexander Strahan, 1867), 212–13.

118 Jerry W. Batson, "Nazareth, Nazarene," in *Holman Illustrated Bible Dictionary*, 1177.

119 "Nazareth," in *Baker Encyclopedia of the Bible*, 1531.

120 Tasker, *The Gospel According to St. Matthew*, 140.

121 Robertson, *Word Pictures*, 111.

122 John MacArthur, *Matthew 8–15*, The MacArthur New Testament Commentary (Chicago: Moody, 1987), 416.

123 Herodias's daughter's name, Salome, isn't mentioned in the New Testament, but the first-century Jewish historian Josephus gives us her name. See "Salome," in *New International Dictionary of the Bible*, 886.

124 Robertson, *Word Pictures*, 115.

125 Lorman M. Petersen, "Money," in *New International Dictionary of the Bible*, 669–70.

126 Johnson, "Exegesis of the Gospel According to St. Matthew," in *The Interpreter's Bible*, 431.

127 Bauer, et al., *Greek-English Lexicon*, 168.

128 See France, *Matthew*, 238.

129 Bauer, et al., *Greek-English Lexicon*, 990–91.

130 Ibid., 444.

131 Lange, *Matthew–Luke*, 277.

132 France, *Matthew*, 243.

133 Bauer, et al., *Greek-English Lexicon*, 575.

134 France, *Matthew*, 247.

135 John R. W. Stott, *God's New Society: The Message of Ephesians*, The Bible Speaks Today (Downers Grove, IL: InterVarsity Press, 1979), 116.